T0330381

Environmental Protection, Security and Armed Conflict

A Sustainable Development Perspective

Onita Das

University of the West of England, UK

Edward Elgar

Cheltenham, UK • Northampton, MA, USA

Published by
Edward Elgar Publishing Limited
The Lypiatts
15 Lansdown Road
Cheltenham
Glos GL50 2JA
UK

Edward Elgar Publishing, Inc.
William Pratt House
9 Dewey Court
Northampton
Massachusetts 01060
USA

A catalogue record for this book
is available from the British Library

Library of Congress Control Number: 2012944473

ISBN 978 1 78100 467 8

Typeset by Columns Design XML Ltd, Reading
Printed and bound by MPG Books Group, UK

Contents

Foreword   vi
Acknowledgements   viii
List of abbreviations   ix
Table of cases   xv
Table of legislation   xvii

1   Introduction   1
2   Sustainable development, security and armed conflict –
    developing a theoretical framework for a legal analysis of
    war and the environment   8
3   Failing sustainable development? Early warning, early action,
    and preventing environmental security threats   66
4   Sustainable development and the protection of the environment
    during times of armed conflict   120
5   Post-conflict: breaking the cycle for a better future – sustainable
    development and environmental protection relevant to security
    and armed conflict   183
6   Conclusions and challenges   248

Index   255

Foreword

Environmental harm in almost any form is inimical to the human experience when it rises above *de minimis* levels. To that extent, significant environmental degradation always has consequences for humanity, be they economic, social, cultural or political. What has become apparent is that there is also often a further dimension to such harm, namely that which is security-related. Environmental harm is thus increasingly recognised as both a consequence of military conflicts and, as significant, a trigger factor in the creation and/or exacerbation of civil strife, inter-State tensions and armed disputes. Resource scarcity, in particular, has shown itself to be a major cause of human insecurity. The birth of the world's newest country – South Sudan – continues to be mired, for instance, in bitter controversies over natural resources.

Environmental security is thus a pivotal matter for communities, States and the wider international community. However, as with all concepts, it is in danger of becoming a buzzword; critics would say full of 'political-ese' and rhetoric but with no real substance. Nevertheless, environmental security threats – both geographically discrete concerns as well as the more pervasive links between environmental harm / natural resource stresses and human conflict (both actual and putative) – are no less real simply because they can also be conceptualised and modelled. What Dr Das achieves in this monograph is to highlight the true extent of the problem without becoming overly-descriptive of particular issues; to reflect the broader context whilst concurrently relying on key instances to reveal the diverse nature of the threats.

She also underlines the role of international law and international organisations in mediating this complex problem. International law and international organisations are, however, no panacea; they cannot be 'activated' in some on/off fashion to resolve the world's ills. International law and international organisations are as imperfect, inchoate and frac-tured as the human causes of environmental insecurity – they can do no more, or no less, than political will allows. Nevertheless, within the substantive and procedural norms of international law and within the mission statements of international organisations, there is the potential for something more, something better – an aspiration for more harmonious co-existence both between peoples, and between peoples and nature. Concepts such as environmental security and sustainable development, which must be considered as integrally related, may indeed be buzzwords but the principles they reflect are worth upholding and pursuing. Indeed, if worst case future scenarios are anywhere near correct, we have no choice but to continue to seek new and additional ways to implement still further the measures necessary to tackle the underlying causes of environmental harm.

Professor Duncan French
Lincoln
May 2012

Acknowledgements

There are a few people to whom I am deeply indebted to for their help and support in writing this book. First I would like to thank Dr Ben Pontin and Dr Noëlle Quénivet for their invaluable guidance with regard to my research and Professor Duncan French and Dr Jona Razzaque for their helpful comments on several points of my work. Dr Razzaque deserves special thanks for her guidance and support throughout the monograph process. The framework for this book benefited considerably from her comments, having read drafts with great perseverance. I would also like to thank Dr Pontin for his guidance on preliminary drafts and Evadne Grant for her invaluable comments on final revisions of parts of the manuscript. In addition, I would like to express my thanks to Keith Feeney and Simon Heavisides, both of whom I am deeply indebted to for painstakingly proofreading my manuscript.

I would also like to thank Edward Elgar for accepting my proposal and a huge thanks to John-Paul McDonald, Laura Seward and Elizabeth Clack at EEP for their assistance at every stage of the process and their patience in answering all my publishing queries. In addition, thank you to the reviewers for their useful comments and observations.

Last, but not least, thank you to my family and friends for their unwavering support and encouragement throughout the monograph process.

Onita Das
Bristol, 2012

Abbreviations

ACP	African, Caribbean and Pacific Group of States
AJIL	American Journal of International Law
Art.	Article
ASEAN	Association of South East Asian Nations
BBC	British Broadcasting Corporation
BTF	Balkan Task Force
CIA	Central Intelligence Agency
CISDL	Centre for International Sustainable Development Law
Cl. Ct.	(US) Court of Claims Reports
CNN	Cable News Network
CSD	Commission on Sustainable Development
CUP	Cambridge University Press
DAC	(OECD) Development Assistance Committee
DEFRA	(UK) Department for Environment, Food and Rural Affairs
DEWA	Division of Early Warning and Assessment
DOD	(US) Department of Defense
DSB	(WTO) Dispute Settlement Body
DSU	(WTO) Dispute Settlement Understanding
EC	European Commission
ECJ	European Court of Justice
ECOWAS	Economic Community of West African States
ECOSOC	(UN) Economic and Social Council

ECHR	European Convention on Human Rights
EEC	European Economic Community
EEA	European Environment Agency
EIA	Environmental impact assessment
ELI	Environmental Law Institute
ENVSEC	Environment and Security Initiative
EPA	(US) Environmental Protection Agency
ETS	European Treaty Series
EU	European Union
EW	Early warning
F.2d	(US) Federal Reporter, Second Series
FAO	(UN) Food and Agriculture Organization
FRY	Federal Republic of Yugoslavia
F.Supp.	(US) Federal Supplement
GAOR	General Assembly Official Records
GATS	General Agreement on Trade in Services
GATT	General Agreement on Tariffs and Trade
GEF	Global Environment Fund
GOS	Government of Sudan
GOSS	Government of the Republic of South Sudan
HC	House of Commons
HL	House of Lords
HMSO	Her Majesty's Stationary Office
IASC	Inter-Agency Standing Committee
ICC	International Criminal Court
ICISS	International Commission on Intervention and State Sovereignty
ICJ	International Court of Justice

ICJ Rep	International Court of Justice Reports
ICTR	International Criminal Tribunal for Rwanda
ICTY	International Criminal Tribunal for the Former Yugoslavia
IELMT	International Environmental Legal Material and Treaties
IISD	International Institute for Sustainable Development
ILA	International Law Association
ILC	International Law Commission
ILM	International Legal Materials
ILR	International Law Reports
IOM	International Organization for Migration
ITLOS	International Tribunal for the Law of the Sea
IUCN	International Union for Conservation of Nature
LNOJ	League of Nations Official Journal
LNTS	League of Nations Treaty Series
MDGs	Millennium Development Goals
MEA	Millennium Ecosystem Assessment
MEAs	Multilateral Environmental Agreements
MUP	Manchester University Press
NAFTA	North American Free Trade Agreement
NATO	North Atlantic Treaty Organization
NGOs	Non-Governmental Organizations
OAU	Organization of African Unity
OCHA	(UN) Office for the Coordination of Humanitarian Affairs
OJ	Official Journal of the European Communities
OJL	Official Journal Legislation

OECD	Organisation for Economic Co-operation and Development
OR	Ontario Reports
OSCE	Organization for Security and Cooperation in Europe
OUP	Oxford University Press
PBC	(UN) Peacebuilding Commission
PCDMB	(UNEP) Post-Conflict and Disaster Management Branch
PCEA	(UNEP) Post-Conflict Environment Assessment
PCA	Permanent Court of Arbitration
PCIJ	Permanent Court of International Justice
PCIJ Ser. A	Permanent Court of International Justice, Collection of Judgements (1922–1930)
REC	Regional Environmental Center for Central and Eastern Europe
RIAA	Reports of International Arbitral Awards
RUF	Revolutionary United Front
SC	(US) Supreme Court
SCOR	(UN) Security Council Official Records
S. Ct.	(US) Supreme Court Reporter
SDC	Swiss Agency for Development and Cooperation
SPLM	Sudan People's Liberation Movement
Stat.	United States Statutes at Large
UCDP	Uppsala Conflict Data Programme
UK	United Kingdom
UN	United Nations
UNAMID	African Union/United Nations Hybrid Operation in Darfur
UNAMSIL	United Nations Assistance Mission in Sierra Leone

UNCBD	United Nations Convention on Biological Diversity
UNCC	United Nations Compensation Commission
UNCCD	United Nations Convention to Combat Desertification
UNCED	United Nations Conference on Environment and Development
UNCLOS	United Nations Convention on the Law of the Sea
UNDAC	United Nations Disaster Assessment and Coordination
UNDESA	United Nations Department of Economic and Social Affairs
UNDG	United Nations Development Group
UNDP	United Nations Development Programme
UN-DPA	United Nations Department of Political Affairs
UNECE	United Nations Economic Commission for Europe
UNEP	United Nations Environment Programme
UNESCAP	United Nations Economic and Social Commission for Asia and the Pacific
UNESCO	United Nations Educational, Scientific and Cultural Organization
UNFCCC	United Nations Framework Convention on Climate Change
UNGA	United Nations General Assembly
UN-HABITAT	United Nations Human Settlements Programme
UNHCR	United Nations Refugee Agency
UNICEF	United Nations International Children's Emergency Fund
UNISDR	United Nations International Strategy for Disaster Reduction
UNMIK	United Nations Interim Administration Mission in Kosovo

UNMIS	United Nations Mission in Sudan
UNMISS	United Nations Mission in Southern Sudan
UNOPS	United Nations Office for Project Services
UNOSAT	United Nations Operational Satellite Applications Programme
UNOSOM	United Nations Operation in Somalia
UNRISD	United Nations Research Institute for Social Development
UNSC	United Nations Security Council
UNTS	United Nations Treaty Series
US	United States of America
USAID	United States Agency for International Development
USC	United States Code
WCED	World Commission on Environment and Development
WEU	Western European Union
WHO	World Health Organization
WTO	World Trade Organization
WWII	World War II

Table of cases

Case Concerning Armed Activities on the Territory of the Congo (DRC v Uganda) (Judgement) General List No 116 [2005] ICJ Rep 1 135
Case Concerning the Factory at Chorzów (Germany v Poland) (Merits) (1928) PCIJ Rep Series A No. 17..186, 190, 191, 202
Commonwealth of Puerto Rico v The SS Zoe Colocotroni 628 F. 2d 652 (1st Cir. August 12 1980) 197
Corfu Channel (UK v Albania) (Merits) [1949] ICJ Rep 4 190
Exxon Shipping Co. v Baker 554 US and 128 S. Ct. 2605 (2008) 196
Fuel Retailers Association of Southern Africa v Director-General: Environmental Management, Department of Agriculture, Conservation and Environment, Mpumalanga Province, and Others (2007) (6) SA 4 (CC), 2007 (10) BCLR 1059 (CC) 55
Gabčikovo-Nagymaros Project (Hungary/Slovakia) (Judgement) [1997] ICJ Rep 7 ....10, 33, 41, 42, 53, 54, 187, 190
I'm Alone Case (Canada v USA) (1935) RIAA III 1609 208
Interpretation of Peace Treaties with Bulgaria, Hungary and Romania (Second Phase) (Advisory Opinion) [1950] ICJ Rep 221 153
Iron Rhine ('Ijzeren Rihn') Railway Arbitration (Belgium/The Netherlands) Award of the Arbitral Tribunal (24 May 2005) 42, 43, 54
Judgement of the International Military Tribunal for the Far East (Tokyo) 1948 [1949] AD 356...135
Judgement of the Nuremberg International Military Tribunal 1946 (1947) 41 AJIL 172 135
Lac Lanoux Arbitration (Spain v France) (1957) 24 ILR 101, (1957) 12 RIAA 281 23
LaGrand Case (Germany v USA) (Judgement) [2001] ICJ Rep 466 ....186, 208
Legality of the Threat or Use of Nuclear Weapons (Advisory Opinion) [1996] ICJ Rep 226 ....23, 27, 53, 125, 126, 127, 139, 140, 141
Legality of the Use of Force (Yugoslavia v NATO States) (Provisional Measures) [1999] ICJ Rep 132 ....166, 216
M/V 'Saiga' (No 2) (Saint Vincent and The Grenadines v Guinea) (Admissibility and Merits) (1999) 120 ILR 143 187
Maritime Delimitation in the Area Between Greenland and Jan Mayen (Denmark v Norway) [1993] ICJ Rep 38 27
Military and Paramilitary Activities in and Against Nicaragua (Nicaragua v USA) (Merits) [1986] ICJ Rep 14 140
Minors Oposa v Secretary of the Department of Environment and Natural Resources (DENR) (Phillipines Supreme Court) 30 July 1993, reprinted in (1994) 33 ILM 173 ....27, 55

Narmada Bachao Aandolan v Union of India and Others (18 October 2000) AIR
    2000 SC 3751 5
Premium Plastics v LaSalle National Bank 904 F. Supp. 809, 25 Chem. Waste Litig.
    Rep 537 (N.D. Ill. 1995) 196
Prosecutor v Kordic and Cerkez (Judgement) ICTY-95–14/2-T (26 February 2001)
   158
Prosecutor v Martic (Judgement) ICTY-95–11-R61 (8 March 1996) 140
Prosecutor v Bagilishema (Judgement) ICTR-95–1A-A (3 July 2002) 160
Pulp Mills on the River Uruguay (Argentina v Uruguay) (Request for Indication of
    Provisional Measures, Order of 13 July 2006) [2006] ICJ Rep 1 54
Rainbow Warrior (New Zealand v France) (Arbitration Tribunal) (1990) 82 ILR
    499 208
Reparation for Injuries Suffered in the Service of the United Nations (Advisory
    Opinion) [1949] ICJ Rep 174 153
Request for an Examination of the Situation in Accordance with Paragraph 63 of the
    Court's Judgement of 20 December 1974 in the Nuclear Tests (New Zealand v
    France) (Order) [1995] ICJ Rep 288 27
Southern Bluefin Tuna Cases (New Zealand v Japan, Australia v Japan) (Requests
    for Provisional Measures, Order) (27 August 1999), reproduced in (1999) 38 ILM
    1624 and 117 ILR 148 33
State of Ohio v U.S. Dept. of the Interior 880 F.2d 432 (D.C. Cir. 1989) 198
The Mox Plant Case (Ireland v UK) (Request for Provisional Measures, Order) (3
    December 2001), reproduced in (2002) 41 ILM 405 and 126 ILR 259................33
Trail Smelter Arbitration (US v Canada) 3 RIAA 1911 (1938), reprinted in (1939)
    33 AJIL 182 and 3 RIAA 1938 (1941), reprinted in (1941) 35
    AJIL 684 ....23, 126, 191, 202
United States – Import Prohibition of Certain Shrimp and Shrimp Products (12
    October 1998) WTO Doc. WT/DS58/AB/R (Appellate Body Report) 54
United States – Import Prohibition of Certain Shrimp and Shrimp Products,
    Recourse to Article 21.5 by Malaysia (15 June 2001) WTO Doc. WT/DS58/RW
    (Report of the Panel) 30
United States Diplomatic and Consular Staff in Tehran (USA v Iran) [1980] ICJ
    Rep 3 187
United States v Aceto Agricultural Chemical Corp. 872 F. 2d 1373, 1380 (8th Cir.
    1989) 196
United States v Alcan Aluminium Corp. 964 F.2d 252 (3d Cir. 1992) 196
United States v List (The 'Hostages Case') (1949) 11 CCL No. 10 Trials 1230...135,
                                                                              138, 142, 159

Table of legislation

1863 Instructions for the Government of Armies of the United States in the Field (Lieber Code) General Orders No. 100 (24 April 1863) 141

1899 Hague Convention (II) with Respect to the Laws and Customs of War on Land (29 July 1899) 32 Stat 1803 ....130, 135, 136, 139

1907 Hague Convention (IV) Respecting the Laws and Customs of War on Land (18 October 1907) 36 Stat 2277 ......121, 129, 130, 135, 136, 137, 143, 147, 149, 158, 159, 170

1945 Charter of the United Nations (1945) 1 UNTS xvi 26, 86, 154

1949 Geneva Convention (IV) Relative to the Protection of Civilian Persons in Time of War (1949) 75 UNTS 287 ....121, 129, 135, 137, 138, 143, 149, 157, 158, 159, 170

1954 International Convention for the Prevention of Pollution of the Sea by Oil, London (1954) 327 UNTS 3 148

1969 International Convention on Civil Liability for Oil Pollution Damage, Brussels (1969) 973 UNTS 3, (1970) 9 ILM 45 199

1972 Convention on International Liability for Damage Caused by Space Objects, London (1972) 961 UNTS 187 207

– Declaration of the United Nations Conference on the Human Environment, Stockholm (16 June 1972) UN Doc. A/CONF.48/14/ Rev.1, reprinted in (1972) 11 ILM 1416 .... 12, 13, 14, 23, 26, 41, 48, 49, 184

1975 Final Act of the Helsinki Conference on Security and Co-operation in Europe (1975) 14 ILM 1292 23

1976 Convention on the Prohibition of Military or Any Other Hostile Use of Environmental Modification Techniques (1976) 31 UST 333, (1977) 16 ILM 88 .... 130, 131, 132, 134, 147

1977 Clean Water Act (1977) Pub. L. No. 95–217, 91 Stat. 1566 197

– Protocol Additional to the Geneva Conventions of 12 August 1949, and Relating to the Protection of Victims of International Armed Conflicts (1977) 1125 UNTS 3 (Pt. I), 1125 UNTS 609 (Pt. II), 16 ILM 1391 ....121, 139, 140, 141, 143, 147, 149, 166, 168, 169, 170, 171, 176, 179

1980 Comprehensive Environmental Response, Comprehensive, and Liability Act (CERCLA) (1980) Pub. L. No. 96–510, 94 Stat. 2767 ....45, 195, 197, 198, 209

– Convention on the Conservation of Antarctic Marine Living Resources (1980) 19 ILM 841 24

1981 Lima Convention for the Protection of the Marine Environment and Coastal Area of the South-East Pacific (12 November 1981) UN Doc UNEP/GC/INF.11, 185 23

1982 United Nations Convention on the Law of the Sea (1982) 21 ILM 1261 .... 24, 32, 148

1983 International Undertaking on Plant Genetic Resources, Rome (1983) FAO Resolution 8/83 .... 24, 25, 27

1985 ASEAN Agreement on the Conservation of Nature and Natural Resources, Kuala Lumpur (1985) 15 EPL 64 .... 44, 50

– Convention on the Protection of the Ozone Layer, Vienna (1985) 26 ILM 1529 69

1986 Natural Resource Damage Assessments, Final Rule, 51 Fed. Reg. 27674–01 (1986) 27, 720–7, 721 (codified at 43 C.F.R. § 11.83 (d)(5)(i) (1988) 198

– Superfund Amendments and Reauthorization Act (SARA) Pub. L. No. 99–499, 100 Stat. 1613 (1986) (codified as amended at 42 U.S.C. §§ 9601–9675 (2000)) 197

1991 Norwegian Forurensningsloven, Section 57, 13 March 1991, No. 6 (Norwegian Pollution Act) 187

– Convention on the Protection of the Alps, Salzburg (7 November 1991), (1992) 32 ILM 767 44

1992 Convention on Biological Diversity, Rio de Janeiro (1992) 1760 UNTS 79 .... 24, 26, 32, 36, 41, 51

– Convention on the Protection of the Marine Environment of the Baltic Sea Area, Helsinki (1992), 2099 UNTS 197 44

– Convention for the Protection of the Marine Environment of the North-East Atlantic (OSPAR Convention), Paris (1992), (1993) 32 ILM 1072 44

– Convention on the Protection and Use of Transboundary Watercourses and International Lakes, Helsinki (17 March 1992) UN Doc. E/ECE/1267 (1992) 31 ILM 1312 51

– North American Free Trade Agreement (NAFTA) (Canada-USA-Mexico) (17 December 1992) (1993) 32 ILM 289 51

– United Nations Conference on Environment and Development (1992) UN Doc. A/CONF.151/26/ Rev.1 (Agenda 21) 14, 36

– United Nations Declaration on Environment and Development, Rio de Janeiro (14 June 1992) UN Doc. A/CONF.151/5/Rev.1 (1992), reprinted in (1992) 31 ILM 876 .... 14, 21, 23, 26, 29, 30, 32, 33, 36, 38, 41, 44, 107, 126, 184

– United Nations Framework Convention on Climate Change (1992) 1771 UNTS 107, (1992) 31 ILM 849 .... 24, 26, 29, 30, 31, 32, 36, 41, 50, 112

1993 Convention for the Protection of the Marine Environment of the North-East Atlantic, Paris (1993) 32 ILM 1069 24

– Convention on Civil Liability for Damage Resulting from Activities Dangerous to the Environment, Lugano (1993) 32 ILM 1228 .... 44, 187, 199

– Statute of the International Tribunal for the Former Yugoslavia (25 May 1993) UN Doc S/RES/827 (1993) 32 ILM 1192 156

1994 Agreement Establishing the World Trade Organization, Marrakesh (1994) 33 ILM 1125 51

– Convention on Cooperation for the Protection and Sustainable Use of the Danube River, Sofia (29 June 1994), reprinted in 994 IELMT 49 44

– Danish Act on Compensation for Environmental Damage (ACED) No. 225 (6 April 1994) 187

– International Tropical Timber
Agreement, Geneva (1994) UN Doc
TD/TIMBER.2/Misc.7/GE.94–
50830, (1994) 33 ILM 1014 24
– Natural Resource Damage
Assessments, Final Rule, 59 Fed.
Reg. 14,262 (25 March 1994)
(codified at 43 C.F.R. §§ 11.10–11.93
(2004)) 198
– Statute of the International Criminal
Tribunal for Rwanda (8 November
1994) UN Doc S/RES/955 (1994) 33
ILM 1598 156
– United Nations Convention to Combat
Desertification in those Countries
Experiencing Serious Drought and/or
Desertification, Particularly in
Africa, Paris (1994) 1954 UNTS
3 .... 30, 36, 41, 51, 112
1995 Agreement on the Cooperation for
the Sustainable Development of the
Mekong River Basin, Chiang Mai
(1995) 34 ILM 864 51
– Finnish Environmental Damage
Compensation Act (EDCA) (737/
1994) (1 June 1995) 187
– Protocol to the United Nations
Framework Convention on Climate
Change, Kyoto (1997) 38 ILM
22 .... 24, 26, 29, 30, 31, 32,
36, 41, 50, 112
– United Nations Convention on the
Non-Navigational Uses of
International Watercourses (1997) 36
ILM 700 51
1998 Convention on Access to
Information, Public Participation in
Decision-Making and Access to
Justice in Environmental Matters,
Aarhus (1998) 2161 UNTS
447 .... 36, 171
– Rome Statute of the International
Criminal Court (17 July 1998) UN
Doc A/CONF 183/9, 2187 UNTS
3 .... 157, 158

– Swedish Environmental Code
(adopted 1998, entered into force 1
January 1999) SFS 1998:808
Miljöbalk 187
2000 Cartagena Protocol on Biosafety
to the Convention on Biological
Diversity (2000) 39 ILM 1027 33
– Partnership Agreement between the
Members of the African, Caribbean
and Pacific Group of States of one
part, and the European Community
and its Member States, of the other
part, Cotonou (23 June 2000) 2000
OJ (L 37) 3 39
– Revised Protocol on Shared
Watercourses in the Southern African
Development Community (7 August
2000) (2001) 40 ILM 321 51
2001 International Treaty on Plant
Genetic Resources for Food and
Agriculture, Rome (3 November
2001) 2001 IELMT 28 27
2002 Convention for Co-operation in
the Protection and Sustainable
Development of the Marine and
Coastal Environment of the
North East Pacific (2002) IELMT
14 51
– German Environmental Liability Act
(Umwelthaftungsgesetz), 10
December 1990 (BGB1. I 1990,
2634), as amended on 19 July 2002
(BGB1. I 2002, 2674) 187
2003 Protocol on Civil Liability and
Compensation for Damage Caused
by the Transboundary Effects of
Industrial Accidents on
Transboundary Waters to the 1992
Convention on the Protection
and Use of Transboundary
Watercourses and International
Lakes and to the 1992 Convention
on the Transboundary Effects of
Industrial Accidents, Kiev (21 May
2003) 44

– United Nations Convention against
   Corruption (6 August 2003) UN Doc.
   A/RES/58/4, (2004) 43 ILM 37 39
2004 Directive 2004/35/CE of the
   European Parliament and of the
Council of 21 April 2004 on
Environmental Liability with Regard
to the Prevention and Remedying of
Environmental Damage (30 April
2004) OJL 143/56 187

1. Introduction

1. SCOPE OF THE BOOK

Threats to the environment, in all their diversity, are a growing concern for societies, States and the international community as a whole. Environmental threats in relation to security and armed conflict are amongst them. These environmental pressures can, in some circumstances cause violent or armed conflict[1] and such conflict can, in turn, cause devastating damage and destruction to the environment. This vicious circle can have both short-term and long-lasting impacts on not only the environment, but also on the communities that depend on it. Such environmental pressures and damage are no longer isolated incidents that affect only a small section of society. These environmental problems often extend beyond the territories of conflict-affected States, threatening the lives and livelihoods of people across communities and borders.

In the context of this book, threats to ecosystems well known to environmental lawyers are addressed with reference to an aspect of human conduct – war and armed conflict – that has not received the attention it deserves.[2] This is a challenging topic because of the cyclical relationship between environmental insecurity and human insecurity. As the United Nations Environment Programme (UNEP) recently reported, not only have violent conflicts been fuelled by natural resource exploitation and related environmental stresses[3] but the environment itself 'continues to be a silent victim of armed conflicts worldwide.'[4]

---

[1] 'A dispute involving the use of armed force between two or more parties.' UNEP, 'Protecting the Environment During Armed Conflict: An Inventory and Analysis of Law' (UNEP, Switzerland 2009) at p. 55 [hereinafter, UNEP International Law].

[2] In this study, the terms 'war' and 'armed conflict' are used interchangeably.

[3] UNEP, 'From Conflict to Peacebuilding: The Role of Natural Resources and the Environment' (UNEP, Switzerland 2009) at p. 5 [hereinafter UNEP Conflict to Peacebuilding].

[4] UNEP International Law (n 1) at p. 4.

1

With regard to what is meant by the 'environment', definition of this term varies.[5] For the purpose of this book, the definition of 'environment' used is as described by UNEP:

> The sum of all external conditions affecting the life, development and survival of an organism ... environment refers to the physical conditions that affect natural resources (climate, geology, hazards) and the ecosystem services[6] that sustain them (e.g. carbon, nutrient and hydrological cycles).[7]

Although the term 'environment' will be used in the context of the broad definition above, it is worth noting that in a more holistic anthropocentric approach, the Millennium Ecosystem Assessment (MEA), in its assessment of the links between ecosystems and human well-being, describes an 'ecosystem' as a 'dynamic complex of plant, animal, and microorganism communities and the nonliving environment interacting as a functional unit.'[8] The MEA further defines 'ecosystem services' as:

> the benefits people obtain from ecosystems. This includes *provisioning services* such as food, water, timber, and fiber; *regulating services* that affect climate, floods, disease, wastes, and water quality; *cultural services* that provide recreational, aesthetic and spiritual benefits; and *supporting services* such as soil formation, photosynthesis, and nutrient cycling.[9]

These more comprehensive definitions provide some idea as to what could constitute an 'environment' or an 'ecosystem service'.[10] As is explained in early chapters of this book, the possibility of environmental factors causing armed conflict is not a new idea and the negative consequences of armed conflict on the environment have been well documented. What is relatively new is the idea that protecting the

---

[5] On the differing definitions of the environment, see e.g. Aust, A., *Handbook of International Law* (CUP, Cambridge 2005) at pp. 329–32 (particularly in relation to the wording of individual treaties); Sands, P., *Principles of International Environmental Law I: Frameworks, Standards and Implementation* (MUP, Manchester 1995) at pp. 17–19.

[6] UNEP uses the same definition for 'ecosystem services' as the MEA, see text to (n 8).

[7] UNEP International Law (n 1) at p. 56.

[8] MEA, *Ecosystems and Human Well-Being: Synthesis* (Island, Washington, DC 2005) at p. v. See also Blanco, E. and Razzaque, J. 'Ecosystem Services and Human Well-Being in a Globalised World: Assessing the Role of the Law' (2009) 31 Human Rights Quarterly 692, at 693.

[9] Ibid.

[10] Ecosystem services are discussed further in Chapter 5 in the context of liability for environmental damage.

environment is the foundation on which a society and an economy depends, and the most popular way of conceptualising this is the overarching concept of sustainable development that is at the heart of this book. Thus, this study aims to use this overarching principle, and the 'sub-principles'[11] subsumed within it, to draw conclusions concerning whether law and its enforcement are strong, weak, or somewhere in between in order to answer the question of, how compatible with the norms of sustainable development is policy and law for the protection of the environment in the field of armed conflict?

Sustainable development, a still evolving concept in international law, has been steadily gaining ground over the last few decades, being used by governments, academics, lawyers and other non-state actors. The concept of sustainable development generally refers to development or the process of improving the quality of life of the present generation without compromising the future generation's. It is a holistic concept increasingly being cited worldwide as a guideline to govern both domestic issues and international relations, though arguably has yet to achieve full international legal status.[12] As sustainable development is a concept being integrated within both the realms of international law and international relations and is seen as a goal to strive for by the international community, it seems practical to also apply this concept in relation to the protection of the environment relevant to security[13] and armed conflict.[14]

---

[11] For example, the duty of states to ensure sustainable use of natural resources; equity and the eradication of poverty; common but differentiated responsibilities; precautionary principle; participation; good governance; integration and interrelationship; and the polluter pays principle.

[12] See, e.g. French, D., 'Sustainable Development' in Fitzmaurice, M., Ong, D.M. and Merkouris, P. (eds), *Research Handbook in International Environmental Law* (Edward Elgar, UK 2010) at pp. 51–68; Viikari, L., *The Environmental Element in Space Law: Assessing the Present and Charting the Future* (Koninklijke Brill NV, The Netherlands 2008) at p. 134.

[13] '"State or national security" refers to the requirement to maintain the survival of the nation-state through the use of economic, military and political power and the exercise of diplomacy. "Human security" is a paradigm for understanding vulnerabilities, which argues that the proper reference for security should be individual rather than the state. Human security holds that a people-centred view of security is necessary for national, regional and global stability. "Environmental security" refers to the area of research and practice that addresses the linkages among the environment, natural resources, conflict and peacebuilding.' See UNEP Conflict to Peacebuilding (n 3) at p. 7.

[14] The terms 'security' and 'armed conflict' are not used as a complementary phrase but will each be discussed separately. 'Security' is reflected in Chapter 3

This study assesses the evolution of sustainable development and how the concept and its principles have gradually gained a key place in both international and domestic policy and law, particularly within the environmental arena. The book thus adopts a distinctive perspective on a growing body of literature in two main ways. First, it takes a broad holistic view of armed conflict issues, examining three stages in the 'life cycle' of conflict as it affects and is affected by the environment – pre-conflict, in-conflict and post-conflict:

- The 'pre-conflict' stage assesses what system, if any, the international community has in place under international law to prevent, mitigate and manage environmental problems such as environmental degradation and resource scarcity, in order to prevent possible environment-induced armed conflict.
- The 'in-conflict' stage examines the efficacy of the largely familiar rules under international law relevant to the environment during war and armed conflict.
- The 'post-conflict' stage reviews whether, in the current international law regime, appropriate 'reparations' (broadly) or restoration measures are available for war-related environmental damages.

As well as its distinctively holistic focus on the stages at which the environment, security and armed conflict converge, this book is distinctive in a second sense in its use of 'sustainable development' as a normative tool or objective applicable to this field. There is nothing new in the use of sustainable development as a device for measuring success or failure in environmental policy and law.[15]

(pre-conflict) in the context of environmental and other issues causing environmental insecurity and possible conflict; 'armed conflict' is reflected in Chapter 4 (in-conflict) where the existing international legal regime is examined to ascertain whether the environment is protected during times of armed conflict; and both 'armed conflict' and 'security' are considered in Chapter 5 (post-conflict) in the context of post-conflict environmental damage and the prevention of such damage from causing further environmental insecurity and possible re-conflict.

[15] See, e.g. UK, 'Sustainable Development in Government' DEFRA, www.defra.gov.uk/sustainable/government/ (accessed 24 February 2012); UK, 'UK Government Sustainable Development Framework Indicators' DEFRA, http://sd.defra.gov.uk/progress/national/ (accessed 24 February 2012) (primarily used in relation to environmental issues, policy and law); EU, 'Sustainable Development: Environment' European Commission, http://ec.europa.eu/environment/eussd/ (accessed 24 February 2012); OECD, *Measuring Sustainable*

2. AIM AND OUTLINE OF THE BOOK

As mentioned, this research is set in the context of security and armed conflict as relevant to the environment and the book's scope covers three stages: pre-conflict, in the context of prevention of environment-induced armed conflict; during armed conflict, in the context of environmental protection in actual battle; and post-conflict, in the context of how and who 'fixes' the war-damaged environment. This research does not confine itself to a specific geographical area, but it does concentrate on some conflicts in more depth than others.

Chapters 3–5 look at the specific life cycle of armed conflicts – pre-conflict, in-conflict and post-conflict by considering five case-studies to assess the applicability of the sustainable development concept in relation to the protection of the environment in the context of armed conflict. The case-studies selected concern recent relevant conflicts in Iraq; Kosovo; Darfur, Sudan; Somalia; and Sierra Leone. The aim of using these case-studies is to demonstrate the operation of law and policy in practical settings. These case-studies not only give a descriptive view of the subject researched, they are also intended to reflect the human experience in those situations. As Stake notes, '[v]icarious experience is an important basis for refining action option and expectations.'[16]

In addition, the scope of this book encompasses the international community as a whole[17] although in some circumstances it focuses on particular institutions and agencies that are most relevant, notably the United Nations (UN), United Nations Security Council (UNSC) and UNEP. It is worth pointing out that when this research initially began, the focus was entirely on the UNSC. However, as the research progressed, it became clear that no State, institution or agency could stand alone in dealing with environmental problems and protection relevant to security and armed conflict. The view being that through collective international efforts, responsibility or action in this regard would be most effectively

Development: Integrated Economic, Environmental and Social Frameworks (OECD, Paris 2004).

[16] Stake, R.E., 'Qualitative Case Studies' in Denzin, N.K. and Lincoln, Y.S., *The Sage Handbook of Qualitative Research* (3rd edn SAGE, California 2005) at p. 460.

[17] Includes States, international organisations and increasingly encompasses 'persons (both legal and natural) within and among those states.' See Sands, P. and Peel, J., *Principles of International Environmental Law* (3rd edn CUP, UK 2012) at p. 13. See also Annan, K.A., 'The Meaning of International Community' UNIS/SG/2478 (30 December 1999).

pursued. As Schrijver points out, '[n]o single world environmental organization or world sustainable development organization exists.'[18]

This book is thus divided into four substantive chapters. The aim of these chapters is to highlight the progress being made (or not) and the challenges the international community still faces in seeking to formulate a meaningful approach to the legal and institutional implementation of sustainable development in the context of this study.

- Chapter 2 introduces the general theoretical framework of sustainable development and its sub-principles that will continue to be used in Chapters 3–5. To reiterate, this study seeks to assess the debate surrounding the concept of sustainable development and take the concept forward in terms of the practical implementation of sustainable development in the context of environmental protection in security and armed conflict. Taking this step is only possible by acknowledging the underlying uncertainty that lies within the concept itself. Chapter 2 thus begins by tracing the origins and historical development of the concept of sustainable development; explores the definition of sustainable development; and then, addresses the legal status of the sub-principles under this overarching concept: the duty of states to ensure sustainable use of natural resources; the principle of equity and the eradication of poverty; the principle of common but differentiated responsibilities; the precautionary principle; the principle of participation; the principle of good governance; the principle of integration and interrelationship; and the polluter pays principle.
- Chapter 3 explores the pre-conflict stage in the context of the prevention of environment-induced armed conflict. It investigates the possible link between environmental factors and armed conflict in theory and in practice, through the evaluation of three case-studies: Somalia; Darfur, Sudan; and Sierra Leone. This chapter then reviews within the concept of sustainable development and the appropriate principles, the responses and actions of the international community in preventing environmental-induced armed conflict specifically in relation to the case-studies; followed by an appraisal as to whether in light of lessons learned, the international community has a system in place for preventing environmental-induced conflict.

---

[18] Schrijver, N., *Development without Destruction* (Indiana University, Indiana 2010) at p. 114.

- Chapter 4 considers the environment in the heat of armed conflict. It examines the protection of the environment during armed conflict as provided by international humanitarian law (IHL) – from the rules limiting the damage to the environment, to affixing liability for the damage concerned. This is examined within the context of two case-studies: the First Gulf War and the Kosovo conflict. The chapter focuses on whether the protection afforded to the environment by the relevant rules under IHL, allows for the environment to be protected in line with the concept of sustainable development.
- Chapter 5 explores the post-conflict stage where damage to the environment has already been done. This is considered from a crucial aspect of the post-conflict stage: finances. It reviews the international law reparations available for conflict-related environmental damage; possible valuation methods for environmental damage; how these methods are applied in practice by reviewing the US domestic system and in particular, by considering the UN Compensation Commission (UNCC) in relation to environmental damage as a consequence of the First Gulf War; and finally, considers the possible alternative of the polluter pays principle in holding parties financially liable for conflict-related environmental damage. This chapter then analyses post-conflict environmental recovery from a sustainable development perspective, after apportioning reparations (or not) in three post-conflict case-studies: the First Gulf War, Kosovo and Sudan.
- Chapter 6 concludes the book with a discussion of the main arguments; lessons learnt from the case-studies for possible reforms in relation to environmental protection relevant to armed conflict and suggestions for future research stemming from this study. It is argued, in the broadest terms, that at every stage in which it is analysed, policy, law and enforcement fall short of the sustainable development model, and this is something that needs to be addressed as a matter of urgency. The book suggests that among the greatest priorities is to develop an early warning provision that facilitates tackling the causes of armed conflict as they arise from human stress on the natural environment, although there are other priorities which will become clear as the book progresses.

2. Sustainable development, security and armed conflict – developing a theoretical framework for a legal analysis of war and the environment

1. INTRODUCTION

> Sustainable development is commonly defined as a process that improves today's quality of life without compromising tomorrow's. In many respects, war can be defined as the opposite of sustainable development. This is because, whatever its causes and justifications, war inevitably has a destructive effect... Armed conflicts disrupt society both socially and psychologically. They divert useful economic resources to destructive aims and often cause long term damage to natural resources.[1]

In recent decades, the international community has become increasingly aware of the ever more complex and pressing problems arising from growing pressure on the environment by humankind, calling for a reappraisal of international law and policy that is central to this study. In response to such developments is materialising a body of emerging rules and a multitude of treaty regimes which are today being implemented within the framework of the overarching policy concept of sustainable development. As Dernbach comments, '[g]rowing human demands on the environment have interfered with conventional development and cannot be sustained indefinitely. Sustainable development is a constructive response to this problem.'[2]

---

[1] Petitpierre, A., International Committee of the Red Cross (ICRC) Statement made at the World Summit on Sustainable Development, Johannesburg, South Africa (ICRC, 29 August 2002), www.un.org/events/wssd/statements/icrcE.htm (accessed 26 February 2012).

[2] Dernbach, J.C., 'Targets, Timetables and Effective Implementing Mechanisms: Necessary Building Blocks for Sustainable Development' (2002) 27 William and Mary Environmental Law and Policy Review 79, at p. 83.

Sustainable development embodies the requirement for 'accommodation, reconciliation and integration between economic growth, social justice (including human rights) and environmental protection objectives, towards participatory improvement in collective quality of life for the benefit of both present and future generations.'[3] It is a concept that integrates three core pillars – social, economic and environmental interests.[4] This book considers the extent to which the implementation of law and policy promotes this multi-faceted concept in the context of environmental protection relevant to security and armed conflict. Therefore the focus is with protecting the environment in a way that respects not only the environment in itself but also the environment in integration with social and economic conditions. As the Brundtland Commission observed,

> [t]he environment does not exist as a sphere separate from human actions, ambitions, and needs, and attempts to defend it in isolation from human concerns have given the very word "environment" a connotation of naivety in some political circles.

> But the "environment" is where we all live; and "development" is what we all do in attempting to improve our lot within that abode. The two are inseparable.[5]

In light of the observation that development and the environment are inseparable, this chapter explores the potential for viewing sustainable development as a concept relevant to security, armed conflict and the

---

[3] 'What is Sustainable Development Law?' Centre for International Sustainable Development Law (CISDL) Concept Paper (Montreal 2005) [hereinafter 2005 CISDL] (based on legal research in Cordonier Segger, M.C. and Khalfan, A., *Sustainable Development Law: Principles, Practices, and Prospects* (OUP, Oxford 2004) [hereinafter Segger and Khalfan]).

[4] For further analysis on sustainable development and the integration of economic growth, social justice, and environmental protection, see e.g. Segger and Khalfan (n 3); Cordonier Segger, M.C. and Weeramantry, C.G. (eds), *Sustainable Justice: Reconciling Economic, Social and Environmental Law* (Martinus Nijhoff, Leiden 2004); Gehring, M. and Cordonier Segger, M.C. (eds), *Sustainable Development in World Trade Law* (Kluwer Law, The Hague 2005); French, D., *International Law and Policy of Sustainable Development* (MUP, Manchester 2005) [hereinafter 2005 French]; Strange, T. and Bayley, A., *Sustainable Development: Linking Economy, Society, Environment* (OECD, France 2008).

[5] World Commission on Environment and Development (WCED, 1987), Our Common Future, 'Chairman's Foreword' [hereinafter Our Common Future].

environment. To achieve this objective the concept or paradigm of 'sustainable development', its legal status and its relevance and nexus to security and armed conflict is reviewed. In particular, Section 2 sketches the evolution of sustainable development; Section 3 considers the definition and elements of the term 'sustainable development', considering the 'sub-principles' integral to the overarching sustainable development concept; Section 4 explores the dilemma as to the ambivalent status of sustainable development from a lawyers' perspective, that is, is it merely a political concept or does it have legal significance and in particular, can it offer a normative framework for the critique of existing law and policy? Finally, Section 5 addresses sustainable development within the context of environmental protection relevant to international security and armed conflict.

2. EMERGENCE OF THE MODERN CONCEPT OF SUSTAINABLE DEVELOPMENT

While the 1987 report of the World Commission on Environment and Development (WCED) – 'Our Common Future', also known as the Brundtland Report, might have popularised the concept of sustainable development globally,[6] the theory that the human species need to live and proceed with development 'within the carrying capacity of the earth and to manage natural resources so as to meet both current demand and the need of future generations is not new.'[7]

According to Vice-President Weeramantry in *Gabčikovo-Nagymaros*,[8] the concept of sustainable development, integrating environmental considerations into economic activity and development needs, can be traced as far back as two millennia.[9] The concept of reconciling the needs of development with the protection of the environment was consciously and

---

[6]   Our Common Future (n 5).

[7]   Marong, A.B., 'From Rio to Johannesburg: Reflections on the Role of International Legal Norms in Sustainable Development' (2003) 16 Georgetown International Environmental Law Review 21, at p. 22 [hereinafter Marong]. For further discussion on the origins of 'sustainable development', see, e.g. Adams, W.M., *Green Development: Environment and Sustainability in the Third World* (2nd edn Routledge, London 2001) at pp. 22–53 [hereinafter Adams]; Strong, W.A. and Hemphill, L., *Sustainable Development Policy: Directory* (Blackwell, Oxford 2006) at pp. 1–2.

[8]   *Case Concerning the Gabčikovo-Nagymaros Project (Hungary/Slovakia)* (Judgement) [1997] ICJ Rep 7 [hereinafter *Gabčikovo-Nagymaros*].

[9]   Ibid., at pp. 97–110 (Separate Opinion of Vice-President Weeramantry).

meticulously practiced by the ancient tribes of Ceylon, Sub-Saharan Africa, Iran and China.[10] 'Sustainable development is thus not merely a principle of modern international law. It is one of the most ancient ideas in the human heritage.'[11] The concept of sustainable development can arguably be seen even during the eighteenth and nineteenth century Agricultural Revolution where subsistence farming gave way to more modernised farming and agricultural techniques that did not waste farmland or destroy the land completely, leaving behind barren plots of wasteland.[12]

Unfortunately, with the emergence of European colonialism and the late nineteenth century Industrial Revolution, environmental concerns were pushed to the background while States and private entities raced ahead to conquer the world.[13] This industrial revolution, a revolution built upon the erosion of the environment, changed Western society at the turn of the twentieth century in numerous fundamental respects.[14] Included within this is the emergence of 'developed' and 'developing' nations – a Western society of industrialised countries that have now become developed nations, and other countries seeking in broad terms to emulate the Western development process.[15]

In the early 1970s, the international community recognised that States, whether developed or developing, were increasingly applying their energies and efforts to the goal of development without regard to the environmental consequences.[16] This prompted within the international community the beginnings of an attempt to redefine development. Prior

---

[10]   Ibid.

[11]   Ibid., at p. 110.

[12]   Overton, M., 'Agricultural Revolution in England 1500–1850' (last updated 5 November 2009), www.bbc.co.uk/history/british/empire_seapower/agricultural_revolution_01.shtml (accessed 26 February 2012). See also Pearce, D.W. and Turner, R.K., *Economics of Natural Resources and the Environment* (John Hopkins University, Baltimore 1990) at pp. 6–7.

[13]   See, e.g. Duiker, W.J. and Spielvogel, J.J., *World History – Volume II: Since 1500* (6th edn Wadsworth, USA 2007) at pp. 549–80.

[14]   See, e.g. Krozer, Y., *Innovations and the Environment* (Springer-Verlag, London 2008) at p. 1.

[15]   Although the world has been split into two categories in this sense, in reality the line between rich and so-called poor countries has become somewhat blurred as there are various ways of determining whether a nation is 'developed' or 'developing'. See 'A Survey of the World Economy: A Question of Definition', *The Economist* (16 September 2006) at p. 6.

[16]   Chapter 1, 'The Founex Report on Development and Environment' (Founex, Switzerland, 4–12 June 1971).

to this, development was seen as high rates of economic and industrial-ised growth that would ease and solve most urgent social and human problems. However, the world soon came to the realisation that in many countries high growth rates had been achieved at a price – development accompanied by increasing unemployment, rising disparities in incomes both between groups and between regions, the deterioration of social and cultural conditions and increasing global environmental problems.[17]

The process of redefining the concept of development at this time led to greater emphasis being placed on the attainment of social and cultural goals as part of the development process and crucially, acknowledgement of the central importance of environmental issues. This emphasis was to be 'part of a more integrated or unified approach to the development objective.'[18]

The notion of development which could be reconciled with and was not incompatible with conserving the environment was brought up in 1971 at the Seminar on Environment and Development held in Founex, Switzerland.[19] As one commentator put it, '[a]t the Founex seminar, the notion was advanced that environmental concerns should not be a barrier to development, but part of the process; the goal was to achieve ecologically sound development, or eco-development. This notion even-tually developed into the concept of sustainable development.'[20] Such an approach to development and environmental issues unified the inter-national community to some extent, bridging the gap between the developed and developing countries in the realisation that these problems affect all.[21]

Following on from the Founex Seminar and Report, the 1972 Stock-holm Conference resulting in the Stockholm Declaration, is particularly important.[22] Although the Conference did not specifically use the term

---

[17]   Ibid.

[18]   Ibid.

[19]   Ibid.

[20]   Ntambirweki, J., 'The Developing Countries in the Evolution of Inter-national Environmental Law' (1991) 14 Hastings International and Comparative Law Review 905, at p. 907 [hereinafter Ntambirweki]. See also UNEP, 'The State of the Environment: 1972–1982' (UNEP, Nairobi 1982) at pp. 6–7; Hägerhäll, B. and Gooch, G.D., 'Sustainability as a Centrally-induced Swedish Local Discourse' in Svedin, U. and Aniansson, B.H. (eds), *Sustainability, Local Democracy and the Future: The Swedish Model* (Kluwer, The Netherlands 2002) at p. 51 [hereinafter Hägerhäll and Gooch].

[21]   Ibid.

[22]   Declaration of the UN Conference on the Human Environment, A/CONF.84/14 (1972) [hereinafter Stockholm Declaration].

'sustainable development', the Conference and subsequent Declaration laid the groundwork for the concept by endorsing the conclusion reached in the Founex Report that environmental and development issues are invariably connected. The Stockholm Declaration further recognised the concerns of developing nations regarding environmental protection and conservation.[23] Therefore developing countries, in directing their efforts towards development, bearing in mind their priority in alleviating poverty were urged to factor in the need to safeguard and improve the environment at the same time.[24] To sum it up, attended by 113 States, '[t]his first International Conference on Man and His Environment achieved its goal: to place the environment on the international agenda.'[25]

Evidence of the international community's increasing preoccupation with the nexus between the environment and development was explored further in 1983 when the WCED (also known as the Brundtland Commission) was established. This commission was convened by the UN in response to the 1983 UN General Assembly (UNGA) Resolution[26] which suggested that the Special Commission, when established, should focus primarily on long-term environmental strategies for achieving sustainable development; recommend ways to enhance international environmental and development cooperation as well as consider the means to effectively deal with global environmental concerns.[27] Five years later, the Commission submitted the Brundtland Report which came to the conclusion that critical global environmental problems were primarily the result of the enormous poverty of the South (developing nations) and the non-sustainable patterns of consumption and production in the North (developed nations).[28] The Brundtland Report, also known as 'Our Common Future' sets out the first official definition of sustainable development which is development aimed at 'meeting the needs of the present without compromising the ability of the future generations to meet their own needs.'[29] 'Our Common Future', urging the international community to play its part in putting the world onto sustainable paths,

[23] Preamble and paras. 4, 8, 9, 10, 11, 13, ibid.

[24] Ibid. See also Adams (n 7) at pp. 56–7.

[25] André, P., Delisle, C.E. and Revéret, J.-P. (trans.), *Environmental Assessment for Sustainable Development: Processes, Actors and Practice* (École Polytechnique de Montréal, Canada 2004) at p. 3 [hereinafter André].

[26] UNGA Resolution 38/161 (19 December 1983).

[27] Ibid.

[28] Our Common Future (n 5).

[29] Ibid.

attracted widespread support and initiated a global debate, renewing the world's interest in environmental and development issues.[30]

The Report was further debated within UNGA in 1989, which led to the organising of the 1992 UN Conference on Environment and Development (UNCED)[31] in Rio de Janeiro, Brazil. UNCED, often colloquially known as the 'Rio Conference' or the 'Earth Summit', sought to reaffirm and build upon the 1972 Stockholm Declaration. According to French, 'the primary purpose of the conference itself was the political endorsement of sustainable development as an international objective.'[32] Accordingly, the Rio Conference produced three non-binding texts: the Declaration on Environment and Development (Rio Declaration),[33] the Non-Legally Binding Authoritative Statement of Principles for a Global Consensus on the Management, Conservation and Sustainable Development of all Types of Forests (Forest Principles)[34] and a plan of action entitled Agenda 21,[35] which were adopted by more than 179 governments. French comments that, 'States were particularly conscious that despite these documents being non-binding in nature, the political commitments contained in them would set the parameters of the subsequent international political debate.'[36] The UN Commission on Sustainable Development (CSD) was created in December 1992 to ensure effective follow-up of UNCED, to monitor and report on implementation of the agreements at the local, national, regional, and international levels.[37]

In August 2002, the full implementation of Agenda 21, the Programme for Further Implementation of Agenda 21, and the Commitments to the Rio principles were reaffirmed at the World Summit on Sustainable

---

[30]   Ibid. See also Marong (n 7) at pp. 26–8.

[31]   For more information on 'sustainable development' and UNCED, see, e.g. Adams (n 7) at pp. 80–101; Pallemaerts, M., 'International Environmental Law in the Age of Sustainable Development: A Critical Assessment of the UNCED Process' (1996) 15 Journal of Law & Commerce 623.

[32]   2005 French (n 4) at p. 18.

[33]   UN Doc. A/CONF.151/26/REV.1, Vol. I (12 August 1992) [hereinafter Rio Declaration].

[34]   UN Doc. A/CONF.151/26/REV.1, Vol. III (14 August 1992).

[35]   UN Doc. A/CONF.151/26/REV.1, Vol. I (12 August 1992) [hereinafter Agenda 21].

[36]   2005 French (n 4) at p. 18.

[37]   See UN Department of Economic and Social Affairs (UNDESA), Division for Sustainable Development, 'About the UN Commission for Sustainable Development (CSD)', www.un.org/esa/dsd/csd/csd_aboucsd.shtml (accessed 26 February 2012).

Development (WSSD) held in Johannesburg, South Africa. The WSSD's intended purpose was to hold a ten-year review of the 1992 Rio Conference. States negotiated and agreed to adopt two documents: the Johannesburg Declaration[38] and its associated Plan of Implementation (JPOI).[39] The Johannesburg Declaration, though not a binding treaty was nevertheless an indication of an emerging commitment by the global community to sustainable development as a framework for both international law as a whole and international environmental law specifically.[40] As Gray comments,

> [i]n order to assess the outcome of WSSD, one has to be mindful of its mandate to identify to implement the Rio Agreements, accomplishments and areas where more effort and action oriented decision is needed, as well as new challenges and opportunities. What evolved was something different, with less focus on reviewing previous activities and more attention directed towards how governments will address the sustainable development challenges in the future.[41]

At this point, although strides had been made towards the emergence of the concept of sustainable development within the international legal community, the general consensus was that the results thus far had not achieved their full potential.[42] Moreover, despite the continuing relevance within the realms of international relations and international environmental law of many of the declarations and international statements embracing sustainable development,[43] there nevertheless remained a

---

[38] Johannesburg Declaration on Sustainable Development (4 September 2002), UN 'Report of the World Summit on Sustainable Development', Johannesburg, South Africa (26 August–4 September 2002) UN Doc. A/CONF.199/20.

[39] Ibid., at p. 6.

[40] See, e.g. Mayeda, G., 'Where Should Johannesburg Take Us? Ethical and Legal Approaches to Sustainable Development in the Context of International Environmental Law' (2004) 15 Colorado Journal of International Environmental Law and Policy 29 [hereinafter Mayeda]; Gray, K.R., 'World Summit on Sustainable Development: Accomplishments and New Directions?' (2003) 52 International and Comparative Law Quarterly 256, at pp. 256–7 [hereinafter Gray] (on discussions and conclusions of the WSSD).

[41] Gray (n 40) at p. 267. See also UNGA Resolution 55/199 (20 December 2000) (ten-year review of progress achieved in the implementation of the UNCED outcome).

[42] 2005 French (n 4) at p. 71.

[43] See Segger and Khalfan (n 3) at pp. 15–44 (for a more comprehensive review of the declarations and statements reflecting the concept of sustainable development; which from Stockholm to Johannesburg, are soft-law instruments).

'need for a comprehensive international law perspective on integration of social, economic, financial, and environmental objectives and activities.'[44] As French notes, 'it was in this spirit that the Committee on Legal Aspects of Sustainable Development of the International Law Association (ILA) formulated its 2002 New Delhi Declaration of Principles of International Law relating to Sustainable Development.'[45] The New Delhi Declaration is based on seven core principles:

1.   The duty of states to ensure sustainable use of natural resources.
2.   The principle of equity and the eradication of poverty.
3.   The principle of common but differentiated responsibilities.
4.   The principle of the precautionary approach to human health, natural resources and ecosystems.
5.   The principle of participation and access to information and justice.
6.   The principle of good governance.
7.   The principle of integration and interrelationship.

The Declaration identifies the seven principles above, without claiming them to be exhaustive.[46] The 2002 New Delhi Declaration of Principles still remains one of the high watermarks in the general development of the concept of sustainable development as it provides a clear and succinct list which could be used as a set of guidelines with which to pursue and

---

For further explanation on 'soft-law', see, e.g. Hillgenberg, H., 'A Fresh Look at Soft Law' (1999) 10 European Journal of International Law 499 (on the importance of soft law in international relations); Keller, H., 'Codes of Conduct and their Implementation: the Question of Legitimacy' in Wolfrum, R. and Röben, V. (eds), *Legitimacy in International Law* (Springer, Berlin 2008) at pp. 248–9 (on the legal relevance of 'soft-law' in influencing State and non-State actors in the international arena).

[44]   Preamble, 'ILA New Delhi Declaration of Principles of International Law Relating to Sustainable Development, 2 April 2002' (2002) 2 International Environmental Agreements: Politics, Law and Economics 211 [hereinafter New Delhi Declaration]. See also ILA's International Law on Sustainable Development Committee, International Law on Sustainable Development, Fifth and Final Report, New Delhi Conference 2002 [hereinafter 2002 ILA New Delhi Report]. The Declaration was formulated after 10 years of research and study. See 2005 CISDL (n 3).

[45]   French, D., 'International Law in the Field of Sustainable Development: the Elaboration of Legal Principles' (2004) 16 Environmental Law and Management 296, at p. 297 [hereinafter 2004 French].

[46]   2005 CISDL (n 3). See also ILA, 'Report of the Seventieth Conference, New Delhi' (ILA 2002) at pp. 861–2 (citing Nico Schrijver: 'The body of the Declaration contained in the Report did not claim to be exhaustive').

achieve sustainable development.[47] As the preamble to the New Delhi Declaration states, 'the application and, where relevant, consolidation and further development of the following principles of international law relevant to the activities of all actors involved would be instrumental in pursuing the objective of sustainable development in an effective way.'[48]

In recent years, the international community once again reaffirmed their commitment to the sustainable development paradigm, although the ILA statement above remains the cornerstone of any legal analysis. From the UN releasing the Millennium Development Goals Report[49] in May 2005, reporting on progress made (if any), towards achieving the Millennium Development Goals (MDGs)[50] including States committing to principles of sustainable development within their national policies, to the adoption of the 2005 World Summit Outcome[51] by UNGA, the sustainable development concept continues to be fleshed out at a strategic level. The World Summit Outcome reaffirmed the Millennium Declaration and recognised sustainable development as a key element of UN

---

[47]   See also Segger and Khalfan (n 3); Schrijver, N., *The Evolution of Sustainable Development in International Law: Inception, Meaning and Status* (Martinus Nijhoff, Leiden 2008) at pp. 171–207 [hereinafter 2008 Schrijver].

[48]   Preamble, New Delhi Declaration. The ILA's International Law on Sustainable Development Committee's work continues. See, e.g. ILA's International Law on Sustainable Development Committee, International Law on Sustainable Development, First Report, Berlin Conference 2004 [hereinafter ILA Berlin Report]; ILA's International Law on Sustainable Development Committee, International Law on Sustainable Development, Second Report, Toronto Conference 2006 [hereinafter ILA Toronto Report]; ILA's International Law on Sustainable Development Committee, International Law on Sustainable Development, Third Report, Rio De Janeiro Conference 2008 [hereinafter ILA Rio Report]; ILA's International Law on Sustainable Development Committee, International Law on Sustainable Development, Fourth Report, The Hague Conference 2010 [hereinafter ILA Hague Report].

[49]   UN, *Millennium Development Goals Report* (UN, New York 2005) at p. 30 (Goal 7: Ensure Environmental Sustainability).

[50]   The eight MDGs were set out in the Millennium Declaration drawn up in September 2000 at the Millennium Summit, participated by 189 States and UNGA. See Millennium Declaration, UN Doc. A/RES/55/2 (18 September 2000). For further information on the MDGs, see UN Development Programme (UNDP), 'Human Development Report 2003' (OUP, New York/Oxford 2003); UN Millennium Website, www.un.org/millennium/ (accessed 26 February 2012); and annual MDGs Reports (UN, New York), www.un.org/millenniumgoals/reports.shtml (accessed 26 February 2012).

[51]   2005 World Summit Outcome, UNGA Resolution 60/1 (24 October 2005).

activities.[52] As Magraw and Hawke note, '[t]aking the 2005 World Summit Outcome as a whole, together with the other instruments mentioned earlier and the fact that day-to-day discourse at the United Nations and elsewhere routinely use the term 'sustainable development', sustainable development … remains the overarching paradigm for both development and environmental protection.'[53] This is still in evidence today as sustainable development continues to have a presence on the global agenda. As the twenty year anniversary of the Rio Earth Summit (also referred to as Rio+20) takes place in Rio de Janeiro, Brazil in 2012, the world once again focuses on sustainable development.[54]

In summary, these international conferences and subsequent declarations over the last four decades have encouraged and developed global discourse and debate on the concept of sustainable development. Furthermore these global summits, as Schrijver notes, 'have stimulated the modification of existing law and the development of new law.'[55]

3. DEFINITION AND ELEMENTS OF SUSTAINABLE DEVELOPMENT

This section briefly explores the definition of sustainable development in international law and the eight principles under the overarching concept of sustainable development (as set out in the New Delhi Declaration and an additional principle – 'polluter pays'). As mentioned above, these New

---

[52]   Paras. 3 and 10, ibid.

[53]   Magraw, D.B. and Hawke, L.D., 'Sustainable Development' in Bodansky, D., Brunnée, J. and Hey, E. (eds), *The Oxford Handbook of International Environmental Law* (OUP, Oxford 2007) at p. 618 [hereinafter Magraw and Hawke] [Bodansky (eds)].

[54]   See RIO+20, UN Conference on Sustainable Development, 20–22 June 2012, www.uncsd2012.org/rio20/index.html (accessed 11 March 2012) [hereinafter RIO+20 Conference]; Earth Summit 2012, www.earthsummit2012.org/ (accessed 2 March 2012).

[55]   2008 Schrijver (n 47) at p. 99. For more discussion on the evolution of sustainable development, see, e.g. Drexhage, J. and Murphy, D., 'Sustainable Development: From Brundtland to Rio 2012' Background Paper prepared for consideration by the High Level Panel on Global Sustainability at its first meeting, 19 September 2010 (UN, New York 2010); Adams (n 7) at pp. 54–101; Cordonier Segger, M.C., 'The Role of International Forums in the Advancement of Sustainable Development' (2009) 10 Sustainable Development Law & Policy 4 [hereinafter 2009 Segger]. See also International Institute for Sustainable Development (IISD), 'Sustainable Development Timeline', www.iisd.org/rio+5/ timeline/sdtimeline.htm (accessed 26 February 2012).

Delhi principles of international law 'would be instrumental in pursuing the objective of sustainable development in an effective way'[56] and they are not meant to be exhaustive. Thus this study introduces in addition, an eighth principle of 'polluter pays' to be grouped under the umbrella of the sustainable development concept. As this book considers environmental protection relevant to security and armed conflict in light of sustainable development, it is explored whether these principles (if any) can be used as guidelines or objectives to achieve sustainable development in that context.

3.1. Definition of Sustainable Development

Development[57] in the traditional sense has clearly brought many benefits. However, it has also resulted in environmental damage and deterioration and an ever widening global poverty gap between the wealthy and the poor. These problems are inevitably linked. Environmental degradation in certain instances is a result of poverty and environmental degradation in turn contributes to poverty.[58] The international community, by adding 'sustainable' to 'development' was attempting to address and solve all these problems by making development sustainable. As Dernbach points out in an argument that is central to the present concerns,

> [t]he essential idea is to protect and restore the environment at the same time as we foster peace and security, economic development, and social development... Sustainable development redefines progress to include environmental protection or restoration as something to be achieved along with other goals, not something to be sacrificed in order to reach these goals.[59]

Overall, the phrase 'sustainable development' is understood globally to incorporate the environment, peace and security, economic development, social development and human rights.[60] There has been considerable debate as to the definition of sustainable development within these broad

---

[56]   Preamble, New Delhi Declaration.

[57]   'Development can be defined as a collective process of change toward improvements in quality of life for human beings and their communities'. See 2005 CISDL (n 3).

[58]   Our Common Future (n 5).

[59]   Dernbach, J.C., 'Achieving Sustainable Development: The Centrality and Multiple Facets of Integrated Decisionmaking' (2003) 10 Indiana Journal of Global Legal Studies 247 [hereinafter 2003 Dernbach].

[60]   Dernbach, J.C., 'Sustainable Development as a Framework for National Governance' (1998) 49 Case Western Reserve Law Review 1, at pp. 9–14.

parameters.[61] For example, McCloskey argues that the 'basic notion of sustainable development implies that development would be guided by physical and environmental constraints (i.e., development which is 'sustainable').'[62] Sands, on the other hand defines sustainable development as a principle that 'requires states to ensure that they develop and use their natural resources in a manner which is sustainable.'[63] There are varying definitions and interpretations of sustainable development as '[f]inding one accepted, universal definition of sustainable development that is appropriate for all cultures and regions of the world is not straightforward.'[64]

From the foundation of the Founex Report, where the groundwork for the current notion or concept of sustainable development was first laid out, to the 2004 ILA Berlin Conference and beyond, the debate over the definition of sustainable development continues.[65] Nonetheless, the definition and objective of sustainable development in the Brundtland Report was recognised and referred to in the New Delhi Declaration and the subsequent Berlin Conference in 2004, and it is a definition used well into the new millennium, and has thus proved remarkably resilient. The Brundtland Report put forth what is currently the most commonly used and probably the most compelling (if broad) basic definition of sustainable development.[66] Scholars have commented that the report 'broke new conceptual ground.'[67] It defined sustainable development, to reiterate, as 'development that meets the needs of the present without compromising

---

[61]   See, e.g. McNeill, D., 'The Concept of Sustainable Development' in Lee, K., Holland, A. and McNeil, D. (eds), *Global Sustainable Development in the 21st Century* (Edinburgh University, Edinburgh 2000) at p. 11; Cooper, P.J., and Vargas, C.M., *Implementing Sustainable Development: From Global Policy to Local Action* (Rowman & Littlefield, USA 2004) at p. 24 [hereinafter Cooper and Vargas].

[62]   McCloskey, M., 'The Emperor Has No Clothes: The Conundrum of Sustainable Development' (1999) 9 Duke Environmental Law & Policy Forum 153, at p. 154 [hereinafter McCloskey].

[63]   Sands, P., 'Environmental Protection in the Twenty-First Century: Sustainable Development and International Law' in Revesz, R.L., Sands, P. and Stewart, R.B. (eds), *Environmental Law, the Economy and Sustainable Development* (CUP, Cambridge 2000) at p. 345 [hereinafter 2000 Sands].

[64]   2009 Segger (n 55).

[65]   See, e.g. Park, S., 'The World Bank, Dams and the Meaning of Sustainable Development in Use' (2009) 5 Journal of International Law & International Relations 93.

[66]   2004 French (n 45).

[67]   McCloskey (n 62) at p. 154. See also Cooper and Vargas (n 61) at p. 24.

the ability of future generations to meet their own needs.'[68] This definition has been widely quoted by the international community.

The Brundtland Report's definition of sustainable development was later incorporated in Principle 4 of the Rio Declaration, which states that, '[i]n order to achieve sustainable development, environmental protection shall constitute an integral part of the development process and cannot be considered in isolation from it.' It has nevertheless been argued that the Brundtland definition is vague and lacking in substantive meaning.[69] Overall however, scholarship here is best summed up by Reid, who comments that 'despite its vagueness – indeed perhaps because of it – the Brundtland definition makes an important statement ... it has more of the character of a moral principle than a precise definition.'[70] Its vagueness in itself enables this definition to be used as a guiding definition for sustainable development in differing circumstances, yet it is not so hopelessly vague that it cannot guide decision-making in these various contexts.

3.2. Sustainable Development in the Field of International Law

Sustainable development is a concept that consists of a number of elements. As Vice-President Weeramantry points out, the notion of sustainable development 'represents a delicate balancing of competing interests.'[71] Sands argues that as a principle of international law, sustainable development requires recognition of inter- and intra-generational equity, the sustainable use of natural resources, common but differentiated environmental responsibilities and the integration of environmental decision-making.[72] Voigt's sustainable development concept for example includes amongst others, the precautionary principle, polluter pays principle and the principle of common but differentiated responsibilities.[73]

---

[68]   Our Common Future (n 5).

[69]   2005 French (n 4) at p. 16.

[70]   Reid, D., *Sustainable Development – An Introductory Guide* (Earthscan, London 1995) at p. xvi.

[71]   Weeramantry, C.G., 'Foreword' in Segger and Khalfan (n 3).

[72]   2000 Sands (n 63) at pp. 369–79.

[73]   Voigt, C., *Sustainable Development as a Principle of International Law: Resolving Conflict between Climate Measures and WTO Law* (Koninklijke Brill NV, The Netherlands 2009) at p. 37 [hereinafter Voigt].

Different scholars have varying views on the principles that make up sustainable development.[74] In the context of this book however, it is suggested that the set of principles that could constitute a framework for achieving sustainable development is the compilation of seven principles within the New Delhi Declaration touched on above as well as the addition of the 'polluter pays' principle. As this study aims to use these principles as instruments or guidelines to achieve sustainable development in the context of the protection of the environment in relation to security and armed conflict, it is worth briefly exploring the status or legal relevance (if any) of these substantive principles of international law related to sustainable development. It should be stressed that, in this section of the chapter, the concern is with setting out these principles largely in abstraction apart from the armed conflict theme. That theme is picked up in the remainder of the chapter and the book as a whole.

3.2.1. The duty of States to ensure sustainable use of natural resources

Traditionally, State territory and State sovereignty were considered supreme, where activities or issues occurring within national jurisdiction could not be challenged by other States. However, as Boyle and Freestone point out,

> [i]t is no longer easy to accept that States may do whatever they please within their own territory or on the high seas when we know that certain types of activity – such as the release of ozone-depleting chemicals or the burning of fossil fuels – may well cause damage to global environmental systems.[75]

Simply put, States' sovereign rights over their natural resources are no longer absolute. This is set out by this principle which consists of three elements. First, it maintains that while States have sovereignty over their own natural resources, they have a duty to ensure they do not cause undue damage to the environment of other States and beyond their own territorial jurisdiction.[76] Second, this principle also goes on to state that States have a duty to manage their natural resources in a sustainable

---

[74]   See, e.g. 2005 French (n 4) at p. 53; Sands, P., *Principles of International Environmental Law* (2nd edn CUP, Cambridge 2003) at p. 253 [hereinafter 2003 Sands].

[75]   Boyle, A. and Freestone, D., 'Introduction' in Boyle, A. and Freestone, D. (eds), *International Law and Sustainable Development: Past Achievements and Future Challenges* (OUP, New York 2001) at p. 2 [hereinafter Boyle and Freestone (eds)].

[76]   Principle 1.1, New Delhi Declaration.

manner, taking into account current and future generations[77] and third, that 'protection, preservation and enhancement of the natural environment … are of common concern to humankind.'[78] As Handl comments, 'sovereignty signals no longer a simple *status negativus,* a legal basis for exclusion, but has become a legal basis for inclusion, or a commitment to co-operate for the good of the international community at large'.[79]

The first element of this principle, the obligation imposed on States not to allow their territory to be used in such a manner so as to cause harm to the territory of other States or to common global areas, can be traced back to the *Trail Smelter Arbitration*[80] where Canada was held liable for transboundary air pollution.[81] This is reflected within Principle 21 of the Stockholm Declaration which provides that although States have a sovereign right to exploit their own resources, they also have an obligation to ensure that activities under their jurisdiction or control do not cause harm or damage to the environment of other States or to areas beyond national jurisdiction. Principle 21, which was further reaffirmed by Principle 2 of the Rio Declaration, is considered to be part of customary international law.[82] Both principles were endorsed by the International Court of Justice (ICJ) in the *Nuclear Weapons* Advisory Opinion[83] where it expressed its view that States have an obligation not to cause transboundary environmental harm to other States or to areas beyond their territorial jurisdiction. This principle can also be seen incorporated within numerous treaties and conventions.[84] For example,

---

[77] Principle 1.2, ibid.

[78] Principle 1.3, ibid.

[79] Handl, G., 'Environmental Security and Global Change: The Challenge to International Law' (1990) 1 Yearbook of International Environmental Law 3, at p. 32.

[80] *Trail Smelter Arbitration (US v Canada)* 3 RIAA 1911 (1938), reprinted in (1939) 33 AJIL 182; 3 RIAA 1938 (1941), reprinted in (1941) 35 AJIL 684.

[81] Ibid. See also *Corfu Channel (UK v Albania)* [1949] ICJ Rep 4, 22; *Lac Lanoux Arbitration (Spain v France)* 12 RIAA 281, 23 ILR 101, 123 (1957).

[82] See, e.g. Schrijver, N., *Permanent Sovereignty over Natural Resources: Balancing Rights and Duties* (CUP, Cambridge 1997) at pp. 390–92; 2005 French (n 4) at p. 58.

[83] *Legality of the Threat and Use of Nuclear Weapons* (Advisory Opinion) [1996] ICJ Rep 266, at pp. 241–2 [hereinafter Nuclear Weapons].

[84] See, e.g. Art. 30, Charter of Economic Rights and Duties of States, UNGA Res. 3821, UN GAOR, 29th Sess., Supp. No. 31, 50, UN Doc. A/9631 (1974); Final Act of the Helsinki Conference on Security and Co-operation in Europe (1975) 14 ILM 1292; Art. 3(5), Lima Convention for the Protection of the Marine Environment and Coastal area of the South-East Pacific, UN Doc

Article 193 of the UN Convention on the Law of the Sea (UNCLOS)[85] provides that 'States have the sovereign right to exploit their own natural resources pursuant to their environmental policies and in accordance with their duty to protect and preserve the marine environment.' In addition to this, Article 194(2) requires States to take the necessary measures to prevent causing transboundary environmental harm to other States as well as beyond their territorial jurisdiction.[86] Another example can be seen from the Preamble of the UN Framework Convention on Climate Change (UNFCCC)[87] which refers to this principle in light of protecting the global climate.

The second and third element of Principle 1 of the New Delhi Declaration: the duty of States to manage their natural resources sustainably and that conserving the natural environment is of common concern, as French notes, is 'more progressive than current international law'.[88] Nevertheless, support for the requirement for 'sustainable use' and 'common concern' can be seen from its incorporation within a number of treaties and conventions.[89] For example, the Preamble of the UN Convention on Biological Diversity (UNCBD)[90] affirms 'that the conservation of biological diversity is a common concern of humankind' and that 'States are responsible for conserving their biological diversity and for using their biological resources in a sustainable manner.' The second and third elements of this principle broaden the first element by integrating that in addition to having the right to manage their own resources subject to

---

UNEP/GC/INF.11, 185 (12 November 1981). For a list and review of treaties reflecting this principle, see Segger and Khalfan (n 3) at pp. 109–22.

[85]   UN Convention on the Law of the Sea (adopted 10 December 1982, entered into force 16 November 1994) (182) 21 ILM 1261 [hereinafter UNCLOS].

[86]   Art. 194(2), ibid.

[87]   UN Framework Convention on Climate Change (adopted 9 May 1992, entered into force 21 March 1994) (1992) 31 ILM 849 [hereinafter UNFCCC].

[88]   2005 French (n 4) at p. 59.

[89]   For 'sustainable use' see, e.g. Preamble, Convention for the Protection of the Marine Environment of the North-East Atlantic (adopted 22 September 1992, entered into force 25 March 1998) (1993) 32 ILM 1069; Art. 1(h), International Tropical Timber Agreement, (10 January 1994), UN Conference on Trade and Development, UN Doc TD/TIMBER.2/Misc.7/GE.94–50830 (1994). For 'common concern' see, e.g. Preamble, Convention on the Conservation of Antarctic Marine Living Resources, (20 May 1980) (1980) 19 ILM 841; Art. 1, FAO International Undertaking on Plant Genetic Resources, FAO Res 8/83 (1983).

[90]   UN Convention on Biological Diversity (adopted 5 June 1992, entered into force 29 December 1993) (1992) 31 ILM 822 [hereinafter UNCBD].

avoiding undue transboundary environmental harm, States should bear in mind the need to sustainably manage their natural resources as well as the 'collective concern for the management of certain resources.'[91] This has been reflected by the international community in its willingness to refer or incorporate these broadening objectives into recent treaties and conventions.[92]

3.2.2. The principle of equity and eradication of poverty

The principle of equity, as set out in the New Delhi Declaration:

> refers to both *inter-generational equity* (the rights of future generations to enjoy a fair level of common patrimony) and *intra-generational equity* (the right of all peoples within the current generation of fair access to the current generation's entitlement to the Earth's natural resources).[93]

The second element of this principle: 'eradication of poverty', extends the principle of equity, requiring States to meet the environmental and developmental needs of the current and future generations in an equitable and sustainable manner and also to cooperate to eradicate poverty.[94] Simply put, this principle calls for States to endorse fair and equitable utilisation of resources amongst the population of the present generation with primary focus on the needs of the poor, in addition to taking into account the rights of future generations in relation to those resources. As Gundling sums up our global challenge, 'without equity within the present generation, we will not be able to achieve equity among generations.'[95]

This principle, as Segger argues, 'finds its roots in Chapter IX of the *Charter of the United Nations*, where the United Nations has the role of promoting higher standards of living, full employment, conditions of economic and social progress and development, respect for human rights,

---

[91] Cordonier Segger, M.C. and others, *Weaving the Rules for Our Common Future: Principles, Practices and Prospects for International Sustainable Development Law* (CISDL, Montreal 2002) at p. 45 [hereinafter 2002 Segger].

[92] For further discussion on this principle, see Segger and Khalfan (n 3) at pp. 109–22; 2008 Schrijver (n 47) at pp. 173–5. See also 2005 French (n 4) at pp. 57–9 (on the principle of sustainable use).

[93] Principle 2.1, New Delhi Declaration.

[94] Principles 2.3 and 2.4, ibid.

[95] Gundling, L., 'Our Responsibility to the Future Generations' (1990) 84 American Journal of International Law 207 at p. 208 [hereinafter Gundling].

among others'.[96-97] Tellingly, the UN Charter also makes reference to responsibility towards future generations by stating its intent in the Preamble: 'to save succeeding generations from the scourge of war'.[98]

This principle or elements of it can thereafter be seen in a number of multilateral declarations. The Brundtland Report for instance, sets out that the attainment of sustainable development is to be understood as development that includes economic, social and environmental interests, taking into account the needs and interests of the current generation as well of those of generations to come.[99] The Stockholm Declaration for example, proclaims that, '[m]an has the fundamental right to ... equality and adequate conditions of life ... and he bears a solemn responsibility to protect and improve the environment for present and future generations.'[100] This principle was further reaffirmed by the Rio Declaration which sets out that, '[t]he right to development must be fulfilled so as to equitably meet developmental and environmental needs of present and future generations.'[101] Principle 5 goes on to state that the international community 'shall cooperate in the essential task of eradicating poverty as an indispensable requirement for sustainable development.'[102]

This principle is also reflected in various international treaties relevant to sustainable development.[103] For example, the UNFCCC refers to the need to take into account 'the legitimate priority needs of developing countries for the achievement of sustained economic growth and the eradication of poverty'[104] as well as the intention to 'protect the climate system for the benefit of present and future generations, on the basis of equity'.[105] The UNCBD is another example, where sharing benefits equitably and intra- and inter-generational equity are referred to in its preambular paragraphs[106] as well as further encouraging equitable sharing in relation to genetic resources in Article 15(7). In a more practical

---

[96]   Arts. 55 and 56, Charter of the United Nations (adopted 26 June 1945, entered into force 24 October 1945) 1 UNTS xvi [hereinafter UN Charter].

[97]   Segger and Khalfan (n 3) at p. 123.

[98]   Preamble, UN Charter.

[99]   Our Common Future (n 5).

[100]   Art. 1, Stockholm Declaration.

[101]   Principle 3, Rio Declaration.

[102]   Principle 5, ibid.

[103]   For a list and review of treaties, see, e.g. Segger and Khalfan (n 3) at pp. 122–32.

[104]   Preamble, UNFCCC.

[105]   Art. 3(1), ibid

[106]   Preamble, UNCBD.

example, the FAO Plant Treaty[107] for instance, sets out a 'multilateral system of access and benefit', operationalising the sharing of plant genetic resources in a 'fair and equitable way.'[108]

In addition to treaties, this principle can also be seen in case-law. In *Minors Oposa*,[109] the Philippines Supreme Court decided that intra- and inter-generational equity is a legal right.[110] The Court held that the minors (Plaintiffs) seeking to halt large-scale timber licensing in order to prevent deforestation, had the right to file a class action suit 'for themselves, for others of their generation and for the succeeding generations... Their personality to sue in behalf of the succeeding generations can only be based on the concept of intergenerational responsibility insofar as the right to a balanced and health ecology is concerned.'[111]

The Court also stated that the utilisation, exploitation and development of nature and natural resources must be 'equitably accessible to the present as well as future generations.'[112] Reference to the intergenerational equity principle was also made in ICJ cases, though mainly within the separate opinions of Vice-President Weeramantry. Intergenerational equity was referred to as 'an important and rapidly developing principle of contemporary environmental law' in the 1995 *Nuclear Tests (New Zealand v France)* case.[113] References to equitable sharing for intra- and inter-generations were also made in the *Maritime Delimitation (Denmark v Norway)* case.[114]

---

[107]   International Treaty on Plant Genetic Resources for Food and Agriculture (adopted 3 November 2001, entered into force 29 June 2004) [2001] IELMT 28 [hereinafter FAO Plant Treaty].

[108]   Arts. 1.1, 10, 11, 12, 13, ibid.

[109]   Supreme Court of the Philippines, *Minors Oposa v Secretary of the Department of Environment and Natural Resources (DENR)* (30 July 1993) (1994) 33 ILM 173, at p. 185 [hereinafter *Minors Oposa*].

[110]   Ibid.

[111]   Ibid.

[112]   Ibid.

[113]   *Request for an examination of the Situation in Accordance with Paragraph 63 of the Court's Judgement of 20 December 1974 in the Nuclear Tests* (New Zealand v France) *Case (New Zealand v France)* (Order) [1995] ICJ Rep 288, at p. 341 (Dissenting Opinion of Judge Weeramantry) [hereinafter 1995 Nuclear Tests].

[114]   *Case Concerning Maritime Delimitation in the Area Between Greenland and Jan Mayen (Denmark v Norway)* [1993] ICJ Rep 38, at pp. 274–7 (Separate Opinion of Judge Weeramantry). See also *Nuclear Weapons* (n 83) at p. 19, para. 29 (ICJ recognised that 'quality of life' in relation to the environment also affected 'generations unborn').

Although this principle is evident in various declarations, treaties and case-law, its legal status is still uncertain and opinion is divided. Some scholars are of the view that this principle is a legal norm.[115] For example Weiss states that, 'sustainable development implies that future generations have as much *right* as the present generation to a robust environment with which to meet their own needs and preferences.'[116] Others however, are of the opinion that it is 'more an objective than a principle of international law.'[117] As Segger and Khalfan succinctly explain, at present this principle is not as yet entrenched within customary international law 'due in part to difficulties in identifying with certainty the needs of future generations, and the lack of consensus between States on the obligation to ensure distributional justice between States.'[118] It is suggested that regardless of its normative status, as this principle is being increasingly reflected in multilateral declarations, treaties and judicial decisions relevant to sustainable development, this is evidence of not only the international community's growing commitment towards it but also that this principle is a crucial objective or guidance tool for States and the international community in striving for sustainable development.[119]

3.2.3.   The principle of common but differentiated responsibilities

Scholars have determined that this principle 'evolved from the notion of "common heritage of mankind" and is a particular manifestation of general principles of equity in international law.'[120] This principle not only recognises that all States and non-State actors are required to

---

[115]   For a discussion of proponents for the 'principle of equity' as a legal norm, see 2002 Segger (n 91) at pp. 46–7.

[116]   Weiss, E.B., 'Environmentally Sustainable Competitiveness: A Comment' (1993) 102 Yale Law Journal 2123 (emphasis added).

[117]   2008 Schrijver (n 47) at p. 178. See also 2005 French (n 4) at pp. 60–67.

[118]   Segger and Khalfan (n 3) at p. 132.

[119]   For more discussion on this principle relevant to sustainable development, see 2008 Schrijver (n 47) at pp. 175–8; 2005 French (n 4) at pp. 59–67. For more debate on the principle of equity itself, see, e.g. D'Amato, A., 'Do We Owe a Duty to Future Generations to Preserve the Global Environment?' (1990) 94 American Journal of International Law 190; Weiss, E.B., 'Our Rights and Obligations to Future Generations for the Environment' (1990) 84 American Journal of International Law 198 (1990); Gundling (n 95).

[120]   Segger and Khalfan (n 3) at pp. 132–3. See also Sands, P., *Principles of International Environmental Law I: Frameworks, Standards and Implementation* (MUP, Manchester 1995) at p. 217 [hereinafter 1995 Sands Frameworks].

cooperate in their common global responsibility towards the environment[121] but also takes into account the varying degrees of contribution by each developed and developing nation towards current environmental problems.[122] In acknowledging the differing capacities of each State in dealing with current and emerging environmental problems as well as the needs and interests of developing countries in particular,[123] this principle further provides that developed States should bear the responsibility in taking the lead and assisting developing countries in achieving sustainable development.[124] In essence, this principle encourages the international community to effectively cooperate in its 'common responsibility' towards the environment but also equitably demarcates the responsibility to do so on the basis of individual or (developed vs. developing) State capacity.

Accordingly, of particular significance is the Rio Declaration. Principle 6, in addition to acknowledging that all States' interests and needs in relation to the environment and development should be addressed, goes on to proclaim that '[t]he special situation and needs of developing countries, particularly the least developed and those most environmentally vulnerable shall be given special priority'.[125] Principle 7 encourages all States to cooperate in relation to the global environment and goes on to recognise that,

[i]n view of the different contributions to global environmental degradation, States have common but differentiated responsibilities. The developed countries acknowledge the responsibility that they bear in the international pursuit of sustainable development in view of the pressures their societies place on the global environment and of the technologies and financial resources they command.[126]

This principle or elements of it have also been reflected in numerous conventions and treaties.[127] The UNFCCC for example, recognises that

---

121 Principle 3.1, New Delhi Declaration.
122 Principle 3.2, ibid.
123 Principle 3.3, ibid.
124 Principle 3.4, ibid.
125 Principle 6, Rio Declaration.
126 Principle 7, ibid.
127 For a list and review of treaties and conventions incorporating this principle, see, e.g. French, D., 'Developing States and International Environmental Law: The Importance of Differentiated Responsibilities' (2000) 49 International and Comparative Law Quarterly 35 [hereinafter 2000 French]; Segger and Khalfan (n 3) at pp. 132–43.

climate change and its implications are of common concern.[128] The Convention also urges States to not only protect the climate system 'on the basis of equity and in accordance with their common but differentiated responsibilities and respective capabilities' but also for developed States to take the lead in this endeavour.[129] With regard to further references to differentiation in responsibilities, the UNFCCC recognises '[t]he specific needs and special circumstances of developing country Parties, especially those that are particularly vulnerable to the adverse effects of climate change'.[130] Article 4(7) further acknowledges that the effective implementation of developing States' commitments are dependant upon developed States effectively implementing theirs, particularly in relation to technology transfer and financial resources as well as taking into consideration that socio-economic development and poverty eradication are primary priorities for developing countries.[131] Similar language is seen in the UN Convention to Combat Desertification (UNCCD)[132] for example, where Article 3 reflects the principle of common but differentiated responsibilities. The principle is further referred to throughout the Convention: from setting out the obligations for affected and developing countries,[133] prioritising African nations,[134] to recognising differing financial and technology transfer capacity.[135]

Interestingly, this principle was even referred to by the World Trade Organization (WTO) adjudicating body in the *Shrimp-Turtles* case[136] where the Appellate Body in taking note of Principle 7 of the Rio Declaration, urged Malaysia and the US to 'co-operate fully in order to conclude as soon as possible an agreement which will permit the protection and conservation of sea turtles to the satisfaction of all interests involved and taking into account the principle that States have

---

[128] Preamble, UNFCCC.

[129] Art. 3(1), ibid.

[130] Art. 3(2), ibid.

[131] Art. 4(7), ibid.

[132] UN Convention to Combat Desertification in Those Countries Experiencing Serious Drought and/or Desertification, particularly in Africa (adopted 14 October 1994, entered into force 26 December 1996) (1994) 33 ILM 1328 [hereinafter UNCCD].

[133] Arts. 4, 5, 6, ibid.

[134] Art. 7, ibid.

[135] Art. 20, ibid.

[136] *United States – Import Prohibition of Certain Shrimp and Shrimp Products, Recourse to Article 21.5 by Malaysia* (15 June 2001) WTO Doc. WT/DS58/RW (Report of the Panel) at p. 102, para. 7.2.

common but differentiated responsibilities to conserve and protect the environment.'[137]

Although this principle is being increasingly recognised by the international community as evidenced above, it is thus far not in any way of customary nature.[138] French notes it is the lack of clarity of the 'precise ambit of a duty to co-operate' in relation to this principle that makes it difficult for it to be confirmed as having customary status.[139] In practice, with regard to its ambiguity in scope, as seen from the UNFCCC, it is up to each treaty or agreement that integrates this principle to also set out the precise ambit or operational direction in which this principle is to be utilised in the context of the treaty concerned. In fact, it is argued that though the legal status of this principle remains unclear, its 'practical applications ... have, nevertheless, largely been adopted in a legally binding form; for instance, as differentiated emissions reduction targets and specific financial mechanisms.'[140] Thus, it is suggested that though not a customary norm, this principle is an important part of the concept of sustainable development, providing an objective or framework for cooperation and equity in relation to the protection of the global environment between States and the international community as a whole.[141]

3.2.4. The principle of the precautionary approach to human health, natural resources and ecosystems

This principle is considered to be central to sustainable development and is applicable to all levels of the international community.[142] The 'precautionary principle' or 'precautionary approach' as it is also known, is

---

[137] Ibid.

[138] See, e.g. Stone, C.D., 'Common But Differentiated Responsibilities in International Law' (2004) 98 American Journal of International Law 276, at pp. 299–300; Brunée, J. and Toope, S.T., *Legitimacy and Legality in International Law: An International Account* (CUP, USA 2010) at p. 152.

[139] 2005 French (n 4) at pp. 69–70.

[140] Honkonen, T., *The Common but Differentiated Responsibility Principle in Multilateral Environmental Agreements: Regulatory and Policy Aspects* (Kluwer Law, The Netherlands 2009) at p. 297.

[141] For further discussion on this principle, see, e.g. 2008 Schrijver (n 47) at pp. 178–84; Cordonier Segger, M.C., and others, 'Prospects for Principles of International Sustainable Development Law after the WSSD: Common but Differentiated Responsibilities, Precaution and Participation' (2003) 12 Review of European Community & International Environmental Law 54, at pp. 56–61. See also 2005 French (n 4) at pp. 69–70 (on the duty to co-operate).

[142] Principle 4.1, New Delhi Declaration.

based on the idea that it is preferable to prevent the damage or destruction to the environment beforehand despite the lack of scientific information, rather than subsequently trying to deal with the damage or pollution after it has occurred. It is a logical principle long recognised by nations based on the idea that prevention is better than cure.

Scholars maintain that the origin of the precautionary principle entering into the realm of international law was as a result of German proposals based on German legislation (*Vorsorgeprinzip*)[143] at the 1984 International North Sea Conference.[144] The precautionary principle can be seen for example, in UNCLOS[145] and in the 1985 Convention on the Protection of the Ozone Layer.[146] The Rio Declaration further reaffirmed the principle by recognising that,

> [i]n order to protect the environment, the precautionary approach shall be widely applied by States according to their capabilities. Where there are threats of serious or irreversible damage, lack of full scientific certainty shall not be used as a reason for postponing cost-effective measures to prevent environmental degradation.[147]

Following its incorporation in Rio, the precautionary principle continues to be reflected in various treaties and agreements. The UNFCCC's Article 3(3) for instance, states that '[t]he Parties should take precautionary measures to anticipate, prevent or minimise the causes of climate change and mitigate its adverse effects. Where there are threats of serious or irreversible damage, lack of full scientific certainty should not be used as a reason for postponing such measures'. Another example can be seen from the UNCBD, which refers to this principle in its Preamble and Article 14 with regard to minimising adverse impacts on biological diversity, and Article 8(g) in relation to risks associated with living

---

[143] See, e.g. Trouwborst, A., *Evolution and Status of the Precautionary Principle in International Law* (Kluwer, The Hague 2002) at p. 17; Freestone, D., and Hey, E., 'Origins and Development of the Precautionary Principle' in Freestone, D. and Hey, E. (eds), *The Precautionary Principle and International Law: The Challenge of Implementation* (Kluwer Law, The Hague 1996) at p. 4 [hereinafter Freestone and Hey (eds)].

[144] First International Conference on the Protection of the North Sea; Declaration, Bremen (1 November 1984).

[145] Indirectly reflected in Arts. 194, 204, 206, UNCLOS.

[146] Adopted 22 March 1985, entered into force 22 September 1988 (1985) 26 ILM 1529. See Preamble.

[147] Principle 15, Rio Declaration.

modified organisms on the environment. The 2000 Cartagena Protocol[148] is another example that reflects the precautionary principle: from its Preamble that reaffirms Principle 15 of the Rio Declaration's precaution- ary approach;[149] Article 1 which states its objective '[i]n accordance with the precautionary approach in Principle 15 of the Rio Declaration';[150] to the precautionary language set out in Articles 10 and 11 in relation to the potential adverse effects of living modified organisms on biological diversity.[151]

The precautionary principle has also been referred to in case-law. For instance, the precautionary principle was put forward before the ICJ by New Zealand in the 1995 *Nuclear Tests* case to establish that France had an obligation before conducting nuclear tests to ascertain that there was no harm to the environment,[152] and by Hungary in *Gabčikovo-Nagymaros* as a reason for its failure to meet its commitments.[153] Unfortunately, the ICJ did not make any direct rulings based on the principle in either case. This principle was also referred to but not implicitly applied by the judicial body concerned in a number of other cases.[154] It is worth noting that the European Court of Justice (ECJ) also has its own jurisprudence on this point.[155]

With regard to the customary status of the precautionary principle, scholars have differing views. Some scholars argue that at the very least, this principle is an emerging or evolving norm of customary international

---

[148]   Cartagena Protocol on Biosafety to the Convention on Biological Diver- sity (adopted on 29 January 2000, entered into force 11 September 2003) (2000) 39 ILM 1027 [hereinafter Cartagena Protocol].

[149]   Preamble, ibid.

[150]   Art. 1, ibid.

[151]   Arts. 10(6) and 11(8), ibid.

[152]   *1995 Nuclear Tests* (n 113) at p. 290, para. 5.

[153]   *Gabčikovo-Nagymaros* (n 8) at p. 68, para. 97.

[154]   See, e.g. *Southern Bluefin Tuna Cases (New Zealand v Japan)*, Requests for Provisional Measures (Order) (27 August 1999) (1999) 38 ILM 1624; *The Mox Plant Case (Ireland v UK)*, Request for Provisional Measures (Order) (2 December 2001) (2002) 41 ILM 405. For a list and analysis of further cases, see 2008 Schrijver (n 47) at pp. 189–94; Zander, J., *The Application of the Precautionary Principle in Practice: Comparative Dimensions* (CUP, New York 2010) at pp. 33–75 [hereinafter Zander].

[155]   For a review of the precautionary principle integrated within EU case-law, see, e.g. Stokes, E., 'Precautionary Steps: The Development of the Precautionary Principle in EU Jurisprudence' (2003) 15 Environmental Law and Management 8; Zander (n 154) at pp. 103–51.

law, that is, it is *lex ferenda*,[156] 'a principle in the rapid process of becoming international customary law, with persistent objectors properly on record.'[157] Some academics for instance, consider there to be sufficient evidence that the precautionary principle is part of customary international law.[158] Schrijver for example, is doubtful that this principle has reached customary status, partly due to the division in academic view and in part due to the lack of judicial declaration as to its definitive legal status.[159] Ultimately however, the exact legal status of this principle becomes less relevant as it has and continues to be widely used in treaty law.[160] Thus, as such the precautionary principle is a crucial and operational tool for the achievement of sustainable development, particularly to avoid undue damage to the environment as a result of unknown risks.[161]

---

[156] De lege ferenda (the law as it may be, or should be, in the future). See Malanczuk, P., *Akehurst's Modern Introduction to International Law* (7th edn Routledge, USA 1997) at p. 35.

[157] Segger and Khalfan (n 3) at p. 155. See also Cameron, J. and Abouchar, J., 'The Status of the Precautionary Principle in International Law' in Freestone and Hay (eds) (n 143) at pp. 36–7; 1995 Sands Frameworks (n 120) at p. 213; Freestone, D., 'International Fisheries Law Since Rio: The Continued Rise of the Precautionary Principle' in Boyle and Freestone (eds) (n 75) at p. 137.

[158] For a discussion on the clarification of the precautionary principle's status as a customary norm, see Trouwborst, A., 'The Precautionary Principle in General International Law: Combating the Babylonian Confusion' (2007) 16 Review of European Community & International Environmental Law 185 [hereinafter 2007 Trouwborst]. See also McIntyre, O. and Mosedale, T., 'The Precautionary Principle as a Norm of Customary International Law' (1997) 9 Journal of Environmental Law 221, at p. 241; Deloso, R.E., *The Precautionary Principle: Relevance in International Law and Climate Change* (Grin Verlag, Munich 2011) at pp. 31–41.

[159] 2008 Schrijver (n 47) at p. 194. See also Birnie, P. and Boyle, A., *International Law and the Environment* (2nd edn OUP, Oxford 2002) at pp. 119–20; Gundling, L., 'The Status in International Law of the Principle of Precautionary Action' (1990) 5 International Journal of Estuarine & Coastal Law 23, at p. 30.

[160] For more analysis of its reflection within treaty law, see, e.g. Segger and Khalfan (n 3) at pp. 143–55; Zander (n 154).

[161] For further discussion on the precautionary principle relevant to sustainable development, see, e.g. Segger and Khalfan (n 3) at pp. 143–55; 2008 Schrijver (n 47) at pp. 184–97.

3.2.5. The principle of public participation and access to information and justice

This principle effectively requires States 'to ensure that individuals have appropriate access to "appropriate, comprehensible and timely" information concerning sustainable development that is held by public authorities, and the opportunity to participate in decision-making processes, as well as effective access to judicial and administrative proceedings, including redress and remedy.'[162] Public participation can occur through various forms such as 'education, information dissemination, advisory or review boards, public advocacy, public hearings and submissions, and even litigation.'[163] The New Delhi Declaration proclaims that 'public participation' is not only crucial to the attainment of sustainable development but also to good governance. This principle works as a 'two-way street' because not only does public participation assist the relevant authorities in making better decisions by having access to wider 'potential sources of relevant information',[164] it also allows the public the opportunity to be involved in the decision-making process and this 'potentially enhances public trust in government decision making ... and serves to co-ordinate and reconcile various strategies of achieving public interest objectives.'[165] This, in turn, enhances good governance. As Weiss and others aptly comment:

> because measures to attain sustainable development inherently involves behavioural changes, public participation encourages the population to be 'on board' and willing to take part in these measures. In addition, when the public is both informed and engaged in decision-making processes honest, effective and accountable governments are more likely... Transparency and public participation also increase the likelihood that sustainable development policies will be effectively implemented.[166]

The principle of public participation was already evident in the Brundtland Report which states that 'the pursuit of sustainable development

---

[162]   2009 Segger (n 55) at p. 16.

[163]   Richardson, B.J. and Razzaque, J., 'Public Participation in Environmental Decision-making' in Richardson, B.J. and Wood, S. (eds), *Environmental Law for Sustainability: A Reader* (Hart, Oregon 2006) at p. 165 (footnote omitted) [hereinafter Richardson and Razzaque].

[164]   Razzaque, J., *Public Interest Environmental Litigation in India, Pakistan and Bangladesh* (Kluwer Law, The Hague 2004) at p. 402 [hereinafter 2004 Razzaque].

[165]   Ibid (footnotes omitted).

[166]   Weiss, E.B. and others, *International Environmental Law and Policy* (2nd edn Aspen, USA 2006) at p. 330.

requires ... a political system that secures effective citizen participation in decision making',[167] as well as in subsequent declarations. For example, the Rio Declaration encourages public participation at all levels within a State in relation to environmental matters;[168] Agenda 21 sets out that States, through transparency, access to information and justice, must ensure the inclusion of the principle of public participation in any sustainable development initiatives;[169] and the Johannesburg Declaration provides that nations 'recognise that sustainable development requires a long-term perspective and broad-based participation in policy formulation, decision-making and implementation at all levels.'[170]

International treaties and conventions have also begun to reflect the public participation principle. One of the most significant treaties in relation to this principle is the 1998 Aarhus Convention,[171] which provides legally binding obligations on public participation in relation to decision-making, access to information and justice in environmental matters.[172] This principle can also be seen in the UNFCCC for instance, which in regard to climate change and its effects, requires States to promote and facilitate public awareness, public access to information on and public participation in relation to it.[173] Another example can be seen from the UNCBD, which in relation to 'access to information', promotes public education and awareness in Article 13, and refers to public participation in Article 14(1) with regard to minimising adverse impacts on biological diversity. Provisions to ensure public participation is also reflected for example, within Articles 3(a) and 10(2)(f) of the UNCCD in relation to national action programmes in combating desertification.

As for its legal relevance, scholars are of the view that despite increasing recognition of the public participation principle in specific

---

[167] Our Common Future (n 5).

[168] Principle 10, Rio Declaration.

[169] Paras. 8(3)(d), 8(4)(e) and 23(2), Agenda 21 (states that sustainable development requires 'broad public participation in decision-making').

[170] Para. 26, Johannesburg Declaration.

[171] Convention on Access to Information, Public Participation and Access to Justice in Environmental Matters (adopted 25 June 1998, entered into force 30 October 2001) 2161 UNTS 447 [hereinafter Aarhus Convention].

[172] For further discussion on the Aarhus Convention see, e.g. Pallemaerts, M., *The Aarhus Convention at Ten: Interactions and Tensions between Conventional International Law and EU Environmental Law* (Europa Law, The Netherlands 2011); Morgera, E., 'An Update on the Aarhus Convention and its Continued Global Relevance' (2005) 14 Review of European Community & International Environmental Law 138.

[173] Art. 6, UNFCCC.

treaties and national settings, it is at present an emerging norm.[174] However, regardless of its legal status, as seen from its increasing integration into treaties and conventions, there is no doubt that this principle is an inherent part of sustainable development as it requires all actors (State and non-State), to take part and be involved in the decision-making processes that may affect them. A failure to take this principle into account could mean that '[n]either environmental nor developmental strategies are likely to be sustainable'.[175]

3.2.6. The principle of good governance

The principle of good governance (requiring the adoption of democratic, transparent decision-making procedures and financial accountability by States) is closely linked to the principle of participation, access to information and justice.[176] The Declaration expresses that this principle is applicable to States and non-State actors alike and that all sectors of civil society have a right to good governance.[177] Elements of good governance which are considered to be widely accepted include the following components: effective rule of law, transparency and free flow of information, accountability, effective management of public resources, control of corruption, citizen participation, and equity.[178]

---

[174] Segger and Khalfan (n 3) at p. 156; Bruch, C. and Filbey, M., 'Emerging Global Norms of Public Involvement' in Bruch, C. (ed), *The New 'Public': The Globalization of Public Participation* (ELI, Washington, DC 2002) at pp. 9–10; UNEP, 'Protecting the Environment During Armed Conflict: An Inventory and Analysis of Law' (UNEP, Switzerland 2009) at p. 42.

[175] 2002 Segger (n 91) at p. 65. For further discussion on this principle, see Segger and Khalfan (n 3) at pp. 156–66; Richardson and Razzaque (n 163) at pp. 165–94.

[176] Principle 6, New Delhi Declaration.

[177] Principle 6.2, ibid.

[178] Glasbergen, P., 'Setting the Scene: The Partnership Paradigm in the Making' in Glasbergen, P., Biermann, F. and Mol, A.P.J. (eds), *Partnerships Governance and Sustainable Development: Reflection on Theory and Practice* (Edward Elgar, Cheltenham 2007) at p. 99; Kurukulasuriya, L. and Robinson, N.A., *Training Manual on International Environmental Law* (UNEP/Earthprint, UK 2006) at p. 36. See also UN Economic and Social Commission for Asia and the Pacific (UNESCAP), 'What is Good Governance?', www.unescap.org/pdd/prs/ProjectActivities/Ongoing/gg/governance.asp (accessed 26 February 2012).

The use of the term 'governance' is relatively new, having surfaced in the World Bank's 1989 World Development Report.[179] The report categorically declared that, '[u]nderlying the litany of Africa's developmental problems is the crisis of governance.'[180] From here onwards, it became entrenched in the minds of the international community that lack of 'good governance' is the root of hindered economic and social development. Since then numerous organizations have put forth variations of the concept of good governance. For example, the UN Development Programme (UNDP) put forward that, '[g]ood governance is, among other things, participatory, transparent and accountable.'[181] It also included equity, effectiveness and rule of law.[182] The World Bank defined governance as 'the manner in which political power is exercised in the management of a country's economic and social resources for development'[183] and it understood the concept of good governance to include accountability, legal framework for development, transparency and effective public sector management.[184]

Good governance, as set out in the New Delhi Declaration, requires full respect for the 1992 Rio Declaration principles. Good governance was also noted as a priority in the 2002 JPOI which states that,

> [g]ood governance within each country and at the international level is essential for sustainable development. At the domestic level, sound environmental, social and economic policies, democratic institutions responsive to the needs of the people, the rule of law, anti-corruption measures, gender equality and an enabling environment for investment are the basis for sustainable development.[185]

---

[179] World Bank, *Sub-Saharan Africa: From Crisis to Sustainable Growth* (World Bank, Washington, DC 1989) at p. 60 cited in Kilick, T., *The Adaptive Economy: Adjustment Policies in Small, Low-Income Countries* (World Bank, Washington, DC 1993) at p. 353.

[180] Ibid.

[181] UNDP Policy Document, 'Governance for Sustainable Human Development' (January 1997), http://mirror.undp.org/magnet/policy/chapter1.htm (accessed 26 February 2012).

[182] Ibid.

[183] World Bank, *Governance and Development* (World Bank, Washington, DC 1992) at p. 3 cited in Crawford, G., 'The World Bank and Good Governance: Rethinking the State or Consolidating Neo-Liberalism?' in Paloni, A. and Zanardi, M. (eds), *The IMF, World Bank and Policy Reform* (Routledge, Oxon 2006) at p. 118.

[184] Ibid.

[185] Para. 4, JPOI.

The international community has begun incorporating good governance or elements of it into policies and treaties in the last decade. This can be seen for example from the EU's efforts towards incorporating good governance elements in its objectives to enhance European governance[186] as well as strengthening the EU's contribution to global governance.[187] Other examples can be seen from global policies linking good governance and corporate social responsibility: the UN Global Compact,[188] the OECD Guidelines for Multinational Enterprises for instance.[189]

With regard to treaties and agreements, good governance is also evident for example in the Cotonou Partnership Agreement[190] which, having set out the characteristics of good governance,[191] went on to state that '[g]ood governance, which underpins the ACP-EU Partnership, shall underpin the domestic and international policies of the Parties and constitute a fundamental element of this Agreement.'[192] Another main treaty founded on the elements of good governance is the UN Convention against Corruption[193] which in its Preamble recognises that corruption poses a threat 'to the stability and security of societies, undermining institutions and values of democracy, ethical values and justice and jeopardizing sustainable development and the rule of law.' Elements of

---

[186] See, e.g. Commission of the European Communities, 'European Governance: A White Paper' (Brussels, 25 July 2001); Curtin, D.M. and Wessel, R.A., *Good Governance and the European Union: Reflection on Concepts, Institutions and Substance* (Intersentia, Antwerp 2005).

[187] See, e.g. EU, 'Report of Working Group: "Strengthening Europe's Contribution to World Governance"' White Paper on Governance, Working Group No. 5 (May 2001).

[188] SustainAbility and UN Global Compact, 'Gearing Up: From Corporate Social Responsibility to Good Governance and Scalable Solutions' (SustainAbility Ltd 2004).

[189] OECD, 'The OECD Guidelines for Multinational Enterprises' (OECD, Paris 31 October 2001) (promoting the achievement of sustainable development via transparency, accountability, cooperation, effective legal system and effective public sector management).

[190] Partnership Agreement between the Members of the African, Caribbean and Pacific Group of States of the One Part, and the European Community and its Member States, of the Other Part (adopted 23 June 2000, entered into force 1 April 2003) (2000) OJ (L 317) 3 [hereainafter Cotonou Agreement].

[191] Art. 9(3), ibid.

[192] Ibid.

[193] UN Convention against Corruption (adopted 31 October 2003, entered into force 14 December 2005) (2004) 43 ILM 37.

good governance to achieve sustainable development can also be found in the rest of the Convention.[194]

The concept of good governance does not at this stage have any customary legal status within international law.[195] Scholars have noted that overall this is due to the ambiguity of the term 'good governance' itself as well as the 'lack of consensus among States on its actual meaning, normative character, and practical implications.'[196] Though not of express binding legal relevance, as Schrijver notes, '[i]n a relatively short period of time, the principle of good governance has thus become an element of international economic, environmental and development cooperation policy.'[197] Thus, as Chowdhury and Skarstedt observe, 'good governance is largely perceived either as a policy or an action-guiding tool that is applied generally at the nation State level.'[198] Moreover, as discussed above, it is already being referred to by the international community in various 'soft-law' declarations and policies. This arguably demonstrates that the international community is embracing this concept in the growing awareness that some form of good or effective governance is logically necessary in order to achieve sustainable development. After all, without it, it would be difficult, if not impossible for the international community and States concerned to ensure the effective practice of sustainable development.[199]

3.2.7.　The principle of integration and interrelationship

The principle of integration reflects the interrelationship between environmental, social, economic and human rights interests as well as the

---

[194]　Arts. 5(1) and 62(1), ibid.

[195]　Kondoch, B., 'Human rights law and UN peace operations in post-conflict situations' in White, N.D. and Klaasen, D. (eds), *The UN, Human Rights and Post-Conflict Situations* (MUP, Manchester 2005) at p. 39. *Cf.* Bolewski, W., *Diplomacy and International Law in Globalized Relations* (Springer-Verlag, Berlin Heidelberg 2007) at p. 47 (on the view that 'good governance may be considered as an emerging legal principle of customary international law').

[196]　See 2009 Segger (n 55) at footnote 90. See also Segger and Khalfan (n 3) at pp. 166–70; Choudhury, N. and Skarstedt, C.E., 'The Principle of Good Governance' (CISDL Draft Legal Working Paper) (CISDL, Oxford March 2005) [hereinafter Choudhury and Skarstedt].

[197]　2008 Schrijver (n 47) at p. 203.

[198]　Choudhury and Skarstedt (n 196) at p. 21.

[199]　For further discussion on good governance relevant to sustainable development, see 2008 Schrijver (n 47) at pp. 200–203; Choudhury and Skarstedt (n 196); Segger and Khalfan (n 3) at pp. 166–70.

needs of current and future generations.[200] This principle is relevant to all sectors of the international community as well as 'all levels of govern-ance – global, regional, national, sub-national and local.'[201]

The principle of integration was already seen emerging during the earliest discourse on sustainable development. Principle 13 of the Stock-holm Declaration sets out that, '... States should adopt an integrated and coordinated approach to their development planning so as to ensure that development is compatible with the need to protect and improve envir-onment for the benefit of the population.' Principle 4 of the Rio Declaration reaffirmed this by providing that, '[i]n order to achieve sustainable development, environmental protection shall constitute an integral part of the development process and cannot be considered in isolation from it.' Since then, the principle of integration has been incorporated into various treaties and agreements. For example, the Preamble of the UNFCCC recognises that:

> responses to climate change should be coordinated with social and economic development in an integrated manner with a view to avoiding adverse impacts on the latter, taking into full account the legitimate priority needs of developing countries for the achievement of sustained economic growth and the eradication of poverty.

The UNCBD for instance, encourages integration as far as possible with regard to measures for conservation and sustainable use of biological diversity.[202] Another example can be seen from the UNCCD which in its objective to combat desertification and mitigate the effects of drought, provides that effective action should be taken in an integrated approach 'with a view to contributing to the achievement of sustainable develop-ment.'[203] It further goes on to state that, '[a]chieving this objective will involve long-term integrated strategies'.[204]

In addition to treaties, this principle can now be seen within case-law. For instance, the necessity of the integration principle was referred to in *Gabčikovo-Nagymaros* where Vice-President Weeramantry states that,

> [t]he problem of steering a course between the needs of development and the necessity to protect the environment is a problem alike of the law of development and of the law of the environment. Both of these vital and

---

[200] Principle 7.1, New Delhi Declaration.
[201] Principle 7.2, ibid.
[202] Art. 6(b), UNCBD.
[203] Art. 2(1), UNCCD.
[204] Art. 2(2), ibid.

developing areas of law require, and indeed assume, the existence of a principle which harmonizes both needs. To hold that no such principle exists in the law is to hold that current law recognizes the juxtaposition of two principles which could operate in collision with each other, without providing the necessary basis of principle for their reconciliation.[205]

In the 2005 *Iron Rhine* case,[206] the Arbitral Tribunal observed that '[t]oday, both international and EC law require the integration of appropriate environmental measures in the design and implementation of economic development activities.'[207] The Tribunal, in taking the view that the integration of environmental and development concepts are a duty and a principle of general international law, also stated that, '[e]nvironmental law and the law on development stand not as alternatives but as mutually reinforcing, integral concepts, which require that where development may cause significant harm to the environment there is a duty to prevent, or at least mitigate, such harm'.[208]

Thus, based on the incorporation and reference to the integration principle within treaties and now, judicial decisions, there is no doubt that this principle is an inherent part of sustainable development. Though not as yet part of customary international law, the principle of integration as French argues, 'remains both the principle tool to achieve sustainable development'[209] as well as being 'the most practicable legal principle in the area.'[210] This book thus engages closely with the integration of environmental considerations into decisions relevant to security and armed conflict.

3.2.8. The principle of polluter pays

This principle, as its name indicates, effectively requires those who pollute the environment to pay for its polluting activities and damage caused.[211] It is considered by some scholars to be one of the core

---

[205] *Gabčikovo-Nagymaros* (n 8) at p. 90 (Separate Opinion of Vice-President Weeramantry).

[206] *Iron Rhine ('Ijzeren Rihn') Railway Arbitration (Belgium v Netherlands)* (24 May 2005) Award of the Arbitral Tribunal [hereinafter *Iron Rhine*].

[207] Ibid., at p. 59.

[208] Ibid.

[209] 2005 French (n 4) at p. 57.

[210] Ibid. For further discussion on this principle, see 2003 Dernbach (n 59); Segger and Khalfan (n 3) at pp. 103–109; 2008 Schrijver (n 47) at pp. 203–207.

[211] The polluter pays principle is discussed further in Chapter 5 in relation to liability for post-conflict environmental damage.

principles of sustainable development.[212] According to one scholar, the polluter pays principle (PPP) 'is widely seen as a distinctly separate 'twin' of the precautionary principle.'[213] Other scholars argue that this principle complements the principle of common but differentiated responsibilities.[214] It is considered an economic principle that imposes 'the cost of pollution abatement on individual polluters, rather than on the public purse, to be passed on to the consumer, and thus in the end reflected in the price of the product.'[215] In essence, PPP aims to attach liability to the responsible party for causing environmental damage. The growing recognition that pollution comes attached with a price tag – a cost on society, having an impact on future resources and the environment, was first addressed in the 1970s.[216]

The origins of PPP came about from the Stockholm Conference in 1972[217] and in the same year, the principle was expressly referred to and adopted by the Organisation for Economic Co-operation and Development (OECD)[218] as a 'recommendable method for pollution cost allocation.'[219] PPP was also endorsed by the EU,[220] being adopted in its First Environmental Action Programme in 1973. For example, Article 25 of the 1986 Single European Act stipulates that action taken by the European Community relating to the environment are to be based on the principles 'that environmental damage should as a priority be rectified at source, and that the polluter should pay.'

---

[212]   See, e.g. André (n 25) at p. 11; Manzi, T. and others, 'Understanding Social Sustainability: Key Concepts and Development in Theory and Practice' in Manzi, T. and others (eds), *Social Sustainability in Urban Areas: Communities, Connectivity and the Urban Fabric* (Earthscan, London 2010) at p. 7.

[213]   Barrow, C.J., *Environmental Management for Sustainable Development* (2nd edn Routledge, Oxon 1999) at p. 32.

[214]   McInerney-Lankford, S., Darrow, M. and Rajamani, L., *Human Rights and Climate Change: A Review of International Legal Dimensions* (World Bank, Washington, DC 2011) at p. 53.

[215]   Larsson, M-L., *The Law of Environmental Damage: Liability and Reparation* (Kluwer Law, Sweden 1999) at p. 90 [hereinafter Larsson].

[216]   Ibid.

[217]   Elliot, J., *An Introduction to Sustainable Development* (3rd edn Routledge, Oxon 2006) at p. 81.

[218]   OECD, '1972 OECD Council Recommendation on Guiding Principles Concerning the International Economic Aspects of Environmental Policies', http://acts.oecd.org/Instruments/ShowInstrumentView.aspx?InstrumentID=4& Lang=en&Book=False (accessed 22 April 2012).

[219]   Larsson (n 215) at p. 91.

[220]   For more information on the development of PPP within EU law, see 2003 Sands (n 74) at pp. 283–5.

Since then, this principle has been reflected in a number of international instruments. Article 174 of the EC Treaty for instance has formally adopted PPP: 'Community policy on the environment ... shall be based on the precautionary principle and on the principles that preventive action should be taken, that environmental damage should as a priority be rectified at source and that the polluter should pay.' Elements of PPP are also evident for example in Principle 16 of the Rio Declaration:

> National authorities should endeavour to promote the internalization of environmental costs and the use of economic instruments, taking into account the approach that the polluter should, in principle, bear the cost of pollution, with due regard to the public interest and without distorting international trade and investment.

Post-Rio for example, the preambular paragraphs of the 1993 Lugano Convention[221] has 'regard to the desirability of providing for strict liability in this field taking into account the "Polluter Pays" Principle'[222] and the 2003 Kiev Protocol[223] refers to the polluter pays principle 'as a general principle of international environmental law'.[224] Other international treaties have also referred to and endorsed this principle in various ways.[225]

---

[221] Convention on Civil Liability for Damage Resulting from Activities Dangerous to the Environment, Lugano (adopted 21 June 1993, not yet in force) [hereinafter Lugano Convention].

[222] Preamble, ibid.

[223] Protocol on Civil Liability and Compensation for Damage Caused by the Transboundary Effects of Industrial Accidents on Transboundary Waters to the 1992 Convention on the Protection and Use of Transboundary Watercourses and International Lakes and to the 1992 Convention on the Transboundary Effects of Industrial Accidents, Kiev (adopted 21 May 2003, not yet in force) [hereinafter Kiev Protocol].

[224] Preamble, ibid.

[225] See, e.g. Art. 10(d), 1985 ASEAN Agreement on the Conservation of Nature and Natural Resources (ASEAN Convention) (adopted 9 July 1985, not in force) reprinted in (1985) 15 EPL 64; Art. 2(1), 1991 Convention on the Protection of the Alps, Salzburg (1992) 32 ILM 767 (adopted 7 November 1991, entered into force 6 March 1995); Art. 2(2)(b), 1992 Convention for the Protection of the Marine Environment of the North-East Atlantic (OSPAR Convention), Paris (adopted 22 September 1992, entered into force 25 March 1998); Art. 3(4), 1992 Convention on the Protection of the Marine Environment of the Baltic Sea Area, Helsinki (adopted 9 April 1992, entered into force 17 January 2000); Art. 2(4), 1994 Convention on Cooperation for the Protection and Sustainable Use of the Danube River, Sofia (adopted 29 June 1994, entered into force 22 October 1998).

Thus far however, PPP has primarily developed and gained Eurocentric support and there is little evidence of support outside the Eurozone.[226] The US for example, though having a well-developed domestic environmental law system, has not made moves towards codifying PPP.[227] Nevertheless, the principle 'has influenced US environmental law, such as the 1980 Comprehensive Environmental Response, Compensation and Liability Act, which seeks to fulfil the polluter-pays principle by imposing liability for clean-up costs on those parties that are responsible for the pollution.'[228]

PPP is not without its limitations. Scholars argue that this principle is imprecise and difficult to practically implement at times because of the 'confusion surrounding the costs to be charged to the polluter.'[229] Costs may be difficult to allocate for various reasons, for example: problems in pinpointing the polluter;[230] complexity or impossibility (in some circumstances) in calculating the costs of environmental damage;[231] the added complication of State and insurance company involvement, having contributed towards restoration costs, making it difficult to ascertain what the polluter should pay.[232] Simply put, this principle leaves the interpretation of it up to the context in which it is employed. On the one hand, this means it does not provide precise guidelines or uniformity in which the principle is to be used but on the other, gives PPP the flexibility to be tailored to fit any given situation involving environmental damage.

In relation to its legal relevance, scholars (especially in the international environmental law field) are of the view that PPP cannot as yet be classed as part of customary international law.[233] As Chemain argues,

---

[226]   Viikari, L., *The Environmental Element in Space Law: Assessing the Present and Charting the Future* (Koninklijke Brill NV, The Netherlands 2008) at p. 186 [hereinafter Viikari].

[227]   Clò, S., *European Emmissions Trading in Practice: An Economic Analysis* (Edward Elgar, Cheltenham 2011) at p. 103 [hereinafter Clò].

[228]   Ibid.

[229]   Chemain, R., 'The "Polluter Pays" Principle' in Partlet, K. and others (eds), *The Law of International Responsibility* (OUP, New York 2010) at p. 884 [hereinafter Chemain].

[230]   Louka, E., *International Environmental Law: Fairness, Effectiveness, and World Order* (CUP, Cambridge 2006) at p. 51.

[231]   Borzsák, L., *The Impact of Environmental Concerns on the Public Enforcement Mechanism under EU Law: Environmental Protection in the 25th Hours* (Kluwer Law, The Netherlands 2011) at p. 138.

[232]   Chemain (n 229) at p. 884.

[233]   See, e.g. 2003 Sands (n 74) at p. 280; Koebele, M., *Corporate Responsibility under the Alien Tort Statute: Enforcement of International Law Through*

'at present, this principle remains too imprecise to cross the threshold necessary to form the basis of a rule of international law.'[234] As with the other substantive principles, regardless of its definitive legal status, this principle is well-entrenched in international environmental law and certainly is part of achieving sustainable development when circumstances necessitate its use. PPP is particularly useful when environmental damage is inevitable and costs are required to be borne in order to mitigate the damage or restore the environment in it entirety. Moreover, it integrates the economic and environmental pillars of sustainable development. It allows development to be sustainable in that, the polluter does not get away without paying for its pollution; ultimately demonstrating that development and its consequences (especially to the environment) are not cost free.

To sum up, these substantive principles of international law related to sustainable development vary in relation to their legal relevance, 'from the universally-accepted through *de lege ferenda* to those provisions that are ultimately aspirational'.[235] In addition, as Segger concludes, these principles in most cases 'are as yet emerging principles of international law.'[236] Nevertheless, as discussed above, regardless of their legal status, these principles (from the 'duty to ensure sustainable use of natural resources' to the 'polluter pays' principle) are an important part of the concept of sustainable development and would certainly provide helpful objectives in order to achieve it. It is also worth noting that these principles need not be collectively present in order to achieve sustainable development.[237] They can be invoked as necessary, depending on the particular circumstances or context concerned.[238] Having discussed its substantive principles, the following section proceeds to look at the concept of sustainable development as a whole.

US Torts Law (Koninklijke Brill NV, The Netherlands 2009) at p. 162; Viikari (n 226) at p. 186 (argues that 'the polluter-pays principle has obvious legal implications as regards liability for environmental damage' but as it is a principle phrased in aspirational language, was never intended to be a binding normative obligation).

[234]   Chemain (n 229) at p. 884.

[235]   2004 French (n 45) at p. 297 (referring to the seven New Delhi principles). See also Viikari (n 226) at p. 186 (argues that the PPP is phrased in aspirational terms).

[236]   Segger and Khalfan (n 3) at p. 171 (referring to the seven New Delhi principles).

[237]   2002 Segger (n 91) at p. 30. Scholars have varied approaches, see, e.g. 2005 French (n 4) at pp. 53–70; 2003 Sands (n 74) at pp. 252–66.

[238]   2002 Segger (n 91) at p. 30.

4. THE CONCEPT OF SUSTAINABLE DEVELOPMENT: AN EMERGING NORM – A LEGAL OR POLITICAL CONCEPT?

The ILA in the 2004 Berlin Conference notes that, 'the role of the international *legal* system in promoting sustainable development has been a central, if ambiguous, element of this political process since the notion of sustainable development was first introduced.'[239] The 2008 report by the ILA's International Committee on International Law on Sustainable Development reminds us that 'sustainable development is a deeply integrated concept, affecting a diverse array of issues, ranging from climate change to international investment, and the links between such issues are becoming evermore complex and nuanced.'[240] Although sustainable development has become an extremely popular and familiar concept, the debate as to its normative status is very much alive and ongoing.[241] Literature in this field reveals numerous arguments and theories in this respect.[242]

The legal relevance of sustainable development is difficult to discern and conclude in the traditional sense, that is, as being part of customary international law.[243] However, as Lowe comments, 'decision-makers need not wait on state practice and *opinio juris* to develop the concept of sustainable development in the way that a primary rule of international law would be developed. They may take the initiative and develop the

---

[239]   ILA Berlin Report (n 48) at p. 3.

[240]   ILA Rio Report (n 48) at p. 25.

[241]   Ibid. See also 2009 Segger (n 55).

[242]   See, e.g. 2008 Schrijver (n 47); Tladi, D., *Sustainable Development in International Law: An Analysis of Key Enviro-Economic Instruments* (PULP, Cape Town 2007) [hereinafter Tladi]; 2005 French (n 4); Segger and Khalfan (n 3); Marong (n 7); Mayeda (n 40); Boyle and Freestone (n 75) at p. 2; Voigt (n 73).

[243]   Art. 38(1)(b), Statute of the International Court of Justice (adopted 26 June 1945, entered into force 24 October 1945) 33 UNTS 993 [hereinafter ICJ Statute]. See, e.g. Dupuy, P.M., 'Formation of Customary International Law and General Principles' in Bodansky (eds) (n 53) at pp. 452–3 (shows the difficulty in proving the required elements: *opinio juris* and State practice, to establish customary international law); Bodansky, D., 'Customary (and Not So Customary) International Environmental Law' (1995) 3 Indiana Journal of Global Legal Studies 105. For further discussion on the possibility of 'sustainable development' attaining customary international law status, see Tladi (n 242) at pp. 94–104. *Cf.* Lowe, V., 'Sustainable Development and Unsustainable Arguments' in Boyle and Freestone (eds) (n 75) at pp. 19–37 [hereinafter Lowe].

concept themselves.'[244] Therefore, the best way to determine the status
and legal relevance of the concept of sustainable development within
international law and international relations, is to look at it in a
non-traditional way: through the 'soft-law' policy-making over the past
four decades on sustainable development;[245] international treaties that
have integrated sustainable development priorities and/or used the concept of sustainable development as an objective;[246] decisions of international courts and tribunals that have integrated or referred to the
sustainable development concept;[247] as well as exploring the views of
scholars on this debate.[248]

4.1. International Policy-making and Non-binding Instruments: 'Soft-law'

Section 2 above has already discussed the development of 'sustainable
development' through global policy-making over the last four decades,
from the 1971 Founex Seminar to the 2012 Rio+20 Summit.[249] These
international summits, which are in effect 'international "soft-law"
policy-making processes on sustainable development',[250] have given
important momentum to the environmental, socio-economic development
and subsequent sustainable development debates. Moreover, as Segger
argues, the international community through these processes, 'has worked
to refine a common concept of sustainable development, identified
priorities for sustainable development, and found certain elements of
consensus on how these priorities can and should be addressed at
different levels through policy and even law.'[251]

In addition, these global summits on sustainable development brought
the international community together – not just States, but non-State
actors as well, by providing a forum for dialogue on the relevant issues.
In the 1972 Stockholm Conference, NGOs, although not participants in

---

[244] Lowe (n 243) at p. 37.

[245] Art. 38(1)(c), ICJ Statute.

[246] Art. 38(1)(a), ibid.

[247] Art. 38(1)(d), ibid.

[248] Ibid.

[249] For a chronological list of non-binding 'soft-law' instruments related to
sustainable development, see Segger and Khalfan (n 3) at pp. 34–6. See also UN
'The History of Sustainable Development in the United Nations' Rio+20 UN
Conference on Sustainable Development, www.uncsd2012.org/rio20/history.html
(accessed 24 March 2012).

[250] 2009 Segger (n 55) at p. 5.

[251] Ibid.

the main Conference, were allowed for the first time to make official and joint statements towards and in relation to the Conference.[252] In the 1992 Rio Conference, the UN allowed a large group of NGO representatives to attend the conference as observers[253] and in the 2002 WSSD, thousands of actors – from State leaders to representatives from NGOs, corporations and other major groups, participated in the summit.[254] This allowed the global community as a whole to contribute to the sustainable development discourse.

An additional point to note is the fact that these summits resulted in 'soft-law' in the form of declarations, guidelines and resolutions relevant to sustainable development. Although this 'soft-law' does not have direct legally binding relevance, it nevertheless is not 'without legal relevance'[255] as States, having come together in the first place and assumed to have made these declarations in good faith during these international discussions, could perhaps be assumed to be willing to act in accordance to those agreements made, in whole or to some extent, or at least would be hesitant in purposely being in direct violation of those commitments.[256] As Segger notes, 'international law is being redefined to include actors other than States among those who make international norms and who implement and comply with them, and to include legal instruments that may not be formally binding.'[257] Thus, through these

---

[252] Hägerhäll, B., 'The Stockholm Declaration and Law of Marine Environment: An NGO Perspective' in Nordquist, M.H, Moore, J.M. and Mahmoudi, S. (eds), *The Stockholm Declaration and Law of the Marine Environment* (Kluwer Law, The Hague 2003) at pp. 353–4 (the NGOs set up a parallel conference). See also Gendlin, F., 'Voices from the Gallery' (1972) XXVIII Bulletin of the Atomic Scientist 26.

[253] It is estimated that over 20000 NGO representatives attended UNCED. See Gallagher, K.P., 'Overview Essay' in Harris, J.M. and others (eds), *A Survey of Sustainable Development: Social and Economic Dimensions* (Island Press, Washington, DC 2001) at p. 341; Princen, T. and Finger, M., 'Introduction' in Princen, T. and Finger, M. (eds), *Environmental NGOs in World Politics: Linking the Local and Global* (Routledge, London 1994) at p. 4

[254] 2002 Segger (n 91) at p. 18.

[255] 2009 Segger (n 55) at p. 8.

[256] Ibid.

[257] 2002 Segger (n 91) at p. 19 (footnote omitted). Seggers's statement is based on Weiss's argument that international law now includes not only traditional binding legal instruments and customary norms but also 'legally non-binding or incompletely binding norms, or what is called "soft law".' See Weiss, E.B., 'The Emerging Structure of International Environmental Law' in Vig, N.J. and Axelrod, R.S. (eds), *The Global Environment: Institutions, Law and Policy* (Congretional Quarterly, Washington, DC 1999) at p. 98.

global 'soft-law' policy-making processes, 'sustainable development' has been brought to the forefront of international law in the context of integrating environmental and socio-economic interests. This has led to not only robust and continuing academic discourse on the subject but also its use in practical terms as treaty objectives as well as being referred to within judicial decisions.

4.2. International Treaties and Conventions

The concept of sustainable development has been incorporated into a multitude of treaties.[258] One of the earliest treaties where sustainable development is mentioned specifically is the 1985 ASEAN Convention which in its 'fundamental principle' aims 'to maintain essential ecological processes and life support systems, to preserve genetic diversity, and to ensure the sustainable utilisation of harvested natural resources under their jurisdiction in accordance with scientific principles and with a view to attaining the goal of sustainable development.'[259]

Another treaty considered to be one of the key legal instruments in relation to sustainable development is the UNFCCC. For example, the UNFCCC, not only provides that '[t]he Parties have a right to, and should, promote sustainable development'[260] in its 'ultimate objective' in tackling climate change, it also sets out that the stabilisation of greenhouse gasses 'should be achieved within a time frame sufficient to allow ecosystems to adapt naturally to climate change, to ensure that food production is not threatened and to enable economic development to proceed in a sustainable manner.'[261] The UNFCCC sets out its objective as well as providing direction as to how it 'should be achieved.' In addition, sustainable development and its substantive principles as discussed above are further integrated throughout the rest of the Convention.[262]

---

[258] For a chronological list of binding international treaties relevant to sustainable development that was highlighted in the JPOI, see Segger and Khalfan (n 3) at pp. 32–3. For further discussion on treaties relevant to sustainable development, see 2009 Segger (n 55) at pp. 8–12; 2008 Schrijver (n 47) at pp. 102–41.

[259] Art. 1(1), 1985 ASEAN Convention.

[260] Art. 3(4), UNFCCC.

[261] Art. 2, ibid.

[262] See in particular, Arts. 4, 5, 6, 7, 11, 12, ibid.

Another example is the UNCCD which in its objective to 'combat desertification and combat the effects of drought in countries experiencing serious drought and/or desertification, particularly Africa',[263] does so with the aim to take integrated effective action 'with a view to contributing to the achievement of sustainable development in affected areas.'[264] Furthermore, in addition to the Parties committing to cooperate at all levels, to work towards sustainable use of land and scarce water resources in the affected areas,[265] the UNCCD also refers and integrates 'sustainable' development, use, etc. and its principles throughout the Convention.[266]

These examples illustrate the fact that the concept of sustainable development is now part of key operational aims and objectives as well as being integrated throughout various other important international, regional and sub-regional treaties and agreements.[267] Through these instruments, States are able to specifically address 'sustainability challenges related to economic, environmental, and also social aspects of

---

[263] Art. 2(1), UNCCD.

[264] Ibid.

[265] Art. 3(3), ibid

[266] Ibid.

[267] See, e.g. UNCBD; Convention on the Protection and Use of Transboundary Watercourses and International Lakes (adopted 17 March 1992, entered into force 6 October 1996) 1936 UNTS 269; UN Convention on the Non-Navigational Uses of International Watercourses (adopted 21 May 1997, not yet in force) (1997) 36 ILM 700. See also, e.g. trade treaties that promote sustainable development as a preambular objective: North American Free Trade Agreement (NAFTA) (Canada-USA-Mexico) (adopted 17 December 1992, entered into force 1 January 1994) (1993) 32 ILM 289; Agreement Establishing the World Trade Organization (adopted 15 April 1994, entered into force 1 January 1995) (1994) 33 ILM 1125. See also, e.g. regional treaties that integrated sustainable development: Revised Protocol on Shared Watercourses in the Southern African Development Community (adopted 7 August 2000, entered into force 22 September 2003) (2001) 40 ILM 321; Convention for Co-operation in the Protection and Sustainable Development of the Marine and Coastal Environment of the North East Pacific (adopted 18 February 2002, not yet in force) reprinted in (2002) IELMT 14 (which includes a legally binding definition of sustainable development (Art. 3)); Agreement on the Co-operation for the Sustainable Development of the Mekong River Basin (adopted and entered into force 5 April 1995) (1995) 34 ILM 864.

development'.[268] As Schrijver notes, '[n]owadays, the concept of sustainable development can be found in international instruments covering various issue-areas and is solidly embedded in treaty practice.'[269]

4.3. Decisions of International Courts and Tribunals

To varying degrees, international courts and tribunals are beginning to recognise sustainable development and its principles in their decisions or judgements.[270] These 'judicial decisions can be of immense importance'[271] to the global community. However, with regard to ICJ decisions for example, although the ICJ generally aims to refer and follow its previous decisions so as to maintain 'a measure of certainty within the process,'[272] its decisions only have a binding effect on the parties to each particular dispute.[273] Nevertheless, these decisions and even individual opinions of Judges add to the discourse of any particular topic of international law and in the process, facilitate the clarification and development of international law.[274] The decisions of international tribunals and arbitrations for instance, although generally only formally binding on parties to the dispute, have also 'been extremely significant in the development of international law.'[275] In addition, as Segger argues, 'through the peaceful settlement of disputes relating to sustainable development, States are starting to gain valuable guidance from international courts and tribunals on how it is possible to resolve particular

---

[268]   2009 Segger (n 55) at p. 5.

[269]   2008 Schrijver (n 47) at p. 104.

[270]   For more discussion see 2009 Segger (n 55) at pp. 18–23; Sands, P., 'International Courts and the Application of the Concept of Sustainable Development' (1999) 3 Max Planck Yearbook of United Nations Law 389.

[271]   Shaw, M.N., *International Law* (5th edn CUP, Cambridge 2003) at p. 103 [hereinafter Shaw].

[272]   Ibid. See also Clemons, H.V., 'The Ethos of the International Court of Justice is Dependent Upon the Statutory Authority Attributed to its Rhetoric: A Metadiscourse' (1997) 20 Fordham International Law Journal 1479, at pp. 1497–8.

[273]   Art. 59, Statute of the ICJ.

[274]   Lauterpacht, H., *The Development of International Law by the International Court* (CUP, Cambridge 1996) at p. 66.

[275]   Shaw (n 271) at pp. 104–105. See also Guzman, A.T., 'International Tribunals: A Rational Choice Analysis' (2008) 157 University of Pennsylvania Law Review 171.

transboundary problems that invoke a need to balance environmental, economic, and social development priorities.'[276]

The ICJ has made references to sustainable development in a number of cases. In its *Nuclear Weapons* Advisory Opinion, the ICJ though not referring to sustainable development specifically, did broaden the description of the environment by stating that, '[t]he environment is not an abstraction, but represents the living space, the quality of life and the health of human beings, including generations unborn.'[277] In *Gabčikovo-Nagymaros* the ICJ, in recognising the need to balance environmental and developmental interests, specifically addressed sustainable development by stating that,

> new norms and standards have been developed, set forth in a great number of instruments during the last two decades. Such new norms have to be taken into consideration, and such standards given proper weight, not only when States contemplate new activities, but also when continuing activities begun in the past. This need to reconcile development with protection of the environment is aptly expressed in the concept of sustainable development.[278]

Although the Court recognised sustainable development as a concept, it did not clarify its legal status within international law. This is in contrast to Vice-President Weeramantry's separate opinion which referred to sustainable development as having customary status within international law by stating that, '[t]he principle of sustainable development is thus a part of modern international law by reason not only of its inescapable logical necessity but also by reason of its wide and general acceptance by the global community.'[279] In any event, in expecting the State parties to balance environmental and development interests, the Court did state that the Parties 'should look afresh at the effects of the environment'[280] as a result of the operation of the dam and that the Parties 'must find a satisfactory solution.'[281]

---

[276] 2009 Segger (n 55) at p. 24.
[277] *Nuclear Weapons* (n 83) at p. 241.
[278] *Gabčikovo-Nagymaros* (n 8) at p. 78.
[279] Ibid., at p. 95 (Separate Opinion of Vice-President Weeramantry).
[280] Ibid., at p. 78.
[281] Ibid.

More recently, sustainable development in reference to balancing environmental protection and economic development was addressed in the *Pulp Mills* case.[282] The ICJ in its 2006 Order noted that,

> [t]he present case highlights the importance of the need to ensure environmental protection of shared natural resources while allowing for sustainable economic development; whereas it is particularly necessary to bear in mind the reliance of the Parties on the quality of the water of the River Uruguay for their livelihood and economic development; whereas from this point of view account must be taken of the need to safeguard the continued conservation of the river environment and the rights of economic development of the riparian States.[283]

Sustainable development has also been referred to by other international tribunals. For instance, the GATT/WTO Panel in the 1998 *Shrimp Turtle* case,[284] cited the Preamble of the WTO Agreement as illustrating not only the fact 'that the signatories to the Agreement were, in 1994, fully aware of the importance and legitimacy of environmental protection'[285] but also that the Preamble 'explicitly acknowledges the "objective of sustainable development."'[286] The Appellate Body also went on to define the concept of sustainable development in a footnote as being 'generally accepted as integrating economic and social development and environmental protection.'[287]

The concept of sustainable development also appeared in the Permanent Court of Arbitration's 2005 *Iron Rhine* case:[288]

> There is considerable debate as to what, within the field of environmental law, constitutes 'rules' or 'principles'; what is 'soft law'; and which environmental treaty law or principles have contributed to the development of customary international law. Without entering further into those controversies, the

---

[282]   *Case Concerning Pulp Mills on the River Uruguay* (*Argentina v Uruguay*) (Request for Indication of Provisional Measures, Order of 13 July 2006) [2006] ICJ Rep 1.

[283]   Ibid., at p. 19, para. 80. This was reaffirmed in the ICJ's recent judgement. See *Case Concerning Pulp Mills on the River Uruguay* (*Argentina v Uruguay*) (Judgement of 20 April 2010) at p. 52, para. 171; p. 52, paras. 175–7; pp. 55–6, paras. 184–9.

[284]   *United States – Import Prohibition of Certain Shrimp and Shrimp Products* (12 October 1998) WTO Doc. WT/DS58/AB/R (Appellate Body Report) [hereinafter Shrimp Turtle case].

[285]   Ibid., at para. 129.

[286]   Ibid.

[287]   Ibid.

[288]   *Iron Rhine* (n 206) at pp. 28–9.

Tribunal notes that in all of these categories 'environment' is broadly referred to as including air, water, land, flora and fauna, natural ecosystems and sites, human health and safety, and climate. The emerging principles, whatever their current status, make reference to conservation, management, notions of prevention and of sustainable development, and protection for future generations.[289]

The Arbitral Tribunal, though addressing sustainable development and referring to relevant declarations and case-law in the context of reconciling the environment and development, still refrained from specifying its legal status.[290]

National courts and tribunals around the world are also not far behind in recognising and invoking sustainable development or some aspects of it when necessary. This can be seen for example, from *Minors Oposa*[291] as discussed above; the 2000 *Narmada River* case[292] where the Supreme Court of India on its consideration of the precautionary principle in a case concerning the construction of a dam on the Narmada River, acknowledged application of the principle when the extent of environmental damage is unknown, but observed that 'when the effect of the project is known then the principle of sustainable development would come into play' to balance development and ecological interests;[293] and in 2007, the South African Constitutional Court in *Fuel Retailers*,[294] noted that the South African constitution recognised the balance of socio-economic and environmental considerations 'through the ideal of sustainable development'[295] as well as the importance of the role of the judiciary 'in the context of the protection of the environment and giving effect to sustainable development.'[296]

To sum it up, though not clarifying the legal status of sustainable development, these judicial references to and recognition of the concept not only illustrate its general importance but also give the international

---

[289] Ibid., at p. 28.

[290] Ibid., at pp. 28–9.

[291] *Minors Oposa* (n 109) at p. 185.

[292] *Narmada Bachao Aandolan v Union of India and Others* (18 October 2000) AIR 2000 SC 3751, 32, at para. 150.

[293] Ibid., at para. 143.

[294] *Fuel Retailers Association of Southern Africa v Director-General: Environmental Management, Department of Agriculture, Conservation and Environment, Mpumalanga Province, and Others* (2007) (6) SA 4 (CC); 2007 (10) BCLR 1059 (CC) 24–40.

[295] Ibid., at p. 26, para 45.

[296] Ibid., at p. 56, para 102.

community guidance in balancing and resolving disputes relating to environmental and development issues, as well as adding to the continuously developing scholarship and practice of sustainable development within international law. Furthermore, perhaps these decisions are a further indication that 'sustainable development', even without having definitive legal status, can be utilised – used as a practical goal or guideline to reconcile or balance socio-economic, development and environmental interests.

4.4.   Scholarly Publications of Academics

McCloskey, Chairman of the Sierra Club, suggests that the concept of sustainable development lacks any 'operational reality', that is, it is a concept which cannot be extended rationally into the detail of research, planning and application.[297] McCloskey fears 'that "sustainability" will prove to be no more than a boon to publicists who will paste new labels on old bottles and claim that every project that makes their clients richer is sustainable.'[298] McCloskey's fears of the doubtful position of the concept of sustainable development are debatable.

It is highly unlikely that the term 'sustainable development' is merely a buzz word. It is clear from its appearance in various summits, international instruments and academic literature, that sustainable development is an accepted concept of global importance.[299] The concept of sustainable development is no longer avoidable. At all levels of State and civil society, the concept of sustainable development now 'provides the framework for the analysis of environmental problems.'[300] After all, global environmental challenges today – from the depletion of the ozone layer, loss of biodiversity, deforestation, desertification to climate change,

---

[297]   McCloskey (n 62) at p. 154. See also Robinson, J., 'Squaring the Circle? Some Thought on the Idea of Sustainable Development' (2004) 48 Ecological Economics 369; Rogers, P.P., Jalal, K.F. and Boyd, J.A. (eds), *An Introduction to Sustainable Development* (Earthscan, London 2008) pp. 382–3 (for a brief review on sustainable development critics); Lomborg, B., *The Sceptical Environmentalist* (CUP, Cambridge 2001).

[298]   McCloskey (n 62) at p. 159.

[299]   See, e.g. Voigt (n 73) at p. 91 (on sustainable development being implemented as a global concept in order to tackle the challenge of climate change); Gray, R. and Bebbington, J., 'Corporate sustainability: accountability or impossible dream?' in Atkinson, G., Dietz, S. and Neumayer, E. (eds), *Handbook of Sustainable Development* (Edward Elgar, UK 2007) at p. 378.

[300]   André (n 25) at p. 6.

transcend national boundaries.[301] As evidenced throughout this chapter, the concept of sustainable development is invoked by States and non-State actors alike, being promoted as the core of recent environmental principles. It is a very logical concept and is, as Steele and Jewell point out, an 'overarching principle' in light of the environmental problems facing us today.[302]

While the concept of sustainable development is clearly an emerging norm of relevance to legal actors, there remains some doubt as to whether it has fully crystallised into a legal principle. French argues that,

> sustainable development is not a legal concept *per se*, such as one might think of concepts such as *jus cogens*, estoppel and *opinio juris*... Rather, sustainable development ... is a political, socio-economic, even potentially moral, objective which may turn into normative consequences, but its origins lie not so much in jurisprudence as in the argument that economic, environmental and social considerations must be integrated if environmental protection and development are to be mutually supportive.[303]

To reiterate, it is clear that the concept of sustainable development has developed and evolved within the texts of treaties, soft-law and other relevant documentation. Sands for example broadly concludes that, 'environmentally sustainable development is now part of the lexicon of international law.'[304] While the legal status of sustainable development is uncertain, it is arguable that it is a concept with significant legal effect.[305] This legal effect is evidenced by the inclusion of the concept of sustainable development within significant binding and non-binding texts as seen above. As French further points out, '[w]hether it is in the preamble or elsewhere, certain legal implications inevitably follow... By including sustainable development as an objective, State Parties can seek to rely upon it to justify their actions or question the actions of others before other parties or in formal adjudication.'[306]

Hence, the general consensus amongst scholars appears to be that sustainable development is an emerging concept in international law;

---

[301] Millennium Ecosystem Assessment, *Ecosystems and Human Well-Being, Scenarios: Volume 2* (Island Press, Washington, DC 2005) at pp. 4–5.

[302] Steele, J. and Jewell, T., 'Law in Environmental Decision-Making' in Jewell, T. and Steele, J. (eds), *Law in Environmental Decision-Making: National, European, and International Perspective* (Clarendon, Oxford 1998) at pp. 7–9.

[303] 2005 French (n 4) at p. 35. See also 2008 Schrijver (n 47) at pp. 219–20.

[304] 2000 Sands (n 63) at p. 408.

[305] 2005 French (n 4) at p. 36.

[306] Ibid., at p. 44.

though not a legally binding norm as yet, is not without legal relevance either.[307] Moreover, as discovered throughout this chapter, the principles of international law relating to sustainable development are also emergent principles of law. Thus, on the whole, in relation to these principles that are reflected within the umbrella concept of sustainable development, as Segger and Khalfan comment, 'it will be important, over the next decades, to monitor their development, operationalization and recognition by States as sustainable development law becomes better defined and implemented.'[308]

Even though sustainable development and its principles have not reached definitive legal status for the most part, it does not matter. These principles and the overarching concept of sustainable development are nevertheless used by the international community as goals and objectives to balance and reconcile environmental protection and interests with socio-economic development interests and has therefore, reached an important place in international law and continues to develop in this regard.[309]

5. SUSTAINABLE DEVELOPMENT AND THE EMERGING CONCEPT OF 'ENVIRONMENTAL SECURITY' IN LIGHT OF PROTECTION OF THE ENVIRONMENT RELEVANT TO ARMED CONFLICT: EVOLUTION

According to the UN Secretary-General Ban Ki-Moon, '[s]ince problems spill across borders, security anywhere depends on sustainable development everywhere.'[310] The nexus at issue in this study was explicitly recognised in the Brundtland Report, that 'a comprehensive approach to

---

[307]   Ibid., at p. 36; Segger and Khalfan (n 3) at p. 365; 2008 Schrijver (n 47) at p. 29.

[308]   Segger and Khalfan (n 3) at p. 171.

[309]   See 2008 Schrijver (n 47) at pp. 221–30 (on challenges to the further development and application of international law on sustainable development). See also, e.g. 2009 Segger (n 55) at pp. 10–13; ILA Hague Report (n 48) (Part Three that sets out the Committee's two year work programme before the adoption of its final report in 2012; RIO+20 Conference (n 54).

[310]   Ki-Moon, B., 'The Right War' *Time Magazine* (17 April 2008).

international and national security must transcend the traditional emphasis on military power and armed competition. The real sources of insecurity also encompass unsustainable development'.[311]

This section thus follows from much of the above that sustainable development is an overarching concept that applies to all spheres, including security and armed conflict. Although there is at present little literature linking sustainable development and environmental protection relevant to armed conflict explicitly, there is however, a gradual growing body of literature on the connection between environmental security[312] and sustainable development.[313] As the definition of the sustainable development concept has already been explored above, it is worth noting that according to UNEP, '"[e]nvironmental security" refers to the area of research and practice that addresses the linkages among the environment, natural resources, conflict and peacebuilding.'[314]

---

[311] Chapter 11, Our Common Future (n 5).

[312] On literature regarding 'environmental security' itself, see, e.g. Dannreuther, R., *International Security: The Contemporary Agenda* (Polity Press, Cambridge 2007) at pp. 59–99; French, D., 'Environmental Security in an Insecure World' (2005) 17 Environmental Law and Management 159; Brauch, H.G., 'Security and Environment Linkages on the Mediterranean Space: Three Phases of Research on Human and Environmental Security and Peace' in Robertson, L. and Liotta, P.H. (eds), *Security and Environment in the Mediterranean: Conceptualising Security and Environmental Conflicts* (Springer-Verlag, Germany 2003) at pp. 35–144 [hereinafter Brauch]; Dalby, S., *Environmental Security* (University of Minnesota, Minneapolis 2002); Manwaring, M.G. (ed), *Environmental Security and Global Stability: Problems and Responses* (Lexington Books, USA 2002); Barnett, J., *The Meaning of Environmental Security: Ecological Politics and Policy in the New Security Era* (Zed Books, London 2001) [hereinafter Barnett]; Butts, K.H. (ed), *Environmental Security: A DOD Partnership for Peace* (DIANE, USA 1994).

[313] For literature on sustainable development and environmental security, see, e.g. Voigt, C., 'Sustainable Security' (2008) 19 Yearbook of International Environmental Law 163; Gaines, S.E., 'Sustainable Development and National Security' (2006) 30 William and Mary Environmental Law and Policy Review 321 [hereinafter Gaines]; Dodds, F. and Pippard, T. (eds), *Human and Environmental Security: An Agenda for Change* (Earthscan, UK 2005); Barnett (n 312) at pp. 134–56 (on environmental security complementing sustainable development); Brunée, J., 'Environmental Security in the 21st Century: New Momentum for the Development of International Environmental Law?' (1995) 18 Fordham International Law Journal 1742 [hereinafter Brunée].

[314] UNEP, 'From Conflict to Peacebuilding: The Role of Natural Resources and the Environment' (UNEP, Switzerland 2009) [hereinafter UNEP Conflict to Peacebuilding] at p. 7.

More than a decade ago, Brunée notes that, 'environmental degradation and resource scarcity have come to be perceived as threats not only to human well-being and prosperity, but also to international security.'[315] The international community in the 1980s began to see a possible link between environmental conditions and issues of security.[316] Scholars such as Ullman, Myers, Westing and others, began to put forward ideas that environmental pressures and change could be a threat to peace and security and hence, lead to armed conflict.[317]

Since then, it has increasingly been recognised that lack of or an abundance of valuable natural resources, land degradation or water scarcity for example, are some of the environmental problems known to cause or increase tension between or within nations, and even eventually lead to conflict.[318] Furthermore, it is of central importance to this study that environmental problems are also problems for national and global security, that is, in the form of environmental pressures that may fuel conflict, to environmental damage and destruction as a result of armed conflict. On the other hand, looking at it from a more opportunistic point of view as Kraska comments, '[e]nvironmental conservation and cooperation can have a reverse effect by generating greater security, reducing regional tension and avoiding conflict.'[319] To address these environmental problems is to contribute directly to security in this way.

The emerging appreciation of the interrelated character of environmental protection and security has prompted the beginnings of a

---

[315]   Brunée (n 313).

[316]   Although the potential link came to prominence in research circles in the 1980s, Lester Brown did sow the seeds of this idea in 1977. See Brown, L.R., 'Redefining National Security' Worldwatch Institute, Paper No. 14 (Washington, DC 1977).

[317]   See, e.g. Ullman, R.H., 'Redefining Security' (1983) 8 International Security 129, at pp. 139–41; Westing, A.H., 'An Expanded Concept of International Security' in Westing, A.H. (ed), *Global Resources and International Conflict: Environmental Factors in Strategic Policy and Action* (OUP, New York 1986) at pp. 183–200; Myers, N., 'Linking Environment and Security' (1987) 4 Bulletin of the Atomic Scientist 46; Gleick, P.H., 'The Implications of Global Climate Changes for International Security' (1989) 15 Climate Change 309; Mathews, J.T., 'Redefining Security' (1989) 68 Foreign Affairs 162.

[318]   UNEP Conflict to Peacebuilding (n 314).

[319]   Kraska, J., 'Sustainable Development is Security: The Role of Transboundary River Agreements as a Confidence Building Measure (CBM) in South Asia' (2003) 28 Yale Journal of International Law 465, at p. 466.

re-evaluation of both security concepts and concepts relating to sustainable development.[320] From a security perspective, Brunée observes that, '[t]he growing potential for conflict over scarce or degraded resources has prompted domestic and international policy-makers to re-evaluate the traditional concepts of security. It is increasingly recognised that only a broader conception of security can adequately capture the underlying concerns and promote more effective solutions.'[321] This broader conception is taking the form of 'environmental security', central to which is the need to break the vicious cycle of environmental degradation resulting in lack of and shortages of natural resources, leading to conflict as nations fight over scarce resources.

Marong proceeds to point out that, '[e]nvironmental security requires maintaining the ecological balance necessary for performing life-support functions, and for the environment to continue to serve as a source of natural resources for the use of current and future generations.'[322] Marong's implicit references to intra- and inter-generational equity suggest that the concept is also capable of being placed somewhere near the core of the sustainable development agenda that is the focus of this foregoing analysis. This view is reflected by Gaines, in referring to equity, precaution and common but differentiated responsibilities,[323] states that '[e]xploring security linkages in the sustainable development frame of reference thus opens our minds to broader, more complex, and ultimately more meaningful connections between personal security and the patterns of economic activity and social organization that affect human use and abuse of the environment.'[324]

---

[320] See, e.g. Kegley, C.W., *World Politics: Trend and Transformation* (11th edn Cangage, USA 2008) at pp. 364–5; Brauch (n 312) at pp. 81–9; Myers, N., 'Environmental Security: What's New and Different?', The Hague Conference on Environment, Security and Sustainable Development (The Peace Palace, The Hague, The Netherlands, 9–12 May 2004); Bernstein, J., 'Discussion Paper on Environment, Security and Sustainable Development', The Hague Conference on Environment, Security and Sustainable Development (The Peace Palace, The Hague, The Netherlands, 9–12 May 2004); McGlade, J., 'Towards a World Summit on Sustainable Development 2012: Environmental Security – the Other Challenge for Sustainable Development' European Environment Agency, www.eesc.europa.eu/resources/docs/mcglade-en.pdf (accessed 26 February 2012).

[321] Brunée (n 313) at p. 1742.

[322] Marong (n 7) at p. 40.

[323] Gaines (n 313) at pp. 366–9.

[324] Ibid., at p. 324.

On the face of it, security is not *per se* development, nor is armed conflict itself. Of course, if development is defined in terms of an economic activity, as it widely is, then anything which costs money, however constructive or destructive, is development.[325] That would appear to bring the two concepts together. Furthermore it is widely accepted that environmental problems are the catalyst for insecurity and that such problems are invariably the product of unsustainable development decisions and practices.[326] Given too that the armed conflict industry is factored into most calculations of development,[327] in much the same way as treating victims of road accidents shows up as a positive in calculations of national Gross Domestic Product, and the interconnectedness of issues in the field of security, the link and integration of the environment and sustainable development become more apparent.[328]

However, this is not to say that environmental security and sustainable development are entirely interchangeable concepts. Scholars comment that,

---

[325] See, e.g. Contreras, R., 'Competing Theories on Economic Development' (1999) 9 Transnational Law and Contemporary Problems 93; Damle, J., *Beyond Economic Development* (Mittal, India 2001); Todaro, M.P. and Smith, S.C., *Economic Development* (Pearson, England 2009). *Cf.* Bradlow, D.D., 'Development Decision-Making and the Content of International Development Law' (2004) 27 Boston College International and Comparative Law Review 195 (analysis on the 'traditional view' of development which is about economic growth and the 'modern view' of development which incorporates the integration of economic, social, cultural, political and environmental dimensions); Yongo-Bure, B., *Economic Development of Southern Sudan* (University Press of America, USA 2007).

[326] Gaines (n 313); Atapattu, S., 'Sustainable Development and Terrorism: International Linkages and a Case Study of Sri Lanka' (2006) 30 William and Mary Environmental Law and Policy Review 273, at pp. 291–2 (considers conflict as a cause of unsustainable development).

[327] See, e.g. Collier, P., 'War and military expenditure in developing countries and their consequences for development' (2006) 1 The Economics of Peace and Security Journal 10; SIPRI, 'Measuring Military Expenditure' SIPRI Military Expenditure project, www.sipri.org/research/armaments/milex/research issues/measuring_milex (accessed 25 March 2012); The World Bank, 'Military expenditure (% of GDP)', http://data.worldbank.org/indicator/MS.MIL.XPND. GD.ZS (accessed 25 March 2012).

[328] Bragdon, S.H., 'The Evolution and Future of the Law of Sustainable Development: Lessons from the Convention on Biological Diversity' (1996) 8 Georgetown International Environmental Law Review 423, at p. 436 (concludes that the integration of environmental concerns in addition to the socio-economic dimension of security 'lies at the heart of the concept of sustainable development').

[t]here is confusion about the difference between environmental security and sustainable development. Although sustainable development and environmental security are mutually reinforcing concepts and directions for policy, they are not the same thing. Sustainable development focuses on environmentally sound socio-economic development, while environmental security focuses on preventing conflict related to environmental factors, as well as the additional military needs to protect their forces from environmental hazards and repair military-related environmental damages.[329]

Implicit within this account is a view of environmental security as a distinctive concept that relates exclusively to the prevention of conflict related to environmental factors, and the restoration of environmental damage after the conflict so as to prevent further conflict. By contrast, the threshold for action on the basis of sustainable development may be set lower; environmental problems may need to be addressed within the parameters of sustainable development well before they become catastrophic enough to be a security threat. Sustainable development is in this sense aptly described as more exacting than environmental security.[330]

Another possible difference between environmental security and sustainable development concerns the relevance of such matters as public participation and other 'sub-principles' of the ILA noted above. Many of the sub-principles may be described as process related (good governance, for example, as well as public participation), whereas the concept of environmental security relates more exclusively, on the face of it, to a specific outcome (security).

Finally, there is the argument that collective security generally, and environmental security in particular, are narrower in their concern with the 'life cycle' of armed conflict than sustainable development. For example, they arguably do not encompass issues relating to the conduct of armed conflict. This is an area which the international lawyer would tend to bracket off as belonging to more humanitarian law fields.[331] The sustainable development concept deals with the prevention, reduction and

---

[329]   Glenn, J.C., Gordon, T.J. and Perclat, R., 'Environmental Security Study: Emerging International Definitions, Perceptions and Policy Considerations', 1997–98, for the US Army Environmental Policy Institute (American Council/UN University), www.acunu.org/millennium/env-sec1.html (accessed 26 February 2012) [hereinafter Glenn].

[330]   See, e.g. Brauch (n 312) at p. 142. *Cf.* Barnett (n 312) at p. 136.

[331]   See, e.g. Hulme, K., *War Torn Environment: Interpreting the Legal Threshold* (Martinus Nijhoff, Leiden 2004); Roberts, A., 'The law of war and environmental damage' in Austin, J.E. and Bruch, C.E. (eds), *The Environmental Consequences of War: Legal, Economic, and Scientific Perspectives* (CUP, Cambridge 2000) at pp. 47–86.

remedying of environmental damage that threatens intra- and inter-generational equity, and to this extent, application of this concept requires a broadening of the environmental security agenda.

This book is thus concerned with how viable in a global context of environmental protection relevant to security and armed conflict at the forefront of which is the sustainable development concept, in the pre-conflict or preventive stage, during actual conflict and the post-conflict stage, is? The focus in doing so concerns the scope that exists (if any) for conveying sustainable development as a body of principles including resource conservation, integration, public participation (amongst others), that require a holistic approach to security and armed conflict oriented around environmental themes. While there is a growing body of literature examining specific aspects of the nexus between war and environment, this book attempts to demonstrate that it is helpful to restructure the analysis around the overarching concept of sustainable development and that it is distinctive and important, for reasons that become clear as the book develops.

6. CONCLUSION

This chapter has provided a brief overview of sustainable development and its principles. As discovered, although sustainable development is probably not a legally binding norm or principle in international law, it is nevertheless a concept with significant legal relevance. Moreover, sustainable development is a constructive goal or objective to strive for in the international political or legal arena.

In the ultimate aim of striving for sustainable development, the sub-principles discussed in this chapter will be used with regard to environmental protection relevant to security and armed conflict in the following three stages: pre-conflict (to prevent environmental pressures from threatening peace and security and fuelling armed conflict); in-conflict (whether international law protecting the environment during armed conflict is in line with the sustainable development concept); and finally, post-conflict (restoring the damaged environment and preventing the cycle of re-conflict).

It is suggested that the appropriate place for sustainable development in scholarship relating to armed conflict is, by way of a synthesis of various strands which are best understood holistically. This book is thus not a detailed engagement with any particular facet of the nexus of armed conflict and the environment; for an increasing amount of studies of this kind are appearing in literature and adding to these is not a priority.

Rather, this study concerns the life cycle of armed conflict and aims to demonstrate how and why sustainable development enables us to approach problems and solutions more constructively than an approach looking at discrete strands of the problem in isolation from others. The remainder of the book is concerned with strengths and weaknesses of law and policy in respect of the stages in the cycle of armed conflict in the context of environmental protection when viewed from the perspective of sustainable development as an overarching concept.

3. Failing sustainable development? Early warning, early action, and preventing environmental security threats

1. INTRODUCTION

> War is inimical to sustainable development and can lay the seeds for future violence... If it is now generally recognised that war causes environmental harm, it is also increasingly accepted that environmental degradation has the potential to produce internal and inter-state conflict by undermining stability and producing mass migrations.[1]

There are numerous laws which are considered in this study which are in place to protect the environment during and in the immediate aftermath of an armed conflict.[2] Yet, despite the plethora of laws and research conducted by scholars on the environment-conflict nexus over the last three decades,[3] the critical issues of understanding and addressing the

---

[1] Kiss, A. and Shelton, D., *Guide to International Environmental Law* (Martinus Nijhoff, The Netherlands 2007) at p. 267.

[2] The relevant laws and international mechanisms will be explored in Chapters 4 and 5.

[3] See, e.g. Ullman, R.H., 'Redefining Security' (1983) 8 International Security 129, at pp. 139–41; Myers, N., 'Linking Environment and Security' (1987) 4 Bulletin of the Atomic Scientist 46; Gleick, P.H., 'Environment and Security: The Clear Connections' (1991) 47 Bulletin of the Atomic Scientist 16; Gleditsch, N.P. (ed), *Conflict and the Environment* (Kluwer, The Netherlands 1997) [hereinafter 1997 Gleditsch (ed)]; Homer-Dixon, T.F., *Environment, Scarcity, and Violence* (Princeton University, Princeton 2001) [hereinafter 2001 Homer-Dixon]; Gleditsch, N.P., 'Environmental Change, Security, and Conflict' in Crocker, C.A. (eds), *Leashing the Dogs of War: Conflict Management in a Divided World* (US Institute of Peace, USA 2007) at pp. 177–96 [hereinafter 2007 Gleditsch], [hereinafter Crocker (eds)]; Cudworth, E. and Hobden, S., 'Environmental Insecurity' in Fagan, G.H. and Munck, R. (eds), *Globalization and Security* (Praeger Security, USA 2009) at pp. 69–100. See also the 'environmental security' discussion in Chapter 2; Ehrlich, A.E. and others, 'Resources

environmental *causes* of conflict have only lately surfaced as worthy of serious attention within the realm of international relations.[4]

The concern in the analysis below is with the nature of the challenge of preventing armed or violent conflict[5] as a result of environmental pressures, that is, by preventing, managing or mitigating environmental issues that may be a threat to international peace and security. This is a challenge rooted in the preventive approach as well as protecting the environment for present and future generations. In order to explore this challenge to the international community, three case-studies are examined: Somalia; Darfur, Sudan; and Sierra Leone. The environment-conflict link in each case is considered first, followed by a review of the international response to that link in relation to conflict prevention in each situation. This chapter explores these preventive issues from a sustainable development perspective as well as attempts to utilise the appropriate sustainable development principles as discussed in the previous chapter, as tools or objectives to prevent environment stimulated conflict. Therefore, Section 2 explores in greater detail the possible connection between the environment and armed conflict as well as case-studies in practice; Section 3 reviews the international responses relevant to environment-conflict prevention in relation to the case-studies; and Section 4 then explores two questions – whether the international community in lieu of lessons learned, has a system or regime in place in relation to environment-conflict prevention and whether it is effective in preventing conflict in light of the overarching concept of sustainable development?

2. ENVIRONMENT AND CONFLICT

Although the possible connection between environmental threats and violent conflict were put forward by scholars in the field some time ago, in the international arena, the nexus between environmental problems and

and Environment Degradation as Sources of Conflict' (September 2001) 2(3) Pugwash Occasional Papers 108, at pp. 122–7 (on the various stages of academic research on the environmental-conflict link) [hereinafter 2001 Ehrlich].

[4]   See, e.g. UN, 'A More Secure World: Our Shared Responsibility' Report of the Secretary-General's High-Level Panel on Threats, Challenges and Change (UN 2004) [hereinafter A More Secure World]; UNEP, 'From Conflict to Peacebuilding: The Role of Natural Resources and the Environment' (UNEP, Switzerland 2009) at p. 5 [hereinafter UNEP Conflict to Peacebuilding].

[5]   The terms 'armed conflict', 'violent conflict' and 'conflict' are used interchangeably in this chapter.

international security came to prominence more recently with the publication of the 2004 UN Report 'A More Secure World'.[6] This report was produced by the High-Level Panel on Threats, Challenges and Change (High-Level Panel) which was created specifically to research and advise the UN on new and potential global threats.[7] The Panel, in expanding the remit of threats to international security to include environmental degradation, expressed concern that 'rarely are environmental concerns factored into security, development or humanitarian strategies. Nor is there coherence in environmental protection efforts at the global level.'[8] In light of this critically important statement, this section explains why the Panel is right to take environmental security threats seriously. Therefore, the link between the environment and armed conflict is well elucidated with reference to case-studies involving Somalia; Darfur, Sudan; and Sierra Leone.

2.1. The Environment-conflict Link

UNEP reports that at least 18 violent conflicts have been fuelled by environmental degradation or natural resource[9] exploitation or both since 1990,[10] and that at least 40 per cent of all intrastate conflicts over the last six decades or so have had some link to natural resources.[11]

---

[6]   A More Secure World (n 4).

[7]   The Panel was assigned with four additional tasks: to examine the current challenges to peace and security, to consider the contribution which collective action can make in addressing these challenges, to review the functioning of the UN system and to recommend ways of strengthening it. See UN, 'The Secretary-General Address to the General Assembly' (New York, 23 September 2003), www.un.org/webcast/ga/58/statements/sg2eng030923 (accessed 7 March 2012).

[8]   A More Secure World (n 4) at p. 26.

[9]   'Natural resources are actual or potential sources of wealth that occur in a natural state, such as timber, water, fertile land, wildlife, minerals, metals, stones, and hydrocarbons. A natural resource qualifies as a renewable resource if it is replenished by natural processes at a rate comparable to its rate of consumption by humans or other users. A natural resource is considered non-renewable when it exists in a fixed amount, or when it cannot be regenerated on a scale comparative to its consumption.' See UNEP Conflict to Peacebuilding (n 4) at p. 7.

[10]   Ibid., at p. 8 and p. 11 (lists recent internal unrest and civil conflicts fuelled by natural resources).

[11]   Ibid., at p. 8. Findings are based on data from the Uppsala Conflict Data Program and Centre for the Study of Civil War (2008). See UCDP/PRIO Armed Conflict Dataset Version 4 (2008), www.prio.no/CSCW/Datasets/Armed-Conflict/UCDP-PRIO/ (accessed 7 March 2012).

Historically, environmental changes resulting in the depletion of natural resources or environmental degradation in a particular area, country or region may have played a role in fuelling armed or violent conflict.[12] Now more than ever, because the global population is living in a time of unprecedented environmental change – from the hole in the ozone layer,[13] climate change,[14] resource scarcity,[15] to the potential increase in environmental refugees,[16] this link between such changes and potential conflicts should be a cause for serious concern. Many of these changes are of a kind that, in some circumstances might be the catalyst that sparks off conflict and in others, exacerbate other pre-existing factors of conflict.[17] It is foreseeable that the pace of environmental change will accelerate as the human population is expected to nearly double in the

---

[12] For historical examples from Mesopotamian times to Easter Island, see, e.g. 2001 Ehrlich (n 3) at pp. 111–12.

[13] For information on the ozone hole and its implications, see, e.g. EU, 'Protection of the Ozone Layer', http://ec.europa.eu/environment/ozone/ozone_layer.htm (accessed 7 March 2012); Hough, P., *Understanding Global Security* (2nd edn Routledge, Oxon 2008) at pp. 156–7.

[14] The abnormal acceleration in climate change that the world is currently experiencing is already causing severe unprecedented effects on the global environment. See Sindico, F., 'Ex-Post and Ex-Ante [Legal] Approaches to Climate Change Threats to the International Community' (2005) 9 New Zealand Journal of Environmental Law 209, at p. 212. See also Webersik, C., *Climate Change and Security* (ABC-CLIO, USA 2010).

[15] See, e.g. 2007 Gleditsch (n 3) at pp. 178–9; 2001 Homer-Dixon (n 3).

[16] See, e.g. Unruh, J.D., Krol, M. and Kliot, N. (eds), *Environmental Change and its Implications for Population Migration* (Kluwer, The Netherlands 2004) [hereinafter Unruh (eds)]; Afifi, T. and Jäger, J. (eds), *Environment, Forced Migration and Social Vulnerability* (Springer-Verlag, Berlin Heidelberg 2010).

[17] This ranges for example, from predicted changing patterns in annual rainfall to climate change. Although there is some disagreement within the scientific community on the issue of climate change, studies have predicted a potential future increase in temperature of 1.5 to 6.4 degrees centigrade by the year 2100. Thus, potentially causing rising sea levels and the redrawing of international boundaries, resulting in gradual population displacement with dire social and economic consequences. Scientists also predict, based on current indications of considerable shifts in the distribution of rainfall over the next 50 years, that this will have a significant impact on the countries and regions affected. See Abbott, C. and others, 'Global Responses to Threats: Sustainable Security for the 21st Century' Oxford Research Group Briefing Paper (June 2006) at pp. 7–8 [hereinafter Abbott], www.oxfordresearchgroup.org.uk/publications/briefing_papers/global_responses_global_threats_sustainable_security_21st_century (accessed 25 March 2012).

next half of this century.[18] The potential for violent conflict is thereby escalating as the ever increasing global population scrambles for dwindling resources and in certain regions struggles to adapt to the environmental stresses affecting them.

There is no doubt that many conflicts over the decades have been fuelled by environmental factors, fighting over natural resources or as a result of environmental degradation or both.[19] The most common natural resources that may cause conflict at present include for example: arable land,[20] water,[21] and in certain circumstances, 'high-value' resources also known as conflict resources[22] such as diamonds,[23] oil[24] and minerals.[25] It should be emphasised that conflicts can be triggered by both the lack of and the relative abundance of such resources.[26] First, either situation can lead to competition over the control of a particular resource and/or

---

[18]   See UN Department of Economic and Social Affairs (UNDESA), Population Division, 'World Population Prospects: The 2010 Revision' Press Release (3 May 2011).

[19]   For further discussion on environmental factors that may cause conflict, see, e.g. Vyrynen, R., 'Environment, Violence, Political Change' (2001) 15 Notre Dame Journal of Law, Ethics and Public Policy 593 [hereinafter Vyrynen]; 2001 Homer-Dixon (n 3); UNEP Conflict to Peacebuilding (n 4).

[20]   See, e.g. Derman, B., Odgaard, R. and Sjaastad, E. (eds), *Conflicts Over Land and Water in Africa* (James Currey, Oxford 2007) (link between land and conflict).

[21]   See, e.g. Fort, T.L. and Schipani, C.A., 'Ecology and Violence: The Environmental Dimensions of War' (2004) 29 Columbia Journal of Environmental Law 243, at pp. 255–60 [hereinafter Fort] (link between water and conflict).

[22]   'Conflict resources are natural resources whose systematic exploitation and trade in a context of conflict contribute to, benefit from, or result in the commission of serious violations of human rights, violations of international humanitarian law or violations amounting to crimes under international law.' See UNEP Conflict to Peacebuilding (n 4) at p. 7.

[23]   See, e.g. Levy, A.V. (ed), *Diamonds and Conflict: Problems and Solutions* (Novinka, New York 2003) [hereinafter Levy (ed)] (link between diamonds and conflict).

[24]   See, e.g. Fort (n 21) at pp. 248–55 (link between competition for oil and conflict).

[25]   For example, States are competing for control over gold, copper, diamonds and other resources in the Democratic Republic of Congo (DRC). See Fort (n 21) at p. 247.

[26]   Vyrynen (n 19) at p. 600. For an introduction into the resource-conflict field also known as the 'resource curse' in some situations, see Collier, P., *The Bottom Billion: Why the Poorest Countries are Failing and What Can Be Done About It* (OUP, Oxford 2007).

inequitable distribution of that resource and thus, cause conflict. This includes conflict that can arise when States or groups within a State or region, compete to control access over 'high-value' resources at the expense of a significant portion of the population.[27] Secondly, while some resources are naturally scarce *per se*, others are scarce because mankind has unsustainably overexploited them. This can cause or exacerbate conflict within countries or regions where the economy of States concerned depend mostly or entirely on a particular scarce or rapidly dwindling resource.[28]

'Environmental degradation' as a trigger of conflict typically means global environmental threats such as climate change that could add to the scarcity of natural resources (for example, freshwater or fertile land).[29] Secondly, it can also denote environmental threats such as water or air pollution which could be either domestic or transboundary.[30] This could cause conflict when, for example, the much needed water resource is too polluted to sustain the livelihoods of the population concerned. Thirdly, it could be unsustainable environmental and agricultural practices employed by the population. For example, 'slash and burn' farming techniques causing deforestation and air pollution or overgrazing by cattle causing land desertification. Such unsustainable environmental damage and degradation can, in certain societies or circumstances, trigger conflict.

To sum up the environment-conflict link (as Homer-Dixon argues), conflict can occur as a result of environmental degradation and scarcity based on two kinds of interaction: 'resource capture', and 'ecological marginalization'.[31] 'Resource capture' occurs when the pressures of environmental degradation and dwindling natural resources interact with population growth. Such interaction can heighten social conflict when the most powerful groups within the society concerned take control of and

---

[27]   Benn, H., 'Trade and Security in an Interconnected World' in Dodds, F. and Pippard, T. (eds), *Human and Environmental Security: An Agenda for Change* (Earthscan, UK 2005) at p. 95 [hereinafter Dodds and Pippard].

[28]   Ross, M., 'The Natural Resource Curse: How Wealth Can Make You Poor' in Bannon, I. and Collier, P. (eds), *Natural Resources and Violent Conflict: Options and Actions* (World Bank, Washington, DC 2003) at pp. 21–2 [hereinafter Bannon and Collier].

[29]   Parry, M. and others (eds), *Climate Change 2007: Impacts, Adaptation and Vulnerability* (IPCC/CUP, Canada 2007) at pp. 443–5.

[30]   Vyrynen (n 19) at p. 611.

[31]   2001 Homer-Dixon (n 3) at pp. 177–8.

practise inequitable distribution of those scarce resources.[32] 'Ecological marginalization' occurs when unequal resource access in combination with population growth, pushes the poorer resource dependant population to migrate. Such migration in turn causes ecological degradation and over exploitation of resources in the new migrated areas thereby potentially causing conflict.[33]

Taking into account Homer-Dixons's findings, it should be borne in mind that changes in the environment alone will not be a threat to international peace and security, that is, it is not likely to be the sole cause of an outbreak of armed conflict. The link between environmental degradation and/or resource scarcity and armed conflict is more complicated in reality. It is environmental factors or changes in combination with existing divisions within society whether political, economic or social in nature, that could lead to violent conflict.[34] To put it simply, environmental changes or pressures are one of many variable factors that may trigger or exacerbate a potential conflict situation because such environmental impacts will not cause elevated conflict risk in all societies. This makes a sustainable development approach all the more crucial.

Regrettably, societies that are most vulnerable to environmentally-induced conflict are the ones that lack any form of sustainable development – the integration and/or balancing of social, economic and environmental interests. Such societies 'are those simultaneously experiencing severe environmental scarcity and various forms of institutional failure (especially failure of states and markets) that hinder social adaptation to scarcity.'[35] Such lack thereof means that these societies do not have the foundation or capacity to adapt to exacerbating or cataclysmic environmental stresses, thereby resulting in possible conflict.

Some scholars argue that, '[i]t is unquestionably true that social variables must be central to any adequate explanation of human conflict,

---

[32]   Ibid.

[33]   Ibid.

[34]   UNEP Conflict to Peacebuilding (n 4) at p. 5. See also Brodnig, G., 'Cultural and Environmental Factors in Violent Conflict: A Framework for Conflict Prevention' in Grandvoinnet, H. and Schneider, H. (eds), *Conflict Management in Africa: A Permanent Challenge* (OECD, Paris 1998) at p. 34 [hereinafter Brodnig].

[35]   Schwartz, D. and others, 'The Environment and Violent Conflict: A Response to Gleditsch's Critique and Some Suggestions for Future Research' (Summer 2000) 6 Environmental Change and Security Project Report 77, at p. 81 [hereinafter Schwartz].

whether in rich or poor countries.'[36] Hence, highlighting the importance of recognising and taking into consideration the role of such causative variables in integration with environmental pressures, particularly with the goal of achieving both sustainable development and conflict prevention. As the Brundtland Report notes, '[t]he real sources of insecurity also encompass unsustainable development, and its effects can become intertwined with traditional forms of conflict in a manner that can extend and deepen the latter.'[37]

The most obvious examples of other underlying factors or intervening variables are population growth, migration, political, economic, and social instability. These factors which may exist singly or in combination in a particular situation and which could, in addition to environmental pressures, trigger or exacerbate armed conflict, are explored below.[38]

The rising global population and increasing pressures on the environment could potentially fuel armed conflict.[39] This is connected in particular to economic and political factors. Scholars have noted that in general, 'one of the most robust findings in the quantitative conflict literature is that impoverished and institutionally weak countries, usually measured by low GDP per capita, have an exceptionally high risk of armed conflict and civil war.'[40] With the added pressure of a rapidly growing population, countries with low adaptive or preventive capacity to environmental degradation and/or resource scarcity are more susceptible to armed or violent conflict.[41] Research also shows that although population growth rates are decreasing at a global level, the population in some continents (sub-Saharan Africa and Asia), particularly in developing low income countries, are increasing at a considerable rate and will

---

[36]   Ibid. See also 2001 Ehrlich (n 3).

[37]   World Commission on Environment and Development (WCED), Our Common Future, 'Chapter 11: Peace, Security, Development and the Environment' (1987) at para. 4.

[38]   These variable factors are non-exhaustive.

[39]   Newbold, K.B., *Six Billion Plus: World Population in the Twenty-First Century* (2nd edn Rowman and Littlefield, Oxon 2007) at pp. 194–9.

[40]   Urdal, H., 'Demographic Aspects of Climate Change, Environmental Degradation and Armed Conflict' UN Expert Group Meeting on Population Distribution, Urbanization, Internal Migration and Development, UNDESA (UN, New York 2008) at p. 3 [hereinafter Urdal]. See also Hegre, H. and Sambanis, N., 'Sensitivity Analysis of Empirical Results on Civil War Onset' (2006) 50 Journal of Conflict Resolution 508.

[41]   Urdal (n 40) at p. 3.

continue do so in the near future.[42] For example, Sub-Saharan Africa, despite HIV/AIDS mortality rates, 'is expected to have the world's fastest population growth'[43] and 'the world's second most populous region, exceeded only by South Asia.'[44] The total population in this region 'is expected to peak around year 2080 at about 1.5 billion, almost two and a half times the population in year 2000.'[45] These areas of predicted accelerated population growth are therefore likely to be the most vulnerable to environmental changes. With the additional factor of ineffective governance failing to take into account intra- and inter-generational equity and mismanagement of these environmental pressures, these stresses could potentially fuel violent local conflicts.[46]

Migration is another example of a causative variable in environmentally related conflict.[47] In this context, migration can be a dual cause and effect issue, that is, it can be 'both a cause and effect of worsening environmental conditions.'[48] Environmental degradation – from pollution, climate change, or unsustainable exploitation of natural resources leading to scarcity – could cause the affected population to move to a better location.[49] This is particularly true in relation to societies that are dependant on environmental elements for their livelihoods such as sufficient rainfall, fresh water, cropland and forests. It is however,

---

[42]   Ibid. See also World Bank, *Atlas of Global Development* (World Bank, Washington, DC 2007) at pp. 24–5; Sen, A., 'Population: Delusion and Reality' in Webber, M. and Bezanson, K. (eds), *Rethinking Society in the 21st Century: Critical Readings in Sociology* (2nd edn Canadian Scholars, Toronto 2008) at pp. 321–2.

[43]   Lutz, W. and others, 'The End of World Population Growth' in Lutz, W., Sanderson, W.C. and Scherbov, S. (eds), *The End of World Population Growth in the 21st Century: New Challenges for Human Capital Formation and Sustainable Development* (Earthscan, London 2004) at p. 45 [hereinafter Lutz].

[44]   Ibid.

[45]   Urdal (n 40) at p. 3; Lutz (n 43) at p. 45.

[46]   2007 Gleditsch (n 3) at pp. 188–9; Stern, N.H., *The Economics of Climate Change: The Stern Review* (CUP, Cambridge 2007) at p. 120. See also Homer-Dixon, T. and Blitt, J. (eds), *Ecoviolence: Links Among Environment, Population, and Security* (Rowman and Littlefield, USA 1998).

[47]   Millennium Ecosystem Assessment, *Ecosystems and Human Well-Being: Scenarios, Volume 2* (Island, Washington, DC 2005) at p. 181.

[48]   Buhaug, H. and others, 'Implications of Climate Change for Armed Conflict' Social Dimensions for Climate Change Program (World Bank, Washington, DC 2008) at p. 27 [hereinafter Buhaug].

[49]   Gibbs, S., 'People on the Move: Population, Migration, and the Environment' in Mazur, L. (ed), *A Pivotal Moment: Population, Justice, and the Environmental Challenge* (Island, Washington, DC 2009) at pp. 57–60.

unlikely that people would migrate solely for environmental reasons.[50] Other underlying factors such as uncertain economic, political and social aspects within a particular country or society, would contribute towards the potential migration. It is thus argued that it is the lack of any form of sustainable development whatsoever, leading to socio-economic, development and environmental stresses that may compel certain societies to migrate.

Such migrations are mostly domestic in nature rather than international and any international movements of people would generally occur in the region of developing countries.[51] In some situations where such migration has occurred, the sharp increase in population in the new location may contribute to local or regional conflicts. Aside from potential ethnic tensions, competing for dwindling environmental resources or contributing to environmental degradation by the migrating population in the new area could be another cause. This undoubtedly obstructs sustainable development, both in terms of the unsustainable use of environmental resources and further damage to the environment. Thus, adding to the inevitable hardship of the population concerned.

Another pre-existing variable that may trigger and fuel the outbreak of armed conflict is political instability wherein a State lacks good or effective governance. While many States have the adaptive capacity to deal with environmental pressures, some States, particularly institutionally fragile and economically unstable ones, are more at risk from 'environmentally related violence.'[52] Urdal sets forth the argument that, 'relatively weaker states are presumably more likely to experience resource scarcity conflicts firstly because they are less capable of mitigating the effects of resource scarcity, and secondly, because they are generally more likely to be militarily challenged by opposition groups.'[53] There is no doubt that 'strong States' are less likely to suffer from internal conflicts as they have better adaptive capacity. Stronger and more stable countries generally have good or effective governance, that is, 'they have effective administrative hierarchies and they control the legitimate use of force, which helps manage potential internal challengers. They also have the capacity to mediate impending conflicts before

---

[50]   Kliot, N., 'Environmentally Induced Population Movements: Their Complex Sources and Consequences' in Unruh (eds) (n 16) at pp. 73–4.

[51]   Barnett, J., 'Security and Climate Change' Tyndall Centre for Climate Change Research, Working Paper No. 7 (October 2001) at p. 8 [hereinafter Barnett].

[52]   Urdal (n 40) at p. 6; 2001 Homer-Dixon (n 3) at p. 179.

[53]   Urdal (n 40) at p. 7.

they turn violent.'[54] Good or effective governance along with sound environmental policies are therefore crucial. With such prerequisites, the country concerned would be better able to weather any environmental stresses or resource problems.

The economic structure of a particular State also plays an important part in preventing environmentally-induced conflict.[55] Equity plays a key role because greater and more equal distribution of income throughout a particular State may mean that its population would be less affected by environmental stresses and less dependant on natural resources. Moreover, the State itself would be less vulnerable to environmental stresses and resource scarcities, and have greater economic capacity to assist its population that may be particularly affected by such stresses.[56] For example, Gleditsch argues that environmental degradation are primarily a result of poverty issues and ultimately, ineffective governance.[57] Environmental problems, 'that at first glance may seem to derive from poor economic conditions are frequently the result of poor economic policy decisions.'[58] This illustrates that good or effective governance is crucial. Gleditsch further argues that,

> [e]conomic development also has a restraining influence on violent behaviour in environmental conflict, since wealth is negatively associated with armed conflict, interstate as well as intrastate. Wealthy individuals and groups stand to lose more if war breaks out. If the wealth is widespread, it is likely to act as a general deterrent to participation in major violence.[59]

Social instability or fragmentation within a State is another causative variable.[60] This includes cultural clashes between divided ethnic and religious groups within a particular society.[61] Simmering pre-existing

---

[54]   Barnett (n 51) at p. 6.

[55]   UNDESA, *World Economic and Social Survey 2008: Overcoming Economic Insecurity* (Academic Foundation, UN 2008) at p. 7. See also Collier, P., 'Economic Causes of Civil Conflict and their Implications for Policy' in Crocker (eds) (n 3) [hereinafter 2007 Collier] at pp. 197–218 (for an economic perspective on the causes of civil war).

[56]   Raleigh, C. and Urdal, H., 'Climate Change, Environmental Degradation and Armed Conflict' 47th Annual Convention of the International Studies Association (San Diego, California 22–25 March 2006) at p. 10.

[57]   2007 Gleditsch (n 3) at p. 184.

[58]   Ibid.

[59]   Ibid.

[60]   UNEP Conflict to Peacebuilding (n 4) at p. 5.

[61]   See e.g. 2007 Gleditsch (n 3) at p. 187; Oberthür, S., 'Preventing Environmentally-Induced Conflicts Through International Environmental Policy'

tensions within such groups which are exacerbated by environmental stresses or resource scarcity can potentially lead to violent conflict.[62] Another possible intervening social variable could be a society that already has a history of armed conflict; a conflict inflicting damage on the environment, which in turn could cause resource scarcity.[63] A war-torn country, in the aftermath of armed conflict may end up in a vicious cycle of socio-economic and political instability, environmental mismanagement coupled with environmental degradation and resource scarcity and as a result, a possible relapse into violence. This negative cycle clearly nullifies any strides towards sustainable development.

These examples show that environmental stresses are never the sole factor in environmental-related conflict. It is environmental problems in combination with one or more of the underlying factors discussed above that could be a threat to security and lead to armed conflict. Thus, awareness of these factors is required by the international community in order to prevent, mitigate or manage environmental-induced conflict. Is it important to add that the inter-connectedness of these varying factors themselves embody the concept of sustainable development, that is, all factors be it social, economic, political or environmental, are integrated.

In conclusion, it is clear that while focusing on preventing environmental-inducing conflict factors, in line with the concept of sustainable development, pre-existing 'causative' or 'intervening variables' in each situation must be considered together. Otherwise any preventive solutions may not be sustainably effective in the long-term. By understanding the sources of conflict, it may then be easier to formulate appropriate methods of prevention. As some scholars comment, '[t]here is strong evidence that our current trajectory of population dynamics, economic expansion, and style of development, is not sustainable; that is, the risks of conflict related to the environment and resources are growing.'[64] Thus, making the utilisation of sustainable development principles as objectives or tools to prevent, mitigate or manage possible environmental-induced conflicts, all the more crucial.

---

in Petzold-Bradley, E., Carius, A. and Vincze, A. (eds), *Responding to Environmental Conflicts: Implications for Theory and Practice* (Kluwer, The Netherlands 2001) at p. 239.

[62]   Ibid.

[63]   2007 Gleditsch (n 3) at p. 187. See also Raknerud, A. and Hegre, H., 'The Hazard of War: Reassessing the Evidence for the Democratic Peace' (1997) 34 Journal of Peace Research 385.

[64]   2001 Ehrlich (n 3) at p. 109.

2.2. Case-Studies

There is no shortage of case-studies to illustrate the issues touched on above, as is clear from the UN report already mentioned.[65] Therefore, the case-studies explored below are selected not as such to typify the common scenario, but to bring out the diverse strands of the environment-conflict nexus.

2.2.1. Somalia

Somalia had already been torn apart by a brutal civil war over the last two decades[66] and continues to suffer from political, economic and social instability.[67] The first phase of the civil war stemmed from rebellion against the repressive government regime of Siad Barre from 1969–1991, which practiced extensive clan and ethnic marginalisation.[68] Barre was ousted in 1991 and violent conflict broke out throughout the country by warring clans.[69] This resulted in a death toll of more than 250 000 Somalis.[70] Somalia also suffered and continues to suffer from famine[71]

---

[65]   UNEP Conflict to Peacebuilding (n 4).

[66]   See, e.g. Ramlogan, R., 'Towards a New Vision of World Security: The United Nations Security Council and the Lessons of Somalia' (1993) 16 Houston Journal of International Law 213, at p. 220 [hereinafter Ramlogan]; Nanda, V.P. and others, 'Tragedies in Somalia, Yugoslavia, Haiti, Rwanda and Liberia – Revisiting the Validity of Humanitarian Intervention under International Law – Part II' (1998) 26 Denver Journal of International Law and Policy 827, at pp. 831–3.

[67]   See, e.g. Cox, D.G., Falconer, J. and Stackhouse, B., *Terrorism, Instability, and Democracy in Asia and Africa* (Northeastern University, USA 2009) at pp. 175–6; Gettleman, J., 'Somalia Tallies the Plagues, Fearing What's Next' *New York Times* (New York 27 September 2007); Gettleman, J., 'Somalia' *New York Times* (updated on 12 March 2010), http://topics.nytimes.com/top/news/international/countriesandterritories/somalia/index.html?scp=1-spot&sq=somalia&st=cse (accessed 20 March 2012) [hereinafter Gettleman 'Somalia'].

[68]   González, R.C., 'Ethiopia' in Derouen, K. and Heo, U.K. (eds), *Civil Wars of the World: Major Conflicts since World War II* (ABC-CLIO, California 2007) at p. 361 [hereinafter Derouen and Heo (eds)]; Ramlogan (n 66) at pp. 219–20.

[69]   Ramlogan (n 66) at p. 220.

[70]   Gettleman, J., 'Chaos in Somalia as Fighting Intensifies and Death Toll Rises' *New York Times* (New York 23 April 2007) (Instability and the increase in the overall death toll in Somalia continues).

[71]   See, e.g. Jones, S., 'Half of all food sent to Somalia is stolen, says UN Report' *Guardian* (UK 10 March 2010); Pflanz, M., 'Millions Face Famine in

and various environmental problems – from land degradation, unsustainable agricultural practices to water scarcity.[72]

In 2004 violent conflict once again erupted and this time, over water resources. The 'war of the well'[73] as it became known, was sparked off after a three year drought.[74] The disastrous drought affected an estimated eleven million people across East Africa but Somalia was hit the hardest, especially with crop yields being the worst in ten years.[75] Extensive violence broke out over the country's limited water resources, exacerbated by the lack of effective government.[76]

Since the collapse of the Barre government in 1991, the country has been left with a vacuum of leadership,[77] thus opening the way to various warlords and their armies to take control of 'informal taxation systems,

---

Somalia' *Telegraph* (UK 27 August 2008); Perlez, J., 'Somalia 1992: Picking Up Pieces as Famine Subsides' *New York Times* (New York 31 December 1992).

[72]   UNEP, 'The State of the Environment in Somalia: A Desk Study' (UNEP, Geneva/Nairobi 2005).

[73]   A name given by villagers in Somalia when referring to these tragic events. See Renner, M., 'The Relentless 3-year Drought in Parts of East Africa Has Turned Water into a Highly-Contested Resource' *Worldwatch Institute* (12 July 2006), www.worldwatch.org/node/4188 (accessed 26 March 2012) [hereinafter Renner].

[74]   Ibid; Wax, E., 'Dying for Water in Somalia's Drought: Amid Anarchy, Warlords Hold Precious Resource' *Washington Post* (Washington DC, 14 April 2006) [hereinafter Wax]. See also Gleick, P.H., 'Pacific Institute's Water Conflict Chronology' (updated November 2009), www.worldwater.org/conflict/list/ (accessed 7 March 2012) [hereinafter Gleick].

[75]   Renner (n 73).

[76]   Wax (n 74). See also Crowe, S., 'Conflict Over Scarce Resources in Drought-Stricken Somalia' UNICEF Newsline (updated 7 June 2006), www.unicef.org/infobycountry/somalia_34426.html (accessed 7 March 2012).

[77]   Somalia was and still is considered to be a 'failed State'. See, e.g. Ripsman. N.M. and Paul, T.V., *Globalization and the National Security State* (OUP, New York 2010) at p. 135; Foreign Policy, 'The Failed States Index 2011', www.foreignpolicy.com/failedstates (accessed 7 March 2012) (Somalia still leads the Failed States Index). The definition of a 'failed State' is 'a condition of "state collapse" – e.g., a state that can no longer perform its basic security, and development functions and that has no effective control over its territory and borders. A failed state is one that can no longer reproduce the conditions for its own existence ... Even in a failed state, some elements of the state, such as local state organisations, might continue to exist.' See, The Crisis States Research Centre (CSRC) of The London School of Economics and Political Science, 'Crisis, Fragile and Failed States: Definitions used by the CSRC' (Crisis States Workshop, London, March 2006), www2.lse.ac.uk/internationalDevelopment/ research/crisisStates/Research/research.aspx (accessed 7 March 2012).

crops, markets and access to water.'[78] The villagers refer to those who control access to the scarce water resources using violent and unscrupulous means as 'warlords of water'.[79] Although observers say that there had been long-standing tensions between the two tribes on the Somali border, they had lived alongside each other in relative peace before the extended drought made water resources scarce.[80] At the end of the conflict two years later, the villagers describe the situation thereafter as 'well widows, well warlords and well warriors.'[81] The conflict over scarce water resources left at least 250 people dead and many more injured.[82]

2.2.2. Darfur, Sudan

UNEP has labelled desertification as 'Sudan's greatest environmental problem.'[83] UNEP went on to report that, '[i]n Sudan, desertification is clearly linked to conflict'.[84] Land degradation and desertification in this case is an example of the consequences of a lack of sustainable environmental policies and implementation within a State.[85] Darfur for example, is Sudan's largest region located in the western part of the country but because of its relative geographic isolation, it has been

---

[78]   Wax (n 74).

[79]   Renner (n 73).

[80]   BBC, 'Somalis Clash Over Scarce Water' *BBC News* (17 February 2006); BBC, '"Dozens Dead" in Somalia Clashes' *BBC News* (16 February 2006) (on the recent history of clashes between clans over pastoral lands and water wells).

[81]   Wax (n 74). See also Gleick (n 74).

[82]   Ibid.

[83]   UNEP, 'Sudan Post-Conflict Environmental Assessment' (UNEP, Nairobi 2007) at pp. 62–4 [hereinafter UNEP Sudan PCEA] (The report points to an overall spread of deserts by an average of 100 km in the last four decades, a loss of almost 12 per cent forest cover in the last 15 years and overgrazing of fragile soil). See also UNEP, 'Environmental Degradation Triggering Tensions and Conflict in Sudan' *UNEP Press Release* (June 2007) [hereinafter UNEP 2007 Sudan PR].

[84]   UNEP Sudan PCEA (n 83) at p. 58.

[85]   See, e.g. Melnick. D. and others, *Environment and Human Well-Being: A Practical Strategy, UN Millennium Project: Task Force on Environmental Sustainability* (Earthscan, UK/USA 2005) at p. 44 [hereinafter Melnick]; Mihyo, P.B., 'Local Governance and Rural Poverty in Africa' in Spoor, M. (ed), *Globalisation, Poverty and Conflict: A Critical 'Development' Reader* (Kluwer, The Netherlands 2004) at p. 165 [hereinafter Mihyo].

neglected by the central Sudanese government in Khartoum.[86] Today, the mere mention of Darfur is enough to bring to mind blood-soaked and barren lands wracked by war and conflict.[87] As UNEP reported, 'regional climate variability, water scarcity and the steady loss of fertile land are important underlying factors.'[88] The conflict in Darfur was triggered by natural ecological adversity[89] which was exacerbated by serious misman-agement of these environmental problems by the government.[90] The rest of Sudan has also suffered from minor to major conflicts over the last 50 years or so, many of which have had some connection to environmental pressures.[91]

About seventy five per cent of the Sudanese population depend directly on indigenous natural resources for their food and livelihoods.[92] Unfortunately, among the various environmental stresses faced by Sudan, the steady loss of fertile land and increasing freshwater shortages are two of the most prominent problems.[93] This is largely due to the decrease in rainfall overall but particularly in northern Darfur, where rain has decreased by a third over the last eighty years.[94] It has been suggested that the declining rainfall can be attributed to a large degree to climate change.[95] This, in addition to unsustainable environmental and agricultural practices by the local population such as deforestation and over-grazing by cattle, have contributed to the gradual degradation and desertification of fertile land.[96]

---

[86] Battiste, L.F., 'The Case for Intervention in the Humanitarian Crisis in Sudan' (2005) 11 Annual Survey of International and Comparative Law 49, at p. 51 [hereinafter Battiste].

[87] See, e.g. Burr, J.M. and Collins, R.O., *Darfur: The Long Road to Disaster* (Markus Wiener, Princeton 2008) [hereinafter Burr and Collins]; Bloomfield, S. and Butler, K., 'Darfur's Return to Hell' *Independent* (UK 12 March 2008); Polgreen, L., 'Grim New Turn Likely to Harden Darfur Conflict' *New York Times* (New York 23 October 2006).

[88] UNEP Conflict to Peacebuilding (n 4) at p. 9.

[89] For further review of the environmental pressures that fuelled conflict, see UNEP Sudan PCEA (n 83) at pp. 72–97.

[90] See, e.g. Melnick (n 85) at p. 44; Mihyo (n 85) at p. 165.

[91] UNEP Sudan PCEA (n 83) at p. 73.

[92] UNEP Conflict to Peacebuilding (n 4) at p. 9.

[93] UNEP Sudan PCEA (n 83) at pp. 59–61.

[94] Ibid. See also Polgreen, L., 'New Depths: A Godsend for Darfur, or a Curse?' *New York Times* (New York 22 July 2007) [hereinafter 2007 Polgreen].

[95] UNEP Sudan PCEA (n 83) at pp. 59–61. See also Moon, B.K., 'A Climate Culprit in Darfur' *Washington Post* (Washington, DC 16 June 2007) [hereinafter Moon].

[96] UNEP Conflict to Peacebuilding (n 4) at p. 9.

Sudan also suffers from a multitude of socio-economic, political and developmental problems.[97] These range from poor governance, demographic pressure, marginalisation of certain groups regarding access to valuable land grazing and water rights, government mismanagement of natural resources, underdevelopment, poverty to ethnic, tribal and religious divisions within society. These factors in combination with natural resource scarcity (fertile land and water in particular) and the recurring drought, 'has fostered violent competition between agriculturalists, nomads and pastoralists in the region'.[98] Violence in Darfur erupted during the drought as a result of a combination of these factors.[99] According to De Waal, '[w]hile Darfur's conflicts smouldered, Sudan was engaged in a large and protracted civil war between the central government and the Sudan People's Liberated Army (SPLA).'[100] A clear example of ineffective governance rendering those in power unable or unwilling to govern and assist its suffering citizens in adapting to such environmental stresses.

Violent conflict broke out in Darfur when local groups rebelled, triggering counter attacks by the Khartoum controlled Sudanese central army and government backed Arab militias, the Janjaweed.[101] By 2003 this escalated into a full-scale tragedy. Nearly four years of armed conflict has killed around 200 000 people and more than five million people have been internally displaced.[102] Some 200 000 Darfurians have also sought refuge in neighbouring Chad.[103] Furthermore, the ongoing civil war also included instances of destruction against natural resources:

---

[97]   See, e.g. Rwomire, A. (ed), *Social Problems in Africa: New Visions* (Praeger, USA 2001); Sidahmed, A.S. and Sidahmend, A., *Sudan* (Routledge, Oxon 2005).

[98]   UNEP Conflict to Peacebuilding (n 4) at p. 9.

[99]   See, e.g. Bankus, B.C., 'Environmental Security in Peacekeeping Operations' in Purkitt, H.E., *African Environmental and Human Security in the 21st Century* (Cambria, New York 2009) at p. 210; Sjöstedt, G., 'Resolving Ecological Conflicts: Typical and Special Circumstances' in Bercovitch, J., Kremenyuk, V. and Zartman, I.W. (eds), *The SAGE Handbook of Conflict Resolution* (Sage, London 2009) at p. 239 [hereinafter Bercovitch (eds)].

[100]   De Waal, A., 'Darfur and the Failure of the Responsibility to Protect' (2007) 83 International Affairs 1039, at pp. 1039–40.

[101]   For more information on the Darfur conflict see, e.g. SIPRI Yearbook 2008, 'Armaments, Disarmament and International Security' (OUP, New York 2008) at pp. 57–63.

[102]   Ibid. See also UNEP 2007 Sudan PR (n 83).

[103]   Jentleson, B.W., 'Yet Again: Humanitarian Intervention and the Challenges of "Never Again"' in Crocker (eds) (n 3) at p. 286.

various water resources, pastoral land, crops and trees within Darfur and the rest of Sudan, which became military tools and targets.[104] It is also worth pointing out that although violence erupted during the drought primarily as a result of pre-existing diverse political and social problems in combination with food and resource insecurity, ethnic tensions in Darfur were simmering just below the surface for years between the mostly nomadic Arabs and pastoralists from local African tribal communities.[105]

While armed conflicts do not occur simply because of environmental stresses, in this case, ecological factors such as climate change, the lack of arable land, drought and water rights, played a major part in instigating conflict. Unfortunately, owing to the displaced Darfurians, the conflict is further exacerbating additional environmental stresses, from water pollution, land degradation to deforestation, potentially threatening to raise future ethnic tensions in the new migrated areas.[106] UNEP also asserts that environmental issues in Sudan such as competition over oil, gas, water, timber and arable land have sparked off conflict in the past and will 'continue to be contributing causes of conflict.'[107] As the UN Secretary-General, Ban Ki-Moon sums up,

> [a]lmost invariably, we discuss Darfur in a convenient military and political shorthand – an ethnic conflict pitting Arab militias against black rebels and farmers. Look to its roots, though, and you discover a more complex dynamic. Amid the diverse social and political causes, the Darfur conflict began as an ecological crisis, arising at least in part from climate change.[108]

2.2.3. Sierra Leone

Sierra Leone is another example of armed conflict fuelled by natural resources, which in this case was conflict over 'high-value' resources –

---

[104] UNEP Sudan PCEA (n 83) at p. 92. See also Gleick (n 74) ('In 2003, villagers from around Tina said that bombings had destroyed water wells. In Khasan Basao they alleged that water wells were poisoned. In 2004, wells in Darfur were intentionally contaminated as a part of strategy and harassment against displaced populations').

[105] Kajee, A., 'The Regional and International Dimensions of the Crisis in Darfur' in Raftopoulos, B. and Alexander, K. (eds), *Peace in the Balance: The Crisis in Sudan* (Institute for Justice and Reconciliation, Cape Town 2006) at p. 87.

[106] UNEP Sudan PCEA (n 83) at p. 104.

[107] Ibid., at p. 78.

[108] Moon (n 95).

diamonds.[109] Sierra Leone was once considered a country 'full of great promise'[110] but since independence in 1961 it had begun to deteriorate. It was plagued by poor governance, debt repayments, inequitable distribution of resources and wealth, corruption, food and energy insecurity and dwindling natural resources.[111] The civil war began when the Revolutionary United Front (RUF) rebelled and staged an attempted *coup d'etat* against the Sierra Leone government in 1991. The invasion and subsequent coup by the RUF was financed and given logistical support by Liberian warlord, Charles Taylor.[112] UNEP reports that Taylor's motivation in supporting the RUF was partly due to his intention in having a hand in Sierra Leone's diamond trade.[113] The RUF began to plunder the country's resources, particularly diamonds, to fund its cause and in the process waged violent warfare across the country, creating havoc and committing atrocities against the defenceless civilian population. However, scholars argue that these insurgents were not primarily motivated by political ideologies but by their greed and intent to control the diamond production.[114] In fact, the RUF never clearly expressed their political objectives.[115]

---

[109]   The warring over 'high-value' resources have also sparked off in a number of countries in West Africa. Moreover, diamonds have not been the only 'precious' commodity being fought over. Other examples include the 'open conflict over cobalt in Zaire in the late 1970s [and the] more recent conflict in the Great Lakes over tantalum supplies (used in mobile phones).' See Abbott (n 17) at p. 13.

[110]   Hummel, J., 'Diamonds are a Smuggler's Best Friend: Regulation, Economics, and Enforcement in the Global Effort to Curb the Trade in Conflict Diamonds' (2007) 41 International Lawyer 1145, at p. 1150 [hereinafter Hummel].

[111]   See, e.g. Hummel (n 110) at p. 1150; Keen, D., *Conflict and Collusion in Sierra Leone* (Palgrave, New York 2005) at p. 298 [hereinafter Keen].

[112]   UNEP Conflict to Peacebuilding (n 4) at p. 10; Human Rights Watch, *Selling Justice Short: Why Accountability Matters for Peace* (Human Rights Watch, USA 2009) at pp. 20–21.

[113]   Ibid.

[114]   Saunders, L., 'Rich and Rare Are The Gems They War: Holding De Beers Accountable for Trading Conflict Diamonds' (2001) 24 Fordham International Law Journal 1402, at p. 1404 [hereinafter Saunders]; See also Gberie, L., 'Fighting for Peace: Sierra Leone' (Summer 2000) XXXVII(2) *UN Chronicle* (maintaining that the war in Sierra Leone was not about politics but over greed for diamonds).

[115]   Saunders (n 114) at p. 1424; Adebajo, A., *Building Peace in West Africa: Liberia, Sierra Leone, and Guinea-Bissau* (Lynne Rienner, USA 2002) at p. 103.

In relation to the natural resource-conflict link, it is worth noting that it did not begin with the RUF. Years prior to the RUF insurgency, the Sierra Leone government and the diamond sector were already plagued by high levels of corruption. The diamond trade was already being brought within the control of a few elites, Siaka Stevens (in power from 1968–1985) and his cronies.[116] As a result, official diamond exports for the country plummeted drastically while profiting only a favoured few. This effectively broke Sierra Leone's economy and set in motion its continuing deterioration under the country's next successor, Joseph Momoh.[117] Simply put, those in power corrupted and weakened the Sierra Leone government over greed for this natural resource. This caused political and economic instability that in turn contributed to violent conflict over further control of the country's diamond production and trade. As UNEP aptly points out, '[t]he looting of the state marginalized large sections of the population, undermined the government's legitimacy and weakened its capacity to maintain peace and stability.'[118] Thus, paving the way for the RUF's brutal and bloody eleven-year conflict where diamonds were once again the heart of the matter.

3. INTERNATIONAL ACTION IN ENVIRONMENT-CONFLICT PREVENTION: ACHIEVING SUSTAINABLE DEVELOPMENT?

As discovered, there is a significant link between environmental factors and armed conflict. This environment-conflict link does however sit on the trajectory of unsustainable development, that is, on the breakdown or degeneration of social, economic, political and development conditions. Although environmental stresses are unlikely to be the sole or direct cause of conflict, current and future environmental stresses are nevertheless a cause for concern. The question is whether the international community has been successful in preventing conflict fuelled by such environmental pressures?

---

[116] UNEP Conflict to Peacebuilding (n 4) at p. 10. See also Iro, A., *The UN Peacebuilding Commission – Lessons from Sierra Leone* (Universitätsverlag Potsdam, Germany 2009) at p. 32; Smillie, I. and others, *The Heart of the Matter: Sierra Leone, Diamonds and Human Security* (Partnership Africa, Canada 2000) at pp. 42–3 [hereinafter Smillie]

[117] Ibid.

[118] UNEP Conflict to Peacebuilding (n 4) at p. 10.

Cousens argues that there are four forms of conflict prevention.[119] First, 'there is the archetype of prevention: namely, preventing conflict before it has broken out in a serious way.'[120] Second, there are conflict prevention efforts after the conflict has begun, that is, mitigation efforts to prevent the conflict from escalating.[121] Cousens further argues that within this category there are two types of conflict-escalation prevention. The first type 'pertains to UN actions taken at the very onset of conflict' and the second type 'relates to UN actions within an ongoing conflict, especially where there is already a UN political or military presence.'[122] The third form of conflict prevention consists of preventive 'actions taken to prevent a humanitarian crisis';[123] and the fourth, 'are actions taken to prevent recurrence of conflict'[124] or 're-conflict'.

From an environment-conflict and sustainable development perspective, the first and fourth forms of conflict prevention: prevention prior conflict and prevention of re-conflict are the most desirable. The first, because through diplomacy and negotiations, solutions to environmental problems in consideration with other possible variable issues may still be integrated and implemented. The fourth, because through the peace processes of peacemaking,[125] peacekeeping[126] and peacebuilding,[127] present ideal opportunities to integrate necessary environmental policies in

---

[119]   Cousens, E.M., 'Conflict Prevention' in Malone, D.M. (ed), *The UN Security Council: From the Cold War to the 21st Century* (Lynne Rienner, USA 2004) at pp. 105–6 [hereinafter Cousens].

[120]   Ibid., at p. 106.

[121]   Ibid.

[122]   Ibid.

[123]   Ibid., at p. 107.

[124]   Ibid.

[125]   See UNEP Conflict to Peacebuilding (n 4) at p. 7 (The term 'peacemaking' in itself 'is the diplomatic process of brokering an end to conflict, principally through mediation and negotiation, as foreseen under Chapter VI of the UN Charter').

[126]   Ibid. ('Peacekeeping is both a political and a military activity involving a presence in the field, with the consent of the parties, to implement or monitor arrangements relating to the control of conflicts (cease-fires, separation of forces), and their resolution (partial or comprehensive settlements), as well as to protect the delivery of humanitarian aid').

[127]   Ibid. ('Peacebuilding comprises the identification and support of measures needed for transformation toward more sustainable, peaceful relationships and structures of governance, in order to avoid a relapse into conflict. The four dimensions of peacebuilding are: socio-economic development, good governance, reform of justice and security institutions, and the culture of justice, truth and reconciliation').

conjunction with other socio-economic development and political policies in order to effectively manage environment-inducing conflict problems. Moreover, from an environment-conflict perspective, both forms exemplify to some extent, elements of the precautionary approach, by integrating the appropriate environmental measures from the outset, environment-conflict or re-conflict could perhaps be prevented and as such, prevent further risks or threats of scientifically uncertain environmental degradation as a consequence of such conflict.

Unfortunately, solving and managing environmental problems become trickier once a conflict has escalated as other non-environmental priorities are more likely to take precedence. This section therefore reviews the international response in preventing, mitigating or managing the environmental-conflict related factors as set out in the case-studies above and then, from a sustainable development perspective, explores whether the international community has a conflict prevention system in place in relation to preventing environmental-induced conflict?

3.1. Case-Studies

It may be objected that the question of the success with which the international community is able to prevent environmental-induced conflict cannot be fully comprehended through analysis of armed conflicts which, by definition, have not been prevented. However, it is nonetheless important to reflect on the efforts that were taken, if any, to address the problem at the heart of this chapter. That is therefore the limited but crucial concern below, to elucidate the lessons to be learned concerning prevention from past experience in the field.

3.1.1. Somalia

As mentioned above, internal conflict has been ongoing in Somalia since the late 1980s. After Barre was ousted from power in 1991, the vacuum left by the lack of functioning central government caused the country to sink into further anarchy, chaos and 'creeping warlordism'.[128] Against this background of significant socio-economic, political and development instability, a clear lack of any form of sustainable development, the 'war of the wells', was but a small part of the ongoing conflict in Somalia.[129] Yet, it is evidence of conflict sparked off and exacerbated by environmental factors such as fighting over scarce water resources particularly

---

[128] Wilson, K., 'Somalia (1988–1991 and 1992–Present)' in Derouen and Heo (eds) (n 68) at pp. 679–80. See also Gettleman 'Somalia' (n 67).

[129] Wax (n 74). See also Gleick (n 74).

exacerbated by severe drought. Furthermore, many water systems throughout the country were destroyed during the continuous civil conflict[130] and the lack of any form of effective government meant that there were no authorities 'to build new wells, pipes and pumps or to look for new underground water resources.'[131] This is one example illustrating the complete halt of any form of sustainable development in this country.

By international standards, the 'war of the well' is considered a minor conflict. However, this could be an example of future conflicts to come and it is worth bearing in mind that this minor conflict in particular, was part of a series of continuous conflicts over scarce water within the failed State of Somalia.[132] This illustrates the importance of taking steps to achieve sustainable development. Failure to do so could mean that the weakening or breakdown in social, economic, political and development conditions with added environmental stresses could lay the foundation for potential conflict. There is little point in questioning whether this particular conflict could have been prevented by the international community. Instead, the question to be asked is whether the international community could have prevented the collapse of this State and the succeeding violent conflict that raged throughout the country? A collapsed State and ensuing violent conflict, both of which have no doubt contributed to conflict over already scarce natural resources, which was further exacerbated by drought and environmental degradation.

Clearly the international community was unsuccessful in preventing these events from unfolding. The UN and the UNSC in particular, were heavily criticised for not intervening in Somalia's affairs much sooner.[133] Scholars argue that the international community missed out on many possible opportunities to set in motion preventive action 'in the waning

---

[130]   Hamilton, J., *Somalia in Pictures* (Learner, USA 2007) at p. 15.

[131]   Ibid.

[132]   Samuels, K., 'Constitution-Building during the War on Terror: The Challenge of Somalia' (2008) 40 New York University Journal of International Law and Politics 597, at p. 601. See also EU, 'European Commission Strategy for the Implementation of Special Aid to Somalia: 2002–2007' (European Community, Development and Cooperation – EUROPEAID 2002–2007) at p. 10.

[133]   See, e.g. Lyons, T., and Samatar, A.I., *Somalia: State Collapse, Multilateral Intervention, and Strategies for Political Reconstruction* (Brookings Institution, Washington, DC 1995) at p. 67 [hereinafter Lyons and Samatar]. See also Zartman, W., 'Cowardly Lions: Missed Opportunities for Dispute Settlement' (2002) 18 Ohio State Journal on Dispute Resolution 1, at p. 4 [hereinafter 2002 Zartman]; Walker, P. and Maxwell, D., *Shaping the Humanitarian World* (Routledge, Oxon 2009) at pp. 64–5 (criticising the fact that the UN did not even have a field-base in Somalia and was slow to respond to the mounting crisis).

years of Siad Barre's rule or in the early months of following his departure'.[134] Taking those opportunities would have perhaps meant that sustainable political solutions or policies could have been put in place to stabilise Somalia's governance and these actions 'might have halted the descent into complete collapse and thereby limited the degree of political reconciliation and institutional reconstruction necessary.'[135] By ignoring or missing these opportunities,[136] the international community completely failed to take a preventive approach, which due either to their reluctance to get involved or a miscalculation on their part, allowed Somalia to descend into chaos and thus, for this failed State, completely halting sustainable development in its tracks.

Admittedly, the failed State of Somalia being in a state of complete anarchy makes it difficult and even dangerous for the international community to take any action towards it. Primarily, it is the lack of government, that is, the lack of effective governance and the fragmented nature of the country that makes it difficult, if not impossible for the international community to assist the Somalis to put in place any short or long-term environmental and resource mitigating or managing strategies. For example, in numerous cases it has been almost impossible for the international community to even deliver emergency food and water as 'aid convoys and water trucks are frequently attacked',[137] let alone attempt to integrate any long-term resource strategies. As further reported, relief efforts by NGOs throughout Somalia are 'made difficult by a lack of proper roads and the absence of a functioning central government, with control of the country divided among rebel militia groups'.[138] This goes back to the point that concerted and collective

---

[134]   Lyons and Samatar (n 133) at p. 67. See also 2002 Zartman (n 133) at p. 4.

[135]   Ibid.

[136]   For an analysis of international action and missed opportunities, see Menkhaus, K. and Ortmayer, L., 'Somalia: Misread Crisis and Missed Opportunities' in Jentleson, B.W. (ed), *Opportunities Missed, Opportunities Seized: Preventive Diplomacy in the Post-Cold War World* (Rowman and Littlefield, USA 2000) at pp. 223–31; Lyons and Samatar (n 133) at pp. 25–35.

[137]   Wax (n 74). Even recently food aid is stolen and diverted away from the starving masses. See Tran, M., 'Scale of reported Somalia food aid theft implausible, insists UN' *Guardian* (UK 16 August 2011); Rugman, J., 'UN Food Stolen from the Starving in Somalia: Fake Camp Fraud' *Times* (UK 15 June 2009); Jones, S., 'Half of all food sent to Somalia is stolen, says UN Report' *Guardian* (UK 10 March 2010).

[138]   BBC, 'Somalis Die of Thirst in Drought' *BBC News* (UK 16 February 2006).

international preventive efforts should have been conducted much earlier. This situation also illustrates the importance of integrating the elements or principles of sustainable development (for example, good governance, public participation, equity) in order for a country to be able to function effectively to some extent. Otherwise the failed State is permanently stuck in a vicious loop of unsustainable development.

The international community and the UN in particular were heavily criticised for detaching themselves from the political issues central to Somalia's problems. After much criticism and media coverage of the disintegration of Somalia, the UN finally intervened in 1992 by sending in UN troops.[139] As one scholar notes, 'one year of chaos and starvation elapsed in Somalia before the United Nations passed its first resolution; almost two more years elapsed before the United States was willing to support the effort.'[140] Unfortunately, the UN missions proved disastrous.[141] The UN 'humanitarian intervention in the collapsed state of Somalia ... ultimately withdrew without stabilizing a unified Somali state.'[142]

Both the UN and the UNSC have been criticised for their involvement in Somalia as having been 'appalling, incompetent, mismanaged'[143] and

---

[139] For further review of international and UN intervention in Somalia, see, e.g. Gundel, J., 'Humanitarianism and Spoils Politics in Somalia' in Juma, M.K. and Suhrke, A. (eds), *Eroding Local Capacity: International Humanitarian Action in Africa* (Grafiur Artes Gráficas, Spain 2002) at pp. 134–58; Rutherford, K.R., *Humanitarianism under Fire: The US and UN Intervention in Somalia* (Kumarian, USA 2008) (an analytical review on the complexity of the intervention).

[140] Cassidy, R.B., 'Sovereignty Versus the Chimera of Armed Humanitarian Intervention' (1997) 21 Fletcher Forum of World Affairs 47, at p. 58 (footnotes omitted).

[141] For an explanation for the UN's failure, see Knight, W.A. and Gebremariam, K., 'UN Intervention and Peacebuilding in Somalia: Constraints and Possibilities' in Knight, W.A. (ed), *Adapting the United Nations to a Postmodern Era: Lessons Learned* (Palgrave Macmillan, New York 2001) at pp. 87–8.

[142] Sriram, C.L. and Nielson, Z., 'Introduction: Why Examine Subregional Sources and Dynamics of Conflict?' in Sriram, C.L. and Nielson, Z. (eds), *Exploring Subregional Conflict: Opportunities for Conflict Prevention* (Lynne Rienner, USA 2004) at p. 8 [hereinafter Sriram and Nielson (eds)].

[143] Ramlogan (n 66) at p. 226. See also Murphy, S.D., *Humanitarian Intervention: The United Nations in an Evolving World Order* (University of Pennsylvania, USA 1996) at p. 385 [hereinafter Murphy]; Clarke, J., 'Debacle in Somalia: Failure of the Collective Response' in Damrisch, L.F. (ed), *Enforcing Restraint: Collective Intervention in Internal Conflicts* (Council on Foreign Relations, USA 1993) at pp. 205–40.

having come as 'too little too late'.[144] By this stage Somalia's population had suffered immeasurably[145] and continues to suffer from political and socio-economic instability, food crises, environmental pressures, to conflict over scarce resources.[146] Sustainable development is non-existent and the current and future generations of Somalis are paying the price for the international community's failure to take the preventive approach through early action. It is viewed that while miscalculations or errors in judgement in international action can occur, there is no excuse for the abject failure on the part of the international community to take any form of preventive measures. Now, faced with the mess in Somalia, this case-study demonstrates, particularly from an environmental dimension of resource scarcity and increasing environmental pressures, the importance of conflict-prevention strategies by the international community that take into consideration all relevant variable factors. As one former senior UN representative, Mohammed Sahnoun comments, '[t]he greatest difficulty is we did not try to cope with the situation earlier ... the divisions and antagonisms have deepened and have taken on dimensions that are almost inextricable.'[147] Lack of urgency, above all else, characterises the chief problem with this case-study.

3.1.2. Darfur, Sudan

As discovered earlier, there is a strong link between environmental pressures, especially land degradation, and the conflict in Darfur.[148] Moreover, there is no denying that the Darfur conflict was incredibly complex, fuelled by a population suffering from years of drought,

---

[144] Evans, G., 'The Responsibility to Protect: Rethinking Humanitarian Intervention' (2004) 98 American Society of International Law Proceedings 78. See also Murphy (n 143) at p. 385; Boutin, M.M., 'Somalia: The Legality of UN Forcible Humanitarian Intervention' (1994) 17 Suffolk Transnational Law Review 138, at pp. 154–5.

[145] Ibid.

[146] See, e.g. UN, 'Somalia: 2010 Consolidated Appeal' (30 November 2009); 'Somali clans clash over water and land, 11 killed' *Reuters Africa* (13 March 2010); UN, 'Somalia faces humanitarian crisis in 2010 with aid coffers empty, UN warns' *UN News Centre* (8 December 2009), www.un.org/apps/news/story.asp?NewsID=33188&Cr=somalia&Cr1= (accessed 2 April 2012).

[147] Perlez, J., 'Profile: Mohammed Sahnoun; A Diplomat Matches Wit with Chaos in Somalia' *Washington Post* (Washington, DC 20 September 1992).

[148] UNEP Sudan PCEA (n 83) at p. 80 (There were also strong environmental-conflict links in the rest of Sudan).

desertification, demographic pressure and simmering ethnic tensions.[149] The conflict between the Sudanese government forces, their militia (the Janjaweed) and various rebel factions has been raging since 2003. The question is, whether appropriate preventive measures taken by the international community could have possibly averted such disaster or at least diffused some of the violence?

Regrettably, the UN and the rest of the world were late in intervening.[150] Once again, negating to take a preventive approach and giving no consideration to the present and future generations of Sudan. The international community, in delaying any intervention action was also by default, from a sustainable development perspective, too late to deal with and prevent or mitigate the deteriorating social and political conditions as well as the environmental stresses that triggered and exacerbated conflict in Darfur. Thus, there was clearly no form of conflict prevention efforts by the international community.[151]

The international community was already aware that Sudan as a whole was suffering from environmental, food and governance problems in the 1990s[152] and in 2001 for example, the UN was also aware that tribal conflict had broken out in northern Darfur over scarce land, water and food due to drought and crop failure.[153] However, it is worth pointing out

---

[149]   UNEP, *Africa: Atlas of Our Changing Environment* (UNEP/DEWA, Nairobi 2008) at p. 60; Battiste (n 86) at p. 51 (conflicts have been ongoing in Darfur over the last two decades as much of the peace amongst the region's varied ethnic groups have been 'destroyed due to environmental degradation from the spread of the Sahara desert as a result of ongoing drought, coupled with "divide and rule" tactics of the central government and the influx of modern weaponry').

[150]   Slim, H., 'Dithering Over Darfur? A Preliminary Review of the International Response' (2004) 80 International Affairs 811, at pp. 811–28 [hereinafter Slim]. See also Stewart, E.J., *The European Union and Conflict Prevention: Policy Evolution and Outcome* (LIT Verlag, Berlin-Hamburg-Münster 2006) at p. 239 (the EU was criticised for not taking any action in Darfur).

[151]   See, e.g. Levitt, J.L., 'The Peace and Security Council of the African Union and the United Nations Security Council: The Case of Darfur, Sudan' in Blokker, N. and Schrijver, N. (eds), *The Security Council and the Use of Force: Theory and Reality – A Need for Change?* (Martinus Nijhoff, Leiden 2005) at p. 250.

[152]   Blaikie, P. and others, *At Risk: Natural Hazards, People's Vulnerability, and Disasters* (Routledge, London 1994) at pp. 200–204 [hereinafter Blaikie]; Burr and Collins (n 87) at p. 252.

[153]   Hawley, C., 'New Appeal for Drought-Hit Sudan' *BBC News* (UK 21 January 2001). See also Doyle, M., 'Darfur Misery Has Complex Roots' *BBC News* (UK 26 September 2004).

that in 2001 and even earlier in 1998 for example, international aid in food and water could not reach the starving Sudanese population because in many instances, the Khartoum government refused the UN 'permission to fly into key areas for their relief effort.'[154] With the government in Khartoum unwilling and even denying help to its own people, an international intervention was clearly desperately needed. Without a collective authorised and effective international intervention, there was no way to resolve the conflict let alone resolve, mitigate or manage the contributing socio-economic, governance, food security, and environmental problems.

International attention did not focus on Darfur until the spring of 2004[155] even after it was obvious that the Darfurian conflict had been escalating for months.[156] The UN for example, seemed to have spent an inordinate amount of time and energy dithering over whether or not the conflict in Darfur was 'genocide'.[157] The UN's tardy and gradual response began with the UN Refugee Agency (UNHCR) conducting an investigation and reporting on the conflict in May 2004.[158] This was followed by the UN encouraging peace talks between the warring parties, mediated by the African Union (AU) and the subsequent passing of several resolutions from July 2004 onwards[159] to authorise and support

---

[154] Ibid.

[155] In May 2004, in a presidential statement, the UNSC expressed 'its grave concern over the deteriorating humanitarian and human rights situation in the Darfur region of Sudan'. See UNSC Presidential Statement 18 (2004) UN Doc S/PRST/2004/18.

[156] See Slim (n 150) at p. 813 (Although the international community was late in intervening, once the intervention began, the Darfur emergency did appear to bring out the best in the international community. This was evidenced by the 'continuous and determined diplomacy by individual states, notably Chad, the United States, the Netherlands and the UK, and by Germany mobilising political commitment within the European Union').

[157] Strauss, S., 'Darfur and the Genocide Debate' (2005) 84 Foreign Affairs 123, at p. 128; Apsel, J., 'On Our Watch: The Genocide Convention and the Deadly, Ongoing Case of Darfur and Sudan' (2008) 61 Rutgers Law Review 53, at p. 54.

[158] Tanagho, E. and Hermina, J.P., 'The International Community Responds to Darfur: ICC Prosecution Renews Hope for International Justice' (2009) 6 Loyola University Chicago International Law Review 367, at p. 381 [hereinafter Tanagho].

[159] UNSC Resolution 1556 (30 July 2004); UNSC Resolution 1591 (29 March 2005); UNSC Resolution 1651 (21 December 2005); UNSC Resolution 1665 (29 March 2006); UNSC Resolution 1672 (25 April 2006); UNSC Resolution 1713 (29 September 2006); UNSC Resolution 1769 (31 July 2007);

various UN and joint UN and African Union (AU-UNAMID) peace-keeping missions to stem and manage the violence in Darfur.[160]

Unfortunately, many of these missions were never deployed because they were blocked by the Sudanese government and missions that were successfully deployed, were continuously obstructed and made difficult by the Sudanese government.[161] This shows how difficult it is in some cases, with issues of sovereignty coming into play, to intervene and attempt to resolve a conflict, thereby illustrating the importance of taking the preventive approach before a conflict escalates into an unmanageable state. Although there is no guarantee that preventive or early action by the international community would have prevented or mitigated the Darfurian conflict,[162] the international community, particularly the UN, could have at least made some attempt to do so. Failing to take any preventive action meant that the international community paid no heed to the intra and inter-generational equity of the Darfurians and the Sudanese population as a whole. If the international community had intervened earlier, perhaps violent conflicts over pastoral land and aggravated tensions over drought exacerbated crop and water scarcity may have been mitigated or even prevented.

As the UN has reported, in addition to aiming for 'a comprehensive resolution to the underlying causes of the crisis, to overcome inter-communal hatred caused by war, and to accelerate socio-economic

---

UNSC Resolution 1779 (28 September 2007); UNSC Resolution 1784 (31 October 2007); UNSC Resolution 1812 (30 April 2008); UNSC Resolution 1828 (31 July 2008); UNSC Resolution 1862 (14 January 2009); UNSC Resolution 1870 (30 April 2009); UNSC Resolution 1881 (6 August 2009); UNSC Resolution 1891 (13 October 2009).

[160]   For a review of the UN-AU partnership in response to the Darfur conflict, see Barnidge, R.P., 'The United Nations and the African Union: Assessing a Partnership for Peace in Darfur' (2009) 14 Journal of Conflict & Security Law 93.

[161]   See, e.g. Tanagho (n 158) at p. 382; Bellamy, A.J., 'Responsibility to Protect or Trojan Horse? The Crisis in Darfur and Humanitarian Intervention after Iraq' in Rosenthal, J.H. and Barry, C. (eds), *Ethics and International Affairs: A Reader* (3rd edn Georgetown University, Washington, DC 2009) at pp. 119–21.

[162]   Fenstein, L., 'Darfur and Beyond: What is Needed to Prevent Mass Atrocities' in Lyman, P.N. and Dorff, P. (eds), *Beyond Humanitarianism: What You Need to Know About Africa and Why it Matters* (Council on Foreign Relations, USA 2007) at p. 104.

development',[163] the most important objective is to achieve 'a comprehensive political solution to end Darfur's marginalization and enable its rightful representation in the national political process.'[164] This would entail the relevant Sudanese government, in aiming for good governance, to ensure the integration of key sustainable development principles such as the duty to ensure sustainable use of natural resources, the principle of equity, the precautionary approach and public participation. Further, from an environmental perspective, UNEP reports that environmental degradation and stresses still plague Sudan and will continue to cause conflicts throughout the country unless appropriate and effective action is taken.[165] UNEP further reminds the international community that Sudan as a whole 'faces a number of key challenges. Chief among them are critical environmental issues – such as land degradation, deforestation, and the impacts of climate change – that threaten Sudan's prospects for long-term peace, food security and sustainable development.'[166] From a sustainable development perspective, unless (both North and South) Sudan's socio-economic marginalisation and development issues are addressed in addition to its environmental issues, the situation in Darfur and throughout Sudan will remain tense.[167]

At present, despite the 2005 Comprehensive Agreement that ended the North-South civil war and continuing international efforts including the thousands of UN-AU peacekeepers deployed in the region,[168] Darfur and

---

[163]   UN 'For UN-African Union Mission in Darfur, Most Important Mandates Those Aimed at Helping Achieve Comprehensive Political Solution, Security Council Told – Peacekeeping Official Briefs, Introduces Report on "Benchmarks" for Mission: Mediator Says Urgent to Reach Political Arrangement before 2010 National Elections' UNSC Press Release SC/9800 (30 November 2009).

[164]   Ibid., (statement by Edmond Mulet, Assistant Secretary-General for Peacekeeping Operations).

[165]   UNEP, 'Sudan' UNEP in the Regions, www.unep.org/conflictsand disasters/UNEPintheRegions/CurrentActivities/Sudan/tabid/294/language/en-US/ Default.aspx (accessed 27 March 2012). See also UNEP Sudan PCEA (n 83).

[166]   UNEP Sudan PCEA (n 83) at p. 20. UNEP's post-conflict efforts will be discussed in Chapter 5.

[167]   Ibid. See also Copnall, J., 'Sudan's Darfur Region Dabbles with Peace' *BBC News* (UK 2 March 2012) [hereinafter Copnall Sudan's Peace]; Gettleman, J., 'Fragile Calm Holds in Darfur After Years of Death' *New York Times* (New York 1 January 2010); US Government, 'Current Situation in Darfur' Hearing Before the Committee on Foreign Affairs, House of Representatives, One Hundred Tenth Congress, First Session (19 April 2007) Serial No. 110–53 (US Government, Washington, DC 2007).

[168]   See, e.g. African Union/UN Hybrid operation in Darfur (UNAMID), www.un.org/en/peacekeeping/missions/unamid/index.shtml (accessed 26 March

Sudan remain unstable.[169] The situation improved somewhat since South-ern Sudan's secession on 9 July 2011[170] and the Darfur region began experiencing some sense of fragile peace,[171] but the population continues to live under the threat of tensions and recurring conflict.[172] UNEP warned in its 2007 assessment that environmental resources will continue to cause conflicts in the country,[173] and Sudan, North and South, are once again on the brink of conflict and this time, over another natural resource – oil.[174]

3.1.3. Sierra Leone

As noted earlier, at the centre of the Sierra Leone conflict was control over diamonds. It was not however, the underlying cause of the violent conflict. Sierra Leone's government and economy were already deterio-rating prior to the conflict with control over and profits from the

---

2012); UNMIS, www.un.org/en/peacekeeping/missions/unmis/ (26 March 2012); UN Mission in the Republic of South Sudan (UNMISS), www.un.org/en/peacekeeping/missions/unmiss/ (accessed 26 March 2012).

[169]   See, e.g. Harding, A., 'South Sudan blamed as it gears up for war' *BBC News* (South Sudan, 30 April 2012) [hereinafter Harding]; BBC, 'Sudanese conflict: What you need to know' *BBC News* (UK, 4 May 2012), www.bbc.co.uk/news/world-africa-17958794 (accessed 8 May 2012) [hereinafter Sudanese Con-flict]; Heavens, A. and Abdelaziz, K. (Reuters), 'Darfur Rebels Say Shot Down Sudan Helicopters' *New York Times* (New York 28 March 2010); BBC, 'Darfur Rebel Row Jeopardises Sudan Peace Deal' *BBC News* (15 March 2010); Plaut, M., 'Critical Year Ahead for Sudan Amid Fears of War' *BBC News* (9 January 2010); Pflanz, M., 'Sudan Faces Return to War' *Telegraph* (UK 7 Jan 2010); Cohen, T., 'Darfur Violence Becoming a Forgotten War' *CNN World* (10 December 2009); 'UN Investigators Challenge Khartoum' *Africa Confidential* (20 November 2009). See also BBC, 'Q&A: Sudan's Darfur Conflict' (updated on 23 February 2010), http://news.bbc.co.uk/1/hi/world/africa/3496731.stm (accessed 26 March 2012).

[170]   UNEP, 'Republic of South Sudan', www.unep.org/southsudan/ (accessed 26 March 2012).

[171]   See, e.g. Copnall Sudan's Peace (n 167); Gettleman, J., 'A Taste of Hope Sends Refugees back to Darfur' *New York Times* (26 February 2012).

[172]   See, e.g. 'Dozens of peacekeepers held in Darfur are released' *Telegraph* (UK 20 February 2012); Copnall, J., 'Border battles threaten the new Sudans' *BBC News* (UK 15 November 2011); Kapila, M., 'Is Sudan committing another genocide – against the Nuba people?' *Guardian* (UK 21 March 2012); Addario, L., 'Sudan' *New York Times* (27 February 2012), http://topics.nytimes.com/top/news/international/countriesandterritories/sudan/index.html (accessed 26 March 2012).

[173]   UNEP Sudan PCEA (n 83) at p. 104.

[174]   See Harding (n 169); Sudanese Conflict (n 169).

diamonds being at the heart of the matter. Thus, Sierra Leone was already plagued by fundamental political and socio-economic problems which sowed the seeds for the years of brutal and bloody conflict.[175] This conflict was protracted by the greed to control the diamond industry.[176] The civil war that swept across Sierra Leone since 1991 crippled the country even further. The civil war in neighbouring Liberia further complicated the Sierra Leone conflict.[177] Violent conflict was allowed to continue unabated in Sierra Leone throughout the 1990s[178] as there was no intervention by the international community in the years prior to the conflict, nor was there any intervention during the first stages of the conflict between 1991 and 1996.[179] According to Hirsch,

> in the Sierra Leone case, over its forty-year history as an independent country there were no regional or international efforts to prevent the illegal exploitation of its natural resources or to address the collapse of its state institutions. There was no long-term structural intervention to address the profound gap between the few wealthy and powerful men at the top and the impoverished, malnourished, and uneducated majority. Diplomatic initiatives to prevent the war in Liberia from spilling over into Sierra Leone were negligible or nonexistent... As we have repeatedly seen, inattention at early stages of political collapse almost always brings greater calamity later on.[180]

Clearly the international community had failed to take a preventive approach by not taking any action that could have possibly prevented or mitigated the violent conflict. The international community, by ignoring the degenerating political and socio-economic conditions of Sierra Leone not only stood aside as any possible prospect of sustainable development in a once promising country was completely destroyed, but also gave no

---

[175] Kabia, J.M., *Humanitarian Intervention and Conflict Resolution in West Africa: From ECOMOG to ECOMIL* (Ashgate, England 2009) at pp. 104–105 [hereinafter Kabia].

[176] Ibid.

[177] Adebajo, A., *Liberia's Civil War: Nigeria, ECOMOG, and Regional Security in West Africa* (Lynne Rienner, USA 2002) at pp. 119–20.

[178] Saunders (n 114) at p. 1425.

[179] Samuels, K., 'Jus Ad Bellum and Civil Conflicts: A Case Study of the International Community's Approach to Violence in the Conflict of Sierra Leone' (2003) 8 Journal of Conflict & Security Law 315, at p. 325; Hilaire, M., *United Nations Law and the Security Council* (Ashgate, England 2005) at p. 103 [hereinafter Hilaire] (notes that the UNSC 'was slow to respond to the situation in Sierra Leone').

[180] Hirsch, J.L., *Sierra Leone: Diamonds and the Struggle for Democracy* (Lynne Rienner, USA 2001) at p. 14 [hereinafter Hirsch].

thought to the then present and future generations of Sierra Leone who were left to suffer a bloody and brutal conflict over a natural resource that should have been used to benefit the whole country.

The first stirring of international response was finally in evidence when the UNSC passed Resolution 1132 in October 1997.[181] Resolution 1132 condemned the military coup in Sierra Leone, declaring the conflict to be a threat to peace and security within the region as well as imposing an oil and arms embargo on Sierra Leone. Although the UN did little else at this point, an unexpected sub-regional organisation: ECOWAS, established a multilateral armed force known as ECOMOG (Economic Community of West African States Monitoring Group).[182] ECOMOG played a rather large part in attempting to mitigate and resolve the Sierra Leone conflict.[183] The UN welcomed ECOWAS/ECOMOG involvement and supported its mediation efforts.[184]

ECOMOG took the lead in the first stage of the international intervention in February 1998, managing to take over Freetown and reinstate the previous government.[185] Unfortunately, success was minor as the RUF still continued its brutal campaign of violence across the rural areas of Sierra Leone.[186] In July 1998 ECOMOG was bolstered by UN assistance in the form of a small observer force under the UN Observer Mission in Sierra Leone (UNOMSIL)[187] and in May 1999, a cease-fire agreement: the Lomé Peace Accord, was signed between the RUF and the Sierra

---

[181]   UNSC Resolution 1132 (8 October 1997) [hereinafter UNSC Res 1132].

[182]   ECOMOG was created in 1990 in response to the conflict raging in Liberia. See Akinrinade, B., 'International Humanitarian Law and the Conflict in Sierra Leone' (2001) 15 Notre Dame Journal of Law, Ethics and Public Policy 391, at p. 403; Levitt, J., 'Humanitarian Intervention by Regional Actors in Internal Conflicts: The Cases of ECOWAS in Liberia and Sierra Leone' (1998) 12 Temple International and Comparative Law Journal 333, at p. 343.

[183]   Nuamah, K. and Zartman, I.W., 'Intervention in Sierra Leone' in Lahneman, W.J. (ed), *Military Intervention: Cases in Context for the Twenty-First Century* (Rowman and Littlefield, USA 2004) at pp. 133–50 [hereinafter Nuamah and Zartman]; Kabia (n 175) at pp. 113–6.

[184]   See, e.g. Vesel, D., 'The Lonely Pragmatist: Humanitarian Intervention in an Imperfect World' (2003) BYU Journal of Public Law 1, at p. 28 [hereinafter Vesel]; Hilaire (n 179) at p. 103.

[185]   Vesel (n 184) at pp. 28–9. See also Rupert, J., 'Nigerians Drive Junta from Sierra Leone' *Washington Post* (Washington, DC 14 February 1998).

[186]   Vesel (n 184) at p. 29.

[187]   UNSC Resolution 1181 (13 July 1998).

Leone Government (GoSL).[188] In October 1999 ECOMOG was further reinforced by a much larger UN peacekeeping force under the UN Mission in Sierra Leone (UNAMSIL),[189] which was just in time as in May 2000 the peace agreement broke down and violence continued.[190] On 10 November 2000 the cease-fire Abuja Agreement brokered by ECOWAS was signed by GoSL and the RUF.[191]

ECOWAS worked closely in cooperation with the UN and UNSC throughout to resolve the conflict in Sierra Leone and although they were faced with numerous setbacks, their cooperative efforts did achieve a number of small successes that contributed towards the overall end of the conflict. This demonstrates the need for more cooperation among regional and sub-regional organisations in preventing, mitigating, managing and/or resolving such conflicts.[192] By early 2001 over 50 per cent of Sierra Leone was still under RUF control and the UN deployed UNAMSIL peacekeepers throughout the country.[193] GoSL gradually began restoring its governmental authority throughout the country and by January 2002, the war was declared over.[194]

Returning to the natural resources-conflict link, although the international community was late in responding to the situation in Sierra Leone, they began to acknowledge the role played by the illicit diamond trade in fuelling violent conflict. NGOs for example, were becoming increasingly vocal on the role of 'conflict diamonds' being traded in the international market.[195] Diamonds – that were in effect fuelling conflicts

---

[188]   Abass, A., 'The Implementation of ECOWAS' New Protocol and Security Council Resolution 1270 in Sierra Leone: New Developments in Regional Intervention' (2001–2002) 10 University of Miami International and Comparative Law Review 177, at p. 178 [hereinafter Abass].

[189]   UNSC Resolution 1270 (22 October 1999). See also Nuamah and Zartman (n 183) at p. 143.

[190]   Abass (n 188) at p. 178.

[191]   BBC, 'Timeline: Sierra Leone' *BBC News* (last updated 28 January 2010), http://news.bbc.co.uk/1/hi/world/africa/country_profiles/1065898.stm (accessed 22 March 2012) [hereinafter Sierra Leone Timeline].

[192]   Abass (n 188) at p. 178.

[193]   Yager, L., *International Trade: Critical Issues Remain in Deterring Conflict Diamond Trade* (DIANE, USA 2003) at pp. 38–40 [hereinafter Yager].

[194]   Sierra Leone Timeline (n 191). For a more detailed review of international intervention in Sierra Leone, see, e.g. Nuamah and Zartman (n 183) at pp, 133–50.

[195]   Keen (n 111) at p. 269 (diamonds also fuelled conflict in Liberia, Angola and Congo). See also UNEP Conflict to Peacebuilding (n 4) at p. 11.

in Sierra Leone and other countries.[196] The UNSC, in recognition of this, voted to impose a global ban on the trade of Sierra Leone rough diamonds by prohibiting all UN member States from importing Sierra Leone diamonds unless legitimately certified[197] by the GoSL.[198] A country specific diamond certification system was thereby established in Sierra Leone with technical assistance from the Belgian Diamond High Council (DHC)[199] and financial assistance by the UK and US.[200] It has been difficult to assess whether the certification scheme had an impact on the armed conflict because this system was implemented during the last stages of the conflict, which ended largely due to the international military intervention and peacekeeping missions.[201]

Although not in time to prevent diamonds from fuelling the Sierra Leone conflict, the conflict did bring the international community together in order to formulate 'ways to stop the trade in "conflict diamonds" and ensure that diamond purchases were not funding violence.'[202] The international community came up with the Kimberly Process Certification Scheme (KPCS)[203] which came into effect on 1 January 2003, requiring participants to establish appropriate domestic

---

[196]   Ibid.

[197]   For more information on the Sierra Leone certification system for diamonds, see Cook, N., 'Diamonds and Conflict: Policy Proposals and Background' in Levy (ed) (n 23) at pp. 51–2 [hereinafter 2003 Cook]; El-Khawas, M.A. and Ndumbe, J.A., 'Diamonds, Ethnicity and Terrorism: The Power Struggle in Sierra Leone' in Wusu, O. (ed), *Politics and Economics of Africa* (Nova Science, New York 2006) at pp. 85–6.

[198]   UNSC Resolution 1306 (5 July 2000).

[199]   DHC is the Belgian diamond industry's official representative. See 'HRD Antwerp', http://www.hrd.be/en/home.aspx (accessed 2 April 2012).

[200]   IMF, 'Sierra Leone: Selected Issues and Statistical Appendix' IMF Country Report No. 04/420 (IMF, Washington, DC December 2004) at p. 29; Cortright, D. and others, 'Implementing Targeted Sanctions: The Role of International Agencies and Regional Organizations' in Wallensteen, P. and Staibano, C. (eds), *International Sanctions: Between Words and Wars in the Global System* (Frank Cass, Oxon 2005) at p. 151.

[201]   Le Billon, P., 'Getting it Done: Instruments of Enforcement' in Bannon and Collier (eds) (n 28) at p. 246.

[202]   'Kimberley Process: Background' <http://www.kimberleyprocess.com/background/index_en.html> (accessed 27 March 2012). See also Roberts, J., *Glitter & Greed: The Secret World of the Diamond Empire* (Disinformation, New York 2003) at p. 1; UK: Foreign and Commonwealth Office, 'Human Rights Annual Report 2004' (Stationary Office, London 2004) at pp. 137–8.

[203]   For more information on the KPCS see, e.g. Wetzel, J.E., 'Targeted Economic Measures to Curb Armed Conflict? The Kimberley Process on the

diamond certification standards and schemes, which includes penalties for transgressions.[204] The KPCS aims to increase transparency in the diamond industry to ensure that conflict diamonds are identified and excluded from the legitimate diamond trade. In the process of establishing the KPCS, De Beers[205] and other leading producers within 'the international diamond industry issued a joint resolution declaring "zero tolerance" towards those who traded in conflict diamonds.'[206] The KPCS did not have a direct impact in stopping armed conflict in Sierra Leone because the conflict had essentially ended by the time the KPCS became operational. However, it did make an impact thereafter as it is reported that almost seventy per cent of Sierra Leone's diamond production goes through the KPCS at the post-conflict stage.[207]

Despite the fact that the UN and the rest of the world were slow to intervene in this conflict, by the end of 2006, Sierra Leone: from its ECOMOG and UN interventions to the establishment of the Special Court for Sierra Leone (SCSL),[208] was considered one of the UN's success stories.[209] In addition, the UNSC-mandated government certificate of origin scheme has increased Sierra Leone's '[d]iamond exports

---

Trade in Conflict Diamonds' in Quénivet, N. and Shah-Davis, S. (eds), *International Law and Armed Conflict: Challenges in the 21st Century* (TMC Asser, The Netherlands 2010) at pp. 168–81; Fishman, J.L., 'Is Diamond Smuggling Forever? The Kimberley Process Certification Scheme: The First Step Down the Long Road to Solving the Blood Diamond Trade Problem' (2005) 13 University of Miami Business Law Review 217.

[204] Collier, P. and others, *Breaking the Conflict Trap: Civil War and Development Policy* (World Bank, Washington, DC 2003) at p. 143.

[205] De Beers is one of the world's largest diamond producers and trader of rough diamonds. See, e.g. De Beers, 'FAQs', www.debeersgroup.com/en/Global/FAQs/ (accessed 30 March 2012).

[206] See 'Joint Resolution of the World Federation of Diamond Bourses (WFDB) and the International Diamond Manufacturers Association (IDMA)' (19 July 2000).

[207] UK: Select Committee of Economic Affairs, 'The Impact of Economic Sanctions, Volume II: Evidence' House of Lords (2006–07) 96-II [59].

[208] For more information on SCSL see, e.g. The Special Court for Sierra Leone, www.sc-sl.org/ (accessed 3 April 2012); Pham, J.P., 'A Viable Model for International Criminal Justice: The Special Court for Sierra Leone' (2006) 19 New York International Law Review 37.

[209] Mertus, J.A., *The United Nations and Human Rights: A Guide for a New Era* (Routledge, Oxon 2005) at pp. 128–9; Keen (n 111) at p. 272. See also UNSC, 'Success In Sierra Leone Is Good Example Of Achievement Of UN, Member States Working Together, Says Secretary-General In Remarks To Security Council' (22 December 2006) Press Release SC/8923 [hereinafter PR

and resulting state revenues'.[210] This increase in legal exports have allowed 'substantial revenue from diamond sales to go back to Sierra Leone – a first step in helping the world's poorest country to help rebuild itself after the war.'[211]

With a portion of the tax revenues from the export of diamonds being used for the needs of the Sierra Leone people,[212] this is certainly a step in improving the socio-economic, development and natural resource issues of Sierra Leone, allowing it to be on the track to sustainable development. Since then, the Sierra Leone government with the assistance of UNDP have launched community-based projects that includes building public structures, schools, markets, agriculture improvements and training.[213] UNDP is not alone. UNEP for example, since 2009 has been working in Sierra Leone 'to assess and address the environmental causes and consequences of the 1991–2002 civil war as well as the current environmental challenges facing the country. Together with UNDP, the Food and Agricultural Organization (FAO) and the World Health Organization (WHO), UNEP is delivering capacity-building support and technical assistance through the UN's "Joint Vision of Sierra Leone"'.[214] Such cooperation has contributed and continues to contribute to the sustainable development of the country. The UN does not take this success for granted, as the former UN Secretary-General points out, 'those of us who remember the anxious days of May 2000 know well that this was far from being a foregone conclusion.'[215]

In summary, these three case-studies not only illustrate the link between environmental factors and armed conflict, they also highlight the inadequate international response in relation to conflict prevention as well as the possibility of similar future armed conflict scenarios as a

---

SC/8923]; UNSC, 'Security Council Press Statement on Sierra Leone' (19 September 2007) Press Release SC/9121.

[210]   Cook, N., 'Sierra Leone: Transition to Peace' in Sillinger, B. (ed), *Sierra Leone: Current Issues and Background* (Nova Science, New York 2003) at p. 43.

[211]   USAID, 'Telling Our Story: Sierra Leone – Diamond Revenues Benefit Local Communities' (last updated 18 August 2009), www.usaid.gov/stories/sierraleone/cs_sierraleone_diamond.html (accessed 2 April 2012).

[212]   Ibid.

[213]   Ibid. See also Deegan, H., *Africa Today: Culture, Economics, Religion, Security* (Routledge, Oxon 2009) at p. 167; OECD/DAC, *DAC Guidelines: Natural Resources and Pro-Poor Growth: The Economics and Politics* (OECD, Paris 2008) at p. 140.

[214]   UNEP, 'Sierra Leone', www.unep.org/sierraleone/ (accessed 26 March 2012).

[215]   See PR SC/8923 (n 209).

consequence of environmental pressures, the lack of sustainable development and the lack of appropriate collective conflict prevention by the international community. Somalia illustrates a smaller violent conflict over scarce resources within the bigger picture of a 'failed State'; and Darfur, Sudan illustrates armed conflict over dwindling precious resources such as arable land amidst demographic pressures, ethnic tensions, an ineffective governance system, drought, climate change and other environmental stresses. Both cases demonstrate the possibility of such future conflicts within socio-economically and politically unstable societies, States or regions that are plagued by the added pressures of environmental degradation, dwindling resources and climate change. Finally, the Sierra Leone case-study shows the breakdown of an already vulnerable State, economically and politically, which has led to armed and violent conflict over the control of and profit from a high-value natural resource. Basically, all three case-studies demonstrate that the lack of sustainable development, the disintegration or breakdown of socio-economic, political, environmental and development conditions may allow environmental stresses to fuel or trigger armed conflicts.

It is thus clear from these cases that international assistance is imperative to prevent, mitigate and manage these environmental-induced conflicts as these States, already plagued by instability, were unable to help themselves. However, to reiterate a recurrent criticism, the international community were tardy in all cases, illustrating the reactive rather than proactive or preventive stance that should have been taken. It is submitted that these conflicts could have been avoided or at the very least mitigated if the international community had taken a more preventive approach by providing earlier assistance. Taking early action includes preventing or mitigating the breakdown of socio-economic and political aspects of these States and particularly from an environmental dimension due to the conflicts' environment-conflict link, before the conflicts had escalated to a calamitous stage.

4. INTERNATIONAL SYSTEM: METHODS AND ACTION IN ENVIRONMENT-CONFLICT PREVENTION – ACHIEVING SUSTAINABLE DEVELOPMENT?

The case-studies highlight the serious consequences of a failure to address adequately the preventive dimension to sustainable development. This section considers which of the principles within the umbrella concept of sustainable development can assist most in the evolution of a more robust approach to preventing environmental-induced armed conflict. In other words, granted the truth of Donovan, Jong and Abe's statement that '[p]reventing conflict and reducing its duration and impacts are among the critical challenges today facing advocates and practitioners of sustainable development and environmental conservation',[216] the following section explores how this can be achieved using the sustainable development concept.

4.1. Collective Responsibility in Preventing Environmental-induced Conflict

French set forth the argument that,

> States possess, in the words of the Millennium Declaration, a 'collective responsibility' to achieve global values. At the foundation level, it is the argument that all States share a common path and that – subject to the positivist qualification of sovereign autonomy – all States are under a duty, certainly since 1945, to cooperate for the benefit and advancement of all.[217]

The international community may question why they should help prevent conflict in particular countries or regions that are vulnerable to possible environmental-induced violence? There are a number of reasons. The first and most obvious argument is that many of these potentially environment-conflict societies or States do not have the capacity to help themselves.[218] In light of the principle of common but differentiated responsibilities, the international community, particularly developed

---

[216]   Donovan, D. and others, 'Tropical Forests and Extreme Conflict' in Jong, W.D., Donovan, D., and Abe, K. (eds), *Extreme Conflict and Tropical Forests* (Springer, The Netherlands 2007) at p. 13.

[217]   French, D., *Global Justice and Sustainable Development* (Koninklijke Brill NV, The Netherlands 2010) at p. 10 and pp. 10–13 (for a discussion on collective responsibility – cooperating for sustainability and global justice).

[218]   See also Bellamy, A.J., Williams, P. and Griffin, S., *Understanding Peacekeeping* (2nd edn Polity, Cambridge 2010) at p. 157 (highlight arguments that bring up 'the moral imperative to prevent armed conflict') [hereinafter 2010 Bellamy]; French, D., 'Developing States and International Environmental Law: The Importance of Differentiated Responsibilities' (2000) 49 International and Comparative Law Quarterly 35, at p. 52 (argues that the international community should pay particular attention 'to those States that are the least developed or most environmentally vulnerable') [hereinafter 2000 French].

nations, should collectively participate to address these problems.[219] As French points out, '[a] more recent justification for the use of differentiated obligations within international environmental law is that the international community has entered a new stage of international cooperation, one that obliges those more developed to take on additional responsibility.'[220]

A second argument is that the international community repeatedly makes declarations and statements as well as establishing treaties and agreements that are geared towards environmental protection and global cooperation. For example, declarations and multilateral environmental agreements (MEAs) that integrates and aims for common but differentiated responsibilities, intra and inter-generational equity, the precautionary principle, public participation and sustainable development. These statements and MEAs would be hollow and meaningless if the international community failed to put into action their declarations pledged. As for translating their intentions into action in practice, there is no excuse as various international organisations, chief among them being the UN, are now 'mandated to prevent armed conflict.'[221]

Thirdly, with the increasing and ever more challenging environmental pressures faced by the world today and the fact that in some situations, these pressures may be a threat to security,[222] the international community cannot in good conscience sit idly by and do nothing. Especially since resulting environmental-conflicts that occur in certain societies, countries or regions, have and may in the future, affect the global community. As one scholar comments,

> while such conflicts may not be conspicuous as wars at an international level, there is nevertheless a potential for significant repercussions for the security interests in both the developing and the industrialized countries. Such internal, resource-based conflicts can affect international trade relations, produce humanitarian disasters, and lead to growing number of refugee flows.[223]

---

[219] Sands, P., *Principles of International Environmental Law I: Frameworks, Standards and Implementation* (MUP, Manchester 1995) at p. 217.

[220] 2000 French (n 218) at p. 55.

[221] 2010 Bellamy (n 218) at p. 157.

[222] See 'Chapter 9: Environmental Security' in Glenn, J. and others, *2009 State of the Future* (Millennium Project: Armer Council for the UN, Washington, DC 2009) [hereinafter 2009 Glenn] at pp. 1–17.

[223] Beniston, M., 'Issues Relating to Environmental Change and Population Migrations' in Unruh (eds) (n 16) at p. 12.

An example of potential global consequences, though not directly environmentally related, can be seen from the Somalia case-study, where the failure of the international community to initiate conflict prevention efforts earlier has contributed to the failure of the State. This failed State in turn, has propagated numerous problems, one of them being piracy which is a constant threat to international shipping.[224]

Fourthly, international preventive efforts carry much less risk than when a conflict is already in motion.[225] A 'wait and see' approach by the international community as evidenced from the case-studies 'risks a narrowing of options as a conflict deepens and a resolution becomes increasingly difficult.'[226] Finally, whether or not the international community takes preventive action, the international community especially the 'wealthier' nations eventually have to pick up the tab for peace-keeping and reconstruction.[227] Therefore, taking preventive environment-conflict action might actually be more cost effective as studies have shown that conflict prevention would cost the international community much less than conflict suppression or post-conflict peacekeeping and reconstruction efforts.[228]

Fortunately, the international community is not only becoming aware of the importance of conflict prevention,[229] but also the fact that environmental factors have to be integrated into the conflict prevention agenda in conjunction with other more obvious security, socio-economic

----

[224]   See, e.g. Murphy, M.N., *Small Boats, Weak States, Dirty Money: Piracy and Maritime Terrorism in the Modern World* (Columbia University, USA 2009) at pp. 101–10.

[225]   Muscat, R.J., *Investing in Peace: How Development Aid Can Prevent or Promote Conflict* (ME Sharpe, USA 2002) at p. 26 [hereinafter Muscat]. See also OECD/DAC, *The DAC Guidelines: Helping Prevent Violent Conflict* (OECD, Paris 2001) at p. 14.

[226]   Ibid.

[227]   House of Commons International Development Committee, 'Conflict and Development: Peacebuilding and Post-conflict Reconstruction' Sixth Report of Session 2005–06, Volume II (The Stationary Office, London 2006) at p. 204.

[228]   Leech, J., *Asymmetries of Conflict: War Without Death* (Frank Cass, England 2002) at p. 49 (conclusion based on a study of nine recent conflicts and cost assessment research by the Oxford Research Group). See also Sokalski, H.J., *An Ounce of Prevention: Macedonia and the UN Experience in Preventive Diplomacy* (US Institute of Peace, Washington, DC 2003) at p. 4; Muscat (n 225) at p. 26.

[229]   This includes the UN, 'other UN related agencies such as the World Bank, as well as regional organizations, such as the Organization for Security and Cooperation in Europe (OSCE), the European Union, and the European Commission. Subregional agencies such as the Southern Africa Development

and political factors.[230] The EU for example has already linked and integrated environmental and security issues in its environmental policies and approach to conflict prevention.[231] The EU has integrated this approach through EU environmental legislation, multiple annual Environmental Action Programmes, bilateral and regional environmental cooperation and MEAs.[232] The EU signing up to the KPCS for example, is part of its conflict prevention agenda in the African region as more than eighty per cent of the world's rough diamonds pass through the EU.[233] As Weiss notes,

> [i]t is against the Community's commitment to a common but differentiated responsibility to conserve, protect and restore to the Earth's ecosystem,[234] that the EC's environmental policy and its interface with conflict prevention is built. Based on precaution, prevention and an ecosystem approach, the EC's environmental policy is a predestined long-term tool to minimise environmental problems before they give rise to tensions and conflicts.[235]

Nevertheless, although it is commendable that the EU has integrated effective environment-conflict prevention strategies, the question is, what about the UN? The UN with its 192 member States, is, after all the main international body that is mandated to maintain international peace and security. As one scholar comments, '[f]or all the setbacks it has faced in recent years, the UN remains indispensable to the international community it serves.'[236] Moreover, advocates for UN conflict prevention argue that, '[a]side from declarations of intent, the UN has built up a

---

Community and the Economic Community of West African States, the developmental agencies of several major countries, as well as nongovernmental organizations.' See Ackerman, A., 'The Idea and Practice of Conflict Prevention' (2003) 40 Journal of Peace Research 339, at p. 340 [hereinafter Ackerman].

[230] 2009 Glenn (n 222) at p. 3.

[231] Weiss, A., 'Environmental Policy and Conflict Prevention' in Kronenberger, V. and Wouters, J. (eds), *The European Union and Conflict Prevention: Policy and Legal Aspects* (Asser, The Netherlands 2004) at p. 211 [hereinafter Weiss].

[232] Ibid., at pp. 211–36 (for a review of the EU's integrated environmental and conflict prevention approach).

[233] EU-UN, 'Kimberley Process – United to Fight Blood Diamonds!' European Commission EC07–141EN (11 June 2007).

[234] Principle 7, Rio Declaration (1992) 31 ILM 876.

[235] Weiss (n 231) at p. 234.

[236] Hannay, D., 'A More Secure World: Our Shared Responsibility – Report of the UN Secretary-General's High Level Panel on Threats, Challenges and Change' in Dodds and Pippard (eds) (n 27) at p. 16.

comprehensive panoply of preventive instruments and bodies involved directly or indirectly in conflict prevention.'[237] The crucial question here however, is whether the UN has integrated environmental as well as sustainable development priorities into its conflict prevention strategies?

The UNSC for example, in recognising the broader remit to threats to security and the fact that 'it was necessary to develop new approaches and address the underlying causes of conflicts – and other sustainable solutions',[238] agreed that the UN should increase its capacity for conflict prevention as thus far the UN has had a more reactive approach to armed conflicts around the world.[239] From an environmental security perspective, there have been numerous intentions and efforts. For example, from acknowledging the necessary inclusion of the environmental dimension into the UN's conflict prevention strategies;[240] establishing a UN International Panel for Sustainable Resource Management (IPSRM);[241] proposing a UN Environmental Mediation Programme (UNEMP) to resolve environmental issues between and within States at the request of the

---

[237]   Dufresne, C. and Schnabel, A., 'Building UN Capacity in Early Warning and Prevention' in Schnabel, A. and Carment, D. (eds), *Conflict Prevention from Rhetoric to Reality, Volume I: Organizations and Institutions* (Lexington, USA 2004) at p. 361 and pp. 363–86 (on review of UN cooperation with other actors for conflict prevention) [hereinafter Dufresne and Schnabel], [hereinafter Schnabel and Carment (eds) Volume I].

[238]   UN, 'Security Council Reiterates Commitment to Conflict Prevention in Africa; Presidential Statement Follows Day-Long Debate' (28 August 2007) Press Release UNSC/9105 [hereinafter PR UNSC/9105].

[239]   2009 Glenn (n 222) at p. 40. See also UNGA, 'General Assembly Decides to Continue Consideration of Secretary-General's Report on Preventing Armed Conflict, At Upcoming Sessions' (7 September 2006) UN Doc GA/10487. (The UN has been criticised for spending about $18 billion over a five-year period on peacekeeping efforts but not even close to that amount on preventive efforts, particularly since the large peacekeeping costs were partly due to inadequate preventive measures).

[240]   UN, 'Annan Maps Out Ways to Bolster UN Ability to Prevent Armed Conflict, Save Lives' *UN News Centre* (21 August 2006); Report of the Secretary-General, 'Progress Report on the Prevention of Armed Conflict' (18 July 2006) UN Doc A/60/891.

[241]   See International Panel for Sustainable Resource Management (IPSRM), www.unep.fr/scp/rpanel/ (accessed 6 April 2012). See also 2009 Glenn (n 222) at p. 45.

governments;[242] bringing up security related environmental issues such as climate change at the 63rd session of UNGA in September 2008,[243] to setting up an UN-EU Partnership on Natural Resources and Conflict Prevention.[244] Other actors have also been moving towards integrating environmental security into their agendas; for example, bringing up environmental security issues within the G8,[245] a report on environmental-related security threats and an environmental security forum by NATO,[246] and OSCE-NATO cooperative workshops on environmental security.[247]

Unfortunately, there is thus far little evidence of the international community putting these plans, declarations and intentions into practice.[248] As scholars have pointed out, it is 'generally recognised that when it comes to conflict prevention in practice, there is a long way to go in translating rhetoric to reality. This is especially the case as far as the UN is concerned'.[249] Nevertheless, integrating and prioritising

---

[242]   'Environmental Security: UN Doctrine for Managing Environmental Issues in Military Action; Appendix C: UNEMP', http://www.millennium-project.org/millennium/es-un-app3.html (accessed 3 April 2012). See also 2009 Glenn (n 222) at p. 45.

[243]   See 'General Debate of the 63rd Session of UNGA' (23 September–1 October 2008), www.un.org/ga/63/generaldebate/ (accessed 3 April 2012).

[244]   UN-EU Partnership on Natural Resources and Conflict Prevention, www.un.org/en/events/environmentconflictday/report.shtml (accessed on 3 April 2012).

[245]   'G8 Statement on Climate Change and Environment' *Guardian* (UK 8 July 2008); Steiner, A., 'Environmental Security' G8 Summit (2006).

[246]   Korteweg, R. and Podkolinski, R., 'New Horizons: Finding a Path Away from NATO's De-solidarisation' (NATO/Hague Centre for Strategic Studies (HCSS), The Netherlands, March 2009); 'NATO Security Science Forum on Environmental Security' (Brussels, 12 March 2008), www.nato.int/docu/update/2008/03-march/e0312b.html (3 April 2012).

[247]   OSCE, 'Mediterranean Countries Discuss Environmental Security at OSCE, NATO workshop' OSCE Press Release, www.osce.org/cio/49284 (accessed 3 April 2012); OSCE/NATO, 'Water Scarcity, Land Degradation and Desertification in the Mediterranean Region – Environment and Security Aspects' Background Paper (Valencia, 10–11 December 2007).

[248]   See 2009 Glenn (n 222); 'Chapter 6: Emerging Environmental Security Issues' in Glenn, J.C. and others, *2011 State of the Future* (Millennium Project: Armer Council for the UN, Washington, DC 2011) [hereinafter 2011 Glenn].

[249]   Rambsbotham, O., Woodhouse, T. and Miall, H. (eds), *Contemporary Conflict Resolution* (Polity, Cambridge 2005) at p. 125 [hereinafter Rambsbotham]. See also 2010 Bellamy (n 218) at pp. 155–72; UNGA, *Report of the Secretary-General on the Work of the Organization* (UN, New York 2005) at p. 14.

environmental-conflict threats with other variable socio-economic, political and development factors within a framework of collective international responsibility is certainly a crucial aspect in respect of any conflict prevention efforts as well as contributing to the sustainable development cycle. As Brodnig comments, '[t]he truism that environmental problems do not respect borders has serious consequences for conflict prevention. Given the conflict potential of environmental degradation, any preventative policies call for a multi-level approach which ascribes a large responsibility to international action.'[250]

Simply put, adhering to common but differentiated responsibilities and better cooperation between all actors (both State and non-State) are crucial in any international conflict prevention efforts. Cooperation has to take place at all levels, thus taking into account the public participation principle is also important because formulating effective environmental and natural resource management policies for a potential resource-conflict prone State is challenging. Cooperation is thus required not only between a key international organisation such as the UN and local and grass-root NGOs (that have closer contact with societies that would be most directly affected by any environmental or resource problem),[251] but also cooperation with other organisations that deal with differing environmental, political, socio-economic and development issues within the country or region.[252] Thus, the international community, particularly the UN, with the intention of achieving sustainable development, have to step up and improve their collective conflict prevention efforts to prevent environmental-induced armed conflicts in the future. As Stub concludes, '[o]ur common future calls for both responses at local, national and regional levels *and* a return to multilateralism.'[253]

---

[250]   Brodnig (n 34) at p. 35.

[251]   See, e.g. Razzaque, J., 'Participatory Rights for Communities in South Asia' in Ebbesson, J. and Okowa, P. (eds), *Environmental Law and Justice in Context* (CUP, Cambridge 2009) at p. 134 (asserting that '[t]o manage natural resources sustainably, the disadvantaged communities need to play a more direct role and be part of the whole process').

[252]   Kirton, J.J. and Stefanova, R.N., 'Introduction: The G8's Role in Global Conflict Prevention' in Kirton, J.J. and Stefanova, R.N. (eds), *The G8, the United Nations, and Conflict Prevention* (Ashgate, England 2004) at pp. 2–3; Volberg, T., *The Sovereignty Versus Intervention Dilemma: The Challenge of Conflict Prevention* (Grin Verlag, Germany 2006) at pp. 3–5.

[253]   Stub, S., 'Our Future – Or None At All' in 1997 Gleditsch (ed) (n 3) at p. 3.

4.2. Laws Relevant to Prevent Environmental-induced Conflict

Unlike the 'in-conflict' and 'post-conflict' stage where there actually is an international law regime that protects the environment during armed conflict as well as affixing liability and awards reparations for post-conflict environmental damage,[254] the pre-conflict stage does not have such protection. The pre-conflict or preventive stage is not governed by any international legal system nor does it have a comprehensive legal regime that could prevent environmental-induced conflict.

Nevertheless, the international community does have numerous environmental security related treaties and agreements that although are not specifically directed to preventing environmental-induced armed conflict, do protect certain environmental issues that as a result may potentially prevent conflict.[255] MEAs, some of which not only incorporate and integrate sustainable development principles but also aim to protect the environment by preventing, mitigating or managing potential environmental damage or other environmentally related issues, that if not protected, could in turn trigger, exacerbate or fuel armed conflict. MEAs are thereby crucial in the challenge 'to tackle global environmental and resource problems and to address transboundary environmental impacts by submitting the international community to commonly agreed concepts, principles, rules, norms and practices.'[256] As Soroos points out,

> [m]any environmental threats to human security involve two or more states, which are contributors to the problem, impacted victims, or a combination of both. In such cases, international cooperation is needed to prevent or lessen threats to environmental security. Such cooperation typically takes the form of international agreements, such as treaties or resolutions, in which the countries bear some responsibility for an environmental problem, accept limits on activities within their jurisdictions that are contributing to the problem. The resulting enhancements of environmental security quite often become international collective, or public, goods that benefit countries regardless of whether they made significant contributions towards creating it.[257]

---

[254]   These legal regimes will be discussed in Chapters 4 and 5 respectively.

[255]   2009 Glenn (n 222) at pp. 28–30 (for a list of 'environmental security related regulations that have been or are close to coming into force since August 2002') and at pp. 30–34 (for a list of environmental security related proposed treaties and/or amendments to existing ones). See also 2011 Glenn (n 248).

[256]   Weiss (n 231) at p. 219.

[257]   Soroos, M.S., 'Environmental Change and Human Security in the Caspian Region: Threats, Vulnerability and Response Strategies' in Ascher, W. and Mirovitskaya, N. (eds), *The Caspian Sea: A Quest for Environmental Security* (Kluwer, The Netherlands 2000) at p. 21.

An example of an MEA relevant to environmental security is the UN Convention to Combat Desertification[258] which is geared towards combating desertification and/or mitigating the effects of drought, with a particular focus on the African continent. As discussed in Chapter 2, in addition to making sustainable development an objective and integrating the concept throughout, the convention not only commits the Parties to collectively cooperate to work towards the sustainable use of scarce land and water resources,[259] but also to do so with regard to the interrelationships between other socio-economic and developmental factors.[260] As seen from the case-studies, drought and desertification exacerbated armed conflict in two examples;[261] thereby this MEA, by attempting to address the issues of desertification and drought 'within a framework of sustainable development'[262] particularly in Africa, could contribute towards environmental-conflict prevention efforts and in the process contribute to the achievement of sustainable development. Another significant treaty for example, is the UN Framework Convention on Climate Change[263] which in setting an overall framework for intergovernmental efforts to deal with the challenges of climate change, not only embraces the concept of sustainable development but also addresses the potential environmental factors aggravated by climate change that may trigger, exacerbate or fuel conflict. The 2009 State of the Future Report sets out a list of further MEAs relevant to environmental security and prevention of environmental-induced conflict.[264] A point to note is that the global community should bear in mind that such MEAs must be more than just expressions of well-meaning intentions.

To sum it up, it would be difficult due to the complexities involved in the field of conflict prevention to have a comprehensive legal system for it (including environment-conflict prevention). It is hence suggested that MEAs, some with their recognition and incorporation of integrating socio-economic, development and environmental factors are therefore,

---

[258]   UN Convention to Combat Desertification in those Countries Experiencing Serious Drought and/or Desertification, Particularly in Africa (adopted 14 October 1994; entered into force 26 December 1996) 1954 UNTS 3 [hereinafter UNCCD].

[259]   Art. 3, ibid.

[260]   Preamble, ibid.

[261]   Somalia (conflict over scarce water) and Darfur, Sudan (conflict over arable land).

[262]   Preamble, UNCCD.

[263]   UN Framework Convention on Climate Change (adopted 9 May 1992, entered into force 21 March 1994) (1992) 31 ILM 851 [hereinafter UNFCCC].

[264]   2009 Glenn (n 222) at pp. 28–34. See also 2011 Glenn (n 248).

the best way to gain international cooperation in dealing with potential conflict-inducing environmental problems. These various MEAs which the global community continue to reinforce or supplement, would certainly contribute towards international environmental-conflict prevention efforts and thereby, prevent or mitigate any obstruction towards the achievement of sustainable development within those potentially vulnerable States and regions.

4.3. Early Warning System – Taking the Preventive Approach

The key to effective conflict prevention is effective 'early warning'.[265] An example of a definition of early warning (EW) is 'the systematic collection and analysis of information coming from areas of crises for the purpose of: (a) anticipating the escalation of violent conflict; (b) development of strategic responses to these crises; and (c) the presentation of options to key decision makers.'[266] Simply put, EW, which embodies the preventive approach, identifies situations which have the potential to generate into armed or violent conflict.[267] Scholars and policymakers are aware of the importance of EW in respect of conflict prevention as evidenced by its increasing inclusion in conflict prevention literature[268] and numerous conflict EW efforts by the international community. This

---

[265] See, e.g. Evans, G., *The Responsibility to Protect: Ending Mass Atrocity Crimes Once and For All* (Brookings Institution, Washington, DC 2008) at p. 81 [hereinafter 2008 Evans]; Rummel, R., 'Advancing the European Union's Conflict Prevention Policy' in Kirton, J.J. and Stefanova, R.N. (eds), *The G8, the United Nations, and Conflict Prevention* (Ashgate, England 2004) at p. 115.

[266] Schmid Pioom, A.P., *Thesaurus and Glossary of Early Warning and Conflict Prevention Terms* (Erasmus University 1998) cited in Niño-Pérez, J., 'Conflict Indicators Developed by the Commission – the Check-list for Root Causes of Conflict/Early Warning Indicators' in Kronenberger, V. and Wouters, J. (eds), *The European Union and Conflict Prevention: Policy and Legal Aspects* (TMC Asser, The Netherlands 2004) at p. 7.

[267] For a review on EW in relation to conflict prevention, see, e.g. 2008 Evans (n 265) at pp. 81–7; Ivanov, A. and Nyheim, D., 'Generating the Means to an End: Political Will and Integrated Responses to Early Warning' in Schnabel, A. and Carment, D. (eds), *Conflict Prevention: From Rhetoric to Reality, Volume 2: Opportunities and Innovations* (Lexington, USA 2004) at pp. 163–76 [hereinafter Ivanov and Nyheim], [hereinafter Schnabel and Carment (eds) Volume 2]; Ackerman (n 229) at pp. 342–4; Van Walraven, K. (ed), *Early Warning and Conflict Prevention: Limitations and Possibilities* (Kluwer Law, The Netherlands 1998).

[268] Ibid.

ranges for example: from efforts by the UN,[269] EU,[270] OSCE,[271] ECOWAS,[272] Intergovernmental Authority on Development (IGAD)[273] to NGOs such as the International Crisis Group, International Alerts, Amnesty International and Human Rights Watch that 'monitor and report on areas of the world where conflict appears to be emerging.'[274]

Despite these efforts, there is no doubt that the applicability of EW is a complex matter in practice. As Ivanov and Nyheim note, '[e]arly warning is becoming part of mainstream practice in efforts towards conflict prevention, but the challenge of linking warning to response is also more pronounced.'[275] Unfortunately, the international community has thus far not been able to achieve a comprehensive and systematic global EW conflict-prevention system. Despite ample ideas and proposals

---

[269]   For UN EW efforts, see, e.g. Rusu, S. and Schmeidl, S., 'Early Warning and Early Action in the UN System: UNDP and OCHA' in Council of Europe, *Institutions for the Management of Ethnopolitical Conflict in Central and Eastern Europe* (Council of Europe, Strasbourg 2008) at pp. 149–84 (for a critical analysis of UN early warning efforts and systems); Dufresne and Schnabel (n 237) at pp. 363–86 (for the UN's early warning efforts); Rakita, S., 'Early Warning as a Tool of Conflict Prevention' (1998) 30 New York University Journal of International Law and Politics 539 (for a range of EW systems within the UN system).

[270]   For EU EW efforts, see, e.g. Burgess, N., 'The Council's Early Warning Process' in Kronenberger, V. and Wouters, J. (eds), *The European Union and Conflict Prevention: Policy and Legal Aspects* (TMC Asser, The Netherlands 2004) at pp. 21–32 (for the EU's early warning process); Stewart, E.J., *The European Union and Conflict Prevention: Policy Evolution and Outcome* (LIT Verlag, Berlin 2006) at pp. 115–20 (for the EU's early warning and policy planning capacities).

[271]   Ramsbotham (n 249) at p. 124 (the OSCE has evolved into a 'primary regional organization for early warning, conflict prevention, crisis management and post-conflict rehabilitations' as well as a conflict prevention structure that includes a Conflict Prevention Centre).

[272]   Adejumobi, S. and Olukoshi, A., *The African Union and New Strategies for Development in Africa* (Cambria, USA 2008) at p. 356 (ECOWAS early warning system in the form of a regional observation programme).

[273]   Gebrewold, B. (ed), *Africa and Fortress Europe: Threats and Opportunities* (Ashgate, England 2007) at p. 31 (on IGAD's Conflict Early Warning and Early Response System (CEWARN)).

[274]   International Commission on Intervention and State Sovereignty (ICISS), 'The Responsibility to Protect' Report of the International Commission on Intervention and State Sovereignty (International Development Research Centre, Canada December 2001) at p. 21.

[275]   Ivanov and Nyheim (n 267) at p. 163.

to establish such a system,[276] early warning in this field is still very much conducted on an ad hoc basis.[277] As Zartman comments '[p]revention depends on early warning, and early warnings abound ... '[278] but '[l]ess prolific is early awareness and early action, that is, the ability to listen, hear and act on early warnings.'[279]

Returning to the environmental dimension of EW conflict-prevention, although various factors cause armed conflict, in light of increasing global environmental problems, it is perhaps worth having a specific environmental EW system to identify potential environment-conflict factors. As non-environmental factors are generally considered more serious or traditionally more conflict relevant,[280] a general EW system may get bogged down with these other variable factors. One option could be the international community establishing an environmental-conflict EW unit that is administered and managed by UNEP. UNEP already has the Division of Early Warning and Assessment (DEWA) that monitors the state of the global environment, assesses global and regional environmental trends and provides early warning of emerging environmental threats[281] as well as the Post-Conflict and Disaster Management Branch (PCDMB) which includes an effective post-conflict environmental assessment system and unit.[282] Because UNEP already has the technical expertise and experience in EW as well as assessing the environment in

---

[276] See, e.g. Menkhaus, K., 'Conflict Prevention and Human Security: Issues and Challenges' in Picciotto, R. and Weaving, R. (eds), *Security and Development: Investing in Peace and Prosperity* (Routledge, Oxon 2006) at p. 243; Lefkon, O.P., 'Culture Shock: Obstacles to Bringing Conflict Prevention under the Wing of U.N. Development...and Vice Versa' (2003) 35 New York University Journal of International Law and Politics 671, at p. 709; ICISS, *The Responsibility to Protect: Research, Bibliography and Background* (International Development Research Centre, Canada 2001) at p. 35.

[277] Ackerman (n 229) at p. 342; Boothby, D. and D'Angelo, G., 'Building Capacity within the United Nations: Cooperation on the Prevention of Violent Conflicts' in Schnabel and Carment (eds) Volume 2 (n 267) at p. 259.

[278] Zartman, I.W., 'International negotiation and conflict prevention' in Coyne, C.J. and Mathers, R. (eds), *The Handbook on the Political Economy of War* (Edward Elgar, UK 2011) at p. 571.

[279] Ibid.

[280] UNEP from Conflict to Peacebuilding (n 4) at p. 4 (reports that 'linking "environment" and "conflict" remains contentious in today's international political arena').

[281] See DEWA website, www.unep.org/dewa/Home/tabid/3081/Default.aspx (accessed 26 March 2012).

[282] See UNEP-PCDMB website, www.unep.org/conflictsanddisasters/ (accessed 26 March 2012).

post-conflict situations, it does not seem implausible for an environment-conflict EW unit to be set up within its remit.[283] Moreover, a global environment-conflict EW system requires an effective EW network where various actors, from other UN agencies to participation from local actors (as eyes and ears on the ground) are needed to collect the necessary information to anticipate armed conflict. UNEP, which already has a good track record in post-conflict cooperative efforts with various actors and publishing numerous studies, assessments and reports through its PCDMB,[284] thus appears to be the best suited body to coordinate and monitor this global environment-conflict EW system. Such an environmental-conflict EW system in cooperation with other EW systems dealing with other variable issues within certain societies, States or regions could certainly contribute towards sustainable development and conflict-prevention efforts.

Nonetheless, if a specific environment-conflict EW system is not feasible due to logistical and financial limitations, then as UNEP concluded in its 2009 'From Conflict to Peacebuilding' Report, the international community should ensure that natural resource and environmental issues are effectively incorporated into any broader international and regional EW systems.[285] To not do so, would mean that potential conflict-inducing environmental factors could be missed or overlooked as it may be overshadowed by other variable factors.

As the international community does not as of yet have a comprehensive global EW conflict-prevention system, it comes down to collective conflict-prevention efforts and more cohesive integration and cooperation between all actors that have EW systems – ranging from international, regional, sub-regional to local systems. In fact, despite the lack of a global environment-conflict EW system, other actors that have EW systems have incorporated environment-inducing conflict factors into their systems. IGAD for example, which looks out for States within the Horn of Africa, not only aims to achieve regional food security, the sustainable development of natural resources and environmental protection, combat the consequences of drought and other disasters, but also to

---

[283]   Ibid.

[284]   See 'UNEP in the Regions', www.unep.org/conflictsanddisasters/UNEPintheRegions/tabid/286/language/en-US/Default.aspx (accessed 10 May 2012).

[285]   See UNEP Conflict to Peacebuilding (n 4) at p. 28.

actively engage in conflict prevention efforts within its regional borders.[286] This is a good example of an EW system embracing the concept of sustainable development. To achieve its objectives, IGAD has established it own Conflict Early Warning and Response Mechanism (CEWARN) which aims to prevent cross-border pastoral conflicts, enable local populations to participate in conflict prevention, provide its members with financial and technical support as well as proceeding with the necessary conflict prevention efforts.[287] Given the pervasiveness of conflict in Africa, particularly environmentally related, an EW system within a sub-regional organisation such as IGAD is invaluable. The international community and the UN in particular, should assist and cooperate with such organisations to ensure more effective conflict prevention efforts. As seen from the case-studies, ineffective governance and resulting poor environmental policies have worsened environmental problems which have contributed to conflict. Therefore a better and more systematic EW network utilising the sustainable development concept is necessary for the international community to translate for example, any EW environmental-conflict indicators into early preventive action. As UNEP recommends:

[t]he UN system needs to strengthen its capacity to deliver early warning and early action in countries that are vulnerable to conflicts over natural resources and environmental issues. At the same time, the effective governance of natural resources and the environment should be viewed as an investment in conflict prevention within the development process itself.[288]

To sum it up, 'successful prevention can only be achieved by developing a strong system of early warning, backed by better international tools to tackle the drivers of conflict when they first arise.'[289] Early warning is rendered useless without early action. The international community must therefore enhance their conflict prevention strategies by improving and

---

[286]   Schmeidl, S., 'Conflict Early Warning and Prevention: Toward a Coherent Terminology' in Mwaûra, C. and Schmeidl, S. (eds), *Early Warning and Conflict Management in the Horn of Africa* (The Red Sea, New Jersey 2002) at p. 74.

[287]   Maitima, J. and others, 'Horn of Africa: Responding to Changing Markets in a Context of Increased Competition for Resources' in Gerber, P., Mooney, H. and Dijkman, J. (eds), *Livestock in a Changing Landscape, Volume 2: Experiences and Regional Perspectives* (Island Press, Washington DC, 2010) at p. 19.

[288]   UNEP Conflict to Peacebuilding (n 4) at p. 28.

[289]   UK: Foreign and Commonwealth Office, 'Human Rights Annual Report 2007' Presented to Parliament on March 2008 (Stationary Office, UK 2008) at p. 30.

strengthening their EW system to go hand in hand with early action efforts. This is imperative particularly in relation to States that have low adaptive capacities to deal with environmental pressures and natural resources and thus, may be more prone to conflict. By taking such integrated action, the international community would have stepped up their preventive approach towards environmental protection and conflict-prevention by taking into account all variable factors in such vulnerable societies in the light of the much broader objective of sustainable development. As the UN Secretary-General Ban Ki Moon states, not only '[i]n today's world, prevention must go beyond mere diplomacy'[290] but also that '[c]onflict prevention and sustainable development reinforced each other'.[291]

5. CONCLUSION

There is no doubt that there is a link between environmental pressures and armed conflict. Of course such conflicts have to be viewed with a broad perspective, prioritising not only resource and environmental issues, but also taking into consideration the relationship between these issues and armed conflict in combination with other pre-existing socio-economic, development and political variables within the broader frame-work of sustainable development. While it is not likely that societies would erupt into conflict solely over environmental stresses, such stresses are becoming increasingly crucial triggering or fuelling factors of violent conflict.

The case-studies highlight the reality of the environment-conflict nexus and the poverty of the international law and policy framework in preventing such armed conflicts. The international community must therefore significantly improve its law and policy framework in relation to conflict-prevention. What the law and policy framework would benefit from is the international community's commitment to sustainable development through collective responsibility, cooperation, common but differentiated responsibilities, integration, intra- and inter-generational equity, public participation, good governance and the precautionary principle. Overall, prevention is a weak link in the holistic approach to the life cycle of armed conflict and the environment. To protect the environment

---

[290]   PR UNSC/9105 (n 238).
[291]   Ibid.

and to 'save succeeding generations from the scourge of war',[292] this weakness must be recognised and prioritised together with other pressing environmental challenges on the international agenda.

---

[292] Preamble, Charter of the United Nations (adopted 26 June 1945, entered into force 24 October 1945) 1 UNTS xvi.

4. Sustainable development and the protection of the environment during times of armed conflict

1. INTRODUCTION

Armed conflict has various short-term and long-term consequences not only on development but also on the environment and human well-being.[1] In fact, from the scorched earth tactics used by the Greeks during the Peloponnesian Wars, the nuclear bomb dropped in Hiroshima in 1945 causing unspeakable human and environmental casualties, to the current yet unaccounted environmental damage and destruction as a result of the ongoing war in Afghanistan – the environment has always been an inevitable casualty of armed conflict. Such conflict 'undercuts or destroys environmental, physical, human and social capital, diminishing available opportunities for sustainable development.'[2] There is no doubt therefore that warfare is inimical to sustainable development. As the International Committee of the Red Cross (ICRC) notes,

> armed conflicts can have a long lasting negative impact on many aspects of sustainable development, be it economic growth, health, education or environment. In recent decades, many armed conflicts have involved a wide range of threats to sustainable development in many countries and societies. The consequences may affect not only belligerents, but also civilians and neutral States; and can sometimes continue long after the end of the armed conflict.[3]

---

[1] Saundry, P., 'Environmental Justice: Environmental and Socioeconomic Impacts of Armed Conflict in Africa' in Cleveland, C.J. (ed), *The Encyclopedia of Earth* (National Council for Science and the Environment, Washington, DC 2008) [hereinafter Saundry].

[2] Ibid.

[3] ICRC, 'International Humanitarian Law and Sustainable Development' Information Paper in the Framework of the World Summit of Sustainable Development, Johannesburg, South Africa (26 August–4 September 2002) [hereinafter ICRC Statement].

This chapter thus reviews laws addressed to mitigating the effects of armed conflict on the environment in the context of sustainable development by exploring two case-studies of international armed conflict (IAC):[4] the First Gulf War and the Kosovo conflict, paying particular attention to the response of the international community, especially the UN. These case-studies, which are different from those explored in the preceding chapter, are chosen because they engage a wide range of relevant laws,[5] to which the international community has made a relatively concerted effort at enforcing (albeit theoretically) in the face of serious risks to the environment.[6]

In this context, the chapter examines issues concerning the legality of the environmental damage caused in these conflicts. When considering war-related environmental harm, the international community tends to deal with it through the laws of armed conflict or international humanitarian law (IHL)[7] which come into play once conflict has begun. Simply

---

[4] A review of international humanitarian law (IHL) protection for the environment in non-international armed conflicts (NIAC) is not within the scope of this book. For a review on IHL rules and principles that may provide environmental protection in NIAC, see, e.g. Roberts, A., 'The Law of War and Environmental Damage' in Austin, J.E., and Bruch, C.E. (eds), *The Environmental Consequences of War: Legal, Economic, and Scientific Perspectives* (CUP, Cambridge 2000) at pp. 76–7 [hereinafter 2000 Roberts], [hereinafter Austin and Bruch (eds)].

[5] The first Gulf War focuses on the Hague Convention (IV) Respecting the Laws and Customs of War on Land (signed 18 October 1907) 36 Stat 2277 [hereinafter Hague IV] and Geneva Convention (IV) Relative to the Protection of Civilian Persons in Time of War (adopted 12 August 1949, entered into force 21 October 1950) 75 UNTS 287 [hereinafter GC IV], as well as applicable customary IHL. The Kosovo conflict, on the other hand, focuses on more specific environmentally related IHL laws such as provisions within the Protocol Additional to the Geneva Conventions of 12 August 1949, and Relating to the Protection of Victims of International Armed Conflicts (adopted 8 June 1977, entered into force 7 December 1978) 1125 UNTS 3 [hereinafter AP I], in addition to the relevant customary IHL principles.

[6] In particular, the Iraq case-study highlights the possibility of State responsibility while the Kosovo case-study presents the possibility of prosecuting or affixing individual liability for war-related environmental harm.

[7] Although the primary focus in this chapter is IHL in the context of environmental protection in armed conflict and the interrelationship with sustainable development, see UNEP, 'Protecting the Environment during Armed Conflict: An Inventory and Analysis of International Law' (UNEP, Switzerland 2009) [hereinafter UNEP International Law] (which in addition to its main focus on IHL, concludes that international environmental law could still be applicable during armed conflict and human rights law may 'provide additional guidance

put, the environment during times of armed conflict is protected by IHL principles relating to the means and methods of warfare and by specific provisions relating to the protection of the environment. As the ICRC points out, if the rules and principles of IHL are 'properly respected, it can therefore significantly contribute to the preservation of sustainable development during armed conflicts.'[8]

As there is already voluminous literature focusing on the protection of the environment in times of armed conflict,[9] this chapter concentrates on IHL laws relevant to the two case-studies chosen. As in the previous chapter, these laws and case-studies are considered in light of the protection of the environment from a sustainable development perspective, with particular reference to salient principles within the umbrella of this concept.

The key to the interrelationship between sustainable development and armed conflict is to ensure that any damage to the environment is not to the extent that sustainable development is unduly obstructed or interrupted in the aftermath of conflict. This means efforts should be made to prevent or mitigate environmental risks as a result of such war-related damage. Damage, which in combination with the breakdown of socio-economic, governance and development conditions, could threaten the livelihoods, health and security of the population and ultimately sustainable development.[10] Conflict-related environmental damage for example could have a direct impact on the livelihoods of a war-torn population by negatively affecting their access to the environment and natural resources as a result of pollution, loss of biodiversity and displacement of the

---

about State conduct affecting the environment and natural resources during armed conflict').

[8]   ICRC Statement (n 3).

[9]   See, e.g. Quénivet, N. and Shah-Davis, S. (eds), *International Law and Armed Conflict: Challenges in the 21st Century* (TMC Asser, The Netherlands 2010) at pp. 123–88 [hereinafter Quénivet and Shah-Davis (eds)]; Jensen, E.T., 'The International Law of Environmental Warfare: Active and Passive Damage During Armed Conflict' (2005) 38 Vanderbilt Journal of Transnational Law 145; Hulme, K., *War Torn Environment: Interpreting the Legal Threshold* (Martinus Nijhoff, Leiden 2004) [hereinafter 2004 Hulme]; Rogers, A.P.V., *Law on the Battlefield* (2nd edn MUP, Manchester 2004) at pp. 106–29 [hereinafter 2004 Rogers]; Green, L.C., *The Contemporary Law of Armed Conflict* (2nd edn MUP, Manchester 2000) at pp. 137–46 [hereinafter Green]; Parsons, R.J., 'The Fight to Save the Planet: US Armed Forces, "Greenkeeping", and Enforcement of the Law Pertaining to Environmental Protection during Armed Conflict' (1998) 10 Georgetown International Environmental Law Review 441.

[10]   UNEP International Law (n 7) at p. 4.

population itself; thereby triggering the vicious cycle of environmental degradation and human vulnerability.[11]

From a holistic sustainable development perspective, vulnerability to the population of the war-torn country 'refers not only to the exposure to negative environmental change, but also to the ability to cope with such change through either adaptation or mitigation.'[12] Armed conflict contributes to the vicious cycle of social disintegration and disruption of local public institutions and governance systems which 'in turn may result in established safety nets becoming unavailable.'[13] As seen in Chapter 3, such conflict also heightens socio-economic vulnerability which with the added pressure of environmental degradation, may exacerbate tensions and trigger further conflict over access to vital resources necessary for the survival and livelihoods of the war-torn population. The consequences of armed conflict do not stop there. As Saundry comments,

> [t]he incidence of poverty may increase, not only through the loss of livelihoods but also as a result of a growing inability of people to cope with change. This loss of resilience is also directly linked to diminished access to public services, resulting in, for example, an increasing incidence of ill health, a contraction in formal employment opportunities, the destruction of subsistence livelihoods, and other entitlements failures which affect consumption and nutrition, as well as the weakening of social cohesion and heightening insecurity.[14]

Therefore, in respect of this potential obstruction to sustainable development, the rules and principles of IHL which protect the environment during actual armed conflict play a crucial role. Moreover, taking into consideration the overarching concept of sustainable development, protecting the environment in times of armed conflict embodies in particular, the principles of precaution and intra- and inter-generational equity. The former, by the fact that the risks and consequences of war-caused environmental damage could include scientifically unknown long-term or irreversible harm. In this context, the precautionary principle should not only be taken into account during times of armed conflict, but also in the application of the relevant rules and principles of IHL 'since the duty to

---

[11] Saundry (n 1).
[12] Ibid.
[13] Ibid.
[14] Ibid.

prevent environmental damage is not suspended by the outbreak of hostilities.'[15] As the UN Secretary-General comments,

> it is not easy to know in advance exactly what the scope and duration of some environmentally damaging acts will be; and there is a need to limit as far as possible environmental damage even in cases where it is not certain to meet a strict interpretation of the criteria of 'widespread, long-term and severe'.[16]

With regard to the need to take into account the principle of intra- and inter-generational equity in times of armed conflict, this goes to the heart of the matter as to why we protect the environment in the first place, that is, for the most part, we protect the environment for the benefit of the human population.[17] In the context of armed conflict, there is the notion or expectation that the environment should not be damaged or destroyed to such an extent that both the present and future generations are unable to enjoy and utilise it in the aftermath of war.[18] Furthermore, such conflict-related environmental damage could not only have consequences for many generations to come, but it could also be an additional economic burden on the war-torn country that is already suffering from collapsed institutions and unstable socio-economic conditions; thereby adding obstacles to sustainable development in the aftermath of conflict.

This chapter thus begins by presenting in Section 2, the laws of armed conflict applicable to the protection of the environment during armed conflict (particularly those pertinent to the case-studies); Section 3 explores the First Gulf War; Section 4 reviews the Kosovo conflict; and Section 5 briefly considers recommendations for reform. The relevant IHL rules and principles in relation to their scope in protecting the environment during armed conflict are considered from a sustainable development perspective.

---

[15] Desgagné, R., 'The Prevention of Environmental Damage in Time of Armed Conflict: Proportionality and Precautionary Measures' (2000) 3 Yearbook of International Humanitarian Law 109, at p. 124 [hereinafter Desgagné].

[16] UNGA, 'Report of the Secretary-General on the Protection of the Environment in Times of Armed Conflict' UN Doc A/48/269 (29 July 1993) at p. 7, para. 34.

[17] 2004 Hulme (n 9) at pp. 14–15 (argues that while some do want to protect the environment for its intrinsic value, generally 'the bulk of environmental protection measures are borne out of selfish, anthropocentric motives').

[18] Weiss, E.B., 'Environmentally Sustainable Competitiveness: A Comment' (1993) 102 Yale Law Journal 2123 ('sustainable development implies that future generations have as much right as the present generation to a robust environment with which to meet their own needs and preferences').

2. OVERVIEW OF IHL RELATING TO ENVIRONMENTAL PROTECTION IN ARMED CONFLICT

Before delving into the IHL rules and principles providing protection to the environment, it is worth highlighting the jurisprudence relating to environmental protection in armed conflict. International organisations and NGOs have also contributed to the development of such environmental protection. For example, from the International Law Commission's (ILC) proposals in its 1996 Draft Code of Crimes Against Peace and Security of Mankind,[19] the ICRC's 1994 Guidelines for Military Manuals and Instructions on the Protection of the Environment in Times of Armed Conflict,[20] to the International Union for Conservation of Nature's (IUCN) Draft Convention on the Prohibition of Hostile Military Activities in Protected Areas.[21] Of particular relevance in this instance, is the ICJ's recognition of protection of the environment during armed conflict. One of the most important cases where the ICJ not only recognised but also further contributed to the development of environmental protection in armed conflict is in its 1996 *Nuclear Weapons Advisory Opinion.*[22]

---

[19] For the text, analytical guide and summary, see ILC, 'Draft code of crimes against peace and security of mankind (Part II) – including the draft statute for an international criminal court' (last updated 18 May 2010) http://untreaty.un.org/ilc/texts/7_4.htm (accessed 7 April 2012). For further discussion on its relevance to environmental protection in armed conflict, see Brauch, H.G., 'War Impacts on the Environment in the Mediterranean and Evolution of International Law' in Brauch, H.G. and others (eds), *Security and Environment in the Mediterranean: Conceptualising Security and Environmental Conflicts* (Springer-Verlag, Germany 2003) [hereinafter Brauch War Impacts], [hereinafter 2003 Brauch (eds)] at p. 507.

[20] UN General Assembly (UNGA), without formally adopting these guidelines, invited States to disseminate it widely. See (1996) 311 International Review of the Red Cross 230 at pp. 230–37. For further discussion, see Brauch War Impacts (n 19) at pp. 507–508.

[21] See IUCN, www.iucn.org/ (accessed 7 April 2012). See also Tarasofsky, R.G., 'Protecting specially important areas during international armed conflict: a critique of the IUCN Draft Convention on the Prohibition of Hostile Military Activities in Protected Areas' in Austin and Bruch (eds) (n 4) at pp. 567–8.

[22] *Legality of the Threat or Use of Nuclear Weapons* (Advisory Opinion) [1996] ICJ Rep 226 [hereinafter Nuclear Weapons]. For further discussion on other ICJ cases that provide some reference to protection of the environment in armed conflict, see UNEP International Law (n 7) at pp. 24–6.

In the *Nuclear Weapons* Advisory Opinion, the ICJ recognises that to a certain extent, the environment is protected in times of armed conflict. First, the Court acknowledges that 'the environment is under daily threat' and 'that the environment is not an abstraction but represents the living space, the quality of life and the very health of human beings, including generations unborn.'[23] Second, the ICJ took the opportunity to reaffirm the customary status of the *Trail Smelter* Principle by stating that '[t]he existence of the general obligation of States to ensure that activities within their jurisdiction and control respect the environment of other States or of areas beyond national control is now part of the corpus of international law relating to the environment.'[24] Third, the Court instructs States to take into account environmental considerations when determining the necessity and proportionality of any legitimate military action. The Court recognises that, '[r]espect for the environment is one of the elements that go to assessing whether an action is in conformity with the principles of necessity and proportionality.'[25] In addition, the ICJ makes further reference to Principle 24 of the Rio Declaration that, '[w]arfare is inherently destructive of sustainable development. States shall therefore respect international law providing protection for the environment in times of armed conflict'.[26] Fourth, in respect of Articles 35(3) and 55 of the1977 Protocol Additional to the Geneva Conventions of 12 August 1949, and relating to the Protection of Victims of International Armed Conflicts (AP I),[27] the ICJ states that,

> [t]aken together, these provisions embody a general obligation to protect the natural environment against widespread, long-term and severe environmental damage; the prohibition of methods and means of warfare which are intended, or may be expected, to cause such damage; and the prohibition of attacks against the natural environment by way of reprisals. These are powerful constraints for all States having subscribed to these provisions.[28]

---

[23] *Nuclear Weapons* (n 22) at para. 29.

[24] Ibid.

[25] Ibid., at para 30.

[26] Ibid.

[27] AP I was adopted in 1977 as a supplement to remedy the shortcomings within the 1949 Geneva Conventions. See ICRC, 'Factsheet on the 1977 Protocols Additional to the Geneva Conventions' (updated 31 May 2007), www.icrc.org/web/eng/siteeng0.nsf/html/protocols-1977-factsheet-080607 (accessed 7 April 2012).

[28] *Nuclear Weapons* (n 22) at para 31.

Fifth, the ICJ concludes in this Opinion 'that the threat or use of nuclear weapons would generally be contrary to the rules of international law applicable to armed conflict, and in particular the principles and rules of humanitarian law'.[29] However, that being said, the ICJ went on to unanimously state that due to the current position of international law, it 'cannot conclude definitely whether the threat or use of nuclear weapons would be lawful or unlawful in an extreme circumstance of self-defence, in which the very survival of the State would be at stake.'[30]

The ICJ's conclusions in the *Nuclear Weapons* Advisory Opinion do suggest to some extent guidelines for the protection of the environment in armed conflict. Moreover, the Court encourages States to respect the environment in times of armed conflict. The extent of the respect towards the environment however, remains unclear. At the very least, as the UNEP International Law Report suggests, the customary obligation of States having to ensure that actions in areas within their control do not cause transboundary environmental harm should be applicable in times of armed conflict.[31] Regrettably, the maximum limit or threshold of environmental harm permitted during armed conflict, 'is much less certain, as in this regard the gaps in the law seem to prevent a decision on the question of the use of weapons of mass destruction in extreme scenarios of self-defence.'[32]

Another organisation that should be considered in this context is the ILA and its 2004 Berlin Rules on Water Resources [hereinafter Berlin Rules][33] in particular. The ILA has made major contributions to international law and in this case, international water law specifically.[34] The ILA's Berlin Rules clearly and comprehensively set out an up-to-date assessment of environmental practices on the progressively developing

---

[29] Ibid., at para. 105E.

[30] Ibid.

[31] UNEP International Law (n 7) at p. 25.

[32] Ibid.

[33] Adopted by the ILA at its Seventy-First Conference (Berlin, 2004). The Berlin Rules were adopted to replace the 1966 Helsinki Rules on the Uses of the Waters of International Rivers [hereinafter Helsinki Rules], adopted by the ILA at its Fifty-Second Conference (Helsinki, 1966). For further discussion on the Helsinki Rules, see Salman, S.M.A., 'The Helsinki Rules, the UN Watercourses Convention and the Berlin Rules: Perspectives on International Water Law' (2007) 23 Water Resources Development 625, at pp. 629–31 [hereinafter Salman].

[34] Salman (n 33) at pp. 625–6 and p. 635 (coverage provided by the Berlin Rules extends well beyond the Helsinki Rules and the 1997 UN Convention on the Law of Non-Navigational Uses of International Watercourses).

area of international water law and management,[35] covering not only international fresh surface waters and groundwaters (aquatic environment)[36] but also waters within the national boundaries of a State. The rules include applicable principles of international law such as public participation;[37] the precautionary approach;[38] the obligation for States to use their best efforts to manage such waters;[39] the obligation to take measures to manage waters sustainably[40] and minimise environmental harm;[41] to identifying the rights and duties of States[42] and individual persons.[43] The Rules also require States to undertake the necessary environmental impact assessments;[44] cover extreme situations including pollution accidents, floods and droughts;[45] as well as incorporating extended consideration of IHL rules relevant to the protection of water and water installations during times of armed conflict.[46] The rules are non-binding and are at present intended to be more of a guidance framework in this area.[47]

The Berlin Rules are an important addition to the development of laws relating to environmental protection during armed conflict because in

---

[35]   Dellapenna, J.W., 'The Berlin Rules on Water Resources: A New Paradigm for International Water Law' Statement at the Proceedings of the 2006 World Environmental and Water Resources Congress (Omaha, Nebraska, USA 21–25 May 2006) [hereinafter 2006 Dellapenna]; Staddon, C., *Managing Europe's Water Resources: Twenty-first Century Challenges* (Ashgate, England/USA 2010) at p. 51 [hereinafter Staddon]. *Cf.* ILA, 'Water Resources Committee Report: Dissenting Opinion' ILA Berlin Conference (Berlin, 9 August 2004) (4 out of the 22 members of the ILA Water Resources Committee argue that the rules proposed by the Committee marks 'a radical and unwarranted departure from existing customary law').

[36]   Art. 3, Berlin Rules.
[37]   Arts. 4, 10, 18, 30, Berlin Rules.
[38]   Art. 23, Berlin Rules.
[39]   Arts. 5 and 6, Berlin Rules.
[40]   Art. 7, Berlin Rules.
[41]   Art. 8, Berlin Rules.
[42]   Art. 68, Berlin Rules.
[43]   Art. 17, Berlin Rules.
[44]   Arts. 29–31, Berlin Rules.
[45]   Arts. 32–35, Berlin Rules.
[46]   Arts. 50–55, Berlin Rules.
[47]   See ILA, 'Water Resources Law' Fourth Report of the Berlin Conference (ILA, Berlin 2004) at p. 4 [hereinafter Berlin Water Report] (The majority of the Committee conclude that these progressively developed Berlin Rules 'will become settled customary international law in the near future, [and as such] all *Rules* are expressed as present legal obligations ("shall")').

times of such conflict, water can not only be used as a military target or as with other elements of the environment become an invariable victim of collateral damage, but it can also become a source of conflict due to its increasing scarcity. Fresh water sources polluted as a result of armed conflict can severely disrupt sustainable development by damaging the environment and harming the civilian population. Such pollution can disrupt the livelihoods of civilians on many levels, from disrupting economic or industrial activities to affecting the health and survival of the population, thereby increasing human vulnerability by decreasing access to fresh water. Chapter X of the Berlin Rules provides protection for waters and water installations during war or armed conflict,[48] from prohibiting combatants from poisoning water indispensable for the survival of civilians;[49] setting limits on targeting water or water installations[50] including dams and dikes[51] during conflict to prevent widespread, long-term and severe ecological harm prejudicial to the civilian population;[52] stipulating obligations of an occupying State regarding water resources;[53] to stating that peacetime water related treaties are still applicable during times of warfare subject to military necessity.[54]

The Berlin Rules, in reviewing international water law for both peacetime and armed conflict, have thus provided additional standards of protection towards fresh water sources in times of conflict.[55] Furthermore, as Jorgensen put it, '[a]lthough the Berlin Rules do not extend the

---

[48] For commentary on Chapter X provisions, see Berlin Water Report (n 47) at pp. 43–5

[49] Art. 50, Berlin Rules. The prohibition of poisoning drinking water is part of customary international law. This principle is also reflected in Art. 23(a), Hague IV and Art. 54, AP I.

[50] Art. 51, Berlin Rules. This article reflects the general principle of proportionality in armed conflict. See Berlin Water Report (n 47) at p. 43.

[51] Art. 53, Berlin Rules. Also reflected in Arts. 56(1) and (2), AP I.

[52] Art. 52, Berlin Rules. Also reflected in Arts. 35 and 55, AP I.

[53] Art. 54, Berlin Rules. By requiring an occupying State to ensure sustainable use of water resources and to minimise environmental harm, this article extends the duties set out in Art. 55, GC IV, which stipulates obligations of an occupying power regarding food and medical supplies for the population. See Berlin Water Report (n 47) at p. 45.

[54] Art. 55, Berlin Rules. See Berlin Water Report (n 47) at p. 45.

[55] Jorgensen, N., 'The Protection of Freshwater in Armed Conflict' (2007) 3 Journal of International Law & International Relations 57, at p. 89.

primary norms applicable to fresh water in armed conflicts, they contribute to raising awareness'[56] and as such, add to the consciousness of the international community as to the level of water-related environmental damage that is not acceptable in times of conflict. This is an important advance in the protection of water and the aquatic environment as a whole. In addition, in the process, this contributes to the cycle of sustainable development by limiting the damage permitted to this precious natural resource so that it does not threaten peoples' health and livelihoods, as well as mitigating the negative impact on development and the environment itself.

Focusing again on the rules and provisions within IHL that provide environmental protection in armed conflict, numerous scholars argue that there are very few IHL laws that specifically do so.[57] This in itself goes against the concept of sustainable development because once armed conflict is set in motion, the only way to achieve or continue the cycle of sustainable development is to alleviate the destructive impact of such conflict.[58] In this regard, the rules and principles of IHL are the only guardians standing between the environment and conflict-related destruction. Unfortunately, only one treaty, the 1976 Convention on the Prohibition of Military or Any Other Hostile Use of Environmental Modification Techniques (ENMOD),[59] and a couple of provisions within AP I are specifically designed to protect the environment during armed conflict. This could indicate a limited degree of interest in protecting the environment in armed conflict or as with any other area in relation to the environment, environmental awareness let alone development of environmental protection have been slow and gradual. In the field of armed conflict and IHL where the environment is clearly not top priority, it is perhaps not surprising that such development is limited. Nevertheless, it is equally necessary to have regard to other non-specific environmental norms which do nonetheless converge on the present subject matter, notably the Hague Regulations.[60]

---

[56] Ibid.

[57] See (n 9) above.

[58] Das, O., 'The Impact of Armed Conflict on Sustainable Development: A Holistic Approach' in Quénivet and Shah-Davis (eds) (n 9) at p. 133.

[59] (Adopted 10 December 1976, entered into force 18 May 1977), 167 ILM 88 [hereinafter ENMOD].

[60] Hague IV; Hague Convention (II) with Respect to the Laws and Customs of War on Land (29 July 1899) 32 Stat 1803 [hereinafter Hague II].

The first of the two conventions dealing explicitly with the environment – ENMOD,[61] does not essentially deal with damage to the environment during armed conflict but with the deliberate manipulation of the natural environment. ENMOD is thus limited in its scope of application.[62] ENMOD protects the environment from being used as a weapon during armed conflict by prohibiting military or any other hostile use of 'environmental modification techniques[63] having widespread, long-lasting or severe effects as the means of destruction, damage or injury to any other State Party.'[64] Thus, ENMOD has a threshold set up, becoming applicable only if in a given situation, the environment is manipulated causing either widespread, long-lasting *or* severe effects in the alternative.[65] This means acts manipulating the environment can only be considered unlawful if the environmental damage encompasses several hundred square kilometres, takes place over a period of months (approximately a season) or involves 'serious or significant disruption or harm to human life, natural and economic resources or other assets.'[66] The latter arguably embodying some elements of the sustainable development concept.

---

[61] ENMOD was formulated in response to US attempts during the Vietnam War to manipulate the environment as a weapon, the ensuing environmental destruction and the growing awareness that advances in technology could cause greater harm to the environment. See Schwabach, A., *International Environmental Disputes: A Reference Handbook* (ABC-CLIO, California 2006) at p. 200 [hereinafter 2006 Schwabach].

[62] For further discussion on ENMOD, see, e.g. Hulme, K., 'Natural Environment' in Wilmhurst, E. and Breau, S. (eds), *Perspectives on the ICRC Study on Customary International Humanitarian Law* (CUP, Cambridge 2007) at pp. 233–6 [hereinafter 2007 Hulme], [hereinafter Wilmhurst and Breau (eds)]; Yuzon, E.F.J., 'Deliberate Environmental Modification Through the Use of Chemical and Biological Weapons: "Greening" the International Laws of Armed Conflict to Establish an Environmentally Protective Regime' (1996) 11 American University Journal of International Law and Policy 793, at pp. 804–9 [hereinafter Yuzon].

[63] 'Refers to any technique for changing – through the deliberate manipulation of natural processes – the dynamics, composition or structure of the Earth, including its biota, lithosphere, hydrosphere and atmosphere, or of outer space.' See Art. II, ENMOD. For further clarification as to the type of phenomena that could be caused by environmental modification techniques, see Understanding to Article II, ENMOD.

[64] Art. 1, ENMOD.

[65] Ibid.

[66] See Understanding to ENMOD.

In the event the Convention is breached, ENMOD does not have provisions that specifically set out liability for State Parties that violate it. However, under Article V, State Parties are required to consult and cooperate with each other to solve any problems arising from this Convention.[67] In addition, State Parties suspecting other State Parties of breaching the Convention are encouraged to lodge a complaint with the UN Security Council (UNSC) and proceed to cooperate with the UNSC in any subsequent investigation.[68] State Parties also undertake to assist any State Party that 'has been harmed or is likely to be harmed as a result of violation of the Convention.'[69] Although ENMOD does not afford direct liability for breaches of the convention, it does provide means of consultation, cooperation, investigation and assistance for any problems or breaches that arise. Thereby, providing State Parties with the means to potentially prevent or minimise harm to the environment. Thus ENMOD, with its requirements to cooperate and take preventive precautionary measures as well as the precautionary nature of the Convention as a whole, does in particular embody elements of the 'common but differentiated responsibilities'[70] and 'precautionary' principles. The former, in light of the cooperative elements within the Convention and the latter, by the fact that ENMOD aims to protect the environment from being manipulated as a weapon potentially causing scientifically uncertain serious or irreversible environmental harm or effects.

The other relevant convention – AP I[71] has provisions: Articles 35 and 55[72] that deal specifically with the issue of damage to the natural environment. Within AP I, Article 35(1) imposes limitations on the conduct of warfare and Article 35(3) prohibits the employment of 'methods and means of warfare which are intended, or may be expected,

---

[67]   Art. V(1), ENMOD.

[68]   Art. V (3), ENMOD.

[69]   Art. V(5), ENMOD.

[70]   See, e.g. French, D., *International Law and Policy of Sustainable Development* (MUP, Manchester 2005) at pp. 69–70 (on the duty to co-operate).

[71]   AP I was also formulated after the consequences of the Vietnam War. See 2006 Schwabach (n 61).

[72]   These two provisions are complementary. For detailed commentary, see Sandoz, Y. and others (eds), *Commentary on the Protocol Additional to the Geneva Conventions of 12 August 1949, and relating to the Protection of Victims of International Armed Conflicts (Protocol I)* (Martinus Nijhoff, Geneva 1987) [hereinafter Sandoz] at pp. 389–420 (for Art. 35) and pp. 661–4 (for Art. 55).

to cause widespread, long-term and severe damage to the natural environment.'[73] The prohibition set out in Article 35(3) is absolute and 'it even continues to apply in the absence of any direct threat to the population or to the flora and fauna of the enemy State. It is the natural environment itself that is protected. It is common property, and should be retained for everyone's use and be preserved.'[74] Article 35 thus not only protects the environment for its intrinsic value but also acknowledges that the environment is of common concern to mankind and should be protected during armed conflict; thereby exemplifying elements of the intra- and inter-generational equity principle. Elements of the precautionary principle are also embodied in this Article in that limits are placed on the means and methods of warfare where there are uncertain risks or threats of serious or irreversible environmental harm in the form of 'widespread, long-term and severe damage to the natural environment'.

Similarly, Article 55 refers specifically to environmental damage but with a further link to humanitarian concerns. Article 55(1) stipulates that, '[c]are shall be taken in warfare to protect the natural environment against widespread, long-term and severe damage. This protection includes a prohibition of the use of methods or means of warfare which are intended or may be expected, to cause such damage to the natural environment and thereby to prejudice the health or survival of the population.' Article 55(2) goes on to prohibit '[a]ttacks against the natural environment by way of reprisals.' From an anthropocentric point of view, Article 55 embodies elements of the precautionary principle in protecting the environment during armed conflict by placing limits on the means and methods of warfare to prevent or mitigate the threat of serious or irreversible damage to the environment, which may also cause harm to the human population.

Although these articles within AP I theoretically provide specific environmental protection obligations during armed conflict and embody elements of the principles under the overarching concept of sustainable development, these principles and ultimately sustainable development are somewhat obstructed by the stringent criteria set out in Articles 35 and 55. Unfortunately, for any environmental damage to be prohibited, the damage must reach the threshold criteria of AP I: 'widespread, long-term

---

[73] AP I does not provide the definition of 'natural environment'. However, the ICRC commentary suggests that '[t]he concept of natural environment should be understood in the widest sense to cover the biological environment in which a population is living' which includes 'fauna, flora and other biological or climatic elements.' See Sandoz (n 72) at p. 662 (commentary on Art. 55).

[74] Ibid., at p. 420 (commentary on Art. 35).

and severe' cumulatively.[75] Therefore, though innovative by directly protecting the environment intrinsically during warfare, these provisions within AP I with their high cumulative threshold of harm, would be difficult to apply in practice.[76]

In attaching liability for causing environmental harm during armed conflict for breaches of relevant AP I provisions,[77] Article 86 imposes criminal liability on military superiors for their failure to prevent or repress breaches to the Conventions and AP I if it was within their power to do so; Article 87 obliges military commanders to prevent, suppress, and report breaches of the Convention and to initiate disciplinary action where appropriate; and Article 91 attaches responsibility to State Parties for any violations of the Conventions and AP I by its armed forces as well as requiring States to be liable for compensation if the situation demands it. This means that breaches of the environmental provisions of Articles 35 and 55 of AP I could entail criminal and civil liability in certain circumstances. In addition, these provisions of liability could be seen as encouraging some level of precaution in causing damage to the environment in times of armed conflict.

Nevertheless, despite ENMOD and AP I providing the most direct environmental protection in armed conflict to date, not all States involved in the conflicts examined in the case-studies below are contracting parties to either of them.[78] It is therefore necessary to explore other means to

---

[75] Legal scholars maintain that the threshold criteria of AP I: 'widespread, long-term *and* severe' is open to interpretation. 'Long-term' is interpreted as a period of decades but thus far, there has been no agreement as to the interpretation of the terms 'widespread' and 'severe'. See Sandoz (n 72) at p. 417 (commentary on Art. 35).

[76] It appears that the authors of AP I did not intend 'acts of warfare which cause short-term damage to the natural environment' and 'battlefield damage incidental to conventional warfare' to be normally prohibited by these provisions. 'What the article is primarily directed to is thus such damage as would be likely to prejudice, over a long term, the continued survival of the civilian population or would risk causing major health problems.' See Sandoz (n 72) at p. 417 (commentary on Art. 35) referring to the Rapporteur's Report, *O.R.* XV 268, CDDH/215/Rev.1, para. 27.

[77] It is worth noting that Art. 82, AP I requires State parties to ensure legal advisors are available to advise military commanders when necessary and Art. 83, AP I requires State Parties to disseminate the Geneva Conventions and this Protocol as widely as possible.

[78] For example, Iraq is not party to AP I and is only a signatory to ENMOD. See Iraq, 'IHL – Treaties and Documents' ICRC, www.icrc.org/ihl.nsf/ Pays?ReadForm&c=IQ (accessed 7 April 2012). The USA has ratified ENMOD

bind those parties, via conventions or provisions which may not specifically protect the environment in armed conflict but that may be used to
indirectly do so. The following section thus briefly presents the relevant
provisions within the Hague Regulations of 1899 (Hague II) and 1907
(Hague IV), the fourth Geneva Convention of 1949 (GC IV) and then
examines customary IHL applicable to the protection of the environment.
Both the Hague[79] and Geneva Conventions[80] are now considered to be
part of customary international law and accordingly, they are binding on
all States.[81]

The Hague Regulations do not have provisions that directly protect the
environment in armed conflict but they do have provisions that limit the
means and methods of warfare.[82] Such provisions may indirectly protect
the environment. Article 23(g) of Hague IV for example, prohibits the
destruction or seizure of enemy property 'unless such destruction or
seizure be imperatively demanded by the necessities of war.'[83] This
provision, by prohibiting the destruction or seizure of enemy property
subject to military necessity, in addition to limiting the damage to
property of the conflict-State itself, could perhaps prevent or minimise

---

but is only a signatory to AP I. See USA, 'IHL – Treaties and Documents' ICRC
www.icrc.org/ihl.nsf/Pays?ReadForm&c=US (accessed 7 April 2012).

[79]   The 1907 Hague Regulations were first recognised as reflecting customary international law in Nuremberg. See the *Judgement of Nuremberg International Military Tribunal* 1946 (1947) 41 American Journal of International
Law 172, at pp. 248–9. This was echoed by *Judgement of the International
Military Tribunal for the Far East (Tokyo)* 1948 [1949] Ad 356, at p. 366. Their
customary status was recently reaffirmed by the ICJ. See *Case Concerning
Armed Activities on the Territory of the Congo (DRC v Uganda)* [2005] ICJ Rep
1, at p. 70, para. 217.

[80]   For further discussion on the customary nature of the Geneva Conventions, see Meron, T., 'The Geneva Conventions as Customary Law' (1987) 81
American Journal of International Law 348.

[81]   For affirmation of the customary status of these Conventions, see
Henckaerts, J-M. and Doswald-Beck, L., *Customary International Humanitarian
Law: Volume I* (CUP, New York 2005) [hereinafter Henckaerts and Doswald-
Beck]; Wilmhurst and Breau (eds) (n 62).

[82]   Art. 22, Hague II; Art. 22, Hague IV.

[83]   See, e.g. *US v List* (The 'Hostages Case') (1949) 11 CCL No. 10 Trials
1230 at pp. 1295–7 (in WWII, German General Rendulic, to evade advancing
Russian troops, adopted a scorched earth policy in Norway. General Rendulic
also ordered the evacuation of all inhabitants in the province of Finland and
destroyed all villages and surrounding facilities. The Nuremberg Military Tribunal charged Rendulic with wanton destruction of property but later acquitted him
on the basis that military necessity justified his actions).

potential environmental harm that may be caused by such destruction or seizure.[84] Such protection for the natural and non-natural environment in turn, could indirectly mitigate the impact on human vulnerability both environmentally and socio-economically.

The environment is also indirectly protected by Article 55 of Hague IV which states that, '[t]he occupying State shall be regarded only as administrator and usufructuary of public buildings, real estate, forests, and agricultural estates belonging to the hostile State, and situated in the occupied territory. [The occupying State] must safeguard the capital of these properties, and administer them in accordance with the rules of usufruct.'[85] This provision allows the occupying State to use and benefit from public property in the occupied territory, but prohibits 'permanent alteration or destruction of it.'[86] Therefore, 'an occupier may reasonably exploit natural resources in occupied territory, but may not act irresponsibly or maliciously in doing so.'[87] Schmitt also argues that this provision 'is limited to abuse or destruction of the four categories delineated.'[88]

---

[84]   UNEP International Law (n 7) at p. 16 ('"enemy property" could include protected areas, environmental goods and natural resources'). See also 2004 Hulme (n 9) at p. 177 (where Art. 23(g) was considered in the context of the Kuwaiti oil-wells in the First Gulf War).

[85]   Art. 55, Hague II; Art. 55, Hague IV.

[86]   Schmitt, M.N., 'War and the Environment: Fault Lines in the Prescriptive Landscape' in Austin and Bruch (eds) (n 4) at p. 95 [hereinafter 2000 Schmitt].

[87]   Ibid.

[88]   Schmitt, M.N., 'Green War: An Assessment of the Environmental Law of International Armed Conflict' (1997) 22 Yale Journal of International Law 1, at p. 64 [hereinafter 1997 Schmitt]. See also 2004 Hulme (n 9) at p. 118: '[t]his provision allows the occupying state to exploit the fruits (literally) of these environmental components but does not allow the wholesale destruction of the assets'; Perez, A.F., 'Legal Frameworks for Economic Transition in Iraq – Occupation under the Law of War vs. Global Governance under the Law of Peace' (2004) 18 Transnational Lawyer 53, at p. 55: provides a broader interpretation of this provision by stating that, '[a]lthough the language is not clear, it seems well-understood internationally and even acknowledged by the United States that these rules, at the very least, cover the exploitation of all state-owned natural resources in the occupied territory – including oil'; *Rules of Land Warfare 1914: Issue 467 of Document, US War Department* (Kessinger, USA 2004) at pp. 124–6: lists properties that must be administered by the occupying State in accordance with the rules of usufruct as well as examples of what the occupying State may utilise. For instance, the occupying State as an administrator or usufructuary, may not be negligent or wasteful so as to 'seriously impair its value' but 'may, however, lease or utilize public lands or buildings, sell the crops, cut and sell timber, and work the mines.'

Nevertheless, this article does contribute to the sustainable development cycle in that its limits could mitigate the negative impact on not only the environment but also on the development and human well-being of the occupied State.

In relation to liability mechanisms, the Hague Regulations set out State responsibility for violations of its provisions. For instance, Article 3 of Hague IV provides that, '[a] belligerent party which violates the provisions of the said Regulations shall, if the case demands, be liable to pay compensation. It shall be responsible for all acts committed by persons forming part of its armed forces.' Therefore, responsible parties may be liable to pay compensation for violation of the Hague provisions that indirectly protect the environment.[89] Moreover, Article 53 of Hague IV also requires an occupying State to restore or pay compensation for seizures of State owned or personal property by an occupying army. Unfortunately, the Convention does not provide for individual criminal liability or any mechanism for enforcing its civil penalties.[90]

There are also incidental provisions for environmental protection during war within GC IV. One of the key provisions of GC IV that provides some form of environmental protection is Article 53 which prohibits the occupying power from destroying real or personal property except when subject to military necessity. This provision provides a similar scope of protection in relation to property as Article 55 of Hague IV. Although Article 53 of GC IV is only limited to destruction by the occupying State within the occupied territory, it does offer some scope for environmental protection especially as environmental damage often occurs in these situations.[91] Therefore, subject to military necessity, destruction of property that may cause damage to the environment – for example, destruction of a chemical factory or an oil-well, may be prohibited.[92]

---

[89] Arts. 23(g) and 55, Hague IV.

[90] Bantekas, I., *Principles of Direct and Superior Responsibility in International Humanitarian Law* (MUP, Manchester 2002) at p. 22.

[91] Damage can occur during an occupying army's retreat from the occupied territory. See, e.g. *The Hostages Case* (n 83) at pp. 1295–7 (the retreating German army (occupying army), adopted scorched earth tactics in Norway (occupied territory) and destroyed villages and surrounding facilities in Finland (occupied territory)).

[92] For further information on the scope of property protected by Art. 53, see 'ICRC Commentary (Art. 53, GC IV)', www.icrc.org/ihl.nsf/COM/380–600060?OpenDocument (accessed 8 April 2012).

The means of attaching liability for breach of Article 53 of GC IV is set out in Articles 146 to 148 of GC IV. The most relevant is Article 147 which provides that 'extensive destruction and appropriation of property, not justified by military necessity and carried out unlawfully and wantonly' is a grave breach of the convention.[93] Thus, a violation of Article 53 becomes a grave breach if the destruction of property involved is 'extensive' and not justified by military necessity. To complete Article 147, Article 146 of GC IV recognises individual criminal responsibility for violation of grave breaches as defined within Article 147.[94] Article 146 thus requires States to pass legislation necessary to provide effective penal sanctions, to carry out searches on individuals alleged to have violated such grave breaches, and also requires States either to try the individual responsible before its own domestic courts or hand him over for trial to another State party.[95] Finally, Article 148 acknowledges State civil liability for grave breaches of the convention, that is, a State remains responsible for and liable to pay compensation for breaches of the convention as set out within Article 147.[96]

IHL treaties are not the only source of environmental protection in armed conflict. Customary principles[97] of IHL may also provide the same. The relevant customary international law principles are the principles of humanity, discrimination, distinction, proportionality and military necessity.[98]

---

[93]   Art. 147, GC IV lists out acts that may amount to grave breaches. For further commentary on 'grave breaches' within this Convention, see 'ICRC Commentary (Art. 147, GC IV)', www.icrc.org/ihl.nsf/COM/380–600169? OpenDocument (accessed 8 April 2012).

[94]   For further commentary, see 'ICRC Commentary (Art. 146, GC IV)', www.icrc.org/ihl.nsf/COM/380–600168?OpenDocument (accessed 8 April 2012).

[95]   Ibid.

[96]   See also 'ICRC Commentary (Art. 148, GC IV)', www.icrc.org/ihl.nsf/ COM/380–600170?OpenDocument (accessed 8 April 2012).

[97]   Customary principles or customary international law 'consists of rules of law derived from the consistent conduct of States acting out of the belief that the law required them to act that way.' See Rosenne, S., *Practice and Methods of International Law* (Oceana, New York 1984) at p. 55.

[98]   For affirmation and further discussion of their customary status, see Henckaerts and Doswald-Beck (n 81); Hensel, H.M. (ed), *The Legitimate Use of Military Force: The Just War Tradition and the Customary Law of Armed Conflict* (Ashgate, UK 2008) at pp. 117–218.

The principle of humanity[99] does not have a defined specific meaning.[100] However, the principle does include, amongst other interpretations, the prohibition of 'methods and means of warfare that are inhumane.'[101] In addition, damage and destruction to the environment during armed conflict should not be to an extent that it causes unnecessary suffering[102] to the human population.[103] Consequently, by protecting human beings and limiting the means and methods of warfare, the principle of humanity may ultimately protect the environment. Undoubtedly, this approach of environmental protection is anthropocentric.

---

[99] The principle of humanity is set out as the 'laws of humanity' in the 1899 Martens Clause which reads, '[u]ntil a more complete code of laws of war is issued, the High Contracting Parties think it right to declare that in cases not included in the Regulations adopted by them, populations and belligerents remain under the protection and empire of the principles of international law, as they result from the usages established between civilized nations, from the laws of humanity, and the requirements of the public conscience.' See Preamble, Hague II. This Clause is meant to fill the gaps of IHL. For example, citing the Martens Clause, the German defence manual states, '[i]f an act of war is not expressly prohibited by international agreements or customary law, this does not necessarily mean that it is actually permissible.' See 'Humanitarian Law in Armed Conflicts-Manual' (Federal Republic of Germany, Federal Ministry of Defense) at para. 129 (ZDv 15/2, 1992).

[100] *Corfu Channel (UK v Albania)* (Merits) [1949] ICJ Rep 4, at p. 22 [hereinafter Corfu Channel] (ICJ's reference to the 'elementary considerations of humanity'). This was reaffirmed in *Nuclear Weapons* (n 22) at p. 257, paras. 78–9 and p. 406 (Dissenting Opinion of Judge Shahabuddeen). For further discussion on this principle, see Meron, T., 'The Martens Clause, Principles of Humanity, and Dictates of Public Conscience' (2000) 94 American Journal of International Law 78, at pp. 82–3.

[101] 1997 Schmitt (n 88) at p. 61.

[102] Unnecessary suffering means that military forces must take all necessary steps to avoid 'inflicting superfluous suffering, injury or destruction causing harm not actually necessary for the accomplishment of legitimate military purposes.' See McClintock, A.D., 'The Law of War: Coalition Attacks on Iraqi Chemical and Biological Weapon Storage and Production Facilities' (1993) 7 Emory International Law Review 633, at p. 645. See also Art. 35(2), AP I which prohibits means and methods of warfare that 'cause superfluous injury or unnecessary suffering.'

[103] 1997 Schmitt (n 88) at pp. 61–2 (on applicability of this principle to the environment).

The principle of distinction imposes upon combatants the legal obligation to distinguish between combatants and civilians and between military objectives and civilian objects.[104] This principle also incorporates the principle of discrimination which specifies that only legitimate military objectives[105] must be targeted. Simply put, the principle of discrimination provides that care must be taken in selecting targets, means and methods of warfare.[106] The principle of discrimination also includes the fact that both sides at war are also required to clearly distinguish combatants from non-combatants[107] and civilian objects from military objectives.[108] Failure to discriminate and distinguish between a legitimate military target and a civilian object would make the attack indiscriminate[109] and thus, a violation of this customary principle.[110] In an environmental context, this would include civilian targets that are environmental in nature or civilian targets (e.g. chemical factory, oil-well) which if damaged or destroyed could cause harm to the environment.

The principle of proportionality[111] requires that the extent of armed force employed by combatants in armed conflict must be reasonably

---

[104]   This customary principle is reaffirmed in Art. 48, AP I and further reaffirmed in *Nuclear Weapons* (n 22) at p. 257, para. 78 and *Prosecutor v Martic* (Judgement) ICTY-95-11-R61 (8 March 1996) at para. 10.

[105]   Art. 52(2), AP I: 'military objectives are limited to those objects which by their nature, location, purpose or use make an effective contribution to military action and whose total or partial destruction, capture or neutralization, in the circumstances ruling at the time, offers a definite military advantage.' For further discussion see 2004 Rogers (n 9) at pp. 58–85.

[106]   2000 Roberts (n 4) at p. 50.

[107]   Arts. 44(3) and (7), AP I.

[108]   For further discussion on the principle of discrimination, see Beier, J.M., 'Discriminating Tastes: 'Smart' Bombs, Non-Combatants, and Notions of Legitimacy in Warfare' (2003) 34(4) Security Dialogue 411, at pp. 415–23.

[109]   Art. 51(4), AP I sets out what involves an 'indiscriminate attack'.

[110]   On the customary validity of the principle of discrimination, see Oeter, S., 'Methods and Means of Combat' in Fleck, D. (ed), *The Handbook of International Humanitarian Law* (2nd edn OUP, New York 2008) at p. 128 [hereinafter Oeter], [hereinafter Fleck (ed)]. For further discussion on the principle of distinction, see Chetail, V., 'The Contribution of the International Court of Justice to International Humanitarian Law' (2003) 850 International Review of the Red Cross 253, at pp. 252–6.

[111]   The principles of necessity and proportionality were considered by the ICJ in *Military and Paramilitary Activities in and Against Nicaragua (Nicaragua v USA)* (Merits) [1986] ICJ Rep 14, at p. 112, para. 237 [hereinafter Nicaragua]. The ICJ also considered these principles in the context of the environment. See *Nuclear Weapons* (n 22) at p. 821, para. 30 ('Respect of the environment is one

proportionate to the military objective for which the use of force is necessary. This is 'proportionality in relation to the adversary's military actions or to the anticipated military value of one's own actions.'[112] Any harm or damage caused to civilians and civilian objects, incidental or otherwise which would be considered excessive in relation to the actual and direct military advantage[113] anticipated, is prohibited.[114] In respect of the environment, this principle equally applies to any military objective relating to the environment or any military objective where the use of force may cause disproportionate damage to the environment.[115] All four customary principles are of course subject to the principle of military necessity.

The principle of military necessity[116] provides that a combatant is justified in applying any force necessary to secure the complete surrender of an adversary as soon as possible, as long as the means are not prohibited by the law of war provisions.[117] Military necessity is a 'subjective doctrine which "authorises" military action when such action is necessary for the overall resolution of a conflict, particularly where the continued existence of the acting State would otherwise be in jeopardy.'[118] In an environmental context, any military target or means or methods of warfare, whether it is an environmental target or means and

---

of the elements that go to assessing whether an action is in conformity with the principles of necessity and proportionality').

[112] 2000 Roberts (n 4) at p. 50.

[113] 'The term "military advantage" refers to the advantage which can be expected from an attack as a whole and not only from isolated or specific parts of the attack.' See Oeter (n 110) at p. 185.

[114] Art. 51(5)(b), AP I .This article is complemented by Art. 57, AP I in relation to precaution in attack.

[115] See 1997 Schmitt (n 88) at pp. 55–61 (on the applicability of this principle to the environment).

[116] This principle was considered by the ICJ in the *Nicaragua* (n 111) and *Nuclear Weapons* (n 22) cases.

[117] See Art. 14, Instructions for the Government of Armies of the United States in the Field (Lieber Code), General Orders No. 100 (24 April 1863): 'Military necessity, as understood by modern civilized nations, consists in the necessity of those measures which are indispensable for securing the ends of the war, and which are lawful according to the modern law and usages of war.' See also, e.g. Art. 54(5), AP I which permits 'derogation from the prohibitions contained' within the Article 'where required by imperative military necessity.'

[118] Caggiano, M.J.T., 'The Legitimacy of Environmental Destruction in Modern Warfare: Customary Substance Over Conventional Form' (1993) 20 Boston College Environmental Affairs Law Review 479, at p. 496 [hereinafter Caggiano] (footnotes omitted). For further discussion on military necessity, see

methods that will affect the environment, will be subject to this principle.[119] It has to be borne in mind however, that military necessity is the reasonable assessment or judgement of a military strategist or commander in the heat of battle.[120] Thus, reliance on this provision for protection of the environment is subjective.[121] Nonetheless and that being said, '[t]he mere plea of military necessity ... is not sufficient to evade compliance with the laws of war.'[122]

Ultimately, 'in the absence of specific rules of war addressing environmental matters in detail',[123] these fundamental customary principles fill in the gaps, preventing actions in armed conflict that would result in significant environmental damage, particularly 'when they do not serve a clear or important military purpose.'[124] Furthermore, the relevant rules and principles within IHL as a whole, do theoretically afford environmental protection in armed conflict to some extent and from a sustainable development perspective, these laws do highlight the need to weigh the immediate and long-term effects of any means and methods of warfare. Thus, such protection could, if respected, lessen the impact on the already vulnerable civilian population and the conflict-State, not only from an environmental dimension but also as a result, from a socio-economic and development perspective during the conflict and after (in particular, reducing the cost of post-conflict reconstruction).

The primary question that emerges is whether these IHL laws are sufficient in practice? Therefore, whether or not these laws are adequate in practice from an environmental and sustainable development perspective is considered by the analysis and conclusions drawn from the case-studies to follow. The next two sections thereby apply the relevant laws to the case-studies: Iraq's actions in the First Gulf War and NATO's actions in the Kosovo conflict.

Greenwood, C., 'Historical Development and Legal Basis' in Fleck (ed) (n 110) at pp. 35–8.

[119]   1997 Schmitt (n 88) at pp. 52–5 (on applicability of this principle to the environment).

[120]   Caggiano (n 118) at p. 497.

[121]   See *The Hostages Case* (n 83) at pp. 1295–7: stating that 'although, in retrospect, General Rendulic may have erred in his assessment of military necessity, he was not guilty of a criminal act because the doctrine of military necessity may be justified by one's reasonable assessment of the situation'.

[122]   Green (n 9) at p. 123.

[123]   2000 Roberts (n 4) at p. 51.

[124]   Ibid.

3. THE 1990–91 GULF WAR (FIRST GULF WAR)

On 1 August 1990, Iraq invaded and occupied Kuwait.[125] The invasion and conflict illustrated in this case-study, highlights the fact that almost an entire conflict revolved around natural resources. Oil was the primary factor motivating Iraq's invasion of Kuwait[126] and the subsequent destruction of oil resources led to significant damage to the environment as a result. Scholars claim that Iraq used the allegation that Kuwait was mining oil on Iraqi territory as a pretext to annex Kuwait and go to war.[127] 'Furthermore, as the momentum for Security Council action gathered pace, Iraq threatened to wash Kuwaiti oil into the sea should an attempt be made to oust its troops from Kuwait.'[128]

Towards the end of the Gulf War,[129] on 23 January 1991, Iraqi armed forces 'began pumping Kuwaiti oil into the Persian Gulf; first by opening

---

[125]   Iraq's annexation of Kuwait was effectively an occupation. See Art. 42, Hague IV: a '[t]erritory is considered occupied when it is actually placed under the authority of the hostile army'; Art. 2(2), GC IV: the rules of belligerent occupation apply in situations where the territory is partially or totally occupied and even when the 'occupation meets with no armed resistance'. IHL governing occupation and the duties of the occupying power are mainly set out in Arts. 42–56, Hague IV; Arts. 27–34 and 47–48, GC IV; AP I and customary international law. For further discussion on Iraq's occupation of Kuwait, see Benvenisti, E., *The International Law of Occupation* (Princeton, USA 2004) at pp. 150–51.

[126]   See, e.g. Rhea, H.M., 'An International Criminal Tribunal for Iraq after the First Gulf War' (2009) 19 International Criminal Justice Review 308; Abubakar, D., 'Rethinking the Rentier Syndrome: Oil and Resource Conflict in the Persian Gulf' in Omeje, K. (ed), *Extractive Economies and Conflicts in the Global South: Multi-Regional Perspectives on Rentier Politics* (Ashgate, England 2008) at p. 240; Gleditsch, N.P., 'Environmental Change, Security, and Conflict' in Crocker, C.A. and others (eds), *Leashing the Dogs of War: Conflict Management in a Divided World* (US Institute of Peace, USA 2007) at p. 180; Little, A., 'Saddam Hussein – Obituary' *Times* (UK, 30 December 2006) which reports that by late July 1990 relations between Kuwait and Iraq disintegrated, 'partly because of a long standing border dispute (in which Iraq had a strong case) and because of a more recent disagreement over oil drilling rights.'

[127]   2004 Hulme (n 9) at p. 163. See also Boustany, N., 'Saddam Threatens Mideast's Oil Fields: "Choking" Embargo Cited as Justification' *Washington Post* (Washington, DC 24 September 1990); 1997 Schmitt (n 88) at p. 15 (Saddam Hussein also threatened to destroy Kuwaiti oil fields if liberation of Kuwait by the Coalition was attempted).

[128]   Ibid.

[129]   The liberation of Kuwait commenced on 17 January 1991. See 2004 Hulme (n 9) at p. 164.

the valves to the Kuwaiti offshore terminal at Sea-Island.'[130] Within the next few days, Iraqi forces proceeded to deliberately release oil from five Iraqi tankers into the Persian Gulf.[131] Saudi Arabian sources also reported that about 1.5 million barrels[132] of crude oil had been dumped into the Persian Gulf.[133] The oil released mostly caused damage in Kuwait and Iran's territorial waters.[134]

Retreating Iraqi forces also sabotaged more than 700 Kuwaiti oil-wells; reportedly setting an estimated 611 on fire and 79 gushing oil.[135] It is alleged that the retreating Iraqi army ruthlessly and systematically destroyed the oil-wells commencing on 21 February 1991.[136] The oil fires, blazing for months, released vast quantities of soot, smoke and dangerous toxins into the atmosphere daily.[137] In Kuwait, it was reported that the smoke radically reduced visibility in the surrounding areas of the burning oil-wells and reduced day time temperatures by up to 10°C below normal.[138] The effects of the environmental damage were trans-boundary as well, with smoke from the oil fires creating smoke clouds that stretched for miles, blanketing neighbouring Arabic States.[139] The British Meteorological Office also reported a black cloud of smoke over Pakistan and the USSR region.[140] Human beings and wildlife alike

---

[130]   Ibid.

[131]   Ibid; Arkin, W.M. and others, 'On Impact: Modern Warfare and the Environment. A Case Study of the Gulf War' *Greenpeace* (May 1991) at p. 62 (the Pentagon, on 25 January 1991, reported the oil spilled from the tankers).

[132]   A barrel contains approximately 42 gallons of crude oil. See Markovitz, H., *Energy Security* (ABDO, USA 2011) at p. 9.

[133]   Yuzon (n 62) at p. 794.

[134]   2004 Hulme (n 9) at p. 167.

[135]   Ibid., at p. 164.

[136]   Ibid; Caggiano (n 118) at p. 480.

[137]   Kuwaiti officials estimated that the 550 oil-wells still burning long after the end of the Gulf War, were putting allegedly 6 million barrels a day into the atmosphere. See Leggett, J., 'The Environmental Impact of War: A Scientific Analysis and Greenpeace's Reaction' in Plant, G. (ed), *Environmental Protection and the Law of War: A Fifth Geneva Convention on the Protection of the Environment in Time of Armed Conflict* (Belhaven, London 1992) at p. 70 [hereinafter Leggett], [hereinafter Plant (ed)].

[138]   Ibid., at p. 71.

[139]   Earle, S.A., 'Persian Gulf Pollution: Assessing the Damage One Year Later' *National Geographic* (February 1992) at p. 129.

[140]   Leggett (n 137) at p. 70.

suffered from a variety of health problems.[141] Regrettably, the environmental damage did not stop there.

Gushing oil from sabotaged oil-wells resulted in a massive uncontrolled oil flow, creating 'huge, flammable lakes that spread towards highways and threatened residential areas. Beneath these oil basins, crude pockets of gas accumulated.'[142] The oil spill was a severe threat to regional wildlife and to the human population, especially because of its anticipated negative effects upon the Persian Gulf desalination plants which supplied most of the drinking water to the population of the Gulf region.[143] As Caggiano notes, '[e]xperts can only guess at the long-term damage that this wide-spread environmental destruction has wrought.'[144]

The Iraqi forces were not the only ones to inflict environmental damage in the Gulf War. As much as 300 tons of armour-piercing depleted uranium (DU)[145] ammunition used by the Coalition (largely US) forces, are now littered across the Gulf region.[146] Approximately 88 000 tons of ordnance was dropped by the Coalition forces over the 43 day Gulf War period, 'much of which targeted environmental infrastructure,

---

[141] For further information on the effects of the oil fires, see UNEP 'Desk Study on the Environment in Iraq' (UNEP, Nairobi 2003) at pp. 65–6 [hereinafter 2003 UNEP Iraq].

[142] Popovic, N.A.F., 'Humanitarian Law, Protection of the Environment, and Human Rights' (1995) 8 Georgetown International Environmental Law Review 67, at p. 70 [hereinafter Popovic].

[143] Caggiano (n 118) at p. 480.

[144] Ibid., at p. 481 (footnote omitted). See 2003 UNEP Iraq (n 141) at pp. 67–8 (for effects of the oil spill).

[145] DU is radioactive, persists in the environment for a long time due to its long half-life, and readily forms dust that is easily mobilised. The US used DU again in the 1999 Kosovo conflict which caused the international community to question DU as an inhumane weapon. See Bruch, C.E., 'Introduction' in Austin and Bruch (eds) (n 4) at p. 44 [hereinafter 2000 Bruch].

[146] Bloom, S. and others (eds), *Hidden Casualties II: The Environmental, Health and Political Consequences of the Persian Gulf War* (North Atlantic, California 1994) at p. 135. See also 2003 UNEP Iraq (n 141) at pp. 68–9 (on DU use by US Coalition forces during this conflict and its effects); UNEP/UNCHS Balkans Task Force (BTF), 'The Potential Effects on Human Health and the Environment Arising from Possible Use of Depleted Uranium during the 1999 Kosovo Conflict: A Preliminary Assessment' (UNEP/UNCHS-BTF, October 1999) at p. 24 (on DU left on the battlefields of Iraq and Kuwait) [hereinafter UNEP/UNCHS DU].

such as sewage treatment plants, and some of which remained on the ground unexploded.'[147]

In addition to the destruction by the Iraqi and Coalition forces, the collateral damage[148] caused during the conflict was just as extensive. Military vehicles were driven through the deserts, 'destroying foliage, tearing up soil surfaces, and disrupting terrestrial habitats. Hundreds of kilometres of ditches were dug and thousands of makeshift shelters were constructed. Vast quantities of solid, semi-solid, and liquid wastes were merely discarded, causing severe pollution in the terrestrial environment, and millions of landmines were placed throughout the country.'[149]

Severe pollution and habitat destruction are among the most serious forms of environmental threats in this case and with it, a serious challenge to sustainable development. From air pollution to damage to desalination plants, the conflict-related environmental destruction had an environmental, economic and social impact on the Gulf States.[150] Not only were the health and livelihoods of the Gulf population affected,[151] the damage itself and the substantial costs incurred as well as the destroyed oil resources and forgone revenues,[152] had a negative effect on

---

[147]   Austin and Bruch (eds) (n 4) at p. 3 (footnote omitted). For more information on the environmental and health impacts of DU in Iraq, see UNEP/UNCHS DU (n 146) at pp. 26–7.

[148]   Collateral damage is inevitable incidental effects 'around the target attacked' towards persons or objects (including the natural environment). See Doswald-Beck, L. (ed), *San Remo Manual on International Law Applicable to Armed Conflicts at Sea* (CUP, New York 2005) at p. 87.

[149]   Omar, S.A.S. and others, 'The Gulf War Impact on the Terrestrial Environment of Kuwait: An Overview' in Austin and Bruch (eds) (n 4) at p. 317. For more information on unexploded ordnance, hazardous waste and physical degradation of landscapes in Kuwait and Iraq during the first Gulf War, see 2003 UNEP Iraq (n 141) at p. 68.

[150]   2003 UNEP Iraq (n 141) at pp. 56–69 (on the effects of the conflict-related damage).

[151]   Ibid. See also Hoskins, E., 'Public Health and the Persian Gulf War' in Levy, B.S. and Sidel, V.W. (eds), *War and Public Health* (American Public Health Association, USA 2000) at pp. 255–8 and pp. 265–86 [hereinafter Hoskins].

[152]   Askari, H., *Middle East Oil Exporters: What Happened to Economic Development?* (Edward Elgar, UK 2006) at p. 300 [hereinafter Askari] (for, e.g. the burning of more than 60 per cent of Kuwait's oil-wells inflicted about '$5.8 billion worth of damage on the country's oil installations.' This excludes 'the cost of any foregone oil revenues and lost oil reserves').

the development of the Gulf States.[153] For example, as a direct result of the war, the Gulf States 'suffered $710.4 billion in lost GDP.'[154] This clearly illustrates the loss and diversion of a vital resource that could have been used for the positive development of the State and region as a whole instead of war. Thus, the following section considers how, and how adequately, the law addresses this challenge to sustainable development.

3.1. Applicable Laws

In the aftermath of the Gulf War, the international community, appalled by Iraqi excesses, '*wanted* Saddam Hussein and his cohorts to be guilty of offences against the environment.'[155] Despite the fact that the Coalition forces had also caused severe damage to the environment, the UN and legal scholars focused solely on Iraq's responsibility for environmental damage. The following actions in particular are meticulously examined: first, the release of oil into the Persian Gulf from the Iraqi tankers and second, the sabotage of Kuwaiti oil-wells (an estimated 611 set on fire and 79 gushing oil onto Kuwaiti land). It is also worth noting (for the application of the law) that the oil-wells were systematically destroyed from 21 February 1991 during the Iraqi forces' retreat. These actions are assessed in light of the current IHL regime that encompasses, *inter alia*, the Hague Regulations, the Geneva Conventions, and customary international law, for Iraq is neither party to AP I nor ENMOD.

Iraq's actions, in dumping oil from its own five tankers into the Persian Gulf, is considered first. The IHL norm that Iraq may have violated is Article 22 of Hague IV which provides that, 'the rights of belligerents to adopt means of injuring the enemy is not unlimited.' The 'means' in this instance is releasing the oil that caused damage to the Persian Gulf.[156] However, because Iraqi forces released oil from its own tankers, the

---

[153]   Ibid. See also Alnasrawi, A., 'Iraq: Economic Consequences of the 1991 Gulf War and Future Outlook' (1992) 13 Third World Quarterly 335; Hoskins (n 151) at pp. 258–65.

[154]   Askari (n 152) at p. 300 (Iraq's occupation 'cost Kuwait $129.6 billion in public and private sector losses, excluding the cost of foregone oil revenues' and the US led Coalition Operation itself cost an 'estimated $71.3 billion, approximately $62.8 billion of which was paid by other countries: Kuwait, Saudi Arabia, and other Gulf States ($42.6 billion), and Germany and Japan ($18.9 billion)').

[155]   2000 Schmitt (n 86) at p. 91.

[156]   Karleskint, G. and others, *Introduction to Marine Biology* (3rd edn Cengage, USA 2010) at p. 543 (damage continues even till today).

relevant IHL provisions may not be applicable.[157] Nevertheless, their actions are still subject to the customary principles of proportionality and military necessity. Iraq's actions in slicking the Persian Gulf with oil may have been an attempt 'to forestall a possible sea-borne invasion by the Coalition forces.'[158] The Coalition acknowledged that Iraqi actions did affect their naval plans but as the US confirmed, the extent of interference was negligible.[159] If this was Iraq's motive, then perhaps it could be subsumed under the principle of military necessity. However, the principle of military necessity only justifies a combatant applying any force necessary to secure complete surrender of an adversary as soon as possible. In this case, although Iraq's actions may have deterred Coalition naval operations, it would not have resulted in Coalition surrender or overall resolution of the conflict. In relation to proportionality, based on US assertion that the interference to the Coalition naval plans were minimal[160] and thus disproportionate to the military advantage expected, coupled with 'Iraq's initial threats to destroy Kuwait'[161] and awash Kuwaiti seas with oil, it is argued that Iraq's actions in releasing oil from

---

[157]   For further discussion on 'transport of oil by sea' regulations (e.g. London International Convention for the Prevention of Pollution of the Sea by Oil (1954) 327 UNTS 3; 1982 UNCLOS) in respect of Iraq releasing oil from its tankers into the Persian Gulf, see 2004 Hulme (n 9) at pp. 166–8 (However, Hulme concludes that these regulations may not be applicable in times of war).

[158]   Ibid., at p. 185.

[159]   Appendix O on the Laws of War, 'Conduct of the Persian Gulf War' Final Report to Congress Pursuant to Title V of the Persian Gulf Conflict Supplemental Authorization and Personnel Benefits Act of 1992 (Public Law 102–25) (Department of Defense, Washington, DC April 1992) at p. 637 [hereinafter Congress Report].

[160]   On the issue of dumping oil into the Persian Gulf, legal scholars and military lawyers alike have concluded that the military advantage of Iraq having done so was minimal at best. See, e.g. Sharp, W.G., 'The Effective Deterrence of Environmental Damage During Armed Conflict: A Case Analysis of the Persian Gulf War' (1992) 137 Military Law Review 1, at p. 44 [hereinafter Sharp]; Roberts, A., 'Failures in Protecting the Environment in the 1990–91 Gulf War' in Rowe, P. (ed), *The Gulf War 1990–91 In International Law and English Law* (Routledge, London 1993) at p. 120 [hereinafter 1993 Roberts]; di Rattalma, M.F. and Treves, T., *The United Nations Compensation Commission: A Handbook* (Kluwer Law, The Hague 1999) at p. 18; 2000 Schmitt (n 86) at p. 115.

[161]   Sharp (n 160) at p. 45.

the five tankers were disproportionate and possibly malicious.[162] Therefore, it concludes that Iraq violated the customary principles of proportionality and necessity[163] and in the process, contrary to any aspect of sustainable development, failed to take any form of precaution or consideration for the environment and the impact of its damage on the present and future Gulf population.

On the sabotage of the Kuwaiti oil-wells, the IHL norms that Iraq may have infringed in this instance are: Article 22 of Hague IV which limits the means and methods of warfare; Article 23(g) of Hague IV which prohibits the destruction or seizure of enemy property 'unless such destruction or seizure be imperatively demanded by the necessities of war'; and Article 55 of Hague IV which prohibits the occupying State from damaging or destroying real property within the occupied State. The relevant Geneva provision that Iraq may have breached is Article 53 of GC IV which prohibits the destruction of private or public property in an occupied territory 'except where such destruction is rendered absolutely necessary by military operations.'

Iraq, by releasing oil from, destroying and torching Kuwaiti oil-wells (Kuwait's property), has failed to protect the property of its occupied State and thus, acted in contravention of Article 55 of Hague IV. Iraq's actions have also violated Article 23(g) of Hague IV by destroying enemy property (Kuwaiti oil-wells) and Article 53 of GC IV by destroying public property (Kuwaiti oil-wells) in an occupied territory (Kuwait). To ascertain whether Iraq has violated these provisions, Iraq's actions will have to be considered in light of the relevant customary norms of IHL.

First, it must be ascertained whether under the principle of discrimination, the oil-wells qualified as legitimate military targets, that is, 'objects which by their nature, location, purpose or use make an effective contribution to military action and whose total or partial destruction, capture or neutralization, in the circumstances ruling at the time, offers a definite military advantage.'[164] Scholars argue that the oil-wells, if used

---

[162] 1993 Roberts (n 160) at pp. 119–20 (for further exploration of Iraqi actions in dumping oil into the sea).

[163] *Cf.* 2004 Hulme (n 9) at p. 179 and pp. 183–5. Hulme is of the view that Iraqi actions may have 'been a legitimate means of obstructing an imminent attack', that 'the principle of proportionality would not appear to have been breached in this instance' and due to the 'proportionality equation of environmental damage [being] extremely high … the military advantage in obstructing a sea-borne invasion would clearly be important.'

[164] Art. 52(2), AP I.

by enemy military forces, may be regarded as military objectives – the use of which can legitimately be denied to the enemy.[165] However, while oil refining facilities were also targeted during this war, the estimated over 600 oil-wells 'destroyed in Kuwait were mining crude oil, not refining it.'[166] As Hulme further points out, 'whilst refined oil products, such as petroleum, are considered to constitute *munitions de guerre*, crude oil generally is not.'[167] In this case, the crude oil contained within the 600 plus oil-wells would not have been much use to enemy forces in their unrefined state. By their nature, purpose and use, the oil-wells would not have made an effective contribution to military action and their destruction would not have given the Iraqi forces a definite military advantage. Thus, the oil-wells were not legitimate military targets and therefore, were unlawfully destroyed.

However, whether or not the oil-wells were legitimate military targets, the actions of the Iraqi forces in torching the oil-wells and spilling oil from it, would still have to be considered in light of the principles of necessity and proportionality. First, in respect of the sabotage of the estimated 79 Kuwaiti oil-wells which resulted in a massive uncontrolled oil flow, was it militarily necessary? The Iraqi forces' actual intentions are unknown but in hazarding a guess, as Hulme suggests, 'it is possible that the oil being poured onto the desert floor by the open oil wells was designed to make crossing the desert hazardous for any ground forces.'[168] However, as highlighted earlier, the principle of military necessity only justifies a combatant in applying any force necessary to secure the complete surrender of an adversary as soon as possible. Therefore, even if the oil poured onto the dessert floor would have disrupted Coalition ground operations, it would have not have resulted in Coalition surrender or overall resolution of the conflict. In addition, the resulting damage – the uncontrolled oil flow causing 'huge, flammable lakes that spread

---

[165] Dinstein, Y., *The Conduct of Hostilities under the Law of International Armed Conflict* (CUP, Cambridge 2004) at p. 192. [hereinafter Dinstein]. See also Haines, S., 'The United Kingdom and Legitimate Military Objectives: Current Practice … and Future Trends?' in von Heinegg, W.H. and Epping, V. (eds), *International Humanitarian Law: Facing New Challenges* (Springer-Verlag, Berlin 2007) at p. 132 (objects of military value may include oil refineries).

[166] 2004 Hulme (n 9) at p. 179. See also Lauterpacht, H. (ed), *International Law Reports: Volume 23* (Grotius, Cambridge 1989) at p. 823 (on the view that unrefined oil does not constitute *munitions de guerre*).

[167] Ibid.

[168] 2004 Hulme (n 9) at p. 178.

towards highways and threatened residential areas',[169] could not be considered collateral damage as it was disproportionate to the military advantage anticipated. Thus, coupled with the fact that the Iraqi forces were retreating, it is argued that Iraq did violate the customary principles of proportionality and necessity.

With regard to setting fire to the estimated 611 Kuwaiti oil-wells, was it militarily necessary? The question here is whether the smoke from the oil-well fires was sufficient to prevent or deter an imminent Coalition aerial attack. It is not inconceivable the Iraqis used smoke from the burning oil-wells to mask attacks and create problems for the Coalition forces. In respect of being a military advantage, it is arguable that smoke resulting from 'the fires were intended to take advantage of "weaknesses" in high-tech Coalition weapons',[170] that is, the thick smoke could have obscured Iraqi ground forces from being visible to Coalition air forces. If this was Iraq's motive, then perhaps it was militarily necessary. The US admitted that the oil smoke clouds did in fact affect their weapon systems and were perilous to their airborne pilots,[171] but went on to state that this had minimal effect on overall 'Coalition offensive combat operations'.[172] It is thus argued that although the smoke from the torched oil-wells may well have disrupted Coalition aerial operations, it would not have resulted in Coalition surrender or overall resolution of the conflict and hence, was not necessary.

In respect of proportionality, even with the intention of obscuring Coalition aerial visibility, detonating 611 oil-wells, causing not only oil-fires that blazed for months but also serious regional cross-border atmospheric pollution, seemed excessive and disproportionate to any military objective and advantage expected.[173] Moreover, the atmospheric environmental damage appears to have been too excessive to be passed off as collateral damage. Dinstein argues that 'on balance, the Iraqis appear to have been motivated not by military considerations but by sheer vindictiveness.'[174] As one commentator notes, Iraq's maliciousness was emphasised by the fact that its defeated armed forces 'also damaged or destroyed all twenty-six gathering centers that were designed to separate the oil, gas, and water from one another – a process that is essential for

---

[169] Popovic (n 142) at p. 70.
[170] 1997 Schmitt (n 88) at p. 21.
[171] 2004 Hulme (n 9) at p. 178.
[172] Congress Report (n 159) at p. 637.
[173] Dinstein (n 165) at p. 192.
[174] Ibid.

oil production.[175] Iraq also destroyed the technical specifications of each well.'[176] Furthermore, the conclusions drawn about the lack of military advantage of Iraq's actions are compounded by the fact that the Kuwaiti oil-wells were sabotaged by a retreating defeated army.[177] Therefore, it concludes that Iraq had again disregarded the customary principles of proportionality and necessity.

Overall, based on the arguments presented, considering Iraq's initial threats about Kuwaiti oil, and evidence that the extensive destruction was conducted by a retreating army, the destruction seems 'to have lacked the required element of *necessity* to render the destruction lawful.'[178] This leads to the conclusion that Iraq has violated several binding IHL provisions by causing such damage to Kuwait's environment. Furthermore, Iraq's actions in disregarding the rules of armed conflict contributed to the obstruction of sustainable development; negating in particular any form of precaution in causing such extensive environmental damage that incurred the risk of severe or irreversible environmental harm. Moreover, the Iraqi forces did not take into account the consequences of their actions on the present and future population of Kuwait and the rest of the affected Gulf region. The environmental impact and the ensuing ripple effect socially and economically, affecting the health and livelihoods of the population and development of the Gulf region, could be experienced long after the end of the war.[179] The question that follows from this is, what was the international community's response to such IHL infringements during the conflict; such as to highlight issues of enforcement, and perhaps even enforceability, of the law?

---

[175]   'The Environmental Aftermath of the Gulf War' A Report for the US Senate Gulf Pollution Task Force, Committee On Environment and Public Works (Washington, DC 2 March 1992) at p. 6.

[176]   Sharp (n 160) at p. 45 (Sharp's arguments are based mostly on the aforementioned report).

[177]   Dinstein (n 165) at p. 192.

[178]   2004 Hulme (n 9) at p. 184.

[179]   2003 UNEP Iraq (n 141) at pp. 56–69 (on the impact of the conflict-related damage).

3.2.   International Response and Affixing Liability

3.2.1.   State responsibility

The responsibility of States for any internationally wrongful conduct is covered under the category of State responsibility.[180] State responsibility consists of two main elements: attribution[181] and breach of an international law norm.[182] In other words, under the international law of State responsibility, States can be held responsible for violations of international law that can be attributed to them.[183] This includes the State being responsible for all actions or omissions of its State officials and organs,[184] including non-State organs which have been given elements of

---

[180]   The elements required for State responsibility to be invoked are set out in the ILC's Articles on the Responsibility of States for Internationally Wrongful Acts (adopted by the ILC on 10 August 2001); Report on the ILC on the Work of its Fifty-third Session UN Doc A/56/10 (2001) [hereinafter Articles on State Responsibility]. UNGA recognised these articles and subsequently brought them to the attention of States and annexed them to UNGA Resolution 56/83 (12 December 2001).

[181]   Regarding attribution, Art. 1, Articles on State Responsibility provides that, '[e]very internationally wrongful act of a State entails the international responsibility of that State.' The ICJ has applied this principle in a number of cases, e.g. *Corfu Channel* (n 100) at p. 23; *Nicaragua* (n 111) at paras. 283 and 292; *Reparation for Injuries Suffered in the Service of the United Nations* (Advisory Opinion) [1949] ICJ Rep 174, at p. 184; *Interpretation of Peace Treaties with Bulgaria, Hungary and Romania (Second Phase)* (Advisory Opinion) [1950] ICJ Rep 221.

[182]   Regarding violation of an international obligation, what is considered to be a breach of international law by a State, depends entirely on what its international obligations actually are. An international obligation of a State may derive from general principles of law, treaties or laws entrenched in custom. Prior to holding a State responsible, a causal link between the injury caused and an official act or omission by the State alleged to have breached its obligations has to exist. See Crawford, J. and Olleson, S., 'The Nature and Forms of International Responsibility' in Evans, M.D. (ed), *International Law* (OUP, Oxford 2003) at p. 449.

[183]   There must also have been loss, harm or damage from the breach of obligation which then gives rise to a requirement for reparation. The gravity or extent of loss, harm or damage however, is only relevant insofar as it goes to assessing the type of reparation that may be appropriate, in particular the amount of compensation to be awarded to the injured State. This is dealt with further in Chapter 5. For further discussion on State responsibility, see Sucharitkul, S., 'State Responsibility and International Liability under International Law' (1996) 18 Loyola of Los Angeles International and Comparative Law Journal 821.

[184]   Art. 4, Articles on State Responsibility.

154 Environmental protection, security and armed conflict

governmental authority by the State and act in that capacity in that particular instance.[185] The State will be responsible even if the organ, entity, official or individual has acted *ultra vires*.[186] In addition, a breach of an international obligation gives rise to a duty to make reparation.[187]

In this case-study, it is clearly established that Iraq breached norms of IHL by its actions (dumping oil into the sea, spilling oil onto the desert floor, setting oil-wells on fire) that caused significant damage to Kuwait's environment.[188] Moreover, these violations were committed by Iraqi military forces, which would come under the responsibility of Iraq[189] and are thereby, attributable to the State. Consequently, Iraq is responsible under international law and is obliged to make reparations.

In practice, Iraq's invasion of Kuwait led the UNSC to consider for the first time the responsibility of States for the adverse environmental consequences of unlawful military actions. This in itself is remarkable, for it is an unprecedented venture by the UNSC and the international community as a whole. The UNSC reminded Iraq in Resolution 674 'that under international law it is liable for any loss, damage or injury arising in regard to Kuwait and third States, and their nationals or corporations, as a result of the invasion and illegal occupation of Kuwait by Iraq.'[190] The Gulf War ended with Iraq's acceptance of the formal cease-fire contained in UNSC Resolution 687 which reaffirmed that Iraq is 'liable under international law for any direct loss, damage, including environmental damage and the depletion of natural resources, or injury to foreign Governments, nationals and corporations, as a result of Iraq's unlawful invasion and occupation of Kuwait.'[191] Resolution 687 has a binding effect on Iraq, having been adopted under Chapter VII of the UN Charter.[192]

---

[185] Arts. 5 and 8, Articles on State Responsibility.

[186] Art. 7, Articles on State Responsibility.

[187] *Case Concerning the Factory at Chorzów (Germany v Poland)* (Merits) (1928) PCIJ Rep Series A No. 17, at p. 29; Art. 31, Articles on State Responsibility. See also Shelton, D., 'Righting Wrongs: Reparations in the Articles on State Responsibility' (2002) 96 American Journal of International Law 833, at p. 835.

[188] Iraq violated provisions within the Hague and Geneva Conventions and customary IHL norms.

[189] Arts. 4 and 7, Articles on State Responsibility.

[190] UNSC Resolution 674 (29 October 1990).

[191] UNSC Resolution 687 (3 April 1991) at para. 16.

[192] UN Member States are bound by UNSC resolutions via Article 25 of the UN Charter, if the resolutions express the intention to be binding. See De Wet,

Legal scholars have questioned the UNSC's lack of stated legal justification for holding Iraq accountable, that is, the UNSC's failure to specify the laws that Iraq could possibly have violated.[193] First, it is argued that by not doing so, the UNSC lost the opportunity to advance and clarify 'the world community's understanding of belligerents' legal obligations'[194] in respect of the environment in times of armed conflict. Second, although the damage to Kuwait's environment by dumping vast amounts of oil in the Persian Gulf and causing serious atmospheric pollution is clearly attributable to Iraq and Iraq had arguably violated its international obligations, the UNSC did not clearly set out that State responsibility had been invoked for these reasons. Third, it appears the UNSC based its action on Iraq's violation of *jus ad bellum*, rather than *jus in bello* rules. Indeed, the invasion and occupation of Kuwait 'were considered unlawful because Iraq had used force in violation of article 2(4) of the United Nations Charter.'[195] This still does not however, explain why Iraq should be held responsible for violations of IHL.

Yet, despite the fact that the UNSC held Iraq liable for environmental damage based on 'Iraq's aggression rather than on any specific violation of substantive environmental norms',[196] this is still considered to be an advance in international responses to war-related environmental damage. In any event, 'the legal validity of Resolution 687 cannot be refuted'[197] and as this is the first UNSC resolution to impose liability for environmental harm it must be duly acknowledged. From a sustainable development perspective, this contributes substantially by demonstrating that

---

E., *The Chapter VII Powers of the United Nations Security Council* (Hart, Oregon 2004) at pp. 376–8.

[193] UNSC Resolution 687 (3 April 1991). See also, e.g. Stone, C.D., 'The Environment in Wartime: An Overview' in Austin and Bruch (eds) (n 4) at p. 28 [hereinafter Stone]; 1993 Roberts (n 160) at p. 150; Feliciano, F.P., 'Marine Pollution and Spoliation of Natural Resources as War Measures: A Note on Some International Law Problems in the Gulf War' in MacDonald, R.S. (ed), *Essays in Honour of Wang Tieya* (Martinus Nijhoff, The Netherlands 1994) at p. 310.

[194] Stone (n 193) at p. 29. See also Dinstein (n 165) at p. 196.

[195] Low, L. and Hodgkinson, D., 'Compensation for Wartime Environmental Damage: Challenges to International Law after the Gulf War' (1995) 35 Virginia Journal of International Law 405, at p. 412.

[196] 2000 Bruch (n 145) at p. 41.

[197] Dinstein (n 165) at p. 195.

such environmental damage with its ensuing environmental and socio-economic ripple effect[198] is unacceptable in the eyes of the international community. Furthermore, this also shows that the UNSC in particular, has the willingness and power to attach responsibility to such actions; thereby, perhaps acting as a deterrent against repeat or similar actions towards the environment in future armed conflicts.

3.2.2. Individual responsibility

The norms of IHL are binding not only on States but also on individuals. In relation to armed conflict, international responsibility in respect of individuals has so far developed in the criminal field. For instance, 'the individual soldier or civilian who performs acts contrary to humanitarian law is criminally responsible for those acts and liable to trial for a war crime.'[199] Any individual, regardless of his or her rank within the armed forces can be held responsible for violations of IHL.[200]

Individual criminal responsibility was brought to the fore after WWII. In the aftermath of the war, the international community established the International Military Tribunals at Nuremberg and Tokyo 'to enforce personal responsibility for war crimes, crimes against peace and crimes against humanity.'[201] Individual criminal responsibility has evolved since then. In the later part of the twentieth century, the international community via UNSC resolutions took further steps to develop and establish the rules of individual criminal responsibility, by creating the International Criminal Tribunals for Yugoslavia (ICTY) in 1993[202] and Rwanda (ICTR) in 1994.[203] A few years thereafter, in 1998, came the

---

[198] 2003 UNEP Iraq (n 141) at pp. 56–69 (for the effects of such damage). See also McLaren, D. and Willmore, I., 'The Environmental Damage of War in Iraq' *Guardian* (London 19 January 2003).

[199] Greenwood, C., 'Historical Development and Legal Basis' in Fleck (ed) (n 111) at p. 39 [hereinafter Greenwood]. For an overview on individual responsibility and individual criminal responsibility, see Aksar, Y., *Implementing International Humanitarian Law: From the Ad Hoc Tribunals to a Permanent International Criminal Court* (Routledge, London 2004) at pp. 71–112 [hereinafter Aksar].

[200] Greenwood (n 199) at p. 39.

[201] Aksar (n 199) at p. 73.

[202] Statute of the International Tribunal for the Former Yugoslavia (adopted 25 May 1993 by UNSC Resolution 827 (25 May 1993), (1993) ILM 1192, 1203).

[203] Statute of the International Criminal Tribunal for Rwanda (adopted 8 November 1994 by UNSC Resolution 955 (8 November 1994), (1994) ILM 1598).

adoption of the Rome Statute[204] which established the International Criminal Court (ICC).[205]

In relation to individual responsibility, there is no doubt that environmental damage during armed conflict can form the basis of criminal liability under the laws of war.[206] However, in practice this differs. Thus far no individual has been prosecuted for environmental damage since the Nuremberg trials.[207] It is worth noting however, that criminal liability for damage to the environment has now been added to by the Rome Statute. In relation to international armed conflicts, Article 8(2)(b)(iv) of the Rome Statute prohibits '[i]ntentionally launching an attack in the knowledge that such attack will cause incidental loss of life or injury to civilians or damage to civilian objects or widespread, long-term and severe damage to the natural environment which would clearly be excessive in relation to the concrete and direct overall military advantage expected.'[208] Such action damaging the environment may constitute a war

---

[204] Rome Statute of the International Criminal Court (adopted on 17 July 1998, entered into force 1 July 2002) UN Doc A/CONF 183/9, 2187 UNTS 3.

[205] The treaty based ICC was established on 1 July 2002, the same date its founding treaty, the Rome Statute came into force.

[206] See customary IHL norms discussed above and Arts. 146 and 147, GC IV. See also Jensen, E.T. and Teixeira, J.J., 'Prosecuting Members of the U.S. Military for Wartime Environmental Crimes' (2005) 17 Georgetown International Environmental Law Review 651. *Cf.* Marauhn, T., 'Environmental Damage in Times of Armed Conflict – Not "Really" a Matter for Criminal Responsibility?' (2000) 840 International Review of the Red Cross 1029 [hereinafter Marauhn].

[207] See, e.g. XXII Trial of the Major War Criminals Before the International Military Tribunal, Nuremberg (14 November 1945–1 October 1946) at pp. 568–71 (1948): (Scorched-earth policies formed part of the basis for the conviction of Alfred Jodl where the tribunal rejected his defence of superior orders). In addition, nine German officials in occupied Poland were charged with the 'ruthless exploitation of Polish forestry.' See Schwabach, A., 'Environmental Damage Resulting from the NATO Military Action Against Yugoslavia' (2000) 25 Colombia Journal of Environmental Law 117, at p. 125 [hereinafter 2000 Schwabach]. For further discussion on the lack of prosecution for war-related environmental damage, see Weinstein, T., 'Prosecuting Attacks that Destroy the Environment: Environmental Crimes or Humanitarian Atrocities?' (2005) 17 Georgetown International Environmental Law Review 697, at p. 704 [hereinafter Weinstein].

[208] For further discussion on Article 8(2)(b)(iv), Rome Statute and its applicability to the natural environment, see Peterson, I., 'The Natural Environment in Times of Armed Conflict: A Concern for International War Crimes Law?' (2009) 22 Leiden Journal of International Law 325.

crime under the Statute.[209] Unfortunately, this prohibition would not apply in this case-study as the Rome Statute only came into force on 1 July 2002.

Thus, the relevant IHL enforcement provision for individual responsibility regarding environmental damage during the First Gulf War would be Article 147 of GC IV which provides that, 'extensive destruction ... of property, not justified by military necessity and carried out unlawfully and wantonly'[210] is a grave breach of the Geneva Convention. This means individual liability can be attached for this violation of IHL. In relation to the actions of the Iraqi forces, the systematic destruction of an estimated almost 700 oil-wells (both torched and emptied of oil), as Hulme concludes, 'would appear to qualify as sufficiently extensive for the purpose of Article 147.'[211] Moreover, such wanton destruction[212] as a consequence, could arguably place Iraqi military tactics in the realm of recklessness and negligence and therefore, violating Article 147 of GC IV. This means that members of the Iraqi armed forces could have potentially been held individually responsible for their environmentally damaging actions. In addition, Iraqi individuals found responsible could have also been found in violation of Article 23(g) of Hague IV which forbids the destruction or seizure of enemy property not 'imperatively

---

[209]   Mosher, D.E. and others, *Green Warriors: Army Environmental Considerations for Contingency Operations from Planning Through Post-Conflict* (RAND, USA 2008) at pp. 168–9.

[210]   The ICTY, on the prohibition of 'wanton destruction' within Article 3(b) of the ICTY Statute, stipulated this to mean that: 'the elements for the crime of wanton destruction not justified by military necessity charged under Article 3(b) of the Statute are satisfied where:

(i)   the destruction of property occurs on a large scale;

(ii)   the destruction is not justified by military necessity; and

(iii)   the perpetrator acted with the intent to destroy the property in question or in reckless disregard of the likelihood of its destruction.'

See *Prosecutor v Kordic and Cerkez* (Judgement) ICTY-95–14/2-T (26 February 2001) at para. 346.

[211]   2004 Hulme (n 9) at p. 185.

[212]   Art. 53, GC IV. Courts after WWII, on '"scorched earth" policy, i.e., the systematic destruction of whole areas by occupying forces withdrawing before the enemy', in some circumstances permitted such actions when exercised for 'purely for legitimate reasons. On the other hand the same rulings severely condemned recourse to measures of general devastation whenever they were *wanton, excessive or not warranted by military operations*' [emphasis added]. See 'ICRC Commentary (Art. 53, GC IV)', www.icrc.org/ihl.nsf/COM/380–600060?OpenDocument (accessed 10 April 2012).

demanded by the necessities of war'. Hague IV does not provide for individual criminal responsibility. Thus, a violation of Article 23(g) entails civil liability[213] which would not apply to the individual but imposes a clear obligation on the responsible State to provide compensation.[214]

In practice, in July 1991, a conference in Ottawa attended by international experts concluded that Iraq may be held liable for its acts of destruction by violating Article 23(g) of Hague IV and Article 147 of GC IV.[215] In addition, the Office of the Judge Advocate General (JAG) of the US Army was entrusted with the task of assessing Iraqi military actions and collecting evidence of violations of IHL during the Gulf War.[216] JAG found that war crimes, including damage to the environment had been committed.[217] This encompassed the finding that Iraqi forces had violated Articles 23(g) and 55 of Hague IV and Articles 53 and 147 of GC IV for 'unnecessary destruction of Kuwaiti private and public property' in relation to the destruction of the oil-wells, for intentionally releasing oil into the Persian Gulf and sabotaging Kuwaiti oil fields, as well as for failing to safeguard Kuwaiti public property during occupation.[218] The evidence gathered during this investigation established a *prima facie* case in relation to individual responsibility, particularly command responsibility[219] in that 'the violations of the law of war committed against Kuwait

---

[213]   Plant (ed) (n 137) at p. 17. *Cf.* Hannikainen, L., Hanski, R. and Rosas, A., *Implementing Humanitarian Law Applicable in Armed Conflicts: The Case of Finland* (Martinus Nijhoff, The Netherlands 1992) at p. 52 (The Nuremberg Tribunal referred to Art. 23(g), Hague IV with regard to the charge against General Rendulic in *The Hostages Case*); Tanja, G., 'International Adjudication of War Crimes' in Denters, E. and Schrijver, N. (eds), *Reflections on International Law from the Low Countries: In Honour of Paul de Waart* (Kluwer Law, The Netherlands 1998) at p. 217 (for a list of war crimes for violations of IHL provisions, including Art. 23(g), Hague IV).

[214]   See Art. 3, Hague IV.

[215]   Robbins, J.S., 'War Crimes: The Case of Iraq' (1994) 18 Fletcher Forum of World Affairs 45, at p. 54 [hereinafter Robbins].

[216]   US Department of Defense (DOD), 'Report on Iraqi War Crimes' (Desert Shield/Desert Storm) (DOD, Washington, DC 19 November 1992) (unclassified version on file at Department of State) [hereinafter DOD Iraqi War Crimes]. This Report is supported by extensive evidence accumulated by the US War Crimes Documentation Center.

[217]   Ibid., at pp. 10–13.

[218]   Ibid., at pp. 12–13.

[219]   Command responsibility is where 'Military Commanders are responsible for the conduct of operations of their units and subordinates. This includes the obligation to ensure the lawful conduct of the mission. The behaviour of military

civilians and property, and against third party nationals, were so wide-spread and methodical that they could not have occurred without the authority or knowledge of Saddam Hussein'[220] and his subordinates.[221] The actions of the Iraqi forces that caused environmental damage were so widespread and systematic that even if Saddam Hussein had claimed he had no knowledge of such actions, he and his subordinates in command of the forces, could have still been found criminally responsible.[222]

The international community did consider 'establishing an inter-national tribunal to try Iraqi troops for war crimes, including those arising from the environmental devastation wrought by Iraqi troops in Kuwait'[223] but this did not materialise.[224] Kuwait was the only country that 'held trials, and those only against "collaborators" and some Iraqi soldiers.'[225] Ultimately, no charges of individual criminal responsibility were brought against Saddam Hussein and his subordinates for any of the crimes committed, let alone environmental crimes.[226] While some argue the reasons for not doing so were pragmatic rather than legal,[227] others

---

commanders invokes state responsibility and also individual responsibility under criminal and disciplinary law.' See Wolfrum. R. and Fleck, D., 'Enforcement of International Humanitarian Law' in Fleck (ed) (n 110) at p. 691.

[220] DOD Iraqi War Crimes (n 216) at p. 13.

[221] Ibid.

[222] Saddam Hussein and his commanding subordinates did not even have to have had actual knowledge of the acts to be held responsible. Hussein and each of his colleagues only needed to possess 'some general information in his possession, which would have put him on notice of possible unlawful acts by his subordinates.' See *Prosecutor v Bagilishema* (Judgement) ICTR-95–1A-A (3 July 2002) at para. 28. See also Williamson, J.A., 'Some Considerations on Command Responsibility and Criminal Liability' (2008) 90 International Review of the Red Cross 303, at pp. 307–8 [hereinafter Williamson].

[223] Bruch, C.E., 'All's Not Fair in (Civil) War: Criminal Liability for Environmental Damage in Internal Armed Conflict' (2001) 25 Vermont Law Review 695, at p. 716 [hereinafter 2001 Bruch].

[224] The UNSC did however create the UN Compensation Commission (UNCC). This will be discussed further in Chapter 5.

[225] Robbins (n 215) at p. 46.

[226] Weinstein (n 207) at p. 713. See also Robbins (n 215) at p. 46 (Iraq as a State did suffer other consequences – from economic sanctions to 'destruction of its program for weapons of mass destruction, continued international criticism, and of course the war destruction itself').

[227] See, e.g. 1997 Schmitt (n 88) at p. 93; Caggiano (n 118) at p. 504.

believe the reasons to be primarily political.[228] In reality, the reasons and motivation for lack of individual criminal responsibility may have been a combination of both. As Schmitt concludes,

> [f]irst, it would have been nearly impossible to bring Saddam Hussein and his cohorts to trial. As a result, any proceedings would have been held in absentia. Furthermore, the possibility of individual criminal punishment would have made it difficult to negotiate war termination with the Iraqis. Those likely to face criminal proceedings were still in firm control of the country and would not have agreed to truce terms that included their arrest. Finally, the political context at that time was important. That a coalition with memberships ranging from Syria to Canada held together at all is surprising. Since the attitude toward legal proceedings varied widely, particularly in the Arab world, convening trial in the post-war environment, which was laden with politics and emotion, might well have ruptured the fragile relations that had been forged. War aims had been deliberately delimited to make possible the coalition's creation. To bring Saddam Hussein to trial would have represented a clear expansion beyond those aims.[229]

By not taking action against those who were responsible for the atrocities committed against the environment in this war, the international community lost the opportunity to set a precedent for prosecution of environmental war crimes and a future deterrence for such behaviour.[230] From a sustainable development perspective, this does not bode well for future acts of similar environmental damage and destruction, especially from the standpoint of individual responsibility for 'unsustainable' actions that give no consideration to the negative impact on the environment, development and human well-being. However, to reiterate, the UNSC attached State responsibility for the war-related environmental damages to Iraq itself, therefore perhaps this alone could be sufficient to contribute to future deterrence and in the process, mitigate obstacles to achieving sustainable development.

---

[228] See, e.g. Robbins (n 215) at p. 46; Beres, L.R., 'Toward Prosecution of Iraqi Crimes under International Law: Jurisprudential Foundations and Jurisdictional Choices' (1991/1992) 22 California Western International Law Journal 127, at p. 133; Roberts, A., 'The Laws of War: Problems of Implementation in Contemporary Conflicts' (1995) 6 Duke Journal of Comparative & International Law 11, at pp. 51–2.

[229] 1997 Schmitt (n 88) at pp. 93–4.

[230] Caggiano (n 118) at p. 504. See also Weinstein (n 207) (for prosecuting environmental destruction when used in furtherance of another anthropocentric prosecutable atrocity).

4. THE KOSOVO CONFLICT

At the beginning, the situation in Kosovo, a former part of the Federal Republic of Yugoslavia (FRY), was primarily considered a 'low-intensity internal conflict'[231] which rapidly turned international once the North Atlantic Treaty Organization (NATO) became involved.[232] This was a result of the Yugoslav government's failure to agree to and sign the American drafted peace accord for Kosovo.[233] After repeated warnings to the Yugoslav government, NATO subsequently commenced military action against Yugoslavia with US forces taking the lead in the 78-day bombing campaign 'Operation Allied Force'.[234] Operation Allied Force was almost exclusively a large-scale air campaign to destroy Yugoslav targets from high altitudes.[235] The campaign bombed a wide range of industrial complexes and public infrastructure, causing significant amount of damage to the non-natural and natural environment that had a negative impact on development, the environment and well-being of the civilian population.[236]

The situation in Yugoslavia differs significantly from the other two major international armed conflicts (the First Gulf and Vietnam wars), in which the environment was damaged inasmuch as in these conflicts the environment was a direct and deliberate target of attacks (for example, the destruction of Kuwaiti oil-wells and the defoliation of Vietnam's

---

[231] Bruch, C.E. and Austin, J.E., 'The Kosovo Conflict: A Case Study of Unresolved Issues' in Austin and Bruch (eds) (n 4) at p. 648 [hereinafter Bruch and Austin 'Kosovo'].

[232] Ibid. For further review of NATO involvement in the Kosovo conflict, see Rogers, A.P.V., 'Zero-Casualty Warfare' (2000) 837 International Review of the Red Cross 165 [hereinafter 2000 Rogers].

[233] Kirgis, F.L., 'The Kosovo Situation and NATO Military Action' (March 1999) American Society of International Law Insights [hereinafter Kirgis].

[234] For discussion on the legality of NATO's intervention, see Henkin, L., 'Kosovo and the Law of "Humanitarian Intervention"' (1999) 93 American Journal of International Law 824.

[235] Medenica, O., 'Protocol I and Operation Allied Force: Did NATO Abide by Principles of Proportionality?' (2001) 23 Loyola of Los Angeles International and Comparative Law 329 at p. 398 and p. 406.

[236] See, e.g. Council of Europe, 'Environmental Impact of the War in Yugoslavia on South-East Europe' Report by Committee on the Environment, Regional Planning and Local Authorities, Doc. 8925 (10 January 2001) at paras. 18–42 [hereinafter Council of Europe]; Cordesman, A.H., *The Lessons and Non-Lessons of the Air and Missile Campaign in Kosovo* (Praeger, USA 2001) at pp. 95–190.

forests).[237] Whereas in the case of Yugoslavia, NATO's military actions resulted in collateral environmental damage.[238] Factories, power and chemical plants for example, were strategic and tactical targets from a military standpoint.[239] Yet, the environment was harmed. This case-study illustrates the fact that whether or not the environment is a deliberate target during armed conflict, it will inevitably be harmed and in the process, result in negative environmental exposure that could threaten the security, livelihoods and health of the civilian population.

That being said, as Schwabach comments, '[a]s was the case in the Persian Gulf War, the environmental damage in Yugoslavia has turned out to be less severe than was originally feared.'[240] Nonetheless, a certain amount of measurable damage did occur in specific places or 'hot spots' as deduced by UN experts examining the consequences of NATO's bombing of Yugoslavia in 1999. Pekaa Haavisto, head of the Joint UNEP/UNCHS-(Habitat) Balkan Taskforce (BTF) team states that, '[t]here are some hot spots where immediate action has to take place but there is not a countrywide catastrophe. This is our first judgement.'[241] The UN team's 'hot spots' of pollution were in particular the heavily targeted Serb towns of Pančevo, Kragujevac, Novi Sad and Bor.[242] As only damage to Pančevo was considered in the Final Report to the Prosecutor by the Committee Established to Review the NATO Bombing Campaign Against the Federal Republic of Yugoslavia [hereinafter Final Report], in application of the relevant IHL laws, this section focuses on

---

[237]   2000 Schwabach (n 207) at p. 118.

[238]   'Kosovo/Operation Allied Force After-Action Report' Report to Congress (Unclassified) (Department of Defense (DOD), USA 31 January 2000) at p. xiv.

[239]   See 'Final Report to the Prosecutor by the Committee Established to Review the NATO Bombing Campaign against the Federal Republic of Yugoslavia' [hereinafter Final Report] at para. 14. See also Kröning, V. (Germany), 'Kosovo and International Humanitarian Law' NATO Committee Report (15 October 1999) at para. 18, www.nato-pa.int/archivedpub/comrep/1999/as245cc-e.asp (accessed 10 April 2012) (e.g. 'NATO had gone after Serbia's water supplies in a serious way, using high-explosive bombs that are doing permanent damage to water systems. According to city officials, Belgrade was down to less than 10% of its water reserves').

[240]   2000 Schwabach (n 207) at p. 118. See also Gec, J., 'Pollution "Hot Spots" ID'd in Serbia' *Associated Press Online* (27 July 1999), http://nucnews.net/2000/du/99du/990728ap.htm (accessed 10 Aril 2012) [hereinafter Gec].

[241]   Gec (n 240).

[242]   UNEP/UNCHS-(Habitat), 'The Kosovo Conflict: Consequences for the Environment & Human Settlements' (UNEP/UNCHS 1999) at p. 31 [hereinafter 1999 UNEP/UNCHS Kosovo].

the damage to the natural environment caused by NATO as a result of destroying the industrial complex in Pančevo, Serbia.

Considerable environmental destruction resulted from the bombing of the Pančevo industrial complex which covers several acres consisting of a petrochemical plant, a fertiliser (nitrogen processing) plant, a large oil refinery, and an aircraft factory, situated 12 miles from Belgrade.[243] According to NATO, the Pančevo plant was selected as a target because it produced chemicals for both military and civilian use.[244] The Pančevo industrial complex is located where the River Tamis and the Danube meet. According to Pančevo's mayor, Srdjan Mikovic, NATO struck the complex with at least 56 missiles over a period of 23 days between 24 March and 8 June 1999.[245] Particularly devastating damage occurred in the early hours of 18 April 1999 when repeated NATO airstrikes resulted in three massive hits.[246]

NATO bombing destroyed the complex's storage tanks containing thousands of tonnes of toxic chemicals.[247] These chemicals were released into the Danube, polluting the river and the aquatic life within.[248] The toxic pollution of the Danube River had serious consequences as the Danube is a source of drinking water for about ten million people within the region.[249] It was also reported that 'the bombs sent fireballs into the air and enveloped Pančevo in clouds of black smoke and milky white gasses. Flames leapt from the facilities for 10 days.'[250] The fumes that filled the air in Pančevo for several days thereafter caused the local population to suffer from respiratory and stomach problems; the leaves in the area to turn 'yellow or black; fish caught in the Danube to look sickly'.[251] It is also worth noting that BTF did find that some of the

---

[243]   2000 Schwabach (n 207) at p. 119.

[244]   Ibid.

[245]   Ibid.

[246]   Hedges, C., 'Serbian Town Bombed by NATO Fears Effects of Toxic Chemicals' *New York Times* (New York 7 July 1999) [hereinafter Hedges].

[247]   2000 Schwabach (n 207) at p. 119. For more information on the environmental effects of the conflict, see 1999 UNEP/UNCHS Kosovo (n 242); Regional Environmental Center for Central and Eastern Europe (REC), 'Assessments of the Environmental Impact of Military Activity During the Yugoslavia Conflict: Preliminary Findings' (REC, 28 June 1999), www.rec.org/REC/Announcements/ yugo/contents.html (accessed 10 April 2012) [hereinafter REC].

[248]   See 1999 UNEP/UNCHS Kosovo (n 242) at pp. 32–8; 2004 Hulme (n 9) at pp. 188–9 (for detailed description of chemicals leaked).

[249]   Council of Europe (n 236) at para. 21.

[250]   Hedges (n 246).

[251]   2006 Schwabach (n 61) at p. 123.

environmental damage discovered were linked to pre-conflict environmental neglect and damage.[252]

The Pančevo case-study is one example of the significant damage caused by the NATO military campaign. On the whole, NATO military actions had a serious impact on FRY's sustainable development, contributing to the breakdown of its socio-economic development and in many instances, adding pressure to an already fragile environment.[253] NATO military operations that included the destruction of industrial sites and infrastructures, caused hazardous substances to pollute the soil, water and air of FRY and several neighbouring countries.[254] The damage to the environment had serious effects not only on the natural environment itself which until the conflict remained relatively unpolluted,[255] but also had serious impacts on the health and quality of life of the population of FRY and the other affected countries of South-East Europe[256] (for example, the pollution of drinking water sources for more than 10 million people).[257] The destruction and damage of housing, public buildings and infrastructure facilities, the disruption of public utilities coupled with the negative exposure to environmental damage, had not only 'seriously affected human settlement conditions'[258] but also triggered 'an unprecedented flight of refugees.'[259] In addition, the economic and development consequences of the Kosovo conflict were severely affecting the region – the armed conflict and ensuing refugee crisis were 'wiping out growth, destroying commerce, and placing enormous strains on the budgets'[260] of the affected Balkan States.

Coming back to Pančevo, in the aftermath of the repeated NATO airstrikes, a NATO spokesperson confirmed that, 'NATO had two types of

---

[252] 1999 UNEP/UNCHS Kosovo (n 242) at pp. 9–10. It was difficult for the BTF in some circumstances to separate the war-related environmental damage from pre-existing environmental contamination.

[253] UNEP, 'UNEP Annual Report 1999' (UNEP/Earthprint, UK 2000) at p. 5. See also 1999 UNEP/UNCHS Kosovo (n 242) at pp. 22–7 (on the state of the FRY environment prior to the conflict).

[254] Council of Europe (n 236) at paras. 18–42.

[255] Ibid., at para. 35.

[256] Ibid., see summary.

[257] Ibid., at para. 21.

[258] 1999 UNEP/UNCHS Kosovo (n 242) at p. 68.

[259] Council of Europe (n 236) at paras. 43–5.

[260] World Bank, 'Economic Consequences of Kosovo Crisis' Beyond Transition (World Bank 2001) (for more information on the economic impact of the Kosovo conflict). See also IMF/World Bank, 'The Economic Consequences of the Kosovo Crisis: A Preliminary Assessment of External Financing Needs and

targets. There were tactical and strategic targets. The oil refinery in Pancevo was considered a strategic target. It was a key installation that provided petrol and other elements to support the Yugoslav army. By cutting off these supplies we denied crucial material to the Serbian forces fighting in Kosovo.'[261] The spokesperson went on to state that environmental damage was taken into consideration during these air strikes.[262] According to another NATO spokesperson, Jamie Shea, the reports on environmental damage by NATO were greatly exaggerated.[263]

The question is, did the NATO member States violate the rules of IHL by causing such environmental damage?

4.1. Applicable Laws

In the midst of the Kosovo conflict, FRY brought an action before the ICJ against ten NATO States involved in the conflict: Belgium, Canada, France, Germany, Italy, the Netherlands, Portugal, Spain, the UK and the US.[264] The most relevant provisions within IHL in respect of the environmental damage caused would be Articles 35 and 55, AP I. At the time of the Kosovo conflict however, although most of the NATO Member States were party to AP I, France,[265] Turkey and the US were not.[266] Therefore AP I would only be applicable to those States party to it. Of course, for the conduct of the NATO countries to be found in violation of these provisions within AP I, the environmental damage

---

the Role of the Fund and the World Bank in the International Response' (16 April 1999) http://www.imf.org/external/pubs/ft/kosovo/041699.htm (accessed 10 April 2012).

[261] Hedges (n 246) (The NATO spokesperson asked not to be named).

[262] Ibid.

[263] See 'NATO HQ press conference by Dr Jamie Shea and Brigadier General Guiseppe Marani' (NATO HQ 30 April 1999), www.nato.int/kosovo/press/p990430a.htm (accessed 10 April 2012).

[264] *Legality of the Use of Force (Yugoslavia v NATO States)* (Provisional Measures) [1999] ICJ Rep 132 [hereinafter *Yugoslavia v NATO States*]. FRY could not file a case directly against NATO because the ICJ only has jurisdiction over States. See also UNEP International Law (n 7) at p. 25 (for review of the ICJ decisions).

[265] France though not party to AP I during the Kosovo conflict, has since acceded to it on 11 April 2001.

[266] See ICRC website that lists treaties by country, www.icrc.org/ihl.nsf/Pays?ReadForm (10 April 2012).

would first have to satisfy the cumulative threshold of 'widespread, long-term and severe'.[267]

The initial element to consider is whether the 'widespread' criteria was satisfied? The air and river pollution as a result of the Pančevo complex bombings by NATO, led to toxic contaminants being carried away up to other areas within FRY as well as into neighbouring Albania, Bulgaria, Macedonia and Romania.[268] It was reported that clouds of toxic smoke about 15 square kilometres lasting for more than 10 days, hovered around the Pančevo area.[269] Furthermore, an increase in acid rain was also reported within FRY and its affected neighbours.[270] In relation to the water pollution, the Danube as an international waterway, exacerbated the transboundary water pollution.[271] For instance, traces of oil (below the maximum concentration) and heavy metals such as copper, cadmium, chromium and lead (double the permitted maximum concentration), were found in Romania's Danube waters.[272] Thus, based on this evidence, it is argued that the environmental damage – the water and air pollution caused by NATO's airstrikes against the Pančevo industrial complex, could be considered 'widespread'.

The second element to consider is whether the environmental harm would have resulted in long-term damage? Hulme succinctly sets out a list of possible sources of long-term harm as a result of NATO's actions.[273] These include for example: toxic metals found on the Danube canal riverbeds (especially petrochemicals and mercury);[274] pollution of Danube's underground aquifers caused by bioaccumulation and seepage of heavy metals through riverbank sediments and from surface waters;[275] extremely high-levels (beyond the permitted rate) of toxic and carcinogenic air-borne pollutants (especially by the release of more than 1000

---

[267]   Arts. 35 and 55, AP I. For further discussion on whether NATO breached the 'widespread, long-term and severe environmental harm' threshold, see 2004 Hulme (n 9) at pp. 194–7.

[268]   Chapter 4, REC (n 247). See also 2004 Hulme (n 9) at p. 194.

[269]   Chapters 1.1.2 and 4.1.6, REC (n 247).

[270]   Chapter 1.1.6, REC (n 247).

[271]   2004 Hulme (n 9) at p. 194.

[272]   Chapter 1.1.1, REC (n 247).

[273]   2004 Hulme (n 9) at p. 195.

[274]   BTF found chronic levels of mercury and oil products in Danube mussels, see 1999 UNEP/UNCHS Kosovo (n 242) at p. 37.

[275]   It is estimated that 90 per cent of Serbia's domestic and industrial water supply comes from groundwater, see Chapter 4.1.1, REC (n 247).

tonnes VCMs);[276] biodiversity loss in the surrounding area including the Danube River itself;[277] 'black rain' in the Pančevo area as a result of the plumes of toxic smoke from the bombed and burning installations, with the potential for short and long-term negative effects on crops, soil, groundwater and human health;[278] as well as 'some physical destruction to habitats.'[279]

However, despite these possible sources of harm, BTF concluded the environmental damage caused did not amount to a catastrophe and therefore would not result in '"long-term" ecological consequences.'[280] Based on such findings, Hulme comments that, 'the damage is arguably not irreversible, and should largely be reversed within the decade.'[281] Thus, it would be difficult to attribute measuring the damage caused by the conflict as 'long-term' environmental damage, particularly since the BTF did find pre-dated 'long-term' damage already in existence.[282]

In relation to the third criteria, the severity of the environmental damage, the Regional Environmental Centre (REC) did find that a significant amount of toxic pollutants: ammonia (NH_3), ethylene-dichloride (EDC), chlorine (C_{12}), hydrochloric acid (HC_1), propylene (C_3H_6), sodium hydroxide (NaOH), vinyl chloride monomers (VCD), metallic mercury (Hg),[283] had been released into the water, soil and atmosphere as a result of the bombings of the Pančevo industrial complex.[284] For instance, more than 100 tonnes of liquid NH_3; more than

---

[276]   Vinyl Chloride Monomer (VCM) is a highly toxic substance. For more details of its effects, see Chapter 4.1.2, REC (n 247).

[277]   See Chapter 4.1.4, REC (n 247).

[278]   1999 UNEP/UNCHS Kosovo (n 242) at p. 32.

[279]   2004 Hulme (n 9) at p. 195.

[280]   Ibid. See also 1999 UNEP/UNCHS Kosovo (n 242) at p. 10 and pp. 31–7 (for Pančevo); Krieger, H. (ed), *The Kosovo Conflict and International Law: An Analytical Documentation 1974–1999* (CUP, Cambridge 2001) at p. 342 [hereinafter Krieger].

[281]   2004 Hulme (n 9) at p. 195.

[282]   Some of the contaminating toxic pollutants found were from the 1960s, 1970s, and 1980s. See 1999 UNEP/UNCHS Kosovo (n 242) at pp. 8–10. See also Krieger (n 280) at p. 342.

[283]   8 tonnes of metallic mercury was released into the surrounding environment. Mercury can bioccumulate in the food chain when transformed to organic form in the environment. See US Environmental Protection Agency (EPA) 'Mecury' (last updated 17 February 2012), www.epa.gov/hg/exposure.htm#1 (accessed 16 April 2012).

[284]   Chapter 3.1, REC (n 247).

1 000 tonnes of EDC;[285] a few thousand tonnes of a 40% NaOH solution; and nearly a thousand tonnes of a 33% HC1 solution, leaked directly into the Danube.[286] REC went on to conclude that these pollutants would be a 'serious' threat to human health and ecological systems within the Balkan region.[287] Before the conflict, the Danubian waters and surrounding banks were rich in biodiversity.[288] The serious pollution caused by the released toxic chemicals from burning Pančevo installations during the conflict, undoubtedly jeopardised this biologically rich and abundant ecosystem.[289]

REC also noted that by 'Yugoslav estimates, some 70 000 [species] have been endangered locally'[290] and referred to pollution as being 'very severe in the vicinity of targeted industrial complexes, such as Pancevo'.[291] BTF however, concluded that '[t]here is no evidence of an ecological catastrophe for the Danube as a result of the air strikes during the Kosovo conflict.'[292] Unfortunately, BTF did not clarify as to what amounted to an 'ecological catastrophe'. The same applies to the REC, which failed to clearly define what they meant by 'very severe' pollution. This makes it difficult to come to the conclusion that the environmental damage caused amounted to 'severe harm' within the context of AP I. Hulme however, argues that the small 'pockets' of environmental harm in Pančevo and its surrounding areas could perhaps be classified as 'severe' harm, within the threshold of AP I.[293] In contrast, it is submitted that although small 'pockets' of environmental damage may amount to severe harm, it is unlikely that as a whole it would amount to 'severe' and 'widespread' harm within AP I. Moreover, based on the complications encountered by BTF in measuring long-term damage, it would have been difficult to determine that these small 'pockets' of damage satisfy the 'long-term' criteria.

Thus, in addition to the small 'pockets' of environmental damage around Pančevo not having reached the cumulative AP I threshold, based

---

[285] EDC is toxic to terrestrial and aquatic organisms and more 'sensitive species may die as a result of exposure to lower concentrations of only 1 mg/l'. As EDC is a volatile chemical compound, it can also cause human health problems. See 1999 UNEP/UNCHS Kosovo (n 242) at Annex II.

[286] Chapter 4.1.1, REC (n 247).

[287] Chapter 3.1, REC (n 247).

[288] 2004 Hulme (n 9) at p. 189.

[289] Ibid.

[290] Chapter 3.1, REC (n 247).

[291] Chapter 1, REC (n 247).

[292] 1999 UNEP/UNCHS Kosovo (n 242) at p. 60.

[293] 2004 Hulme (n 9) at p. 196.

on the available facts and findings by REC and BTF, it is concluded that having only reached 'widespread' harm, the environmental damage as a whole caused by the NATO airstrikes did not reach the AP I threshold of 'widespread, long-term *and* severe' harm. Consequently, the NATO States party to AP I have not violated Articles 35 and 55 thereof.

As the US, Turkey and France were not bound by AP I at the time of the conflict and the fact that the NATO States' airstrikes-related environmental damage did not violate the relevant provisions within AP I, alternative provisions are explored. This section proceeds to explore whether those States may have breached other relevant provisions within IHL, namely Hague IV and GC IV as they both contain norms of customary nature. The most relevant provision within Hague IV that is applicable to this situation is Article 23(g) which prohibits the destruction of enemy property unless imperatively demanded by military necessity. As discussed above, NATO's repeated bombings did destroy the FRY Pančevo complex. However, whether or not the NATO States have breached this provision would depend on whether it was militarily necessary? With regard to GC IV, as the relevant provisions[294] that indirectly provide some form of environmental protection are directed towards the 'occupying power', these provisions would not apply in this case.

That being said, NATO's actions must be considered against the customary principles of discrimination, distinction, proportionality and military necessity. First, looking at the principle of distinction,[295] the NATO States conducting the aerial bombardment would have had to determine whether the Pančevo industrial complex was a civilian object or a military one?[296] Furthermore, under the principle of discrimination, the complex would have to be a legitimate military target, that is, a target that by its destruction would afford the attacking belligerent party a definite military advantage.

To justify its decision to aerially bombard the complex, NATO argued that first the Pančevo complex, in addition to producing civilian products, 'supplied gasoline and other essential materials to the Serb army, and

---

[294]   GC IV (Art. 53 and the penal sanctions set out within Arts. 146, 147, 148).

[295]   For further discussion on the principle of distinction and the Kosovo conflict, see David, E., 'Respect for the Principle of Distinction in the Kosovo War' (2000) 3 Yearbook of International Humanitarian Law 81 [hereinafter David].

[296]   Art. 48, AP I. See also Art. 24(1), 1923 Hague Rules which states that '[a]erial bombardment is legitimate only when directed at a military objective.'

thus was a legitimate military target'[297] and second, 'Pancevo was considered to be a very, very important refinery and strategic target, as important as tactical targets inside Kosovo.'[298] To reiterate, in relation to the attacks, there were three main facilities within the Pančevo industrial complex: an oil refinery, a petrochemical plant and a fertiliser plant. The oil-refining facilities could constitute a military objective due to their military 'nature, purpose or use'.[299] It is not known for a fact what precise intelligence the NATO commanders actually had on Pančevo[300] but based on their statements of the dual civilian and military purpose of the complex,[301] the assessment made by the NATO commanders was that the Pančevo complex constituted a legitimate military target. In addition, certain chemical facilities could also constitute a military objective and hence, a legitimate military target – which in this case, the petrochemical facility would have been.[302]

With regard to the fertiliser plant, chemicals for the production of fertilisers could also be used to make explosives.[303] However, Hulme argues that classifying the Pančevo fertiliser plant as a military objective is doubtful.[304] Hulme's argument is based on the reasoning that destroying a fertiliser factory that may (or may not) supply the farming industry, which unless the factory in question was wholly converted for military use, would most likely fall outside the definition of Article 52(2) of AP I.[305] In addition, Hulme sets out the statement by Dr Ing Slobodan Tresac, the general director of the HIP Petrochemical plant at Pančevo 'that the plant was not making products for military use.'[306] Nevertheless, NATO's statement that the complex 'supplied gasoline *and other essential materials*[307] to the Serb army'[308] would indicate that NATO assessed that the oil refinery, the petrochemical plant and the nitrogen-processing plant (fertiliser plant) to be military objectives and legitimate military

---

[297]   Bruch and Austin 'Kosovo' (n 231) at p. 649.
[298]   Quoting an unnamed NATO spokesperson, see Hedges (n 246).
[299]   Art. 52(2), AP I.
[300]   Bruch and Austin 'Kosovo' (n 231) at p. 649.
[301]   See text to (n 297) and (n 298).
[302]   Final Report (n 239) at para. 22. See also 2004 Hulme (n 9) at p. 201.
[303]   2004 Hulme (n 9) at p. 200.
[304]   Ibid., at p. 199.
[305]   Ibid.
[306]   Ibid.
[307]   This could perhaps indicate the fertiliser factory's dual purpose within the Pančevo complex.
[308]   Bruch and Austin 'Kosovo' (n 231) at p. 649 [emphasis added]. See also Hedges (n 246).

targets. Thus, based on the facts and NATO's assertions, it would appear that the principle of distinction was not violated in respect of the oil-refinery and petrochemical plant but may have been breached in respect of the fertiliser plant. Perhaps if the ICTY Prosecutor had commenced investigations, we may have had a clearer picture, but this is not the case.

Furthermore, irrespective of whether or not the complex was a legitimate target, the actions of the NATO States involved in the bombardment are still subject to the principles of proportionality and necessity. According to the Final Report, '[t]he targeting by NATO of Serbian petro-chemical industries may well have served a clear and important military purpose.'[309] Arguably, although the oil-refinery and petrochemical facility were clear military targets, the fertiliser plant does not appear to be one. However, whether or not destroying the complex was militarily necessary is an entirely different matter. This is not easy to establish, particularly since NATO only gave vague statements such as 'Pancevo was considered to be a very, very important refinery and strategic target',[310] without actually providing clear reasons.[311] Thus, based on NATO's statements to the international community as well as the conclusion in the Final Report, it is decided that the NATO States have not breached the principle of military necessity in respect of the petrochemical and oil-refining plants. In contrast, with respect to the fertiliser plant, if NATO did not intend to attack it, it could be viewed as collateral damage. Even if NATO did mistakenly hit the fertiliser plant in the belief that it was militarily necessary, as the Committee in the Final Report concludes, the conduct would still be insufficient to incur the criminal liability of the commanders in charge.[312]

The final question would be whether the attack came within the principle of proportionality? The proportionality of the incidental environmental damage caused by NATO's bombardment of the complex would depend entirely on the military advantage expected to be gained. It would certainly have been reasonably foreseeable to NATO that an attack on the Pančevo complex holding hazardous chemicals would result in the inevitable or at least high risk of release of toxic substances into the surrounding environment,[313] thereby potentially causing harm to the

---

[309] Final Report (n 239) at para. 22.
[310] Quoting unnamed NATO spokesperson, see Hedges (n 246) [emphasis added].
[311] See criticisms set out in Bruch and Austin 'Kosovo' (n 231) at p. 650.
[312] Final Report (n 239) at para. 23.
[313] 2004 Hulme (n 9) at p. 200.

natural environment and the civilian population as a result. There is no doubt that a significant amount of toxic pollutants were released and this would have to be weighed against NATO's anticipated military advantage. According to the Final Report the military advantage expected to be gained would have to be 'very substantial',[314] which the Report failed to define. Therefore, the substantiality of the anticipated military advantage can only be deduced from NATO's ambiguous statements.[315]

In addition to not knowing the exact military advantage expected, we also have no knowledge of the actual information possessed by NATO on the Pančevo industrial complex, nor do we know what steps NATO actually took to minimise collateral damage in the attacks.[316] However, NATO with its state of the art technology and weaponry as well as having probably the 'most sophisticated intelligence capability'[317] should have possibly known the risks of heavily attacking such a hazardous facility that was nearly 30 years old[318] or at least exercised some element of the precautionary approach. Unfortunately, although it was acknowledged in the Final Report that in order to fully evaluate the situation and the environmental damage caused it was necessary to know the extent of NATO's knowledge regarding the nature of the enemy targets and the likelihood of resulting environmental damage from the attacks,[319] the Committee did not recommend further investigation into the matter.[320] Nonetheless, despite the Committee's disinclination to recommend further investigation in respect of the collateral environmental damage caused by NATO,[321] based on NATO's statements that Pančevo was an important military target[322] and the UNEP-BTF's conclusion that there was no 'environmental catastrophe',[323] it is concluded *prima facie* that the NATO States did not violate the customary principle of proportionality.

This case-study, from the perspective of sustainable development and the environment itself, illustrates the problems and complexities involved

---

[314] Final Report (n 239) at para. 22.

[315] See text to (n 297) and (n 298).

[316] See, e.g. 2004 Hulme (n 9) at p. 201.

[317] Ibid., at p. 202.

[318] 1999 UNEP/UNCHS Kosovo (n 242) at p. 34. See also 2004 Hulme (n 9) at p. 201.

[319] Final Report (n 239) at para. 24.

[320] Ibid., at para. 25.

[321] Ibid.

[322] See text to (n 261) and (n 262).

[323] Gec (n 240).

in protecting the environment during armed conflict – from the stringent and ambiguous IHL laws that were formulated to expressly protect the environment, to the 'get out' clause of military necessity. Furthermore, it is difficult in the heat of battle to fulfil or even consider any elements within the precautionary or intra- and inter-generational equity principles with regard to the environment during armed conflict. Thus, these weaknesses in environmental protection result in the inevitable damage to the environment during conflict that has a negative impact not only on the environment itself but also on development and human well-being; thereby, obstructing sustainable development.

In this case, although NATO has not violated the relevant IHL provisions, its military operations did had a negative impact on sustainable development within the affected countries. Pančevo was one of the locations attacked by NATO. There were various others – from the damage to the 'hot-spots', bombed craters in National Parks to the indirect effects of administrative, social and economic disruption in the former FRY and the region (for example, reduced income from tourism; increased use of wood for heating due to electricity disruptions, resulting in further natural resources loss; etc.).[324] Obstruction to sustainable development was also evidenced by the UNCHS (Habitat) team in their analysis of Kosovo: damage and disruption to settlement and housing infrastructure as well as disruption of local governance and administration;[325] thereby, illustrating the damaging effects of war on sustainable development.

Next, the following section explores (albeit theoretically), that if NATO's actions had violated the applicable rules and principles within IHL, as Bruch and Austin comment, 'then the thorny issue arises of how responsibility, and possibly liability, should be determined.'[326]

4.2. International Response and Affixing Liability

4.2.1. State responsibility

To invoke the doctrine of State responsibility for the environmental damage caused by NATO's actions, the NATO States would have had to have violated the applicable international law, and those violations would have to be attributed to them. As concluded, the NATO States do not appear to have violated any of the IHL provisions that afford direct or

---

[324]   1999 UNEP/UNCHS Kosovo (n 242) at pp. 54–67.

[325]   Ibid., at pp. 68–71.

[326]   Bruch and Austin 'Kosovo' (n 231) at p. 650.

indirect environmental protection in respect of the aerial attack on Pančevo.[327] Therefore, none of the NATO States can be held liable for their actions.

In reality, while the armed conflict was still going on, FRY brought a case before the ICJ, filing separate complaints against the ten NATO countries.[328] FRY requested that the Court declare the bombing illegal and to order immediate cessation of the operation.[329] The ICJ immediately declared that it manifestly lacked jurisdiction against the US and Spain, and in 2004 found that it lacked *prima facie* jurisdiction against the other eight countries.[330] Some scholars argue it remains questionable whether the ICJ, even if it had jurisdiction at the time, would have found NATO States in violation of IHL norms, especially environmental law provisions.[331] Such a scenario may have been unexpected because unlike the significant level of international outrage and condemnation at Iraq's actions in the First Gulf War, in contrast, there seems to have been much less international support for any serious consideration of legal responsibility for the NATO nations.[332]

4.2.2. Individual responsibility

While the conflict was still in progress, the Office of the Prosecutor (OTP) of the ICTY established an investigative fact-finding committee to determine and report on war crimes allegedly committed by NATO during the conflict,[333] including the bombardment of the Pančevo

---

[327]   See 2004 Hulme (n 9) at p. 204; Bruch and Austin 'Kosovo' (n 231) at p. 650. *Cf.* Alexander, N.G., 'Airstrikes and Environmental Damage: Can the United States Be Held Liable for Operation Allied Force?' (2000) 11 Colorado Journal of International Environmental Law and Policy 471, at p. 491 [hereinafter Alexander].

[328]   See *Yugoslavia v NATO States* (n 264).

[329]   Ibid.

[330]   Ibid.

[331]   See, e.g. Bruch and Austin 'Kosovo' (n 231) at p. 651; 2006 Schwabach (n 61) at p. 124.

[332]   See, e.g. Final Report (n 239). See also Laursen, A., 'NATO, The War over Kosovo, and the ICTY Investigation' (2002) 17 American University International Law Review 765, at p. 811.

[333]   See, e.g. Boelaert-Suominen, S., 'The International Criminal Tribunal for the Former Yugoslavia and the Kosovo Conflict' (2000) 82 International Review of the Red Cross 217, at p. 247 ('the Prosecutor acknowledged that she had received requests from persons and groups urging her to indict various NATO and other officials for war crimes in relation to the air strikes conducted in

complex.[334] Despite references being made to Articles 35(3) and 55 of AP I, Article 8(b)(iv) of the ICC as well as the principles of military necessity, proportionality and distinction, the Committee advised against any investigation by the OTP on 'NATO's bombing campaign or incidents occurring during the campaign,'[335] including any collateral environmental damage caused.[336] Finally, in July 2000, the new ICTY Prosecutor announced her decision against initiating 'a full investigation into NATO's conduct of the conflict.'[337] The Final Report and the Prosecutor's decision were both controversial and drew a high degree of criticism.[338] First of all, despite the urging of numerous States and other actors for the ICTY to hold the NATO States and various officials involved responsible, the ICTY would not have been able to do so with regard to the States as the ICTY only has jurisdiction over individuals. In respect of affixing individual responsibility to NATO forces' actions that caused environmental damage, it would most likely be against the pilots conducting the airstrikes over Pančevo or based on command responsibility, the military commanders that gave the orders.[339]

However, based on *prima facie* evidence that individual members belonging to the NATO forces did not violate norms and provisions of IHL, attaching liability to them would be difficult. As discussed previously, it is unlikely the ICTY would have found any of the environmental damage resulting from the attack on the Pančevo complex to amount to a

---

Serbia.' Boelaert-Suominen lists a few of the individuals and groups that sent such requests).

[334]   2006 Schwabach (n 61) at p. 124.

[335]   Final Report (n 239) at para. 91.

[336]   Ibid., at para. 25.

[337]   Cryer, R., *Prosecuting International Crimes: Selectivity and the International Criminal Law Regime* (CUP, Cambridge 2005) at p. 215.

[338]   For support of the report (by one of its authors) see Fenrick, W.J., 'Targeting and Proportionality during the NATO Bombing Campaign Against Yugoslavia' (2001) 12 European Journal of International Law 489. For criticism against, see, e.g. David (n 300); Benvenuti, P., 'The ICTY Prosecutor and the Review of the NATO Bombing against the Federal Republic of Yugoslavia' (2001) 12 European Journal of International Law 503; Bothe, M., 'The Protection of the Civilian Population and NATO Bombing on Yugoslavia: Comments on a Report to the Prosecutor of the ICTY' (2001) 12 European Journal of International Law 531; Ronzitti, N., 'Is the Non Liquet of the Final Report by the Committee Established to Review the NATO Bombing Campaign Against the Federal Republic of Yugoslavia Acceptable?' (2000) 840 International Review of the Red Cross 1017; Marauhn (n 206).

[339]   Alexander (n 327) at p. 487.

war crime.[340] Errors of judgement would not entail responsibility[341] and as according to NATO targets were selected carefully, no individual NATO members would likely be found liable.[342] Furthermore, any charges let alone charges for environmental damage may be politically difficult to carry out. Indeed, despite the complaints and criticisms, no indictment or action was taken against individual members of NATO forces for the environmental damage. One of the reasons could be 'it is unlikely that the court is willing to face the repercussion of indicting a high level NATO official.'[343] Alexander further comments that,

> [w]hile the Office of the Prosecutor has shown a high degree of independence,[344] the repercussions of indicting the leader of a NATO country, especially the United States would be tremendous. What western industrialised nation would be willing to contribute military forces to an action motivated by humanitarian concerns if it thought that there was even the slightest chance that its officials could be indicted based on collateral damage to the environment? It is highly doubtful that the ICTY or any future ad hoc war crimes tribunal will be willing to take this step.[345]

Indeed, when posed the question as to what would happen if NATO (individuals) were ever brought before the ICTY, NATO spokesman Jamie Shea replied that,

> [w]ithout NATO countries there would be no International Court of Justice, nor would there be any International Criminal Tribunal for the former Yugoslavia because NATO countries are in the forefront of those who have established these two tribunals, who fund these tribunals and who support on

---

[340]   Ibid.

[341]   2000 Rogers (n 232) at p. 178.

[342]   'The targets were exclusively military – every effort was made to avoid collateral damage – planes only fire at targets when we are confident that we can strike accurately – some aircraft in the first operation returned without dropping ordnance. Targets are carefully selected and continuously assessed to avoid collateral damage.' See 'NATO Press Conference by NATO Spokesman, Jamie Shea and Air Commodore David Wilby, SHAPE' (NATO HQ 26 March 1999), www.nato.int/kosovo/press/p990326a.htm (accessed 18 May 2012).

[343]   Alexander (n 327) at pp. 487–8.

[344]   See, e.g. Hundley, T., 'Indictment Limits Yugoslav Leader's Ability to Barter' *Chicago Tribune* (Belgrade 30 May 1999).

[345]   Alexander (n 327) at pp. 487–8. See also Kerr, R., *The International Criminal Tribunal for the Former Yugoslavia: An Exercise in Law, Politics and Diplomacy* (OUP, Oxford 2004).

a daily basis their activities. We are the upholders, not the violators, of international law.[346]

To sum it up, States and their military forces should recognise the importance of protecting the environment during armed conflict because such conflict, in a matter of days or even a few hours can destroy '[s]table ecosystems that have required eons of evolution.'[347] As illustrated for example by the case-studies above – the environmental damage to the Persian Gulf by the actions of Iraqi forces in the First Gulf War and even the damage to the aquatic life in the waters of the Danube as a result of NATO airstrikes. Such environmental damage and the possibility of even more devastating damage in the future due to the ever increasing sophistication and destructiveness of the means and methods of warfare and its potential negative impact on the environment, human well-being and socio-economic development, highlight the reasons as to why armed conflict is the very 'antithesis of sustainable development.'[348]

5. HEAT OF THE BATTLE – CONTRIBUTING TO THE CYCLE OF SUSTAINABLE DEVELOPMENT

At the end of the day, in this part of the armed conflict life cycle – 'in conflict', the ethos of protagonists involved in the war is key, that is, respecting the rules of IHL. Indeed, both case-studies draw attention to the need for better respect by States' military forces of the existing IHL provisions that provide direct and indirect environmental protection during armed conflict. Even in the face of high thresholds of 'widespread, long-term and severe', States and their forces should endeavour to take precautionary measures to mitigate and limit damage to the environment as much as feasibly possible during armed conflict. Undoubtedly, the rules of IHL in armed conflict and the situation of conflict itself are different to times of peace, making it the most difficult in the lifecycle of armed conflict to use and adhere to sustainable

---

[346] 'Press Conference given by NATO Spokesman, Jamie Shea and SHAPE Spokesman, Major General Walter Jertz' (NATO HQ 17 May 1999), www.nato.int/kosovo/press/p990517b.htm (accessed 18 May 2012).

[347] Richardson, J., 'Why Should Proponents of Sustainable Development Care About Deadly Conflict and Terrorism?' *RMI Solutions Newsletter* (Rocky Mountain Inst., Colorado Spring 2003) at p. 20.

[348] Cooper, P.J. and Vargas, C.M., *Sustainable Development in Crisis Conditions: Challenges of War, Terrorism, and Civil Disorder* (Rowman & Littlefield, USA 2008) at p. 1.

development principles and contribute towards the concept. However, it is also part of the life cycle that can do the most damage – environmentally, socially and economically. Thus, better respect of and adherence to the relevant IHL rules could certainly 'reduce the destructive impacts of armed conflicts on sustainable development.'[349] As the ICRC stresses, efforts 'should be undertaken to better respect and ensure respect for the rules of international humanitarian law, which aim at protecting ... the natural environment, either against attacks on the environment as such or against wanton destruction causing grievous environmental damage.'[350]

Better respect for the relevant IHL rules comes with knowing what the rules actually are, but expecting military forces (especially the average soldier) to take note and remember all the relevant rules and principles to protect the environment in armed conflict is impractical. Thus, it is suggested that there is a strong case for the relevant existing IHL laws to be taken together and set out clearly and comprehensively within a new set of guidelines or rules, enabling the relevant rules for protecting the environment during conflict to be more easily digested by members of the armed forces. This new set of guidelines could take its cue from the ILA's Berlin Rules[351] by clearly and comprehensively setting out up-to-date guidelines prescribing the obligations towards the environment during conflict, be it an international, non-international or hybrid conflict. These guidelines could also take the opportunity to integrate salient sustainable development principles, and whilst not intended to extend the primary norms within IHL applicable to environmental protection in armed conflict, they could contribute to raising awareness and as such, add to the consciousness of the international community especially belligerents as to the level of environmental damage that is not acceptable during warfare.

Other than these suggestions, this chapter does not seek to make further recommendations for improvements in respect of environmental protection in armed conflict, except to point out that UNEP in conjunction with leading experts in the field, have already come up with several recommendations in its comprehensive report on international law and protection of the environment during armed conflict.[352] The recommendations range for example, from a clearer definition of the threshold criteria in Articles 35 and 55 of AP I; better clarification, codification and

---

[349]   ICRC Statement (n 3).
[350]   Ibid.
[351]   Berlin Rules (n 33).
[352]   UNEP International Law (n 7).

expansion of the laws governing environmental protection in armed conflict by the UN's ILC; to the creation of a permanent UN body to monitor violations and address compensation for conflict-related environmental damage.[353] Hopefully, the international community, particularly the UN, will take these UNEP recommendations on board and proceed to improve and strengthen the laws and procedures to protect the environment during times of armed conflict and in the process, mitigate the obstruction to sustainable development. As UNEP's Executive Director, Klaus Toepfer aptly comments:

> If we are to take the path towards sustainable development in the years to come, we must address the root causes that prevent us from achieving it. The ambivalence between increasing global environmental cooperation and intensified environmental damage associated with armed conflicts is one of the major points in this regards.

> It is our responsibility to protect and enhance the environment, which enables people to enjoy a healthy and productive life in harmony with nature. As part of the process towards sustainable development, we need to consider issues associated with the environmental consequences of war, and identify realistic, innovative policy responses. A solution to this challenge will provide us with a key to the gate leading to a peaceful and sustainable world that we owe to future generations.[354]

The case-studies explored and the conclusions drawn thereof support these exhortations.

6. CONCLUSION

The first part of this chapter deals with the laws of armed conflict that relate specifically to the environment as well as wider IHL customary norms which are considered to encompass the environment. In the process, some problems regarding these laws were identified, noticeably the stringent and high thresholds in which environmental harm is set as well as the convenient loophole of military necessity. In the following sections, two case-studies were examined which proceeded to confirm the inherent difficulty in satisfying the high threshold of laws protecting the environment during armed conflict. For example, in Kosovo, though serious 'pockets' of environmental harm were found, the harm was not

---

[353] Ibid., at pp. 51–4.
[354] Toepfer, K., 'Foreword' in Austin and Bruch (eds) (n 4).

considered having satisfied the cumulative 'widespread, long-term and severe' threshold. The Iraq case-study, although it highlights the significant devastation on the environment wrought by Iraqi armed forces during armed conflict and the subsequent actions of the international community in holding Iraq responsible, it also demonstrates the lack of clarification of IHL provisions providing environmental protection during warfare by only holding Iraq liable under *jus ad bellum* rules.

One of the key messages of these case-studies is that politics and diplomacy can get in the way of environmental protection in armed conflict. These case-studies bring to the fore the poor track record of the international community seeking to hold States and individuals responsible for environmental harm caused during armed conflict, barring the one notable exception: the First Gulf War. The Kosovo conflict in contrast to the First Gulf War case-study illustrates the difficulty and reluctance in holding certain State parties responsible for war-related environmental damage, owing to pragmatic or political reasons. Another hurdle, this time relating to individual liability relates to impunity from prosecution, particularly in circumstances when the promise not to prosecute can be a key to cease-fire agreements in which case politicians are more than likely to sacrifice the environment for peace and again, political motivating factors prevent the indictment of responsible individuals where States seem reluctant to hold individuals, particularly from the more powerful States, responsible. Ultimately however, perhaps holding individuals responsible for conflict-related environmental damage or environmental war crimes have not yet reached the necessary level of consciousness within the international community.

Nevertheless, there is no doubt that the international community should seek to increase environmental protection during armed conflict especially since armed conflict will never cease. As seen in Chapter 3, the world is already facing various environmental pressures and challenges – from environmental degradation, resource scarcity to demographic pressures (amongst others). Therefore, it is hardly justifiable to put the added pressure of war-ravaged environments on the growing list of global environmental problems. There is no doubt improving environmental protection during armed conflict and preventing obstruction to sustainable development would be a hard challenge for the international community. Therefore, the overall conclusion of this 'in-conflict' chapter is that the difficulty in mitigating the effects of armed conflict on the environment and thus, attempting to achieve sustainable development, highlights the importance of prevention (Chapter 3) and post-conflict reparations and reconstruction (Chapter 5). To give credence to the statement that 'war is inimical to sustainable development', strides towards achieving sustainable development should be stepped up before a conflict even begins and in the event prevention fails, ensuring its integration after conflict.

5. Post-conflict: breaking the cycle for a better future – sustainable development and environmental protection relevant to security and armed conflict

1. INTRODUCTION

> Despite the protection afforded by several important legal instruments, the environment continues to be the silent victim of armed conflicts worldwide... armed conflict causes significant harm to the environment and the communities that depend on natural resources. Direct and indirect environmental damage, coupled with the collapse of institutions, lead to environmental risks that can threaten people's health, livelihoods and security, and ultimately undermine post-conflict peacebuilding.[1]

The preceding chapter reviews environmental protection during armed conflict, coming to the conclusion that the environment is directly or indirectly harmed by warfare and that war inexorably halts sustainable development in its tracks. Regrettably, as the law stands, little can be done to protect the environment in a sustainable way during an armed conflict.[2] This makes the post-conflict stage even more vital to not only mitigate and restore the war damaged environment but as following on from Chapter 3, to also alleviate and manage environmental pressures. Environmental pressures, that have to be considered together with other socio-economic and development factors, which in combination have triggered and fuelled armed conflicts. Therefore, it is important to integrate environmental and natural resource issues into the post-conflict peacebuilding stage. Prospects of peace and post-conflict reconstruction

---

[1]   UNEP, 'Protecting the Environment During Armed Conflict: An Inventory and Analysis of Law' (UNEP, Switzerland 2009) at p. 4 [hereinafter UNEP International Law].
[2]   See Chapter 4.

can be undermined if environmental and natural resource issues are not properly managed at this stage.[3] The UNEP Conflict to Peacebuilding Report aptly highlights the importance of sustainable development and effective environmental and natural resource management (NRM) in post-conflict situations:

> The recognition that environmental issues can contribute to violent conflict underscores their potential significance as pathways for cooperation, transformation and the consolidation of peace in war-torn societies. Natural resources and the environment can contribute to peacebuilding through economic development and the generation of employment, while cooperation over the management of shared natural resources provides new opportunities for peacebuilding. These factors, however, must be taken into consideration from the outset.[4]

Thus, this chapter examines the third component in a 'comprehensive system' for addressing through law and policy the remedies for environmental damage as well as mitigating conflict-related environmental issues in integration with other variable factors,[5] to prevent a relapse into conflict or 're-conflict'. This is explored in the context of integrating the concept of sustainable development in the post-conflict recovery stage.

The subjects covered by the final element in this analysis are as wide ranging as they are conceptually complex. The evolution of sustainable development and the references to sustainable development and environmental protection in the context of armed conflict have been discussed in previous chapters as set out, for example, in the Stockholm Declaration,[6] the World Charter of Nature[7] and the Rio Declaration.[8] However, as Okowa points out, 'these instruments did not envisage a specific

---

[3]　UNEP, 'From Conflict to Peacebuilding: The Role of Natural Resources and the Environment' (UNEP, Switzerland 2009) at p. 5 [hereinafter UNEP Conflict to Peacebuilding].

[4]　Ibid.

[5]　See Chapter 3, Section 2.1. (for discussion on socio-economic and political variable factors).

[6]　Principle 26, Declaration of the UN Conference on the Human Environment, A/CONF.84/14 (1972).

[7]　UN General Assembly (UNGA) Resolution 37/7 (28 October 1982).

[8]　Principle 24, Declaration of the UN Conference on Environment and Development, UN Doc. A/CONF.151/26/REV.1, Vol. I (12 August 1992).

programme of enforcement, nor do they concern themselves with apportioning responsibility or redressing environmental harm.'[9] There is no doubt that these crucial factors: enforcement, allocating responsibility and remedying environmental harm, need to be accounted for. Therefore, this chapter considers the post-conflict stage where the damage has already been done and explores in that context, via international law – the reparations affixed to State responsibility and via international environmental law – the polluter pays principle, to respond to conflict-related environmental damages and in the process, explore the integration (or not) of sustainable development principles in the reconstruction stage.

It has to be remembered that reparations under international law are only applicable to international conflicts. To reiterate, there is great dearth in the application of international law for non-international armed conflicts (NIACs) let alone laws in respect of conflict-related environmental damage. Thus, following on from Chapter 3, this chapter also explores post-conflict environmental damage and management of conflict-inducing environmental pressures in relation to NIACs. This chapter is divided into two parts: Section 2 and Section 3. Section 2 gives an overview of remedies for conflict-related environmental damage. First, by considering the types of reparations available under international law; second, by exploring the possible economic valuation methods available for assessing environmental damage; third, by examining the valuation methods in relation to the US domestic system for environmental damages; fourth, by reviewing the UNCC system as a model for war-related environmental damages; fifth, by determining the best possible model for calculating conflict-related environmental damages; and finally, by considering the polluter pays principle as an alternative to or complementary means for reparations under international law. Section 3 analyses post-conflict environmental recovery after apportioning reparations (or not) for both conflict-related environmental damages and environmental-inducing conflict pressures in order to prevent re-conflict, in relation to international armed conflicts (IACs) and NIAC respectively. This is analysed from a sustainable development perspective in the context of three case-studies: the First Gulf War, the Kosovo Conflict and Sudan.

---

[9] Okowa, P., 'Environmental Justice in Situations of Armed Conflict' in Ebbesson, J. and Okowa, P. (eds), *Environmental Law and Justice in Context* (CUP, Cambridge 2009) at p. 239.

2. AFFIXING (OR NOT) POST-CONFLICT LIABILITY: REPARATIONS AND THE POLLUTER PAYS PRINCIPLE

Having explored the laws applicable to environmental protection in armed conflict and attaching liability for environmental damage caused in Chapter 4, this part considers the next stage: reparations under international law and the polluter pays principle under international environmental law and the umbrella concept of sustainable development.

2.1. International Law: Reparations

It must be stressed that with regard to remedies offered for environmental damages, whether the result of armed conflict or not, there is no specifically dedicated mechanism. Indeed, '[n]o attempt has yet been made, either in the Commission's articles on State responsibility, or in those on the prevention of transboundary harm, to develop forms of reparation specifically adapted to particular kinds of damage, such as environmental damage.'[10] Thus, any breach of an international obligation that is environmental in nature would have to be remedied by general international law.

Under international law, if a State fails to comply with its international law obligations and it is proven that the damage is attributable to the State, the State is under the obligation to cease the internationally wrongful act (if it is continuing), and if the circumstances require it, to guarantee or offer assurances of non-repetition[11] as well as to make full reparation for the injury caused.[12] The injury here would be environmental damage. Generally, '[t]he aim of reparation is to eliminate, as far

---

[10]   Boyle, A., 'Reparation for Environmental Damage in International Law: Some Preliminary Problems' in Bowman, M. and Boyle, A. (eds), *Environmental Damage in International and Comparative Law: Problems of Definition and Valuation* (OUP, Oxford 2002) at p. 22 [hereinafter 2002 Boyle], [hereinafter Bowman and Boyle (eds)].

[11]   Art 30, ILC's Articles on the Responsibility of States for Internationally Wrongful Acts (adopted by the ILC on 10 August 2001) [hereinafter Articles on State Responsibility]. See also Report on the ILC on the Work of its Fifty-Third Session, UN Doc A/56/10 (2001); *LaGrand Case (Germany v USA)* (Judgement) [2001] ICJ Rep 466, at pp. 510–16 (on States offering assurances of non-repetition) [hereinafter *LaGrand*].

[12]   Art 31, Articles on State Responsibility. The principle of reparation was laid down in the *Case Concerning the Factory at Chorzów (Germany v Poland)*

as possible, the consequences of the illegal act and to restore the situation that would have existed if the act had not been committed.'[13] Reparation can take a variety of forms, including restitution, compensation or satisfaction.[14] Each remedy can be applied singly or in combination in response to a particular violation of international obligation.[15]

That being said, as Boyle points out, '[t]here is no inherent difficulty in applying any of these concepts [restitution, compensation or satisfaction] to cases of environmental damage: examples of restoration of a damaged environment, compensation for the value of an irreparably damaged environment, or monetary satisfaction for breaches of environmental obligations which cause no quantifiable loss can already be found in state practice or national law'.[16] Boyle further notes that the ILC acknowledges that the application of international law on remedies needs to be flexible.[17] For instance, the ILC commentary states that, '[t]he most suitable remedy can only be determined in each instance with a view to

---

(Merits) (1928) PCIJ Rep Series A No. 17, at pp. 47–8 [hereinafter *Chorzów Factory*]. See also *Case Concerning United States Diplomatic and Consular Staff in Tehran (Unites States of America v Iran)* [1980] ICJ Rep 3, at p. 41, para. 90 (ICJ concluded that Iran did have a duty to make reparation to the US). The principle was further reaffirmed in a number of cases, including for, e.g. by the ICJ in *Gabčíkovo-Nagymaros (Hungary v Slovakia)* [1997] ICJ Rep 7, at p. 55 [hereinafter *Gabčíkovo-Nagymaros*]; and by ITLOS in *M/V 'Saiga' (No.2) (Saint Vincent and The Grenadines v Guinea)* (Admissibility and Merits) (1999) 120 ILR 143, at p. 199.

[13] Gillard, E.C., 'Reparations for Violations of International Humanitarian Law' (2003) 85 International Review of the Red Cross 529, at p. 531 [hereinafter Gillard].

[14] Art. 34, Articles on State Responsibility.

[15] See Arts. 31–4, ibid.

[16] 2002 Boyle (n 10) at p. 22. See, e.g. EU legislation: Directive 2004/35/CE of the European Parliament and of the Council of 21 April 2004 on Environmental Liability with Regard to the Prevention and Remedying of Environmental Damage, OJL 143/56 (30 April 2004); Convention on Civil Liability for Damage Resulting from Activities Dangerous to the Environment (1993) 32 ILM 1228 [hereinafter Lugano Convention]. National legislation: Finnish Environmental Damage Compensation Act (EDCA) (737/1994) (1 June 1995); Chapters 10 and 32, Swedish Environmental Code (adopted 1998, entered into force 1 January 1999) SFS 1998:808 Miljöbalk; Norwegian *Forurensningsloven*, Section 57 (13 March 1991) No. 6 (Norwegian Pollution Act); Danish Act on Compensation for Environmental Damage (ACED), No. 225 (6 April 1994); German Environmental Liability Act (Umwelthaftungsgesetz) (10 December 1990) (BGB1. I 1990, 2634) as amended on 19 July 2002 (BGB1. I 2002, 2674).

[17] 2002 Boyle (n 10) at p. 22.

achieving the most complete satisfaction of the injured state's interest in the "wiping out" of all the injurious consequences of the wrongful act.'[18] Simply put, this calls for a mix and match of international remedies on a case-by-case basis. This section thereby explores restitution, compensation and satisfaction with respect to damage to the environment as a result of armed conflict.

2.1.1. Restitution

Article 35 of the Articles on State Responsibility provides that a State found 'responsible for an internationally wrongful act is under an obligation to make restitution, that is to re-establish the situation which existed before the wrongful act was committed.'[19] Of course, restitution is only an obligation insofar as it is not materially impossible to do so.[20] Moreover, in certain circumstances, restitution as a remedy may be inappropriate especially 'if the benefit to be gained from it by the victim is wholly disproportionate to its cost to the violator.'[21]

From a sustainable development standpoint, restitution is an ideal remedy as the damaged environment would have to be restored to its original state. This not only exemplifies the precautionary principle in that scientifically uncertain threats or risks of serious or irreversible environmental damage are prevented or mitigated,[22] but also allows the current and future generations to enjoy the environment in its restored pre-damaged state.[23] This remedy also embodies elements of the duty of States to ensure sustainable use of natural resources, in that, States are obliged to restore the damaged environment or natural resource particularly to ensure that it does not cause any transboundary harm as well as ensuring its sustainable preservation and protection for the development

---

[18] 'Report of the Commission to the General Assembly on the Work of its Forty-Fifth Session: United Nations' (1993) II Yearbook of the International Law Commission Part 2, at p. 63 [hereinafter ILC Report].

[19] For further discussion on restitution in the context of State responsibility, see Shelton, D., 'Righting Wrongs: Reparations in the Articles on State Responsibility' (2002) 96 American Journal of International Law 833, at pp. 849–51; Crawford, J., *The International Law Commission's Articles on State Responsibility: Introduction, Text and Commentaries* (CUP, Cambridge 2002) at pp. 213–18 [hereinafter 2002 Crawford]; Pronto, A. and Wood, M., *The International Law Commission 1999–2009: Volume IV: Treaties, Final Draft Articles, and Other Materials* (OUP, New York 2010) at pp. 127–348.

[20] Art. 35(a), Articles on State Responsibility.

[21] Gillard (n 13) at p. 531.

[22] Principle 4, New Delhi Declaration.

[23] Principle 2, ibid.

of their population.[24] The remedy of restitution also ensures that any further environmental threat to the environment itself, development and human well-being is prevented or mitigated; thus, contributing to sustainable development.

However, with regard to conflict-related environmental damage, restitution as a form of reparation may be more difficult to apply.[25] The primary reason is because in such circumstances it would be difficult, if not impossible, to restore the damaged environment to its original pre-conflict state. Damage to the environment (natural and non-natural), cannot be restored overnight. Trying to reverse the environmental damage caused in armed conflict may be possible for minor environmental damage but may be less likely where major damage is concerned. The second reason is the fact that responsibility for the exact damage caused cannot always be pinpointed or isolated from pre-existing environmental damage. For example, restitution would have been difficult to apply to the Pančevo incident because the damage to the environment found by UNEP-BTF was not only as a result of NATO bombings but also the result of pre-existing environmental harm.[26] Thus, it would have been almost impossible to apply the remedy of restitution to the NATO States.

Nevertheless, as noted above, each remedy can be tailored to the situation in combination with other remedies. Therefore, as restitution in kind is always the first remedy sought,[27] in cases of environmental damage where cleaning up the environment and restoring it as much as possible is preferred, perhaps restitution in combination with another remedy, such as compensation (as financial support is required to restore the environment in any event) might be the best possible solution and also in line with achieving sustainable development.

2.1.2. Compensation

This section examines compensation in relation to environmental damage, with a focus on State responsibility. With regard to individual

---

[24]   Principle 1, ibid.

[25]   For further discussion on restitution and environmental damage, see Larsson, M.L., *The Law of Environmental Damage: Liability and Reparation* (Kluwer Law, Stockholm 1999) at pp. 115–570.

[26]   UNEP/UNCHS-HABITAT, 'Kosovo Conflict: Consequences for the Environment & Human Settlements' (UNEP/UNCHS-HABITAT, Switzerland 1999) at pp. 8–10 [hereinafter UNEP/UNCHS Kosovo].

[27]   ILC Report (n 18) at p. 63.

responsibility,[28] as discovered in Chapter 4, the last time any individual was held liable for war-related environmental damage was during the Nuremberg trials.[29] As it seems to be inherently difficult to attach liability to individuals responsible for such damage, in addition to the fact that there has been relatively little progress in this area,[30] this chapter focuses only on compensation in relation to State responsibility.[31] The previous chapter has already considered how a State may be held liable for war-related environmental damage, therefore this section considers how payment can be made for the environmental damage caused? To do so, it is necessary to explore what the environment is worth in terms of calculating such damages. That said, there is nothing in this discussion of calculating compensation that is not as pertinent to individual responsibility as it is to State responsibility, or indeed broader collective responsibility. Getting the measure of compensation in law right is therefore of far reaching importance.

2.1.2.(a)   Compensation for State liability   Article 36 of the Articles of State Responsibility stipulates that '[t]he State responsible for an internationally wrongful act is under an obligation to compensate for the damage thereby, insofar as such damage is not made good by restitution.'[32] The compensation should cover any financially assessable damage.[33] Of all the forms of reparation, compensation is probably 'the most commonly sought in international practice'.[34] This is perhaps because it

---

[28]   Chapter 4 considered individual responsibility in relation to conflict-related environmental damage in order to determine whether individuals could be held liable for it and used as future deterrence.

[29]   For example, Alfred Jodl was convicted for scorched earth policies in Nuremberg.

[30]   Weinstein, T., 'Prosecuting Attacks that Destroy the Environment: Environmental Crimes or Humanitarian Atrocities?' (2005) 17 Georgetown International Environmental Law Review 697 at pp. 704–5; Bruch, C.E., 'All's Not Fair in (Civil) War: Criminal Liability for Environmental Damage in Internal Armed Conflict' (2001) 25 Vermont Law Review 695, at p. 716.

[31]   In addition, this chapter examines how post-conflict funds for environmental damages and international funding assists the post-conflict environment; funds for the environment which are generally administered through governments and international and national organisations, and not individuals.

[32]   See also, e.g. *Gabčikovo-Nagymaros* (n 12) at p. 81, para. 152; *Chorzów Factory* (n 12) at p. 27; *Corfu Channel Case (UK v Albania)* (Assessment of Compensation) [1949] ICJ Rep 244, at p. 249.

[33]   Art. 36, Articles on State Responsibility.

[34]   2002 Crawford (n 19) at p. 218.

is more convenient and easier to fulfil than any of the other forms of reparation.[35] Furthermore, as Crawford notes, '[e]ven where restitution is made, it may be insufficient to ensure full reparation. The role of compensation is to fill in any gaps so as to ensure full reparation for damage suffered.'[36]

Compensation is probably the most important and practical form of reparation with regard to environmental damage as a result of warfare, particularly since in many cases it would be quite difficult to apply restitution in its entirety and reparation in the form of satisfaction does not actually assist the war-torn environment. However, whether or not compensation actually helps the post-conflict environment is discussed below in Section 3. The essential question here would be on how to financially assess environmental damage as a result of armed conflict? This involves consideration of the following: first, methods of assessing environmental damage; second, the UN Compensation Commission (UNCC)[37] as an example for conflict-related environmental damages; third, the best possible assessment model for future conflict-related environmental damages; and finally, the possibility of States paying compensation for such damages without admitting liability.

2.1.2.(b)   Calculating costs for environmental damage   As there is no precedent for conflict-related environmental damage reparation other than the UNCC, it is worth examining peacetime models of compensation for environmental damage. Due to this dearth in the field of conflict-related environmental damage, peacetime models could provide practical examples on assessing damage to the environment. This in turn, may be used as a basis for comparison with the methods of assessment employed by the UNCC, in order to consider the best possible model for calculating future conflict-related environmental damage.

In most cases regarding liability for environmental damage or the threat of potential damage, compensation is paid towards the victim State for incurring reasonable costs 'in preventing or remedying pollution, or to providing compensation for a reduction in the value of polluted property.'[38] A point to note however, is that environmental damage is not

---

[35]   Ibid., at pp. 218–30 (for more discussion on the range of cases and compensation sought by States for breaches of international obligations).

[36]   Ibid., at p. 218. See also *Chorzów Factory* (n 12) at pp. 47–8.

[37]   The UNCC is a subsidiary organ of the UN Security Council established by UNSC Resolution 687 (3 April 1991) [hereinafter UNSC Resolution 687].

[38]   2002 Crawford (n 19) at p. 223. In the *Trail Smelter Arbitration (US v Canada)* (1938) 3 RIAA 1911; (1941) 3 RIAA 1938 [hereinafter *Trail Smelter*],

always easily quantifiable, that is, it may not have direct market value. Very often, damage to the environment extends to environmental elements such as biodiversity and amenities for example, which are essentially non-quantifiable damage that is generally termed as 'non-use values'.[39] Although not easily quantifiable, such damage, 'is, as a matter of principle, no less real and compensable than damage to property'.[40]

OVERVIEW OF ECONOMIC VALUATION METHODS FOR ENVIRONMENTAL DAMAGES   There are a number of valuation techniques that have been developed to ascertain the value of a particular environmental resource.[41] Some commonly used examples of valuation methods are:

- Market Price: determines the value of a particular natural resource that is only directly traded in commercial markets. For example, natural resource products such as oil, diamonds, gold, timber, fish, cattle, and grain.[42]
- Production Function: may be used to estimate the value of ecosystem services[43] by calculating its contribution to the production of

---

Canada had to pay compensation to the US for damage to land and property caused by sulphur dioxide emissions from a smelter across the border in Canadian territory. Compensation was calculated on the basis of the reduction in value of the affected land.

[39]   2002 Crawford (n 19) at p. 223.

[40]   Ibid.

[41]   For more information on the various environmental economic valuation methods, see van Beukering, P. and Slootweg, R., 'Valuation of Ecosystem Services: Lessons from Influential Cases' in Slootweg, R. and others (eds), *Biodiversity in Environmental Assessment: Enhancing Ecosystem Services for Human Well-Being* (CUP, New York 2010) at pp. 287–397 (uses twenty practical case-studies) [hereinafter Beukering and Slootweg], [hereinafter 2010 Slootweg (eds)]. See also Becker, J.S., 'Valuing the Depletion of Natural Resources under International Law' (1997) 6 Review of European Community & International Environmental Law 181.

[42]   Advantage: relatively simple method to apply. Disadvantage: excludes any natural resources that do not have market value. See Beukering and Slootweg (n 41) at pp. 313–14; Lee, V.A. and Bridgen, P.J., *The Natural Resource Damage Assessment Handbook: A Legal and Technical Analysis* (ELI, Washington, DC 2001) at pp. 305–6 [hereinafter Lee and Bridgen].

[43]   'Ecosystem services' is a term used to describe environmental goods and services i.e., 'goods and services obtained from biodiversity.' See Slootweg, R., 'Interpretation of biodiversity' in 2010 Slootweg (eds) (n 41) at p. 34 (based on the Millennium Ecosystem Assessment (MEA), *Ecosystems and Human Well-being: A Framework for Assessment* (Island Press, Washington, DC 2003)). MEA

commercially marketable goods. An example of this method is determining the changes in the quality of the ecosystem such as water pollution, soil erosion or deforestation, which causes changes in productivity or output in fisheries, agriculture or forestry.[44]

- Net Factor Income: estimates the economic value of ecosystem services that contribute to the production of a marketed product. For example, in valuing a coral reef that sustains a reef-based diving recreation site, the calculation should be: 'the revenue received from selling diving trips to the reef, minus the labour, equipment and other costs of providing the service.'[45]

- Replacement Cost: estimates the value of ecosystem services based on the cost of replacing or restoring the damaged environment or natural resource to its pre-existing state.[46]

- Damage Cost Avoided: measures the value of the ecosystem services based on the cost of avoiding damages due to loss of ecosystem services or the expenditure taken in avoiding the environmental damages in the first place. For example, if mangrove trees provide coastal protection from extreme weather damage, the estimated costs of the damages avoided is 'the value of the coastal protection function of the mangrove forest.'[47]

---

defines ecosystem services as 'the benefits that people obtain from the ecosystem.' See also Blanco, E. and Razzaque, J., 'Ecosystem Services and Human Well-Being in a Globalised World: Assessing the Role of the Law' (2009) 31 Human Rights Quarterly 692, at p. 693.

[44] Advantage: very effective method in theory due to its strong environment-economic benefits link. Disadvantage: in practice, this method requires vast amounts of data and is technically complex. See Lee and Bridgen (n 42) at pp. 307–8; Beukering and Slootweg (n 41) at pp. 315–16.

[45] Advantage: relatively easy method to apply, using readily available date. Disadvantage: most useful for valuing a narrow type of ecosystem services (relating to recreation and tourism). See Beukering and Slootweg (n 41) at p. 314.

[46] Advantage: relatively simple and cost-effective method as it does not need complex analysis or comprehensive surveys. Disadvantage: often it is not easy to acquire the exact substitute or replacement for ecosystem services providing the same level of benefits as the pre-existing ecosystem services. See Santhosh, V. and others, 'Biodiversity and its Valuation Techniques: An Overview' in Sahu, N.C. and Choudhury, A.K. (eds), *Dimensions of Environmental and Ecological Economics* (Universities Press, India 2005) at p. 322; Beukering and Slootweg (n 41) at pp. 314–15.

[47] Advantage: effective for valuing ecosystem services that have some function as natural protection. Disadvantage: this method is generally used in

- Travel Cost: generally used for assessing the value of an ecosystem-based recreational area or site (for example, safari parks, forest reserves, desert parks, wilderness camping sites). The valuation is based on the amount people spend to actually travel to the site, that is, travel expenses which include for example, petrol for private car use, car hire, public transport tickets, entrance fees, and other costs related to the trip.[48]
- Hedonic Pricing: estimates the value of the environment that directly affects the market prices of certain goods or amenities. This method is generally applied to variations in residential properties that reflect the value of their surrounding environment. For example, a house that has a close proximity to a landfill site or a chemical factory will be less valuable than a house that is further away or house prices in an area may decrease due to air or noise pollution.[49]
- Contingent Valuation (CV): estimates the value of ecosystem services by conducting survey interviews based on a hypothetical scenario. The survey asks individuals how much they would be willing to pay for a particular environmental service or resource.[50]
- Habitat Equivalency Analysis (HEA): is essentially a replacement cost method. It assesses the nature and extent of the temporary or interim loss of ecological services from the damaged ecosystem,

---

hypothetical scenarios based on predicting a situation where the environment may deteriorate or be damaged. See Beukering and Slootweg (n 41) at p. 315.

[48]   Advantage: effective for valuing ecosystem-based recreational sites. Disadvantage: dependant on large seasonal data sets collected through interviews and surveys, involves complex analysis and in most cases, relatively expensive and time consuming. See Beukering and Slootweg (n 41) at p. 317; Brans, E.H.P., *Liability for Damage to Public Natural Resources: Standing, Damage, and Damage Assessment* (Kluwer Law, The Netherlands 2001) at p. 104 [hereinafter Brans].

[49]   Advantage: useful for valuing ecosystem services related to residential properties. Disadvantage: requires substantial data, complex analysis and technically difficult to apply. See Lee and Bridgen (n 42) at pp. 310–11; Beukering and Slootweg (n 41) at pp. 316–17.

[50]   Advantage: applicable to value all types of ecosystem services (both use and non-use values). Disadvantage: as based on hypothetical scenarios, the answers received may not be accurate. Requires complex data collection that entails large-scale surveys, which can be time-consuming and expensive. See Brans (n 48) at pp. 105–6; Bateman, I.J. and Willis, K.J. (eds), *Valuing Environmental Preferences: Theory and Practice of the Contingent Valuation Method in the US, EU, and Developing Countries* (OUP, New York 1999).

determining the value of damaged resources based on the cost of replacing or restoring it.[51]

Each valuation method varies and is not always easy to apply, depending on the ecosystem services to be valued, expertise, budget and other potential variables. However, as there are no foolproof valuation methods, in order to ascertain damage costs, each method could be applicable to different types of environmental damage depending on its suitability.[52] Moreover, the valuation methods themselves arguably embody elements of the sustainable development concept, in that in order to valuate the environment, not only environmental but also economic and social factors and costs are taken into account. Having considered examples of methods available, the next sub-section explores the US system for an insight into environmental damage compensation in practice.

THE US: AN EXAMPLE OF A PEACETIME ENVIRONMENTAL DAMAGE COMPENSATION SYSTEM   US domestic laws on compensation for harm to natural resources and the economic valuation techniques used in the process are examined for the following reasons. First, because US law on 'compensation for nonmarket damages to environmental resources clearly exists'[53] and second, because laws on environmental damages have developed considerably[54] as a result of the US experiencing environmental

---

[51]   Advantage: attempts to restore the interim losses of a damaged ecosystem. Disadvantage: relatively complex method to apply. See Lee and Bridgen (n 42) at pp. 300–301.

[52]   See Beukering and Slootweg (n 41) at p. 320 (provides a detailed table of types of ecosystem services and the most commonly applied economic valuation methods).

[53]   Farber, D.A., 'Basic Compensation for Victims of Climate Change' (2007) 155 University of Pennsylvania Law Review 1605, at p. 1621 [hereinafter Farber]. See also, e.g. Tolan, P.E., 'Natural Resource Damages under CERCLA: Failures, Lessons Learned, and Alternatives' (2008) 38 New Mexico Law Review 409 [hereinafter Tolan]; Thompson, D.B., 'Valuing the Environment: Courts' Struggles with Natural Resource Damages' (2002) 32 Environmental Law 57 [hereinafter Thompson]; Brans (n 48) at pp. 65–176.

[54]   See, e.g. Kopp, R.J. and Smith, V.K. (eds), *Valuing Natural Assets: The Economics of Natural Resource Damage Assessment* (Resources for the Future, USA 1993); Kazazi, M., 'Environmental Damage in the Practice of the UN Compensation Commission' in Bowman and Boyle (eds) (n 10) at p. 121 [hereinafter Kazazi]. See also 'US Natural Resources Damage Assessment and Restoration Program (NRDAR)' US Department of Interior (DOI), www.doi.gov/restoration/index.cfm (accessed 30 April 2012).

incidents such as oil spills[55] and the release of hazardous and toxic substances.[56]

It is probably a coincidence that many of the early incidents of environmental contamination which precipitated Federal legislation in this field grew out of the war industry (such as the infamous Love Canal incident, also known as the Love Canal Superfund site in Niagara Falls, New York).[57] Most environmental lawyers will be familiar with the broad contours of Superfund legislation[58] and other such provisions, yet it is nonetheless worth exploring this system in detail, to highlight the scope and the limits of a compensatory approach to the clean-up of the environment after armed conflict. Certainly, the Superfund analogy will not be obvious to armed conflict law experts, and that alone is justification for the depth in which this issue is explored below.

The primary standard suitable for determining environmental damages in oil spill cases for instance, as explained by the US First Circuit,[59] is based on the reasonable expenses likely to be sustained by 'the sovereign or its designated agency' for rehabilitating or restoring the damaged

---

[55] See, e.g. the Exxon Valdez incident in 1989, *Exxon Shipping Co. v Baker* 128 S. Ct. 2605 (2008). For further analysis of the Exxon Valdez incident and the assessment of damages, see Doskow, C.S., 'What Do You Do with a Drunken Sailor? Reprehensibility, the Exxon Valdez, and Punitive Damages' (2009) 27 Quinnipiac Law Review 465; Bardwick, D.S., 'The American Tort System's Response to Environmental Disaster: The Exxon Valdez Oil Spill as a Case Study' (2000) 19 Stanford Environmental Law Journal 259; van Beukering, P. and others, 'Annex: Valuation of Ecosystem Services: Influential Cases' in 2010 Slootweg (eds) (n 41) at pp. 392–7.

[56] See, e.g. *US v Aceto Agricultural Chemical Corp.*, 872 F. 2d 1373 (8th Cir. 1989); *US v Alcan Aluminium Corp.*, 964 F. 2d 252 (3rd Cir.1992); *Premium Plastics v La Salle National Bank*, 904 F. Supp. 809 (N.D. Ill 1995). See also Glicksman, R.L., 'Pollution of Federal Lands IV: Liability for Hazardous Waste Disposal' (1994) 12 UCLA Journal of Environmental Law and Policy 233.

[57] *Love Canal Property Acquisition*, 42 U.S.C. §9661 (1978). See also Fletcher, T.H., *From Love Canal to Environmental Justice: The Politics of Hazardous Waste on the Canada-U.S. Border* (Broadview, Canada 2003) [hereinafter Fletcher].

[58] Fletcher (n 57) at p. 61 (Superfund legislation came about after the serious health threats as a result of the Love Canal incident).

[59] *Com. of Puerto Rico v SS Zoe Colocotroni*, 628 F. 2d 652 (1st Cir. 12 August 1980) (damages were assessed for environmental damage to a Puerto Rican coastline as a result of oil spillage from the defendant's tanker as well as costs for the clean-up) [hereinafter *Puerto Rico*].

environment to it pre-existing state or as close to it as possible without incurring grossly excessive costs.[60] The Court went on to state that,

> [t]he focus in determining such a remedy should be on the steps a reasonable and prudent sovereign or agency would take to mitigate the harm done by the pollution, with attention to such factors as technical feasibility, harmful side effects, compatibility with or duplication of such regeneration as is naturally to be expected, and the extent to which efforts beyond a certain point would become either redundant or disproportionately expensive .[61]

In the latter circumstances, the US First Circuit also stated that '[s]ome other measure of damages might be reasonable in such cases, at least where the process of natural regeneration will be too slow to ensure restoration within a reasonable period'.[62] The Court suggested that, 'one possibility [is] "the reasonable cost of acquiring resources to offset the loss."'[63] Simply put, if restoration efforts become unfeasible or unduly expensive, compensation will be determined based on the reasonable costs required in obtaining resources that could replace or compensate for the environmental damage caused.[64]

Most current US domestic laws in respect of damages to natural resources are linked to hazardous waste liability. The US Department of Interior (DOI), under the 1980 Comprehensive Environmental Response, Comprehensive, and Liability Act (CERCLA)[65] and the Clean Water Act[66] disseminated regulations for compensation based on the diminution in value of natural resources.[67] The DOI developed two types of assessment procedures within these regulations, the 'standard procedures'

---

[60]   Ibid., at pp. 675–6 (footnotes omitted) (quoting the 1977 amendments to the Clean Water Act 33 U.S.C. s 1321 (f)(4)-(5)). See also Farber (n 53) at p. 1621.

[61]   *Puerto Rico* (n 59) at pp. 675–6.

[62]   Ibid.

[63]   Ibid.

[64]   For further discussion on compensation and US oil spill cases, see Farber (n 53) at pp. 1621–3.

[65]   Pub. L. No. 96–510, 94 Stat. 2767, amended by Superfund Amendments and Reauthorization Act (SARA), Pub. L. No. 99–499, 100 Stat. 1613 (1986) (codified as amended at 42 U.S.C. §§ 9601–9675 (2000)).

[66]   33 U.S.C. §§ 1251–1387 (1988).

[67]   Wendel, H., 'Restoration as the Economically Efficient Remedy for Damage to Publicly Owned Natural Resources' (1991) 91 Columbia Law Review 430. For further discussion on the regulations, see Farber (n 53) at p. 1625.

assessment referred to as the 'Type A' model and the 'alternative protocols' as the 'Type B' model.[68] These regulations specify that:

> (A) standard procedures for simplified assessments requiring minimal field observation, including establishing measures of damages based on units of discharge or release or units of affected area, and (B) alternative protocols for conducting assessments in individual cases to determine the type and extent of short and long-term injury, destruction, or loss. Such regulations shall identify the best available procedures to determine such damages, including both direct and indirect injury, destruction, or loss and shall take into consideration factors including, but not limited to, replacement value, use value, and ability of the ecosystem or resource to recover.[69]

In 1989 however, major portions of the regulations set out in Type B were found to be in violation of CERCLA and struck down by the Court of Appeals for the District of Columbia on the basis that CERCLA requires the measure of damages in these actions to be the costs of restoration.[70] The Court did however uphold the DOI's methods of determining the 'use value' of damaged natural resources with no tradable market value.[71] One of the methods used was the CV[72] method which the Court upheld.[73]

After the *Ohio* judgement, the DOI in 1994, circulated new regulations on damage assessments for natural resources[74] which permit trustees of the environment in question to regain their expenses for 'restoration, rehabilitation, replacement, and/or acquisition of equivalent resources in

---

[68]   Farber (n 53) at p. 1625. For further discussion on both types, see Brans (n 48) at pp. 163–71.

[69]   42 U.S.C. § 9651 (c)(2).

[70]   *State of Ohio v US Department of Interior*, 880 F.2d 432 (D.C. Cir. 1989) 444, at p. 448 [hereinafter *Ohio*].

[71]   Farber (n 53) at p. 1627.

[72]   See text to (n 50).

[73]   *Ohio* (n 70) at pp. 475–77 (quoting Natural Resource Damage Assessments, Final Rule, 51 Fed. Reg. 27674–01 (1986), 27, 720–727, 721 (codified at 43 C.F.R. § 11.83 (d)(5)(i) (1988)) (footnotes omitted). See also Cummings, R.G. and Harrison, G.W., 'Was the Ohio Court Well Informed in Its Assessment of the Accuracy of the Contingent Valuation Method?' (1994) 34 Natural Resources Journal 1. The CV method was used in the Exxon Valdez oil spill. See (n 55) and National Research Council (US) Committee on Assessing and Valuing the Services of Aquatic and Related Terrestrial Ecosystems, *Valuing Ecosystem Services: Towards Better Environmental Decision-Making* (National Academies, Washington, DC 2005) at pp. 182–3 [hereinafter US National Research Council].

[74]   Natural Resource Damage Assessments, Final Rule, 59 Fed. Reg. 14,262 (Mar. 25, 1994) (codified at 43 C.F.R. §§ 11.10–11.93 (2004)).

all cases.'[75] To summarise, based on the US compensation assessment system for natural resources, compensation is not limited to damage assessment based on market value environmental resources. In the event of non-use value environmental resources, costs are based on restoration or substitution of the damaged resources. In cases where the restoration or substitution measure of damages becomes unfeasible, the CV method may be used as an alternative.[76] Simply put, the US methods for assessing damage to natural resources are based primarily on restoration costs.[77]

The question is, whether these peacetime criteria for damage to the environment can be applied to conflict-related environmental damages? It is suggested that it is possible for the following reasons. First, the economic valuation methods in relation to the environment can be applied to any ecosystem services depending on the circumstances and the suitability of the method. Therefore, these methods could also be applied to conflict-related environment damage. Second, the US system illustrates a practical example of not only the complexities involved in valuing environmental damage but that despite the difficulties involved, it is possible to assess compensation for damaged ecosystems, taking into consideration both use and non-use values of the environment. The US system, aims in the first instance, to restore the environment by compensating for restoring or substituting the damaged environment and in the event that these methods are not possible (particularly in relation to

---

[75]   Natural Resource Damage Assessments, Final Rule, 59 Fed. Reg. 14,624 (codified at 43 C.F.R. § 11.15 (2004)).

[76]   Farber (n 53) at p. 1629. For further discussion on the development of US use of valuation methods for natural resource damages, see, e.g. US National Research Council (n 73); Lee and Bridgen (n 42); Augustyniak, C.M., 'Economic Valuation of Services Provided by Natural Resources: Putting a Price on the "Priceless"' (1993) 45 Baylor Law Review 389; Tolan (n 53).

[77]   Thompson (n 53) at pp. 87–9. For more information on the evolution of international liability rules regarding 'impairment to the environment', see Mensah, T.A., 'Environmental Damages under the Law of the Sea Convention' in Austin, J.E. and Bruch, C.E. (eds), *The Environmental Consequences of War: Legal, Economic, and Scientific Perspectives* (CUP, Cambridge 2000) at pp. 226–39 [hereinafter Austin and Bruch (eds)]: includes for, e.g. International Convention on Civil Liability for Oil Pollution Damage (29 November 1969) 973 UNTS 3; UN Law of the Sea Convention, UN Doc. A/CONF.62/122 (1982) 21 ILM 1261; Lugano Convention (n 16).

non-use value environmental damage), considers the possibility of alternative methods, primarily the CV method.[78]

Overall, the US system appears to be a comprehensive system[79] which is not only precautionary in itself, but also contributes towards the sustainable development cycle. The former, by aiming at first instance to restore the environment to its pre-damaged state and taking cost-effective measures to do so; thereby preventing and mitigating the threat or risk of serious or irreversible environmental damage, and the latter, by encouraging the restoration of a damaged environment, thereby allowing the present and future generations to enjoy and benefit from a restored and undamaged environment. Nonetheless and that being said, in order to consider the best possible valuation model for damage to the environment as a result of armed conflict, the subsequent section explores the UNCC's method of assessing environmental damages as a consequence of the First Gulf War.

THE UNCC: AN EXAMPLE OF COMPENSATION AWARDED FOR CONFLICT-RELATED ENVIRONMENTAL DAMAGES　　This section explores the methods used by the UNCC to valuate compensation in relation to conflict-related environment damages. In an unprecedented achievement in respect of liability for war-time environmental damage, the UNCC[80] dealt with compensation claims following the UN Security Council (UNSC) establishing Iraq's liability under international law 'for any direct loss,

---

[78]　The CV method 'has formed the basis for a significant amount of policymaking in the US'. See, e.g. Alberini. A. and Longo, A., 'Valuing Environmental Resources using States Preferences' in Alberini, A., Rosato, P. and Turvani, M. (eds), *Valuing Complex Natural Resource Systems: The Case of the Lagoon in Venice* (Edward Elgar, US 2006) at p. 3; Kazazi (n 54) at p. 121.

[79]　For consideration of US models to value war-related environmental damage, see, e.g. Miller, J.G., 'Civil Liability for War-caused Environmental Damage: Models from United States Law' in Austin and Bruch (eds) (n 77) at pp. 264–96; Jones, C.A., 'Restoration-based Approaches to Compensation for Natural Resource Damages: Moving Towards Convergence in US and International Law' in Austin and Bruch (eds) (n 77) at pp. 477–500; Farber (n 53).

[80]　The evolution of the UNCC is well documented. From the voluminous literature, see especially Lillich, R.B. (ed), *The United Nations Compensation Commission* (Transnational, New York 1995); di Rattalma, M.F. and Treves, T. (eds), *The United Nations Compensation Commission: A Handbook* (Kluwer Law, The Hague 1999); Heiskanen, V., 'The United Nations Compensation Commission' (2003) 296 Recuiel des cours de l'Académie de Droit International de la Haye 259. See also UNCC website, www.uncc.ch/ (accessed 30 April 2012) [hereinafter UNCC website].

damage, including environmental damage and the depletion of natural resources ... as a result of its unlawful invasion and occupation of Kuwait.'[81]

The UNCC set up six categories for compensation claims: A-D which cover individual claims, E which covers claims from corporations, and F which covers claims by governments and international organisations.[82] The most relevant category in respect of the environmental damage and depletion of natural resources as a result of the First Gulf War is F (particularly F4).[83] Guidance on liability was never set out by the UNSC but instead, clarified by the UNCC Governing Council (hereinafter UNCC-GC) which specified various heads of damage regarding claims to be covered by F4.[84] F4 covers losses and expenses arising from:

(a) Abatement and prevention of environmental damage, including expenses directly relating to fighting oil fires and stemming the flow of oil in coastal and international waters;

(b) Reasonable measures already taken to clean and restore the environment or future measures which can be documented as reasonably necessary to clean and restore the environment;

(c) Reasonable monitoring and assessment of the environmental damage for the purposes of evaluating and abating the harm and restoring the environment;

(d) Reasonable monitoring of public health and performing medical screenings for the purposes of investigation and combating increased health risks as a result of the environmental damage; and

(e) Depletion of or damage to natural resources.[85]

---

[81]   Para. 16, UNSC Resolution 687.

[82]   See UNCC, 'The Claims', www.uncc.ch/theclaims.htm (accessed 30 April 2012) [hereinafter UNCC Claims].

[83]   F4 claims are claims for damage to the environment. See UNCC, 'Category F Claims' www.uncc.ch/claims/f_claims.htm (accessed 30 April 2012). For further review of the UNCC claims procedure (particularly the F4 category), see Kazazi (n 54) at pp. 111–31; Sand, P.H., 'Environmental Damage Claims from the 1991 Gulf War: State Responsibility and Community Interests' in Fastenrath, U. and others (eds), *From Bilateralism to Community Interest: Essays in Honour of Judge Bruno Simma* (OUP, New York 2011) at pp. 1241–61.

[84]   2002 Crawford (n 19) at p. 223.

[85]   Criteria for Additional Categories of Claims, 'Decision 7 of the UNCC Governing Council' UN Doc S/AC.26/1991/7/Rev.1 (17 March 1992) at para 35.

From a sustainable development perspective, the sub-categories of war-related environmental damages covered within the F4 category exemplifies elements of the precautionary principle, in that it covers measures to abate, prevent, clean-up and restore the environmental damage to prevent it from degrading further. In addition, the F4 category in itself contributes to sustainable development from an environmental, social and economic dimension. Environmentally, it does so by contributing towards the clean-up and restoration of the war-damaged environment to prevent further deterioration of the damaged environment; socially, by the fact that not only does F4 cover the monitoring of public health to combat health risks as a result of the environmental damage, but also that the cover provided for mitigating and restoring the damaged environment will benefit the present and future generations of the affected States and region, allowing them to enjoy a healthy environment; and economically, by the fact that F4 was set up to cover costs on the conflict-related environmental damages including the depletion of or damage to natural resources, thereby lessening the economic burden on the conflict-affected States and its population. Thus, the establishment of the F4 Panel allows for the mitigation of such conflict-related environmental damage as well as reducing its negative impact on the health, security and livelihoods of the Gulf population.

Nevertheless, as seen from the US model above, assessing compensation for damage to the environment can be difficult. The F4 Panel, citing the *Chorzów Factory*[86] and *Trail Smelter*[87] cases in support,[88] took the view that 'international law does not prescribe any specific and exclusive methods of measurement for awards of damages for internationally wrongful acts by states.'[89] The F4 Panel proceeded to take a broad interpretation of 'environmental damage', using the definitions provided by the UNCC-GC as a non-exhaustive guide.[90] The Panel addresses the issue of valuation of ecological losses by 'allocating the appropriate

---

[86] *Chorzów Factory* (n 12) at p. 47.

[87] *Trail Smelter* (n 38).

[88] UNCC-GC, 'Report and Recommendations Made by the Panel of Commissioners Concerning the Fifth Instalment of "F4" Claims' UN Doc /AC.26/2005/10 (30 June 2005) [hereinafter Panel Report F4/5(2005)] at paras. 49–50 and para. 80.

[89] Ibid., at para. 80.

[90] UNCC-GC, 'Report and Recommendations Made by the Panel of Commissioners Concerning the Second Instalment of "F4" Claims' S/AC.26/2002/26 (3 October 2002) [hereinafter Panel Report F4/2(2002)] at para. 22; Panel Report F4/5(2005) (n 88) at para. 67.

damage award according to the use and non-use value of the affected natural resource.'[91] Simply put, the UNCC-GC 'did *not* exclude compensation for damage to natural resources without commercial value' (so-called 'pure' environmental damage); nor did it exclude compensation in cases where there was only a temporary loss of resource use during the period prior to full restoration.[92] [93] The UNCC, in doing so appears to have taken the precautionary approach in relation to assessing compensation for war-related environmental damages in that all types of damage were covered, thereby reducing the risk of long-term or irreversible environmental damage which may cause further significant harm to natural resources, ecosystems or human health. In addition, the F4 Panel decided from the outset that the main focus was going to be on attempting to restore the environment to its pre-conflict state as much as feasibly possible.[94] Thus, the UNCC essentially took the US approach of evaluating damage to the environment that have both use and non-use

---

[91] Juni, R.L., 'The United Nations Compensation Commission as a Model for an International Environmental Court' (2000) 7 Environment Lawyer 53, at p. 69. The use and non-use value method in assessing the compensation to be awarded to environmental damage was endorsed by the UNEP Working Group convened to provide a comprehensive report on environmental damage arising from military activities. See UNEP, 'Report of the Working Group of Experts on Liability and Compensation for Environmental Damage Arising from Military Activities' UN Doc UNEP/Env.Law/3/Inf.1 (1996); UNEP, 'UNEP and the United Nations Compensation Commission (UNCC) sign cooperation deal in the Persian Gulf Region' *UN Press Release* (Geneva, 5 August 2002).

[92] Panel Report F4/5(2005) (n 88) at paras. 55–8. *Cf.* See, e.g. Assembly of the International Oil Pollution Compensation Fund (IOPC), Resolution 3 on Pollution Damage (17 October 1980) IOPC Doc FUND.A/ES 1/13, at para. 11(a).

[93] Sand, P.H., 'Compensation for Environmental Damage from the 1991 Gulf War' (2005) 35 Environmental Policy and Law 244, at p. 249 [hereinafter Sand].

[94] UNCC-GC, 'Report and Recommendations Made by the Panel of Commissioners Concerning the Third Instalment of "F4" Claims' S/AC.26/2003/31 (18 December 2003) [hereinafter Panel Report F4/3(2003)] at para. 48, further reaffirmed in UNCC-GC, 'Report and Recommendations Made by the Panel of Commissioners Concerning Part I of the Fourth Instalment of "F4" Claims' S/AC.26/2004/16 (9 December 2004) [hereinafter Panel Report F4/4/I (2004)] at para. 50; UNCC-GC, 'Report and Recommendations Made by the Panel of Commissioners Concerning Part II of the Fourth Instalment of "F4" Claims' S/AC.26/2004/17 (9 December 2004) [hereinafter Panel Report F4/4/II (2004)] at para. 41; Panel Report F4/5(2005) (n 88) at para. 43.

value[95] as well as placing an emphasis on restoration or remediation of ecosystem services first.[96] By doing so, the UNCC arguably contributed towards continuation of the cycle of sustainable development within the affected Gulf region from an environmental perspective and in the process, also mitigated the negative exposure of such conflict-related environmental damage on socio-economic development and human well-being.

In assessing compensation for such environmental damage, the F4 Panel 'took into account a number of novel methodologies developed for this purpose in contemporary systems of environmental law and eco-nomics, on the basis of informal testimony by leading experts in the field.'[97] For example, the Panel, while giving due consideration to the travel cost method,[98] deemed this method inappropriate in this particular situation (Kuwait and Saudi Arabia's compensation claims for using this method) on the basis that in both cases the circumstances were inadequate to gather reliable information 'for quantifying Kuwait's and Saudi Arabia's alleged loss of recreational shoreline uses.'[99] In another instance however, the Panel though viewing the proposed valuation method as 'relatively novel',[100] accepted HEA[101] as an appropriate method for assessing 'the nature and extent of *compensatory remediation* in order to make up for the loss of ecological services; e.g., of rangeland wildlife habitats in Jordan,[102] and natural shoreline habitats in Kuwait

---

[95]   See also Kazazi (n 54) at p. 121 (for summary of recommendations by the UNEP Working Group to the UNCC on valuation methods – use value: market price, travel cost, hedonic pricing, etc. and non-use value: CV).

[96]   Panel Report F4/3(2003) (n 94) at para. 48, further reaffirmed in Panel Report F4/4/I (2004) (n 94) at para. 50; Panel Report F4/4/II (2004) (n 94) at para. 41; Panel Report F4/5 (2005) (n 88) at para. 43.

[97]   'Including professors Robert Costanza (Vermont) and the late David W. Pearce (London).' See Sand (n 93) at p. 249.

[98]   See text to (n 48).

[99]   See Kuwait's claims: No. 5000401, No. 5000402, part of No. 5000460; and Saudi Arabia's claim: No. 5000365 in UNCC-GC, 'Report and Recommen-dations Made by the Panel of Commissioners Concerning the First Instalment of "F4" Claims' S/AC.26/2001/16 (22 June 2001) [hereinafter Panel Report F4/1(2001)] at paras. 444–50, paras. 584–7; and Panel Report F4/5 (2005) (n 88) at paras. 457–65. See also Sand (n 93) at p. 249.

[100]   Panel Report F4/5 (2005) (n 88) at paras. 81–2.

[101]   See text to (n 51).

[102]   Panel Report F4/5 (2005) (n 88) at paras. 353–66 (see the terrestrial resource unit of Jordan's claim No. 5000304).

and Saudi Arabia.[103,104] In another claim, for example, with regard to Iran's claim for damage or depletion to rangeland resources caused by the presence of refugees, instead of valuing Iran's claim based on the loss of ecological services, the F4 Panel deemed it appropriate to evaluate compensation based on the prices of fodder.[105]

It is clear that the F4 Panel mixed and matched 'novel methodologies' on a case-by-case basis in assessing compensation for environmental damage stemming from the First Gulf War, and as evidenced from the difficulty in accurately evaluating such damage, taking such an approach was necessary. As McGovern notes, '[t]he "F4" panel of Commissioners worked at the cutting edge of environmental science and law to make its decisions on the 168 claims before it.'[106] In such a new and unprecedented area of conflict-related environmental damage, this is certainly a remarkable endeavour and arguably, provides a good and effective precedent for the future.[107]

THE FUTURE: CALCULATION MODEL FOR CONFLICT-RELATED ENVIRONMENTAL DAMAGES Having considered the above valuation methods for environmental damages in theory as well as in practice, it is concluded that thus far, the best possible valuation model for conflict-related environmental damages is to take the UNCC approach. This is because the UNCC, in mirroring the US approach, aims in the first instance, if possible, to restore the damaged environment and in that vein, to evaluate restoration costs for environmental damage (considering both use and non-use value). Furthermore, most importantly, the UNCC in its evaluation process, mixed and matched economic valuation methodologies from developed and current environmental law systems. In essence, the UNCC approach demonstrates that the valuation methods have to be

---

[103] Ibid., at paras. 442–56 (calculated in 'discounted service hectare years' (DSHY). See the shoreline resource unit of Kuwait's claim No. 5000460.

[104] Sand (n 93) at p. 249. See also Payne, C., 'UN Commission Awards Compensation for Environmental and Public Health Damage from 1990–91 Gulf War' American Society of International Law Insights (10 August 2005).

[105] Panel Report F4/5 (2005) (n 88) at para. 165 and paras. 171–81 (see Iran's claim No. 5000288).

[106] McGovern, F.E., 'Dispute System Design: The United Nations Compensation Commission' (2009) 14 Harvard Negotiation Law Review 171, at p. 187 [hereinafter McGovern]. See also Sand (n 93) at p. 245.

[107] See also McManus, K.P., 'Civil Liability for Wartime Environmental Damage: Adapting the United Nations Compensation Commission for the Iraq War' (2006) 33 Boston College Environmental Affairs Law Review 417, at p. 433.

applied on a case-by-case basis, finding the most suitable method for a particular environmental damage situation.

In the UNCC discussion above, these valuation techniques were used in an actual war-related environmental compensation situation, albeit unprecedented. It has to be borne in mind that most conflicts are unlikely to end in such convenient terms as the First Gulf War. As mentioned in Chapter 4, the international community thus far (barring the First Gulf War), has a poor track record when it comes to holding parties responsible for conflict-related environmental damage. The First Gulf War situation was unique, not only in respect of the will of the international community, particularly the UNSC in holding Iraq responsible but also the fact that Iraq was a wealthy oil-rich nation that had the resources to fund the UNCC. This is not the case in most post-conflict situations. Nevertheless, perhaps these valuation methods and the UNCC approach could still be applied to such conflicts. For instance, in the post-conflict stage, when environmental priorities are to be decided upon and integrated, the appropriate valuation method could perhaps be employed to estimate costs of restoring or mitigating the environmental damage in question. Moreover, in cases where environmental pressures have fuelled conflict in the first place, perhaps the valuation method (e.g. market price, damage cost avoided, CV) could be used to determine the value of a particular ecosystem service in order to estimate the costs required to implement post-conflict environmental management programmes.

2.1.2.(c) Compensation without admission of liability   Compensation can also be paid by a State on an *ex gratia* or without prejudice basis, that is, compensatory payment by a State without actually admitting liability for any wrongdoing.[108] For example, the Cosmos-954 incident between Canada and the former Union of Soviet Social Republics (USSR) not only illustrates the fact that States can give compensation without admitting responsibility but also that States may seek compensation for costs incurred as a result of responding to environmental damage.

In this case, the USSR Cosmos-954 satellite crashed into Canadian territory in January 1978. Following the crash, Canadian authorities

---

[108]   See, e.g. the Chinese Embassy incident, where the US did not admit liability but apologised and agreed to make an *ex gratia* payment of US $4.5 million to be handed out to the families of those killed and injured as a result of the bombing of the Chinese Embassy in Belgrade on 7 May 1999. See Merrills, J.G., *International Dispute Settlements* (4th edn CUP, Cambridge 2005) at p. 60.

immediately took 'steps to locate, recover, remove and test the radioactive debris and to clean up the affected areas.'[109] As a result, they incurred expenses totalling Canadian $6,041,174.70,[110] for which they subsequently claimed against the USSR. Canada's compensation claim was based 'jointly and separately on (a) the relevant international agreements ... [111] and (b) general principles of international law.'[112] The claim was settled by an agreement between Canada and the USSR, that the latter shall make an *ex gratia* payment of Canadian $3 million (about half the amount claimed)[113] in full and final settlement.[114]

This could effectively mean that in relation to environmental damage relevant to armed conflict, State parties that may not wish to admit liability, which is the situation in most cases, could perhaps come to an agreement with the victim State regarding *ex gratia* compensation payments. This would be particularly helpful with regard to post-conflict environmental clean-up and remediation costs, not least because it spares scarce resources being consumed by the litigation process; as time and effort goes to addressing the problem directly, rather than hearings deciding who, if anyone, is responsible and therefore liable.

2.1.3. Satisfaction

Article 37 on the Articles of State responsibility provides that a 'State responsible for an internationally wrongful act is under an obligation to give satisfaction for the injury caused by that act insofar as it cannot be made good by restitution or compensation.'[115] The reparation of satisfaction[116] generally covers non-material injury, 'not financially assessable, which amount to an affront to the State.'[117] Satisfaction may for example

---

[109]   Sands, P. and others (eds), *Principles of International Environmental Law, Volume II: Documents of International Environmental Law* (MUP, Manchester 1994) at p. 1549.

[110]   Ibid.

[111]   Particularly, the Convention on International Liability for Damage Caused by Space Objects, London (29 March 1972) 961 UNTS 187.

[112]   See Canada: Claim Against the Union of Soviet Socialist Republics for Damage Caused by Soviet Cosmos 954 (1979) 18 ILM 899, at p. 905.

[113]   2002 Crawford (n 19) at p. 223.

[114]   Protocol between Canada and the USSR (1981) 20 ILM 689.

[115]   Art. 37(1), Articles on State Responsibility.

[116]   For more discussion on satisfaction in the context of State responsibility, see 2002 Crawford (n 19) at pp. 231–4.

[117]   ILC, 'Draft Articles on Responsibility of States for Internationally Wrongful Acts, with commentaries, 2001' (UN, 2008) at p. 106, para. 3 [hereinafter ILC Commentary].

take the form of an expression of regret or an official acknowledgement of the internationally wrongful act or a formal apology.[118] Satisfaction may also take the form of disciplinary or penal action against individuals responsible for the internationally wrongful act[119] as well as assurance or guarantee of non-repetition.[120]

In respect of damage to the environment, the reparation of satisfaction does not help in any material way. Therefore, it is the least useful of all three reparations in relation to conflict-related environmental damage. Nevertheless, in circumstances where the offending State is unwilling or unable to provide restitution or where compensation cannot be assessed in respect of the damage done, an official acknowledgement or even an apology from the violating State could also be satisfactory to the victim State. Of course, in practice, States rarely, if ever, admit to wrongdoing particularly for environmental damage as a consequence of armed conflict. States, as seen from practice, usually brush off such consequences as collateral damage.[121] Unfortunately, this does not do much for the environment from a practical and sustainable development standpoint.

2.2. International Environmental Law: Polluter Pays – a Sustainable Development Perspective

The polluter pays principle (PPP) is explored as an alternative to the reparation system under international law. The evolution and legal status of PPP was explored earlier[122] and to reiterate, it is a principle that requires those responsible for the pollution or environmental damage to bear the costs of that pollution or damage. It is an economic principle that attaches liability to the polluter. The principle is at present more of a

---

[118]   Art. 37(2), Articles on State Responsibility. See also, e.g. *'I'm Alone' (Canada v USA)* (1935) RIAA III 1609; *Rainbow Warrior (New Zealand v France)* (1990) RIAA XX 273, at para. 123; *LaGrand* (n 11) at p. 495, para. 81.

[119]   Gillard (n 13) at p. 531. For further examples of possible forms of satisfaction, see ILC Commentary (n 117) at pp. 106–7.

[120]   ILC Commentary (n 117) at p. 106, para. 5.

[121]   Cordesman, A.H., *The Lessons and Non-Lessons of the Air and Missile Campaign in Kosovo* (Praeger, USA 2001) at pp. 124–5; Seager, J., 'Operation Desert Disaster: Environmental Costs of the War' in Peters, C. (ed), *The 'New World Order' At Home & Abroad: Collateral Damage* (South End, Boston 1992) at p. 198.

[122]   See Chapter 2, Section 3.2. (viii) (for evolution and status of PPP).

Eurocentric principle, having gained more support in Europe than anywhere else.[123] Although the US, as noted above, has a developed domestic environmental law system, it has yet to formally endorse PPP.[124] Nevertheless, there is evidence of the principle influencing some aspects of US domestic environmental law, for example, the stipulations of liability for clean-up costs on polluters within CERCLA 1980.[125] As concluded in Chapter 2, PPP has yet to become part of customary international law. Nevertheless, it is still a principle that has 'attracted broad support, and is closely related to the rules governing civil and state liability for environmental damage...'.[126]

As one scholar comments, PPP 'envisages ... the application of a well-known concept within economics or requiring internalization of environmental costs incurred from polluting activities that are usually left to society as a whole to absorb.'[127] In a post-conflict situation, a war-torn society is unlikely to have the capacity to absorb the costs of conflict-related environmental damage. Thus, internalising environmental costs by making the polluter pay for the expenditure of 'fixing' the conflict-environmental damage caused may be a more just and sustainable solution. This contributes towards sustainable development by restoring or mitigating the damaged environment as well as reducing the economic burden on the conflict-torn society.

As seen above, for remedies under international law, there must be a violation of an international law obligation and as illustrated by the Iraq and Kosovo case-studies, the international community has a poor record of holding parties accountable for conflict-related environmental damage.[128] This is arguably understandable as States may be wary of setting a precedent for environmental damage reparation under international law that could rebound on those States themselves in future conflicts. Thus, it is suggested that PPP, as it is more of a 'soft-law' principle part of

---

[123]   Viikari, L., *The Environmental Element in Space Law: Assessing the Present and Charting the Future* (Koninklijke Brill NV, The Netherlands 2008) at p. 186.

[124]   Clò, S., *European Emmissions Trading in Practice: An Economic Analysis* (Edward Elgar, Cheltenham 2011) at p. 103.

[125]   Ibid.

[126]   Sands, P. and Peel, J., *Principles of International Environmental Law* (3rd edn CUP, New York 2012) at pp. 228–9.

[127]   Ong, D., 'Applying international environmental principles to project-financed transnational investment agreements' in Leader, S. and Ong, D. (eds) *Global Project Finance, Human Rights and Sustainable Development* (CUP, New York 2011) at p. 75.

[128]   See Chapter 4.

international environmental law, is an alternative way for States to hold parties responsible for post-conflict environmental damage both in the aftermath of an IAC, a NIAC or a hybrid conflict (e.g., conflicts that change in status during or throughout the conflict).[129] In fact, PPP not being part of the established international law regime and with its flexibility in application, makes it arguably easier to apply at the post-conflict stage.

However, using PPP in the context of armed conflict is not without its problems. For instance, it may be difficult to identify the polluter or the belligerent who caused the damage; pre-existing environmental damage makes it difficult to isolate and valuate the actual conflict-environmental damage (for example, the pre-war damage found in the Kosovo 'hot spots');[130] the polluter may not have the means to pay for the damage or pollution caused; there is no way of enforcing payment for damage even on a known polluter (for example, as with the US and the UK as a result of NATO's damage caused in the Kosovo conflict);[131] as environmental damage is caused by all belligerents involved in the war, should both sides (loser and the victor of the conflict) be held liable (for example, this clearly was not the case in the First Gulf War as only Iraq was held responsible);[132] should non-belligerents who pollute to avoid more serious consequences during conflict be made to pay (for example, workers of a chemical factory who dump highly flammable toxic chemicals into a river in the belief that it is the 'lesser of two evils' in that, a military attack on the factory could have more severe consequences). In addition, while enforcing PPP on private citizens or operators may be likely, enforcing PPP on liable States may prove more difficult. As with any other breach or attachment of liability at international level, getting unwilling States to admit liability let alone pay for its pollution in a conflict-related situation is likely to be problematic. Enforcement against States very much depends on the willingness of those States themselves to be held liable.

---

[129]   Cooper, P.J. and Vargas, C.M., *Sustainable Development in Crisis Conditions: Challenges of War, Terrorism and Civil Disorder* (Rowman & Littlefield, USA 2008) at p. 22 ('in recent decades, intrastate or hybrid conflicts, in which there are both international and local combatants directly or indirectly involved, are far more common').

[130]   See Chapter 4, Section 4.

[131]   Ibid.

[132]   See Chapter 4, Section 3 (for environmental damage caused by the coalition forces).

Overall, PPP is perhaps not the best solution for liability in relation to post-conflict environmental damage but as seen throughout this study, there is no perfect remedy in law or in policy. It is thus argued that for liability in respect of conflict-related environmental damage, PPP can theoretically be an alternative or complementary means towards remedying the environmental or natural resource damage caused during war. Whether (or not) PPP is applicable in a practical setting of a post-conflict environment remains to be seen. Ultimately, if the end goal is to protect the environment and achieve sustainable development, the global community has to use any means at its disposal to achieve those ends and in the post-conflict stage, making the polluter pay may be another way to do so.

3. POST-CONFLICT ENVIRONMENTAL DAMAGE AND MANAGEMENT OF ENVIRONMENTAL RESOURCES IN LIGHT OF SUSTAINABLE DEVELOPMENT: WHAT HAPPENS NEXT?

As discovered above, reparations in the form of restitution could be very difficult to apply and satisfaction is inappropriate in relation to conflict-related environmental damages. Hence, the reparation of compensation in the form of monetary compensation and/or PPP which makes the polluter pay, are key steps in propagating the virtuous cycle of sustainable development. Most importantly, Section 2 above has explored valuing the environment, that is, what the environment is worth; which is crucial if money is to be obtained to restore or manage it. Without funds, there is not a lot that can be done to fix the post-conflict environment and thus, further obstructing the path to sustainable development.

At the post-conflict peacebuilding stage, there are a variety of challenges 'for the international community by requiring cooperation on many levels whether across disciplines, military, civilian, humanitarian, human rights, political and developmental, between bilateral and multi-lateral actors or in an improved dialogue between national and international authorities.'[133] As discussed throughout this study, to contribute to and achieve the virtuous cycle of sustainable development, all these

---

[133] McAskie, C., 'The International and Peacebuilding Challenge: Can New Players and New Approaches Bring New Results?' UN Peacebuilding Support Office, The Lloyd Shaw Lecture in Public Affairs, Dalhousie University, Halifax, Nova Scotia (22 November 2007) at p. 7 [hereinafter McAskie].

other socio-economic development factors must be integrated with environmental issues. Not only must environmental priorities be considered with other factors from the outset, such post-conflict environmental issues, if not restored or managed appropriately, can in itself have a negative impact on the social, economic and environmental conditions of the war-torn state; thereby, in certain situations potentially fuelling or triggering re-conflict.[134]

Chapter 4 concluded that due to the difficulty in protecting the environment during conflict, the pre-conflict (prevention) and post-conflict stages are most crucial, not only to protect, restore and manage environmental issues but also to do so with the goal of sustainable development in mind. The importance of protecting the environment to achieve sustainable development post-conflict is best summed up by UNEP: 'a healthy environment is a prerequisite for sound and sustainable development. People cannot secure real and sustainable economic development if they are confronted by contaminated water, polluted land and declining natural resources.'[135]

To reiterate, the law of reparations is only applicable for violations of international State responsibility where liability has been established. However, due to the fact that most armed conflicts going on in the world today are NIACs[136] or essentially internal in nature,[137] the application of international law let alone attaching liability becomes trickier; thereby requiring an alternative means to reparations. PPP is suggested as an alternative[138] but as discovered, it is not without problems especially in relation to environmental-conflict damage. Such damage as a result of armed conflict cannot however be left unremedied and restoration or management of the environment are not cost free. Thus, this is where the

---

[134]   UNEP Conflict to Peacebuilding (n 3) at p. 6.
[135]   UNEP, 'UNEP opens Post-Conflict Assessment Unit' *UNEP Press Release* (Geneva, 11 December 2001).
[136]   Approximately 10% of global conflicts today are internationalised internal disputes. See 'Human Security Report 2005' Human Security Report Project, Canada, www.humansecurityreport.info/HSR2005_HTML/Part1/index. htm (accessed 30 April 2012) at p. 20.
[137]   UNEP International Law (n 1) at p. 4. See also Harbom, L. and Wallensteen, P., 'Patterns of Major Armed Conflicts, 1999–2008' in *SIPRI Yearbook 2009: Armaments, Disarmament and International Security* (OUP, New York 2009) at pp. 69–84; MiniAtlas of Human Security, 'Human Security Report Project' Canada (9 October 2008), www.miniatlasofhumansecurity.info/en/ access.html> (accessed 30 April 2012) at p. 9.
[138]   See Section 2 above.

international community in the form of collective responsibility[139] and in the spirit of common but differentiated responsibilities, should step in to assist in the post-conflict process. Thus, this section first explores post-conflict financing with regard to environmental remediation and management; and second, if funds are available, how the money is actually used, that is, whether it is actually used for the environment? These questions are considered in light of the sustainable development concept by reviewing post-conflict case-study examples in practice: the UNCC (First Gulf War), Kosovo, and Sudan.

3.1. Financing the Environment

Without funds, environmental recovery and management at the post-conflict stage are virtually impossible. This would be a major obstacle to achieving post-conflict sustainable development because the damaged and unmanaged environment and natural resources would be a further strain not only on the environment or natural resource, but also on the socio-economic development of the war-torn country.[140] Therefore, a crucial factor in this respect would be the availability of funding. Thus, this section explores the source of funding and whether any funding received is sufficient for its purpose – the post-conflict environment. Furthermore, as this is considered from a sustainable development perspective, consideration is also given to: whether other socio-economic and development factors are taken into account together with the environment?

3.1.1. UNCC

The UNCC is an example where funds for conflict-related environmental damages and post-conflict environmental recovery are obtained via an international liability and compensation system. In addition, from a

---

[139] Simply put, under international law, this means that the international community as a whole has 'collective responsibility'. See, e.g. Kelsen, H., *Principles of International Law* (Lawbook Exchange, New Jersey 2003) at pp. 116–18. 'Collective responsibility' is akin to the newly endorsed international humanitarian principle of Responsibility to Protect (R2P). In fact, some members of the international community have argued that the Peacebuilding Commission (PBC) is a 'crucial instrument to implement the key preventive aspects of the R2P norm'. See International Coalition for the Responsibility to Protect (ICRtoP), 'Report on the General Assembly Plenary Debate on the Responsibility to Protect' (15 September 2009) at p. 9. See also, e.g. Bellamy, A.J., *Responsibility to Protect* (Polity, Cambridge 2009).

[140] UNEP Conflict to Peacebuilding (n 3) at p. 5 and p. 8.

holistic sustainable development perspective, the UNCC as whole,[141] covered a broad range of claims for injury, damage and loss as a result of the conflict. The claims ranged from compensation for individuals having to flee Kuwait or Iraq during the conflict;[142] claims for serious personal injury or death;[143] individual claims for damages up to US$100 000 (includes personal injury, mental pain and anguish, loss of personal property and bank accounts, loss of real property, loss of income, etc.);[144] claims by corporations, other private legal entities and public sector entreprises (for losses from construction, losses and damage to assets, goods and services, oil sector losses, loss of profits, etc.);[145] to claims by Governments and international organisations (includes providing relief to citizens, loss of and damage to government property, damage to the environment, etc.).[146] The range of claims covered and awarded certainly helped mitigate the negative impact of the conflict not only on the post-conflict environment but also on the post-conflict socio-economic and development status of the affected Gulf States and its population.[147]

With regard to actual financing of the UNCC compensation awards,[148] funding was obtained by Iraq giving up a percentage of its oil exports via the Oil-for-Food Programme:[149] 30 per cent share of its oil export

---

[141]   UNCC Claims (n 82).

[142]   ibid, Category A.

[143]   ibid, Category B.

[144]   ibid, Categories C and D.

[145]   ibid, Category E.

[146]   ibid, Category F.

[147]   See, e.g. Schrijver, N., *Development Without Destruction: The UN and Global Resource Management* (Indiana University, USA 2010) at p. 179; Matheson, M.J., *Council Unbound: The Growth of UN Decision Making on Conflict and Postconflict Issues After the Cold War* (US Institute of Peace, Washington, DC 2006) at p. 178; Weisaeth, L., 'War-Related Psychopathology in Kuwait: An Assessment of War-Related Mental Health Problems' in Fullerton, C.S. and Ursano, R.J. (eds), *Posttraumatic Stress Disorder: Acute and Long-Term Responses to Trauma and Disaster* (American Psychiatric, USA 1997) at pp. 97–120.

[148]   For further discussion on the financing mechanism of the UNCC, see Van Houtte, H. and others, 'The United Nations Compensation Commission' in De Grieff, P. (ed), *The Handbook of Reparations* (OUP, New York 2006) at pp. 363–4; von Sponeck, H.C., *A Different Kind of War: The UN Sanctions Regime in Iraq* (Berghahn, Germany 2006) at pp. 174–91 [hereinafter Sponeck].

[149]   See Sponeck (n 148) at pp. 179–91 (although Sponeck acknowledges the justification for international compensation, he also criticised the Oil-for-Food Programme from which much needed funds would have perhaps mitigated the deteriorating humanitarian conditions in Iraq). *Cf.* Fox, M.B., 'Imposing Liability

revenues since 1996,[150] which was subsequently reduced to 25% in 2000[151] and to 5% in 2003.[152] With these available funds, the UNCC awarded compensation in the total sum of $52.5 billion out of the $352.5 billion claimed.[153] The 'F4' environmental claims panel in particular, awarded $5.26 billion compensation on total claims of $85 billion.[154] It has to be borne in mind however, that the UNCC was able to successfully acquire funding because Iraq has a rich tradable resource – oil.[155]

The next question is whether the compensation paid out was sufficient for its purpose: to restore or replace the damaged ecosystem services? The compensation figures arrived at were based on the valuation methods applied by the UNCC as discussed above, and based on Panel Report F4/5 (2005), by 21 February 2005, 53 of the 69 projects compensated were completed.[156] Out of the 16 remaining projects, 12 were given the go ahead by the Panel to continue and the Governments concerned were allowed to use funds awarded from the first F4 instalment to carry on their environmental activities.[157] In respect of the remaining 4 projects, the Panel decided that work on them were no longer necessary and recommended that the UNCC-GC retrieve the remaining funds administered for those projects from the Governments concerned.[158] Arguably, the almost 8 per cent completion rate on the environmental projects

---

for Losses from Aggressive War: An Economic Analysis of the UN Compensation Commission' (2002) 13 European Journal of International Law 201; Caron, D. and Morris, B., 'The UN Compensation Commission: Practical Justice, not Retribution' (2002) 13 European Journal of International Law 183. See also Christoff, J.A., *United Nations: Lessons Learned from Oil for Food Program Indicate the Need to Strengthen UN Internal Controls and Oversight Activities* (DIANE, USA 2006).

[150]   Para. 2, UNSC Resolution 705 (15 August 1991); Para. 8 (c), UNSC Resolution 986 (14 April 1995).

[151]   Para. 12, UNSC Resolution 1330 (5 December 2000).

[152]   Paras. 20 and 21, UNSC Resolution 1483 (22 May 2003); Para. 24, UNSC Resolution 1546 (8 June 2004).

[153]   Sand (n 93) at p. 245.

[154]   McGovern (n 106) at p. 187. See also Sand (n 93) at p. 245.

[155]   Central Intelligence Agency (CIA), *The CIA World Factbook 2010* (Skyhorse, New York 2009) at p. 332; BBC, 'Iraq: Key Facts and Figures' *BBC News* (last updated 7 September 2010) http://news.bbc.co.uk/1/hi/world/middle_ east/7856618.stm (accessed 30 April 2012).

[156]   Panel Report F4/5(2005) (n 88) at para. 782.

[157]   Ibid.

[158]   Ibid.

funded by awards dispensed by the UNCC, plus the continuing observation and assessment on the remaining projects,[159] are a good indication
that the compensation paid out was sufficient for its purpose. Moreover,
the money paid out for the conflict-damaged environment, did allow for
the environment, from the very beginning 'because of its significance for
human health and sustainable post-conflict economic development'[160] to
be given priority.

3.1.2. Kosovo

Unlike the UNCC which was able to obtain its funds from an aggressor
State that has substantial oil resources, most conflicts do not have this
advantage. For example, as demonstrated in the preceding chapter,
liability was never attached to those responsible for environmental
damage during the Kosovo conflict.[161] In this case, the clean-up efforts
orchestrated by UNEP came up to over $12.5 million.[162] UNEP had to
work mainly on its own initiative due to the 'lack of any formal
international response mechanism.'[163]

The clean-up initiative was financed largely by contributions from
donor States (Denmark, Finland, France, Germany, Ireland, Luxembourg,
The Netherlands, Norway, Sweden, and Switzerland).[164] Unfortunately,
the US and the UK, both having played a major role as part of NATO in
the armed conflict, were glaringly absent from the list of State donors

---

[159]   Ibid., at paras. 781–2.

[160]   UNEP, 'Desk Study on the Environment in Iraq' (UNEP, Switzerland 2003) at p. 87 [hereinafter UNEP Iraq Study].

[161]   See Chapter 4, Section 4.2. See also Wren, C.S., 'Yugoslavia Gives NATO $100 Billion Damage Bill' *New York Times* (New York, 29 September 1999).

[162]   'UNEP is not allocated this money through general United Nations funds but rather must raise this money through a mixture of governmental and private donors.' See Sameit, M.D., 'Killing and Cleaning in Combat: A Proposal to Extend the Foreign Claims Act to Compensate for Long-Term Environmental Damage' (2008) 32 William and Mary Environmental Law and Policy Review 569. See also UNEP, 'Kosovo Conflict Hot Spots Cleaned Up' *UNEP Press Release* (Belgrade, 7 May 2004).

[163]   UNEP, 'From Conflict to Sustainable Development: Assessment and Clean-Up in Serbia and Montenegro' (Switzerland, UNEP 2004) at p. 9 [hereinafter UNEP Clean-Up].

[164]   Ibid., at p. 10. FRY also brought actions against France, Germany and the Netherlands, which were dismissed by the ICJ. *Legality of the Use of Force (Yugoslavia v NATO States)* (Provisional Measures) [1999] ICJ Rep 132.

helping to finance the clean-up efforts.[165] Nevertheless, the generous donations by the other European nations (only Finland, Ireland, Sweden and Switzerland are non-NATO members)[166] do demonstrate an effort by the international community to remedy environmental damage caused by armed conflict.

From a sustainable development perspective, these financial contributions from donor countries do show evidence of the international community's awareness of the need to clean-up and restore conflict-related environmental damage which in the process, prevents or alleviates the otherwise negative impact on development, the environment and human well-being. This arguably exemplifies elements of PPP in that six NATO Member States (Denmark, France, Germany, Luxembourg, The Netherlands, Norway) paid for the pollution caused, that is, they contributed to the Kosovo clean-up initiative. Unfortunately, this case also illustrates the problems inherent in PPP and international law in general, in that at international level, it is very difficult to enforce liability on States that do not wish to admit to or remedy any damage caused. The US and the UK's lack of contribution to the clean-up initiative for example. The clean-up operation also illustrates elements of the precautionary principle, in that measures were taken to prevent or mitigate the threat or risk of further environmental harm and degradation as well as the cooperative element in the common but differentiated responsibilities principle, which in the process contributed towards restoring conflict-damaged environments for the benefit of present and future generations within FRY. An additional point to note is that funding[167] was also obtained by UNEP to conduct two post-conflict depleted uranium (DU) assessments.[168]

---

[165]   UNEP Clean-Up (n 163) at p. 10.

[166]   See 'NATO Member Countries' (last updated 10 March 2009), www.nato.int/cps/en/natolive/nato_countries.htm (accessed 30 April 2012).

[167]   Switzerland donated US$ 200 000 for each assessment. See Haavisto, P., 'Environmental Post-Conflict Assessments: A New UN Tool Developed by UNEP' in Brauch, H.G. and other (eds), *Security and the Environment in the Mediterranean: Conceptualising Security and Environmental Conflicts* (Springer-Verlag, Germany 2003) at p. 541 [hereinafter Haavisto].

[168]   UNEP, 'Depleted Uranium in Kosovo: Post-Conflict Environmental Assessment' (Switzerland, UNEP 2001) [hereinafter 2001 UNEP DU]; UNEP, 'Depleted Uranium in Serbia and Montenegro: Post Conflict Environmental Assessment in the Federal Republic of Yugoslavia' (UNEP, Switzerland 2002) [hereinafter 2002 UNEP DU].

The next question that arises is, whether the funding received was adequate? The UNEP/BTF Feasibility Studies[169] set out in detail, 27 proposed clean-up projects in the four main 'hot spot' sites[170] which in total amounted to the estimated cost of $20 million.[171] However, the $12.5 million funding obtained was only sufficient for 16 remediation projects that had the highest priority.[172] With only 60 per cent of the budget obtained, funding was clearly insufficient. Nonetheless, UNEP did manage to go ahead with a further 6 projects with the assistance of other international partners (Swiss Agency for Development and Cooperation (SDC) and Czech development partners)[173] providing bilateral support.[174] Therefore, despite the lack of sufficient funding, UNEP considered the UNEP Clean-up Programme in Serbia and Montenegro to be an overall success, taking into consideration the lesser budget and limited timeframe that UNEP had to carry out its work.[175] It is argued that UNEP's Clean-Up Programme was indeed a success especially taking into account the limitations it faced. However, the insufficient funding received highlights a serious gap in the international post-conflict environmental recovery and response field. A gap, which if not addressed,

---

[169]   UNEP/UNCHS Kosovo (n 26) and the subsequent UNEP/BTF Feasibility Studies were funded by Austria, Belgium, Czech Republic, Denmark, Finland, France, Italy, Netherlands, Norway, Sweden and the UK at the cost of US$ 2.2 million.

[170]   See UNEP/BTF, 'UNEP/BTF Feasibility Studies for Novi Sad, Pancevo, Bor and Kragujevac', www.grid.unep.ch/btf/reports/feasibility/index.html (accessed 30 April 2012) [hereinafter UNEP/BTF Feasibility Studies]; UNEP Clean-Up (n 163) at pp. 28–9.

[171]   Governing Council of UNEP, 'State of the Environment and Contribution of the United Nations Environment Programme to Addressing Substantive Environmental Challenges' UNEP/GC.23/3/Add.2 (2 November 2004) at para. 11 [hereinafter UNEP State of the Environment] (There does not seem to be clear information on how UNEP came up with the figure of $20 million, i.e. there is no available public data on the exact valuation of each environmental remediation project).

[172]   UNEP/BTF Feasibility Studies (n 170); UNEP State of the Environment (n 171) at para. 11.

[173]   UNEP, Ministry of Science and Environmental Protection of the Republic of Serbia, and Ministry of Environmental Protection and Physical Planning of the Republic of Montenegro, 'From Conflict to Sustainable Development: Assessment of Environmental Hot Spots, Serbia and Montenegro' (UNEP, Switzerland 2004) at p. 6 [hereinafter UNEP Hot Spots].

[174]   UNEP Clean-Up (n 163) at p. 10.

[175]   Ibid., at p. 12.

could seriously hinder future environmental recovery and sustainable development in post-conflict States.

As seen throughout this book, environmental problems are rarely isolated issues. In this case, at the conclusion of the Kosovo conflict, in addition to conflict-related environmental damage sustained, FRY 'was in a state of economic and social chaos.'[176] To sum up the situation: half the population had fled as well as being internally displaced, homes and personal property destroyed or stolen, economic activity had stopped, public institutions and structures had collapsed or shut down, there was unsurprisingly still simmering ethnic tensions between the Albanian and Serbian residents, and there was 'no functioning law enforcement system to provide justice.'[177] Therefore, from a holistic sustainable development perspective, while UNEP was tasked with dealing with the environmental damage and ensuing impact of the Kosovo conflict, the UNSC adopted Resolution 1244[178] that set out the decision to deploy UN supported '... international civil and security presences'[179] in Kosovo. The UN Secretary-General subsequently created UNMIK[180] which was divided into four components: civil administration led by UNMIK itself; institution building led by the Organization for Security and Cooperation in Europe (OSCE); humanitarian led by UN High Commissioner for Refugees; and reconstruction (including reconstruction of main infrastructure and other socio-economic systems) led by the EU.[181] Thus, UNMIK, with the cooperation of other States and international organisations in both financial and human resources, proceeded to rebuild the war-torn province.[182]

---

[176]   Matheson, M.J., 'United Nations Governance of Postconflict Societies' (2001) 95 American Journal of International Law 76, at p. 78 [hereinafter 2001 Matheson].

[177]   Ibid. See also Report of the Secretary-General on the UN Interim Administration in Kosovo (UNMIK), UN Doc.S/1999/779 (12 July 1999) at paras. 5–6.

[178]   UNSC Resolution 1244 (10 June 1999).

[179]   Ibid., at para. 5.

[180]   For detailed information on UNMIK in Kosovo, see UNMIK Online, www.unmikonline.org/pages/default.aspx (accessed 30 April 2012).

[181]   2001 Matheson (n 176) at pp. 79–80.

[182]   Ibid., at p. 79. See also Dulic, D., 'Peacebuilding and Human Security: Kosovo Case' 3 HUMSEC Journal 1.

3.1.3. Sudan

After protracted decades-long conflict and the signing of the Comprehensive Peace Agreement (CPA) in 2005,[183] UNEP stepped in to examine the environment-conflict related issues in Sudan. UNEP undertook a comprehensive post-conflict environmental assessment (PCEA) in 2007 which included ten fact-finding field missions and over 2 000 interviews,[184] bringing to international attention the numerous challenges that needed to be met 'to ensure long-term peace, food security and sustainable development for the Sudanese people.'[185] UNEP also made 85 recommendations across the sectors assessed, ranging for example: from investing in environmental management, capacity building 'to ensure that reconstruction and economic development do not intensify environmental pressures and threaten the livelihoods of present and future generations',[186] to ensuring that all post-conflict relief and development programmes in Sudan integrate environmental considerations.[187] The UNEP Report, embracing sustainable development, outlined a detailed government action plan to carry out these recommendations with an estimated expenditure of $120 million over a three to five year period.[188] With regard to funding, UNEP reported that with Sudan's new oil-driven economic boom,[189] the Sudanese government should be able to bear the

---

[183]   The Comprehensive Peace Agreement between The Government of the Republic of The Sudan and The Sudan People's Liberation Movement/Sudan People's Liberation Army (CPA) (signed 9 January 2005).

[184]   UNEP in the Regions, 'Current Activities: Sudan', www.unep.org/conflictsanddisasters/UNEPintheRegions/CurrentActivities/Sudan/tabid/294/language/en-US/Default.aspx (accessed 30 April 2012).

[185]   Ibid. See UNEP, 'Sudan: Post-Conflict Environmental Assessment' (UNEP, Nairobi 2007) at p. 328 [hereinafter Sudan-PCEA] (These recommendations were further reviewed by the Governments of Sudan and both national and international stakeholders).

[186]   Sudan-PCEA (n 185) at p. 330.

[187]   Ibid.

[188]   Ibid., at p. 328.

[189]   Ibid; Gettleman, J., 'War in Sudan? Not Where the Oil Wealth Flows' *New York Times* (New York, 24 October 2006); Tisdall, S., 'Khartoum's Boom' Guardian (UK, 11 March 2008); 'Sudan Oil Revenues for February '08 Reach 397ml' *Sudan Tribune* (Khartoum, 30 March 2008) (Sudan's oil revenues reached $397.78 million on February 2008). *Cf.* BBC, 'Sudan Oil Revenue "Discrepancy"' *BBC News* (UK, 7 September 2009); 'China and Japan have to press Sudan for transparency in oil figures' *Sudan Tribune* (London, 18 September 2009); 'Sudan rejects accusations of manipulations in oil revenue figures' *Sudan*

costs for the 'necessary investment in improved environmental governance.'[190]

Unfortunately, there is a lack of information in the public domain on
whether Sudan's oil industry is contributing towards funding Sudan's
much needed environmental programmes.[191] In general however, the
BBC reports that after the signing of the 2005 CPA, North and South
Sudan have 'split southern oil revenues equally'.[192] Southern Sudan has
since seceded, from July 2011, dividing Sudan into two countries: North
and South Sudan.[193] Most of Sudan's oilfields are located in the South
but most of the refineries, pipelines and the main export terminal are in
the North.[194] Regrettably, there is still a lack of transparency in oil
production and revenues,[195] perpetuating the foundation for corruption
and ineffective governance. Moreover, tensions are once again on the rise
between the North and South, with threats of further conflict imminent as
diplomacy has failed and both countries have been unable to come to an
agreement on 'how to share the vast oil fields that straddle those borders,
and on which both north and south now depend for their economic
viability.'[196]

Tribune (Khartoum, 26 September 2009); McDoom, O., 'Interview: Sudan oil
output falls short of estimates – minister' *Reuters India* (Khartoum, 25 October
2009).

[190]   Sudan-PCEA (n 185) at p. 328.

[191]   Ibid. See also (n 189); Hansohm, D., 'Oil and Foreign Aid: Chances for
Pro-poor Development in Sudan?' in Wohlmuth, K., Alabi, R.A. and Burger, P.
(eds), *New Growth and Poverty Alleviation Strategies for Africa – Institutional
and Local Perspectives* (LIT-Verlag, Germany 2009) at p. 133 [hereinafter
Hansohm]; Youngs, R., *Energy Security: Europe's New Foreign Policy Challenge*
(Routledge, Oxon 2009) at p. 147 [hereinafter Youngs]; Berhanu, D.G., *Institutions and Investment in Sudan: Socio-Economic and Institutional Foundations
of Reconstruction and Development* (Deutsche Nationalbibliothek, Berlin 2011).

[192]   Copnall, J., 'Can Sudan's oil feed north and south?' *BBC News* (Khartoum, 4 July 2011) [hereinafter Copnall].

[193]   UNEP, 'Republic of South Sudan', www.unep.org/southsudan/ (accessed
26 March 2012). See also Chapter 3.

[194]   Shankleman, J., 'Oil and State Building in South Sudan' Special Report
(US Institute of Peace, USA 2011) at p. 1.

[195]   Copnall (n 192). See also 'South Sudan parliament favours oil industry
secrecy over transparency' *Sudan Tribune* (Juba, 6 April 2012).

[196]   Harding, A., 'South Sudan blamed as it gears up for war' *BBC News*
(South Sudan, 30 April 2012) [hereinafter Harding]. See also BBC, 'Sudanese
conflict: What you need to know' *BBC News* (UK, 4 May 2012), www.bbc.co.uk/
news/world-africa-17958794 (accessed 8 May 2012) [hereinafter BBC Sudanese

Coming back to the Sudan's post-conflict environmental initiatives, environmental management programmes in Sudan are currently being funded by international aid.[197] For instance, UNEP's projects in Sudan: a waste management programme in cooperation with Juba County is supported by the Italian Development Cooperation and Japan International Cooperation Agency (JICA) (JICA also fully funded a waste management expert);[198] the Darfur Timber and Energy project is funded by the US Agency for International Development (USAID);[199] the Darfur Integrated Water Resources Management (IWRM), the Darfur Aid and the Environment projects, a long-term waste management program, and the recent five dam rehabilitation projects brokered by UNEP, are being supported and funded by UKAID from the UK's Department for International Development (DFID).[200]

In fact, DFID is currently funding a £20 million programme that commenced in July 2009 in partnership with UNEP and UNOPS to support peacebuilding efforts on an environmentally sustainable basis, by improving 'sustainable and equitable governance' as well as the 'management and use of environmental resources',[201] including the DFID funded

---

Conflict]; Tran, M., 'The $7bn stumbling block to peace between Sudan and South Sudan' *Guardian* (UK, 27 April 2012).

[197]   Sudan already receives US$ 2 billion per annum in aid from the international community. The aid is channelled through 'humanitarian crisis programmes, recovery and development programmes, and peacekeeping operations' and delivered by various organisations. See Sudan-PCEA (n 185) at p. 32.

[198]   UNEP Disasters and Conflicts Programme, 'Sudan Country Programme' Quarterly Progress Report (Jan-Mar 2011) at pp. 6–7 [hereinafter 2011 Jan-Mar QPR].

[199]   UNEP-PCDMB, 'Sudan Programme Overview' (UNEP, June 2008) at p. 1 [hereinafter Sudan Overview]; UNEP/FAO, 'Progress Report: Darfur Timber and Energy Project' (UNEP, July 2008) [hereinafter UNEP/FAO Darfur Timber]. See also USAID-SUDAN, 'Sudan Transitional Environment Program' Final Report (June 2009) at p. 5 [hereinafter USAID-SUDAN STEP].

[200]   2011 Jan-Mar QPR (n 198) at p. 6; Sudan Overview (n 199) at p. 2. See also UNEP, 'President of Southern Sudan Launches Clean-Up of Juba' *UNEP Press Release* (Juba, 23 November 2009) [hereinafter UNEP Juba Clean-up].

[201]   Project start: 1 July 2009 and end: 31 December 2013. See DFID, 'Sudan Integrated Environment Programme (SIEP)', http://projects.dfid.gov.uk/project. aspx?Project=200627 (accessed 8 May 2012) [hereinafter DFID-SIEP Programme]; UNEP, 'UK Government Donor Visits UNEP Environment and Peacebuilding Projects in Sudan' *UNEP New Centre* (Khartoum, 2 March 2012), www.unep.org/newscentre/default.aspx?DocumentID=2676&ArticleID=9060&l =en (accessed 9 May 2012); DFID, 'UNEP Environmental Sustainability Program in Sudan' Sudan Project Details, http://projects.dfid.gov.uk/Project

projects mentioned above. These projects attempt to integrate elements of sustainable development, by prioritising pressing environmental issues in consideration with other relevant socio-economic and development issues within Sudan.[202] DFID continues to fund projects in Sudan (not through either of the Sudanese governments) but via multi-donor pooled funds managed by UN agencies,[203] working closely with various partners (for example, the EU, USAID, USA, Norway, World Bank, International Monetary Fund (IMF), African Development Bank, UN agencies).[204] DFID in the next 3 years (with an expected expenditure of approximately £360 million)[205] will focus on helping Sudan with transitioning 'from humanitarian programmes to longer-term development support'; peace-building between North and Sudan Sudan, within Darfur, and Sudan as a whole within the region; increasing good governance, mitigating corruption, increasing security, peace and justice; and achieving sustainable development.[206]

In respect of environmental programmes within Sudan, UNEP receives no funding from its global or regional operations.[207] Thus far, UNEP receives direct funding support from the Swedish International Development Cooperation Agency (SIDA), USAID and DFID.[208] UNEP admits that the international community has been and still is an important part of Sudan's recovery, particularly in relation to the environment, by providing extensive financial aid.[209] In addition to UNEP and its partner agencies' environmental work in Sudan, USAID also started its own environmental programme. USAID funded the Sudan Transitional Environment Programme (STEP) with a budget of US $5.8 million.[210] STEP, implemented between 12 August 2005 and 31 August 2009, aimed to

---

Details.asp?projcode=200627–101&RecordsPerPage=10&sectorSelect=Sec~ 41030-Bio-diversity&PageNo=4 (accessed 6 February 2012). See also UNEP Juba Clean-up (n 200).

[202]   Sudan Overview (n 199).

[203]   DFID, 'Operational Plan 2011–2015' (DFID, March 2012) at p. 6 [hereinafter DFID Operational Plan].

[204]   Ibid.

[205]   UK Parliament, 'International Development Committee – Fifteenth Report, South Sudan: Prospects for Peace and Development – DFID Programme' (27 March 2012), www.publications.parliament.uk/pa/cm201012/cmselect/cmintdev/1570/157008.htm (accessed 9 May 2012).

[206]   DFID Operational Plan (n 203) at p. 3.

[207]   Sudan Overview (n 199) at p. 3.

[208]   Ibid.

[209]   Ibid. See also UNEP, 'Disaster and Conflicts' 3(2) The Educator 1.

[210]   USAID-SUDAN STEP (n 199) at p. 3.

improve 'Southern Sudan's capacity to assess and monitor environmental impacts of developmental projects and to reduce conflict over the exploitation of natural resources.'[211]

In relation to whether the funding received is sufficient for the projects outlined in UNEP's report, UNEP did state that the figures recommended could increase substantially from the USD \$120 million figure initially recommended.[212] As the programmes and projects are currently ongoing and Sudan (both North and South) is once again in a tense imminent conflict situation, it is difficult to ascertain whether funding is adequate.[213] In relation to USAID's STEP, although most of the targets were achieved, there still remained a number of important uncompleted environmental processes.[214] As to the question of whether the valuation methods used in estimating implementation costs for the programmes recommended are adequate? Neither UNEP nor USAID appear to have published their valuation methods or techniques used to come up with the recommended financial costs for each project.

In this case, UNEP managed to obtain funding sources for specific projects and USAID, in addition to providing funding for UNEP's projects, funded its own environmental programme. This could be considered a success as funding was found to implement environmental projects and programmes in post-conflict Sudan.[215] Nonetheless and that being said, this case-study once again demonstrates the lack of formal international response mechanisms for post-conflict environmental issues in particular, and the reliance of parties concerned in obtaining ad hoc funding in order to integrate post-conflict environmental priorities.

Another major weakness in this case, is the lack of funding from Sudan itself. This could be due to lack of good governance, which includes the lack of transparency within Sudan's booming new oil

---

[211]   Ibid.

[212]   Sudan-PCEA (n 185) at p. 331.

[213]   Sudan Overview (n 199); UNEP Disasters and Conflicts Programme, 'Sudan Country Programme' Quarterly Progress Report (July–September 2009) at pp. 4–5 [hereinafter 2009 Jul–Sept QPR]; 2011 Jan–Mar QPR (n 198) at pp. 6–8.

[214]   For information on unfinished processes, see USAID-SUDAN STEP (n 199) at pp. 36–7.

[215]   UNEP continues to partner with other agencies and organisations (particularly UKAid from DFID) for various environmental and sustainable development projects in Sudan. See UNEP, 'Republic of Sudan', www.unep.org/sudan/ (accessed 3 May 2012) [hereinafter Sudan website].

industry.[216] Sudan should have been able to channel some of its new oil profits back into post-conflict environmental programmes, particularly since environmental pressures were factors in fuelling conflict within the country in the first place.[217] In any event, Sudan has since split and is once again on the brink of conflict.[218] Thus, as Sudan as a whole (both North and South) is still unable to deal with its own problems be it environmental, political, socio-economic or development issues, assistance from the international community is still very much needed.

In respect of Sudan's other variable factors that in combination had fuelled the armed conflict, that is, the crisis in Darfur and Sudan as a whole, the UN in response deployed a multidimensional peace support operation: UNMIS.[219] UNMIS was established on 24 March 2005 to support the 2005 CPA by providing good offices, political support for the peacebuilding process, security, governance, humanitarian and development assistance.[220] UNMIS' work was supported by other UN agencies (including UNEP) and international organisations in order to rebuild and manage Sudan's political, social, economic, development and environmental issues.[221] With the secession of South Sudan however, UNMIS was terminated on 9 July 2011 and a new UN mission: UN Mission in the Republic of South Sudan (UNMISS) has been deployed since.[222]

This case-study illustrates that while the international community and collective responsibility are vital in providing technical, financial and

---

[216] See (n 189). See also Hansohm (n 191) at p. 133; Youngs (n 191) at p. 147.

[217] See, e.g. Sudan-PCEA (n 185); Gleditsch, N.P., 'Environmental Change, Security and Conflict' in Crocker, C.A. and others (eds), *Leashing the Dogs of War: Conflict Management in a Divided World* (US Institute of Peace, USA 2007) at p. 181; Sjöstedt, G., 'Resolving Ecological Conflicts: Typical and Special Circumstances' in Bercovitch., J. and others (eds), *The SAGE Handbook of Conflict Resolution* (SAGE, London 2009) at p. 239.

[218] See Harding (n 196).

[219] UN Mission in Sudan (UNMIS), www.un.org/en/peacekeeping/missions/ unmis/background.shtml (accessed 30 April 2012) [hereinafter UNMIS Sudan].

[220] Ibid.

[221] See UNMIS Mandate, www.un.org/en/peacekeeping/missions/unmis/ mandate.shtml (accessed 30 April 2012). See also UNDP Sudan, 'The UN Millennium Development Goals in Sudan' (UNDP Sudan 2010), www.sd. undp.org/mdg_sudan.htm (accessed 30 April 2012).

[222] See UNMISS website, www.un.org/en/peacekeeping/missions/unmiss/ (accessed 3 May 2012).

human resource assistance in any post-conflict situation,[223] for sustainable development to be achieved, all relevant post-conflict factors must be considered in addition to all stakeholders playing their parts, including the post-conflict State itself.[224]

3.2. Affixing Funds to the Environment

Returning to the environmental dimension of the post-conflict stage, the next question is whether the funds obtained are actually being used for the benefit of the environment? It is important that funding is actually used for the environment in order for the environment to be protected intrinsically, as well as for it to contribute to the cycle of sustainable development. Under general international law, States may use their compensation obtained under State responsibility as they see fit.[225] For example, if a State obtained compensation for an injured national or for damage to their environment, the State has no obligation to either give the compensation to the injured national or to use the compensation to remediate or restore the environment.[226] This of course differs from post-conflict situations where funding is obtained for specific environmental projects. In these circumstances, the funds received have to be used for the purpose it was acquired for. This is explored in the following section in relation to the three case-studies.

3.2.1. UNCC

The UNCC F4 Panel's main focus regarding conflict-related environmental damage within the affected States was 'on restoring the environment to pre-invasion conditions, in terms of its overall ecological functioning rather than on the removal of specific contaminants or

---

[223]   See, e.g. UNEP Conflict to Peacebuilding (n 3) at p. 5; Scharf, R., 'Key Findings of the OECD-DAC Task Force on Conflict, Peace and Development Co-Operation: The Imperative of Conflict Prevention' in Grandvoinnet, H. and Schneider, H. (eds), *Conflict Management in Africa: A Permanent Challenge* (OECD, Paris 1998) at p. 110.

[224]   See French, D.A., 'A Reappraisal of Sovereignty in the Light of Global Environmental Concerns' (2001) 21 Legal Studies 376, at p. 377 [hereinafter 2001 French] (on 'the emerging obligation on a state to protect also its own domestic environment').

[225]   Boczek, B.A., *International Law: A Dictionary* (Scarecrow, USA 2005) at p. 111.

[226]   Ibid.

restoration of the environment to a particular physical condition.'[227] Although there is no such obligation under general international law, any compensation paid out by the F4 Panel in relation to claims for a specific purpose (for example, restoration of environmental damage), has to be used for that specific purpose claimed.[228] If the compensation is not used for its purpose or distributed by the receiving Government accordingly, the UNCC-GC has to take measures to ensure that the Government concerned returns the funds.[229]

The UNCC's decision to restore the damaged environments to its pre-war conditions overall contributed to the protection and remediation of the conflict-damaged environment for the benefit of the present and future generations of the affected States. In addition, the UNCC's policy of making certain that the awards are specifically used for the environment not only ensures that the damaged environment is cleaned-up or restored but also contributes to the achievement of sustainable development in the process. In essence, the UNCC's policy of ensuring that the environment is actually restored, prevents or mitigates the negative impact of the damaged environment on the security, health and livelihoods of the Gulf population.

3.2.2. Kosovo

In this case, the appeal for funds was for specific priority environmental clean-up projects: from urgent remedial action, cleaning-up the heavily contaminated wastewater flowing into the Danube from Pančevo, to preventing further toxic gasses from being released into the air at the Bor ore smelting complex.[230] The funding received was thus specifically used

---

[227]   Panel Report F4/3 (2003) (n 94) at para. 48, further reaffirmed in Panel Report F4/4/I (2004) (n 94) at para. 50; Panel Report F4/4/II (2004) (n 94) at para. 41; and Panel Report F4/5 (2005) (n 88) at para. 43. See also comments by Julia Klee in 'The International Responses to the Environmental Impacts of War' (2005) 17 Georgetown International Environmental Law Review 565, at p. 603 and pp. 598–605; Sand (n 93) at p. 250.

[228]   See Panel Report F4/1 (2001) (n 99); Panel Report F4/2 (2002) (n 90); Panel Report F4/3 (2003) (n 94); Panel Report F4/4/I (2004) (n 94); Panel Report F4/4/II (2004) (n 94); Panel Report F4/5 (2005) (n 88).

[229]   Panel Report F4/5 (2005) (n 88) at para. 782.

[230]   UNEP, 'UNEP-led Balkans Task Force to Continue Its Work in Yugoslavia' *UNEP Press Release* (Geneva/Nairobi, February 2000); UNEP/UNCHS Kosovo (n 26).

for the benefit of the environment.[231] Two of the most urgent environmental 'hot spots' (Kragujevac and Bor) were satisfactorily dealt with
and the other two 'hot spots' (Novi Sad and Pančevo) had been
significantly reduced.[232] Basically, 16 out of 27 projects initially planned
by UNEP had been successfully implemented by 2004.[233] The funding
obtained that was used for urgent and significant conflict-related environmental damage (as prioritised by UNEP-BTF) not only demonstrates
UNEP's precautionary approach but also the international community's
in relation to contributing financial assistance to solve and manage urgent
conflict-related environmental problems. Measures were taken to actually
clean-up or restore the environment (e.g. reduce soil, air and water
pollution) and this prevented or mitigated the negative exposure of a
damaged environment on the security, health and livelihoods of the
war-torn population.

In relation to the DU assessments conducted by UNEP,[234] the assessment conducted in 2001[235] was a follow-up to the earlier DU assessment[236] undertaken. UNEP undertook thorough field work assessments,
working with scientists from the International Atomic Energy Agency
(IAEA) as well as cooperating closely with UN in Kosovo (UNMIK) and
NATO Kosovo Force (KFOR).[237] These UNEP assessments were important because there was not much information on DU contamination prior
to this.[238] These first assessments provided a starting base for information
on DU contamination that could assist in preventing or mitigating future
possible threats or risks to the environment and human well-being.

Although funding was used primarily for the specific purpose of
UNEP's Clean-up Programme: remediation projects reducing the environmental risks in 'hot spots' located in FRY, UNEP also initiated and
integrated post-conflict environmental capacity building.[239] UNEP, in

---

[231]   For more information on the environmental remediation projects and
progress reports, see UNEP Hot Spots (n 173); UNEP Clean-Up (n 163).

[232]   UNEP, 'UNEP Closes Environmental Clean-Up Operations in Serbia and
Montenegro' *UNEP Press Release* (Belgrade/Nairobi, 7 May 2004); UNEP
Clean-Up (n 163) at pp. 32–46.

[233]   UNEP Clean-Up (n 163) at p. 48.

[234]   For more information on UNEP's DU assessments and field missions, see
Haavisto (n 167) at pp. 543–7.

[235]   2002 UNEP DU (n168).

[236]   2001 UNEP DU (n 168).

[237]   Haavisto (n 167) at p. 543.

[238]   Ibid.

[239]   UNEP Clean-Up (n 163) at p. 46. See also UNEP, 'UNEP 2003: Annual
Report' (UNEP, March 2004) at p. 16.

cooperation with local authorities and partners, set up training and workshop activities within the Programme to support effective implementation and follow-up of the environmental clean-up projects as well as strengthening domestic abilities to identify, prioritise and address environmental issues.[240] These capacity building activities 'covered areas such as hazardous waste management, Local Environmental Action Plans, cleaner production and sustainable consumption, foreign direct investment, and Multilateral Environmental Agreements.'[241] These efforts certainly embraced the concept of sustainable development, not only covering environmental issues but also ensuring that the environment would be managed effectively for future development prospects. Thus, funding in this case was used for cleaning-up the conflict-damaged environment as well as integrating environmental awareness and management skills to enable the locals to manage effectively on their own.

UNEP's actions and training activities not only encouraged public participation of local and national actors on post-conflict environmental priorities and management, but it also encouraged good environmental governance. In this case, the initial partnership between UNEP and the relevant national authorities set the foundation for good environmental governance, allowing the new environmental authorities to take over and manage their own environmental priorities and management and in the process, to achieve sustainable development.[242] Basically, better environmental management capacity means that there would likely be a more positive impact on the socio-economic development and environmental sectors in the Balkan region.[243]

Although UNEP had overall responsibility for the Clean-up Programme, it had significant assistance from its implementing partner UN Office for Project Services (UNOPS).[244] UNEP was in charge of 'strategic direction, technical coordination of external relations, and fund

---

[240]   Ibid.

[241]   Ibid.

[242]   For further examples of setting up post-conflict institutional structures for environmental governance in practice, see UNEP, 'UNEP in Iraq: Post-Conflict Assessment, Clean-up and Reconstruction' (UNEP, Nairobi 2007) at pp. 19–20; 2007 Sudan-PCEA (n 185) at pp. 290–307.

[243]   UNDP, 'Environmental Policy in South-Eastern Europe' (UNDP, Belgrade 2007) at pp. 162–70 (for a more recent update on the 1999 war and instability legacy within the region).

[244]   A joint Project Implementation Office (PIO) was established in Belgrade in January 2001. See UNEP Hot Spots (n 173) at p. 89.

mobilization',[245] while UNOPS provided 'management expertise, complementing UNEP's environmental and technical know-how.'[246] UNEP was also given instrumental logistical and institutional assistance by the UN and especially by the UNDP office in Belgrade when in the initial stages of the program in 2000 there were no other international environmental assistance programmes operating in that area.[247] In addition, UNEP was greatly assisted by and cooperated with, throughout the implementation of the programme by local partners (from national authorities to contaminated site owners) at all stages of the operations, including Serbian environmental experts and other specialists in the relevant fields.[248]

All actors involved worked together towards a common concern – fixing the conflict-damaged environment and in the process towards sustainable development, by ensuring that further threats or risks were mitigated for the benefit of the environment itself, development and human well-being. Thus, this case demonstrates not only the importance of cooperative interaction between all relevant stakeholders (both local and international at all stages) in order to successfully implement environmental remediation and management programmes in post-conflict situations; the Clean-up Programme itself and the environmental capacity-building integrated within, are all contributory steps towards achieving sustainable development in a war-torn society.

3.2.3. Sudan

UNEP's PCEA of Sudan included assessments of water, forests, agriculture, natural disasters, desertification, wildlife, the marine environment, population displacement, industrial pollution, the urban environment, environmental governance, international aid and the role of environmental issues in Sudan's conflicts.[249] The PCEA exemplifies the concept of sustainable development, conducting a thorough assessment that considered all relevant areas, not only environmental but also related socio-economic, development and governance aspects.[250] The UNEP's

---

[245]   UNEP Clean-Up (n 163) at p. 30.
Ibid.
[246]   Ibid. See also UNEP Hot Spots (n 173) at p. 89.
[247]   Ibid.
[248]   UNEP Clean-Up (n 163) at p. 13.
[249]   UNEP Sudan-PCEA (n 185). See also UNEP, 'Sudan Environmental Database', http://postconflict.unep.ch/sudanreport/sudan_website/ (accessed 30 April 2012).
[250]   Ibid.

comprehensive PCEA examined all areas of the environment including environmental-conflict links that could flag up possible environmental challenges to the detriment of the Sudanese people living peaceful sustainable lives.[251] The PCEA also led to environmental projects[252] that covers areas such as capacity building for the relevant Sudanese authorities;[253] assisting with environmental management across the country (includes waste management); setting up a reforestation and alternative energy programme; assisting in sustainable water management and governance; and engaging 'with the international community in Sudan to develop environmental and natural resource management as a critical component of conflict resolution, recovery and development.'[254] From a sustainable perspective, these projects and efforts not only encourage cooperation and provide opportunities for peacebuilding through the management of the Sudanese environment and natural resources, but they also generate employment, encourage development, improves environmental protection and contributes positively to the security, health and livelihoods of the population for the benefit of the present and future generations.[255]

UNEP subsequently set up its first Sudan office in Khartoum in December 2007 with the intention of following through and overseeing the PCEA recommendations, to aid the delivery of the 2005 CPA's 'environmental elements ... and other national priorities, and to make

---

[251] Cudworth, E. and Hobden, S., 'Environmental Insecurity' in Fagan, G.H. and Munck, R. (eds), *Globalization and Security* (Praeger, California 2009) at p. 81.

[252] For further information on these projects, see UNEP, 'UNEP and Partners in Sudan Joint Programme on Environment and Natural Resource Management: 2007–2009 Strategy Paper' Version 1.2 (7 November 2007); UNEP Sudan Overview (n 199).

[253] UNEP-PCDMB in partnership with Yale University and more than 120 scientific publishers organised two capacity-building training courses on the Online Access to Research in the Environment (OARE) for both North and South Sudanese environmental institutions in 2008. See UNEP, 'UNEP provides training on environmental developments and best practices in Sudan' *UNEP Press Release* (Nairobi, 12 May 2008).

[254] For more information, see UNEP, 'UNEP in the Regions, Current Activities: Sudan', www.unep.org/conflictsanddisasters/UNEPintheRegions/CurrentActivities/Sudan/tabid/294/language/en-US/Default.aspx (accessed 30 April 2012).

[255] UNEP Conflict to Peacebuilding (n 3) at p. 5. See also 2011 Jan–Mar QPR (n 198) at pp. 6–8.

progress towards the relevant Millennium Development Goals.'[256] UNEP's mission in Sudan is '[t]o assist the people of Sudan in achieving peace, recovery and development on an environmentally sustainable basis.'[257] Therefore, the funding obtained was and is being used for Sudan's post-conflict environment with projects and programmes, some of which have been completed, some still currently underway and new projects commencing.[258] These projects and programmes which range for example, from sustainable timber, forest and alternative energy management;[259] water governance and management with a particular focus on 'the role that water stress plays in conflict and its fundamental role in the livelihoods of the poorest';[260] local capacity building training;[261] studies on 'alternative energy, the market economy for forest products, the available livelihood strategies for pastoralists, alternative construction technologies;[262] to preparing for future projects[263] that will further improve the conditions of the environment and socio-economic development of Sudan, certainly contribute to the virtuous cycle of sustainable development. As for USAID, their $5.8 million budget was used for Sudan's post-conflict environment but as mentioned above, at the end of their STEP programme, there still remained some outstanding environmental issues.[264] USAID at present continues to provide humanitarian aid in financing and human resources in Sudan (particularly Darfur and Southern Sudan), contributing towards socio-economic development, peace efforts, good governance, strengthening public institutions, agriculture, the environment, amongst other sectors.[265]

---

[256]   UNEP Sudan Overview (n 199).

[257]   Ibid.

[258]   Ibid; 2009 Jul–Sept QPR (n 213) at pp. 4–5; 2011 Jan–Mar QPR (n 198) at pp. 6–8. See also UNEP Sudan website (n 215).

[259]   Sudan Overview (n 199) at p. 1

[260]   Sudan Overview (n 199) at p. 2.

[261]   Ibid., at pp. 2–3.

[262]   Ibid., at p. 2.

[263]   See UNEP Sudan website (n 215); DFID-SIEP Programme (n 201); 2011 Jan–Mar QPR (n 198) at pp. 6–8.

[264]   USAID-SUDAN STEP (n 199) at pp. 36–7.

[265]   USAID, 'Congressional Budget Justification: Foreign Operations' (US, Fiscal Year 2010) at pp. 160–66. See also USAID, 'Sub-Saharan Africa', www.usaid.gov/locations/sub-saharan_africa/countries/sudan/ (3 May 2012).

3.3.   Following up on Environmental Recovery and Management

Even after compensation awarded or funding obtained is used towards the post-conflict environment, there still needs to be follow-up procedures in place by the relevant parties to ensure that environmental remediation projects have been effectively completed and/or environmental management programmes that have been implemented are proceeding effectively. Not taking this step could be regressive and hinder the achievement of sustainable development and in some cases, a possible factor towards re-conflict. This section thereby considers the follow-up procedures in relation to the three case-studies.

3.3.1.   UNCC

The GC, after approving the first batch of environmental remediation and monitoring and assessment (hereinafter M&A) claims in 2001,[266] required the F4 Panel to ensure that the recipient Governments submitted periodic progress reports to ascertain that the compensation awarded were actually used to conduct environmental remediation and M&A activities in a reasonable, appropriate and transparent manner.[267] The claimant Governments were required to send in progress reports (every six months) on each of their environmental remediation projects and M&A activities pursuant to the 'special tracking scheme' devised by the F4 Panel.[268] These reports were also regularly reviewed externally by the UNEP's Post-Conflict Assessment Branch.[269] To date, neither UNEP nor the UNCC appear to have made public any reports by UNEP on reviewing the M&A reports by the Governments concerned. In addition

---

[266]   Sand (n 93) at p. 250.

[267]   UNCC-GC Decision 132 (21 June 2001) at para. 6.

[268]   UNCC-GC Decision 248 (30 June 2005) at para. 5.

[269]   See Governing Council of UNEP, 'Implementation of Governing Council Decision 22/1 IV on Post-Conflict Environmental Assessment' UNEP Doc. GC.23/INF/20 (14 December 2004) at paras. 90–96. For further information on the 'M&A tracking reports', see summary in Panel Report F4/5 (2005) (n 88) at paras. 781–2. See also 'Decision concerning follow-up programme for environmental claims awards taken by the Governing Council of the UNCC at its 150th meeting on 8 December 2005' UN Doc. S/AC.26/Dec.258 (2005). The Governing Council adopted the follow-up program guidelines which is annexed to UNCC-GC Decision 258, S/AC.26/Dec.258 (2005) (8 December 2005): (this decision included a detailed set of guidelines for the Follow-Up Programme for the Environmental Awards) [hereinafter GC Decision 258 (2005)].

to these reviews, the UNCC Secretariat's[270] internal financial verification of project expenditures[271] were also included within reports[272] from the F4 Panel to the UNCC-GC.[273]

The UNCC-GC discussed progress reports by the UNCC Secretariat in every UNCC-GC session,[274] covering: claims payments and processing; transparency of the distribution process, including distribution of the awards by the Governments concerned to successful claimants; the return of the undistributed funds to the UNCC; the status of the projects; as well as ensuring the technical reasonableness and financial transparency of the environmental remediation and restoration projects and M&A activities undertaken by the participating Governments under the Follow-up Programme for Environmental Awards.[275] Furthermore, the UNCC, in addition to withholding the mandatory 15 per cent, could also withhold a further discretionary 10 per cent[276] with regard to the funds awarded.[277] This is to ensure that the environmental projects were carried out according to phased plans.[278] For example, the UNCC-GC did withhold a

---

[270]   Provides administrative, technical and legal support services to the GC and panels as well as administers the UNCC Compensation Fund. For more information, see 'The Secretariat' UNCC www.uncc.ch/secretar.htm (accessed 30 April 2012).

[271]   Sand (n 93) at p. 250.

[272]   'Tracking Progress of Environmental M&A Projects Compensated Pursuant to Governing Council Decision 132': First Report of the 'F4' Panel (13 September 2002); Second Report (24 January 2003); Third Report (2 May 2003); Fourth Report (21 November 2003); Fifth Report (27 February 2004); Sixth Report (30 April 2004); Seventh Report (17 September 2004); Eight Report (21 February 2005) as set out in Panel Report F4/5(2005) (n 88) at para. 781.

[273]   Summarised in Panel Report F4/5(2005) (n 88) at paras. 781–2.

[274]   See, e.g. UNCC, 'Governing Council of UNCC Has Concluded Its Sixty-First Session' PR/2006/10 (3 November 2006); UNCC, 'Governing Council of UNCC Has Concluded Its Sixty-Fourth Session' PR/2007/10 (31 October 2007); UNCC, 'Governing Council of UNCC Has Concluded Its Sixty-Fifth Session' PR/2008/1 (9 April 2008); UNCC, 'Governing Council of UNCC Has Concluded Its Sixty-Sixth Session' PR/2008/9 (22 October 2008); UNCC, 'Governing Council of UNCC Has Concluded Its Sixty-Seventh Session and Pays Out US$300 Million' PR/2009/3 (29 April 2009) [hereinafter PR/2009/3]; UNCC, 'Governing Council of UNCC Has Concluded Its Sixty-Eighth Session' PR/2009/7 (12 November 2009).

[275]   GC Decision 258 (2005) (n 269).

[276]   Ibid.

[277]   UNCC-GC Decision 266 (S/AC.26/Dec.266 (2009)) (29 April 2009); PR/2009/3 (n 274).

[278]   Ibid.

portion of one of Kuwait's environmental claims awarded, to be released at a later date.[279] It is argued that these post-award compensation tracking measures were noteworthy, because in an area of law where enforcement is generally difficult to achieve, this tracking scheme, by taking a precautionary 'checks and balances' approach, made attempts to ensure that the money awarded would not be misappropriated and that the environmental restoration and M&A projects claimed for, were conducted appropriately.[280] Similar post-award tracking measures were also applicable to claims in the other categories.[281] Thus, these proactive attempts regarding war-reparations ensure to some extent that the compensation awarded is channelled back to the affected States and their people; thereby, contributing to the virtuous cycle of sustainable development.

The integration of sustainable development can also be seen from the cooperative efforts between the five governments (Iran, Jordan, Kuwait, Saudi Arabia and Iraq) participating in the F4's Follow-up programme.[282] These five Gulf States, with the UNCC Secretariat acting as facilitator,[283] carried out several joint regional meetings[284] to discuss numerous environmental matters such as the follow-up program for monitoring the use of UNCC awards, agreeing on efforts towards future regional environmental cooperation concerning all countries within the region, the new Regional Remediation Programme (RERP),[285] a new regional environmental advisory group as well as a potential regional environmental

---

[279]   PR/2009/3 (n 274).

[280]   For further information on post-award environmental M&As, see Sand (n 93) at pp. 250–51.

[281]   Gattini, A., 'The UN Compensation Commission: Old Rules, New Procedures on War Reparations' (2002) 13 European Journal of International Law 161, at pp. 170–1 [hereinafter Gatini]. See also UNCC, 'Reports and Recommendations of the Panel Commissioners', www.uncc.ch/reports.htm (accessed 30 April 2012).

[282]   See UNEP Iraq Desk Study (n 160) at p. 57. See also Sands (n 93) at p. 250.

[283]   UNCC, 'Governing Council of UNCC Has Concluded Its Fifty-Seventh Session' PR/2005/11 (29 September 2005) at p. 2 [hereinafter PR/2005/11].

[284]   See, e.g. UNCC, 'Governing Council of UNCC Has Concluded Its Fifty-Eight Session' PR/2005/14 (8 December 2005) [hereinafter PR/2005/14]; UNCC, 'Governing Council of UNCC Has Concluded Its Fifty-Ninth Session' PR/2006/3 (9 March 2006) [hereinafter PR/2006/3]; UNCC, 'Governing Council of UNCC Has Concluded Its Sixtieth Session' PR/2006/6 (29 June 2006) at p. 1; UNCC, 'Governing Council of UNCC Has Concluded Its Sixty-Second Session' PR/2007/3 (22 February 2007) at p. 1.

[285]   PR/2005/14 (n 284); PR/2006/3 (n 284).

databank.[286] In addition, Iraq and Kuwait have been having bilateral talks on projects relating to RERP as well.[287] Progress is tangible when considering the cooperative efforts shown by the Gulf States. Their willingness to hold joint meetings and discussions and the attempts to integrate and coordinate efforts in dealing with environmental issues affecting the region are a remarkable achievement. These efforts arguably reflect elements of the 'common but differentiated responsibilities' and 'integration and interrelationship' principles between States that have not always been known to have strong and politically stable relationships with one another.[288]

These cooperative efforts are arguably evidence of these States recognising that environmental issues in the region transcend their own State boundaries. Therefore, for any effective environmental remediation to occur at that stage and in the future, they would need to work together collaboratively to succeed. Simply put, these previously hostile States now had a common goal – the environment. Thus, these post-conflict cooperative efforts over environmental matters do contribute towards fostering better international and political relations between these States. On the whole, the UNCC's environmental programme is not only a significant milestone 'in the practice of international environmental claims settlement, but also an innovative effort in multilateral post-conflict cooperation among former enemy states'[289] and thus, arguably, a

---

[286]   PR/2005/11 (n 283); Sand (n 93) at p. 250. For regional environmental cooperation thereafter, see, e.g. 'Letter dated 11 May 2009 from the Permanent Observer of the League of Arab States to the United Nations addressed to the President of the Security Council' (Section VI: Cooperation on Environmental Affairs and Sustainable Development) S/2009/241 (12 May 2009) at paras. 76–90; 'Joint Ministerial Meeting between Arab States and the Community of South American Nations on Environmental Development' (Nairobi, 6 February 2007) and 'Joint Ministerial Meeting between Arab States and the Community of South American Nations on Water Resources and Combating Desertification' (Riyadh, 16–17 November 2008); Center for Environment and Development for the Arab Region and Europe (CEDARE), www.cedare.int/cedare.int/Main.aspx (accessed 19 January 2012) See also UNDP Arab States: Environment and Energy website, http://arabstates.undp.org/subpage.php?spid=9&sscid=37 (accessed 30 April 2012); UNEP-CEDARE, 'Environment Outlook for the Arab Region: The First Comprehensive Policy-Relevant Environmental Assessment Report for the Arab Region' (UNEP, Bahrain 2009).

[287]   PR/2006/3 (n 284).

[288]   Sand (n 93) at p. 250. See also Spain, A., 'Using International Dispute Resolution to Address the Compliance Question in International Law' (2009) 40 Georgetown Journal of International Law 807, at p. 848 [hereinafter Spain].

[289]   Ibid.

huge step towards achieving sustainable development through environmental cooperation within the region.

The UNCC system illustrates that reparation mechanisms may provide the means to start a new cycle of achieving sustainable development in the aftermath of war.[290] The UNCC was a success overall,[291] the efficiency of it 'was paralleled by its effectiveness in achieving its purpose.'[292] As observed above, the UNCC provided States affected by the First Gulf War, compensation to restore their environment and by doing so, embraced not only the precautionary principle to prevent further deteriorating environmental damage but also the principle of equity, taking into account the environment of the Persian Gulf region for intra and inter-generations. Furthermore, by enabling the affected States to restore their environment, the UNCC to some extent assisted those countries in fulfilling their duty to ensure sustainable use of their natural resources. Moreover, the UNCC, by permitting a wide range of claims,[293] not only contributed to the environment but also to the socio-economic development of these affected States.[294]

3.3.2. Kosovo

The clean-up activities by UNEP in Serbia and Montenegro ended in December 2003.[295] Throughout the programme, UNEP maintained that the primary responsibility for environmental clean-up efforts rested on FRY and although UNEP was in charge of the programme, UNEP worked in close partnership with the Government of Serbia and Montenegro after signing a Memorandum of Understanding between them regarding the overall programme.[296] In addition, to ensure transparency

---

[290] Ibid.

[291] DuBarry Huston, M., 'Wartime Environmental Damages: Financing the Cleanup' (2002) 23 University of Pennsylvania Journal of International Economic Law 899, at p. 917. See also McGovern (n 106) at p. 189.

[292] Spain (n 288) at p. 847.

[293] UNCC Claims (n 82). See also Gatini (n 281).

[294] Cunningham, S., *Rewealth! Stake Your Claim in the $2 Trillion Redevelopment Trend That's Renewing the World* (McGraw-Hill, USA 2008) at p. 199. See also Section 3.1. above; Elias, O., 'Sustainable Development, War Reparations and Environmental Damage' in Fitzmaurice, M. and Szuniewicz, M. (eds), *Exploitation of Natural Resources in the 21st Century* (Kluwer Law, The Netherlands 2003) at pp. 67–90.

[295] Governing Council of UNEP, 'State of the environment and contribution of the United Nations Environment Programme to addressing substantive environmental challenges' UNEP/GC.23/3/Add.2 (2 November 2004) at para. 11.

[296] UNEP Clean-Up (n 163) at p. 49.

of the Programme, throughout its implementation from 2001 to 2003, exemplifying public participation, regular stakeholder meetings were held to report on the Programme's progress and to raise any potential issues.[297]

UNEP worked with national and local stakeholders throughout the programme to ensure a smooth handover of the programme to the relevant partners.[298] The follow-up measures necessary were already assessed and set out in the joint final assessment report between UNEP and the environmental authorities of Serbia and Montenegro.[299] Each site was handed over to its original site owners[300] and the whole programme was transferred to the control of the relevant environmental authorities in Serbia and Montenegro.[301] The transfers for overall programme responsibility and follow-up monitoring were done via formal legal arrangements, where specific legal documents set out detailed tasks regarding each site.[302] The handover was done as efficiently as possible and UNEP, having provided the relevant national authorities with capacity building tools,[303] left the responsibility for the post-conflict environment and sustainable development in the hands of the new restructured country. Any further continuing involvement by UNEP regarding environmental issues in this region is conducted through the Environment and Security Initiative (ENVSEC).[304]

This case-study demonstrates that an effective handover, involving the transfer in responsibility of environmental issues to a war-torn country, is entirely possible. It shows that the international community, in this

---

[297]   Ibid., at p. 30.

[298]   Ibid., at p. 50.

[299]   UNEP Hot Spots (n 173) at p. 89.

[300]   Most were State enterprises or undergoing privatisation processes. See UNEP Clean-Up (n 163) at p. 50.

[301]   Ibid., at p. 30.

[302]   Ibid., at p. 50.

[303]   Ibid., at p. 56. See also UNEP, 'UNEP 2003: Annual Report' (UNEP, March 2004) at p. 16.

[304]   A partnership between UNEP, UNDP, OSCE, NATO, UN Economic Commission for Europe (UNECE) and Regional Environmental Center for Central and Eastern Europe (REC) that 'works to assess and address environmental problems, which threaten or are perceived to threaten security, societal stability and peace, human health and/or sustainable livelihoods, within and across national borders in conflict prone regions.' For further environmental-security projects within Kosovo and Serbia and Montenegro, see ENVSEC, 'South Eastern Europe', www.envsec.org/index.php?option=com_content&view=article&id=77&lang=en&Itemid=95 (accessed 9 May 2012).

instance through UNEP, was not only able to encourage public partici-pation by raising environmental awareness, but was also able to provide local and national actors with the skills necessary to monitor and manage their own environmental issues. From a sustainable development view-point, this is a key step as encouraging a war-torn country to protect and manage its own environment[305] could not only contribute towards the country's post-conflict environmental and socio-economic development by generating employment in the environmental management sector and providing a healthier environment for the post-conflict population, but also make the State less dependant on international assistance.

In relation to the DU assessments undertaken by UNEP, the assess-ments did not find widespread significant ground contamination and therefore there were no significant environmental risks attached to those sites assessed.[306] Thus, there was no follow up by UNEP in relation to cleaning up the DU contaminated sites. However, based on these findings and also the fact that there were still scientific uncertainties regarding the long-term effects of DU on the environment, UNEP recommended a precautionary approach to be taken by relevant national and local authorities within the region.[307] Overall, UNEP recommended that with regard to the Balkan region, stronger and more effective 'environmental management is needed to ensure that short-term economic gains are not detrimental to the longer-term prospects for environmentally sustainable development.'[308]

With regard to the other post-conflict issues in Kosovo, UNMIK, since its establishment in 1999 has maintained a strong presence in the region and with the cooperation of other UN partners, international organ-isations and donor States, has established and continues to oversee 'the development of provisional democratic self-governing institutions to ensure conditions for a peaceful and normal life for all inhabitants of Kosovo.'[309] In doing so, UNMIK and its partners built and improved

---

[305]   2001 French (n 224) at p. 377; Weiss, E.B., 'International Law' in Krech, S. and McNeil, J.R. (eds), *Encyclopaedia of World Environmental History: Volume 2 F-N* (Routledge, New York 2004) at p. 698.

[306]   2002 UNEP DU (n 168) at pp. 33–4.

[307]   UNEP Clean-Up (n 163) at pp. 24–6. See also Haavisto (n 167) at pp. 543–7.

[308]   UNEP Clean-Up (n 163) at p. 10.

[309]   UNMIK Mandate, see UNMIK Online, www.un.org/en/peacekeeping/missions/unmik/mandate.shtml (accessed 30 April 2012) [hereinafter UNMIK Kosovo].

issues within eight crucial sectors:[310] functioning democratic institutions, rule of law, freedom of movement, economy, property rights (including cultural heritage), facilitating Pristina-Belgrade dialogue, and establishing the Kosovo Protection Corps (KPC).[311]

3.3.3. Sudan

As mentioned above, post-conflict environmental projects and programmes in Sudan are currently ongoing.[312] UNEP's Sudan Programme funded by DFID which began in July 2009 continues to focus on effective natural resource management (NRM) and capacity-building within the Sudanese population to address issues of poverty, community resilience and 'support peacebuilding within the region';[313] thereby, contributing to the cycle of sustainable development.[314] Further progress was also made on the USAID funded UNEP-FAO joint timber and energy project[315] as well as the joint UNEP-UNDP natural resource assessment on the potential use for liquid petroleum gas.[316] In addition, progress was also made on the IWRM project with monthly progress meetings between UNEP, DFID and UNOPS; integration of IWRM programmes within local Sudanese communities through UNEP advocacy efforts;[317] a breakthrough in influencing Sudanese government policy, especially on sustainable water management and drought contingency plans for the internally displaced population; the monitoring of 200 wells across the country (especially in Darfur) and the potential dam

---

[310] Ibid (for more information on UNMIK and its partners' work in post-conflict Kosovo).

[311] KPC was a civilian protection body serving under UNMIK from 1999 to 14 June 2009. Its disbandment was prompted by the improvement and modernisation of Kosovo's security. See UNDP Kosovo, 'Kosovo Corps Resettlement Programme (KCP RP)', www.ks.undp.org/?cid=2,90,776 (accessed 8 May 2012).

[312] See, e.g. UNEP, 'Republic of Sudan', www.unep.org/sudan/ (accessed 8 May 2012); 2011 Jan–Mar QPR (n 198) at pp. 6–8; DFID-SIEP Programme (n 201); UNEP/FAO Darfur Timber (n 199); 2009 Jul–Sept QPR (n 213) at pp. 4–5.

[313] 2009 Jul–Sept QPR (n 213) at p. 4.

[314] See DFID-SIEP Programme (n 201). For further UN actions contributing to sustainable development in Sudan, see UNDP, 'The United Nations Serving Sudan for Over A Half-Century', www.sd.undp.org/un_sudan.htm (accessed 30 April 2012) [hereinafter UN in Sudan].

[315] 2009 Jul–Sept QPR (n 213) at p. 5 (for further information).

[316] Ibid.

[317] Ibid.

rehabilitation project.[318] UNEP also continues to implement community environmental actions plans[319] as well as collaborating with the UN International Children's Emergency Fund (UNICEF) on drought preparedness for internally displaced persons and refugee camps.[320] Cooperation and public participation between all actors, from international, national to the grass-root levels, are crucial in integrating these environmental priorities and programmes in post-conflict Sudan; improving not only environmental and natural resource management but also in the process, improving security, livelihoods and human well-being.

UNEP is the focal point for integration of these environmental issues. By having a presence and becoming the primary co-ordinator for other partners for environmental governance in Sudan, UNEP is not only attempting to help the Sudanese people (both in the North and South) to manage their environmental issues for the benefit of the current and future Sudanese generations but also bringing to the fore the principles of common but differentiated responsibilities, integration and interrelationship and public participation with regard to cooperative efforts of all partners involved. These follow-up efforts by UNEP and its partners are steps towards helping both countries achieve sustainable development, exemplifying a precautionary and common concern approach in respect of Sudan's environment.[321]

Moreover, in addition to UNEP's environmental focus in Sudan, since 2005, various UN agencies[322] in cooperation with other international organisations and donor countries have been continuing to work together

---

[318] UNEP is encouraging public participation via community environmental management in partnership with Darfur Development and Reconstruction Agency (DRA). Since 2011, 7 villages in North Darfur have been the first participants for the UNEP-DRA pilot project for community engagement in sustainable activities. See 2011 Jan–Mar QPR (n 198) at p. 6.

[319] Ibid.

[320] 2009 Jul–Sept QPR (n 213) at p. 1.

[321] For earlier summary progress reports, see, e.g. 2011 Jan–Mar QPR (n 198) at pp. 6–8; UNEP Disasters and Conflicts Programme, 'Sudan Country Programme' Quarterly Progress Report (January–March 2009) at pp. 3–4; UNEP Disasters and Conflicts Programme, 'Sudan Country Programme' Quarterly Progress Report (April-June 2009) at pp. 3–4.

[322] World Food Programme (WFP), UN Development Fund for Women (UNIFEM), Joint UN Programme on HIV/Aids (UNAIDS), UN Refugee Agency (UNHCR), UN Industrial Development Organization (UNIDO), Food and Agriculture Organization (FAO), UN Population Fund (UNFPA), UN Office for the Coordination of Humanitarian Affairs (OCHA), UNICEF, UNMID, UNMIS, UNOPS, UN-HABITAT, UNEP.

across various sectors: health; education; food security; livelihood support; public institution and infrastructure rehabilitation; 'support for return and reintegration of internally displaced persons (IDPs) and refugees; protection of IDPs and refugees; rule of law and good governance; water and environmental sanitation; mine action; disarmament, demobilization and reintegration of former combatants.'[323] It is hoped that these decisions and actions by the international community will prevent or mitigate unresolved and festering environmental issues in combination with other socio-economic issues from fuelling the vicious circle of re-conflict. Unfortunately, it appears that efforts have failed. At present, as discovered above, new tensions have arisen between North and South Sudan over another natural resource – oil, primarily the inability of either country to diplomatically share this resource. Sudan is once again on the brink of conflict.[324]

To sum up, there is no doubt that 'sustainable development is critical to ensuring global security, and peace is required for effective development.'[325] Thus, in this respect, the 'international community has a justifiable interest in those domestic issues that prevent a state from achieving sustainable development'[326] and in addition to the more traditional socio-economic development and political issues, this includes the post-conflict environment especially environmental issues with the potential for triggering re-conflict. Thus, in the spirit of cooperation, collective responsibility and common but differentiated responsibilities, States should assist other States not capable of helping themselves[327] to restore, abate or manage such environmental issues in order to prevent or mitigate the negative impact on development, the environment and human well-being of the affected post-conflict State.

The case-studies above have highlighted the weaknesses of environmental recovery and management post-conflict as well as the successes

---

[323]   UN in Sudan (n 314).

[324]   Harding (n 196); BBC Sudanese Conflict (n 196).

[325]   'By awarding the 2004 prize to Kenya environmental activist Wangari Maathai, the Nobel Peace Prize committee also recognized the critical connections among environmental management, local livelihoods, governance, and conflict.' See Dabelko, G.D., 'From Threat to Opportunity: Exploiting Environmental Pathways to Peace' Prepared for 'Environment, Peace and Dialogue Among Civilizations and Cultures', (Tehran, Islamic Republic of Iran, 9–10 May 2006) at p. 1.

[326]   2001 French (n 224) at p. 397.

[327]   See, e.g. French, D., 'Developing States and International Environmental Law: The Importance of Differentiated Responsibilities' (2000) 49 International and Comparative Law Quarterly 35, at p. 45 [hereinafter 2000 French].

of the system. The weaknesses range for example, from the inadequacy of international law in relation to post-conflict environmental damages (from the lack of specific laws of State responsibility for conflict-related environmental damage to the fact that compensation awarded need not be used for the environment); the problems of applying the polluter pays principle in post-conflict situations; the difficulties involved in obtaining funds to assist in post-conflict environmental recovery and management; war-torn States lacking the capacity to protect and manage their own environmental issues; to the lack of priority given to post-conflict environmental issues by the international community. The main successes are: First, the UNCC as a precedent for future reparations and restoration of conflict-related environmental damages (from its environmental-damage valuation methods used, to its environmental award M&A system) as well as bridging the gap between former enemy Gulf States via its Environmental Follow-Up programme. Second, the international community collectively in the spirit of common but differentiated responsibilities contributes towards post-conflict environmental clean-up, recovery, restoration and management as demonstrated by the Kosovo and Sudan case-studies. Third, UNEP's effective PCEAs and coordination efforts in relation to the environment in post-conflict situations.

Another success for the international community in relation to post-conflict peacebuilding and reconstruction is the creation of the UN Peacebuilding Commission (PBC).[328] The PBC, a subsidiary of both UNSC and UNGA, was created in December 2005 to 'address the critical gap in the international community's ability to meet the needs of countries emerging from violent conflict.'[329] The Commission is supported by the Peacebuilding Support Office and the Peacebuilding Fund.[330] The PBC takes the unique role in:

> (1) bringing together all of the relevant actors, including international donors, the international financial institutions, national governments, troop contributing countries; (2) marshalling resources and (3) advising on and proposing integrated strategies for post-conflict peacebuilding and recovery and where appropriate, highlighting any gaps that threaten to undermine peace.[331]

---

[328]   For more information, see UN Peacebuilding Commission, www.un.org/en/peacebuilding/ (accessed 30 April 2012) [hereinafter Peacebuilding Commission]. See also Iro, A., *The UN Peacebuilding Commission – Lessons from Sierra Leone* (Universitätsverlag Potsdam 2009) at pp. 19–27.

[329]   McAskie (n 133) at p. 8.

[330]   Peacebuilding Commission (n 328).

[331]   Ibid.

The PBC was not discussed above as it did not have a role to play in the post-conflict case-studies used. As it is still a fledgling organisation of seven years,[332] thus far, only six countries (Burundi, Sierra Leone, Guinea, Guinea-Bissau, Liberia and the Central African Republic) are on its agenda.[333] Nonetheless, due to it unique and much needed role in the field of post-conflict peacebuilding, the Commission could in future help fragile war-torn States to achieve sustainable peace by rebuilding and integrating all political, security, humanitarian, development, economic and environmental factors. As the UN has admitted that it has 'not effectively integrated environmental and natural resource considerations into its peacebuilding interventions'[334] and often leaving these issues to be addressed at a much later stage,[335] the creation of the PBC 'provides an important chance to address environmental risks and capitalize on potential opportunities in a more consistent and coherent way.'[336]

UNEP has recently analysed the legal regime in relation to environmental protection relevant to armed conflict[337] as well as the role of the environment from armed conflict to the peacebuilding stage.[338] UNEP made several recommendations on protection and management of the environment and natural resources in the post-conflict stage.[339] UNEP recommends that the PBC and the international community as a whole take into consideration its recommendations 'for integrating environment and natural resource issues into peacebuilding interventions and conflict prevention.'[340] The recommendations range from: a permanent UN body akin to the UNCC structure, 'to monitor violations and address compensation for environmental damage'[341] post-IAC and NIAC; integrating NRM and environmental priorities, issues and concessions from the outset of the post-conflict stage;[342] defining conflict resources;[343] 'improving governance capacity to control natural resources' at the

---

[332]   McAskie (n 133).

[333]   UN, 'Review of UN Peacebuilding Activities Will Benefit Post-Conflict Nations, Says Official' *UN News Centre* (New York, 13 April 2010).

[334]   UNEP Conflict to Peacebuilding (n 3) at p. 19.

[335]   Ibid.

[336]   Ibid., at p. 5.

[337]   UNEP International Law (n 1).

[338]   See UNEP Conflict to Peacebuilding (n 3).

[339]   Ibid., at p. 5.

[340]   Ibid.

[341]   UNEP International Law (n 1) at p. 53.

[342]   Ibid., at p. 54; UNEP Conflict to Peacebuilding (n 3) at pp. 30–31.

[343]   UNEP International Law (n 1) at p. 54.

peacebuilding stage;[344] harnessing natural resources for post-conflict environmental recovery;[345] to capitalising on the potential for environmental cooperation in contributing to the peacebuilding process.[346]

This chapter does not seek to duplicate UNEP's recommendations. However, a couple of recommendations are added based on the conclusions drawn from the discussion and case-studies above. First, there needs to be a better system in obtaining funding for post-conflict environmental damages and environmental management programmes. One source of funding, as with most international environmentally-related matters, could come from the international donor community. It could either be ad hoc funding or as with UNEP, a combination of ad hoc funding and voluntary contributions towards a trust fund set up for a future UNCC-like system.[347] For instance, French advocates that, 'the need to take into account the needs of developing States provides further support for the creation of environmental funds'.[348] As there are violent and armed conflicts constantly going on in the world today and most of them within or with developing countries, it is arguably practical to provide voluntary funding to a permanent post-conflict fund. A second option, if a similar UNCC system is used, is that funding could be sourced on a case-by-case basis, depending on whether the country concerned has natural resources that have particularly high market value (for example, oil, diamonds, timber), that could be used to fund a similar compensation system that provides reparation and channels the money awarded back to the conflict-damaged environment or, in the case of the UNCC, not only the environment but also individuals, private entities, governments and international organisations that have suffered losses as a result of conflict. This could help the war-torn country environmentally, socially and economically by permitting the compensation awarded to be channelled back to not only fix the environment, but also to bolster economic and development opportunities as well as improving human

---

[344]   Ibid.

[345]   UNEP Conflict to Peacebuilding (n 3) at p. 31.

[346]   Ibid.

[347]   UNEP receives funding in a combination of voluntary contributions to its main fund: the UN Environment Fund, other trust funds, earmarked contributions and a small portion from the UN Regular Budget. For UNEP funding sources in detail, see UNEP, 'Organization Profile' at pp. 32–3, www.unep.org/PDF/UNEPOrganizationProfile.pdf (accessed 30 April 2012).

[348]   For more information on funds and financing provisions for environmental matters, see 2000 French (n 327) at pp. 42–4.

well-being. A third option could be funding obtained from the UN PBC's Peacebuilding Fund.[349]

Second, as discovered from the discussion regarding the economic valuation methods to assess environmental damages, such methods could also be applied in assessing environmental and ecosystem services in respect of post-conflict situations where environmental pressures had fuelled the conflicts in the first place. The valuation methods could be used to estimate the costs required in order to implement the relevant environmental recovery and management programmes. In increasing transparency with regard to the valuation of environmental issues, that is, by having a breakdown as to why and how money is needed and used, could perhaps encourage funding and at the same time increase environmental awareness amongst the international community.

From the case-studies, barring the UNCC system, funding in respect of the Kosovo and Sudan case-studies were unclear (with regard to the breakdown and valuation of monetary figures needed for the projects) and ad hoc (voluntary funding). There is scope for improving this by creating a better funding system, in addition to setting out and integrating the recommendations formulated by UNEP and improving international cooperation,[350] which would ensure better post-conflict environmental recovery and management in future. Integrating these priorities will not only prevent further disintegration of environmental problems but will also help in achieving sustainable development, potentially removing environmental issues that may 'threaten the livelihoods and health of current and future generations and may constitute an impediment for lasting peace.'[351] Furthermore, armed conflicts that have had some environmental-conflict link could be prevented from falling into the vicious cycle of re-conflict.[352]

---

[349] Peacebuilding Commission (n 328) at p. 298.

[350] For discussion on whether States have an international obligation to protect their own environment and whether the international community as a whole 'have a right to be concerned with environmental issues within the boundaries of an individual state', see 2001 French (n 224) at pp. 391–2.

[351] Bijlsm, M., 'Protecting the Environment' in Junne, G. and Verkoren, W. (eds), *Post Conflict Development: Meeting New Challenges* (Lynne Rienner, USA 2005) at p. 166; Glenn, J. and others, *2009 State of the Future* (The Millennium Project, Washington, DC 2009) at p. 71 [hereinafter Glenn].

[352] 'The UN reports that about half of all conflicts over the past 20 years were "re-conflicts" – those that recurred within five years of peace accords. Many had environmental backgrounds. There is consensus that failed states are the most vulnerable to climate change and possible conflicts due to environment-related issues.' See Glenn (n 351) at p. 71.

4. CONCLUSION

In theory, the international law of reparations and the polluter pays principle are adequate in relation to conflict-related environmental damages from many aspects of the sustainable development perspective. In particular, it allows for a wide range of environmental harm to be 'brought home' to the perpetrator. That includes liability for rebuilding the damaged environment for the present and future generations. In practice however, there are essentially political obstacles in the way of making perpetrators pay for environmental damage as a consequence of armed conflict. That is why the emphasis on collective solutions where members of the UN have recognised the shared responsibility for conflict-related environmental damage is impressive.

This does however, bring to the fore, in the absence of a permanent post-conflict environmental compensation and recovery system for both IACs and NIACs, the need for the international community to prioritise environmental issues in the aftermath of armed conflict. The international community has a collective responsibility towards protecting the environment in consideration with other sustainable development factors, particularly at the post-conflict stage where the war-torn State is vulnerable and may lack the capacity to integrate the necessary environmental priorities itself. It is clear that despite increasing global environmental awareness, the international community still needs to improve its performance, utilising the principles of common but differentiated responsibilities, polluter pays, public participation, integration, precaution and intra- and inter-generational equity, in order to achieve sustainable development. Hence, in order for the cycle of sustainable development to resume and continue, post-conflict environmental priorities need to be integrated effectively from the outset of the peacebuilding stage in any war-torn country together with other more traditional economic, political or social factors.[353] Failure to do so could mean that the post-conflict population will continue to suffer the effects of armed conflict as well as conflict-related environmental damage and natural resources issues long after the end of the war, and in some circumstances, resulting in possible re-conflict.

---

[353]   UNEP Conflict to Peacebuilding (n 3) at p. 19 (on the fact that very few peace negotiations consider environmental priorities from the outset).

6. Conclusions and challenges

> Today we cannot secure security for one state at the expense of the other. Security can only be universal, but security cannot only be political or military, it must be as well ecological, economical, and social. It must ensure the fulfilment of the aspirations of humanity as a whole.[1]

The environment functions well without humanity but humanity cannot survive without the environment. This book argues that legal and policy responses to environmental protection in security and armed conflict situations must be formulated with the guiding principles of sustainable development – an integrated consideration of the environment in the context of other social, economic and development issues.

The key question of 'how consistent is international policy and law in relation to protection of the environment in security and armed conflict from a sustainable development perspective?' is answered by considering three other specific questions representing the three stages of the life cycle of security and armed conflict (pre-conflict, in-conflict and post-conflict): First, are the laws or practices preventive in respect of environmental-induced conflicts? Second, are the controls and limitations on unnecessary and unsustainable environmental harm during actual armed conflict adequate? Third, how effectively is responsibility attached, reparations awarded or funding obtained for the restoration of conflict-related environmental damages and the management of post-conflict environmental issues to prevent re-conflict?

In considering the primary and the ensuing sub-questions, this study leads to an emphasis on the vicious and virtuous circle of sustainable development, the environment, security and armed conflict. It is vicious in the sense that environmental problems coupled with the collapse of institutions and breakdown in socio-economic conditions can be a threat to security, livelihoods and human well-being, leading to or exacerbating

---

[1] Statement by Timoshenko, A.S. (Institute of State and Law, USSR Academy of Sciences), World Commission on Environment and Development (WCED) Public Hearing (Moscow, 11 December 1986).

armed conflict; thereby becoming an obstacle to sustainable development. And, it is a virtuous circle in that sustainable development is a condition for peace and security.

1. CONCLUSIONS: SUSTAINABLE DEVELOPMENT AND PROTECTION OF THE ENVIRONMENT RELEVANT TO SECURITY AND ARMED CONFLICT

The key conclusion is straightforward – law and policy is weak throughout the life cycle of conflict. The findings of this study are summarised as follows:

- Chapter 2 concludes that although sustainable development has not as yet reached the status of a legally binding norm or principle in international law, it is nevertheless a concept with significant legal effect. This chapter also concludes that in the ultimate aim of achieving sustainable development, the substantive principles under the umbrella concept of sustainable development (duty of states to ensure sustainable use of natural resources; equity and the eradication of poverty; common but differentiated responsibilities; precautionary approach; participation; good governance; integration and interrelationship; and polluter pays) could be utilised as tools, objectives or guidelines (not necessarily cumulatively) in order to tackle environmental challenges relevant to security and armed conflict. It is argued that that these principles could be used at all stages of the armed conflict life cycle: at the preventive stage, during conflict and post-conflict.

1.1. Pre-conflict

- Chapter 3 explores the conflict prevention framework of the international community with a particular focus on environmental-induced conflict. This chapter establishes that there is a link between environmental pressures and conflict, in combination with other underlying variable social, economic or political factors. Although the environment-conflict link is clearly highlighted in practice, the case-studies (Somalia; Darfur, Sudan; and Sierra Leone) reviewed, draw attention to the limitations of the international law and policy framework in preventing such violent and

armed conflicts. It is concluded that international conflict prevention as a whole, let alone environment-conflict prevention, is a
significantly weak link in the holistic approach to the life cycle of
armed conflict.

- This leads to the conclusion that to overcome these challenges the
international community should concentrate in particular on
stepping-up collective conflict prevention efforts, going beyond lip
service and putting into practice the relevant Multilateral Environmental Agreements (MEAs) that can prevent, mitigate or manage
environmental issues in consideration with other variable factors
that could, if left untouched, potentially motivate conflict. Moreover, it is necessary to develop a stronger and more comprehensive
early warning (EW) system, supported by a better collective
international early action system. To accomplish this, it is argued
that the international community would benefit from the commitment to sustainable development through collective responsibility,
cooperation, common but differentiated responsibilities, integration,
intra- and inter-generational equity, public participation and good
governance.

1.2. In-conflict

- Chapter 4, which considers protection for the environment during
the heat of armed conflict, reinforces the difficulties in applying the
relevant rules and principles under IHL in relation to environmental
protection. From the stringent and high thresholds of IHL rules
specifically intended to prevent environmental harm to the 'get out'
clause of military necessity, the case-studies (First Gulf War and
Kosovo conflict) demonstrate the practical difficulty in applying the
relevant IHL provisions to protect the environment during conflict.
In relation to even the possibility of attaching responsibility for
environmental harm caused during armed conflicts via indirect
provisions of IHL, this chapter draws attention to the international
community's poor performance in holding States and individuals
responsible for such environmental damage, citing political or
pragmatic reasons for this failure.
- Chapter 4 also sets out the international community's success story
– holding Iraq liable for the environmental damage caused in the
First Gulf War. Although this was an unprecedented and remarkable
achievement in relation to conflict-related environmental damages,
this case failed to clarify the application of the relevant rules and
principles under IHL. Chapter 4 concludes that given the inherent

difficulty in preventing environmental harm during armed conflict and taking into account the negative impact of such harm on development, environmental and human well-being, steps towards environmental protection and achieving sustainable development should be increased prior to a conflict even occurring and in the event that armed conflict breaks out, ensuring the ex post response is effective.

1.3. Post-conflict

- Chapter 5 considers the post-conflict stage in the context of reparations and the polluter pays principle (PPP) for conflict-related environmental damages as well as the remediation of such damage and management of natural resources that may cause possible re-conflict. This chapter concludes that in theory, in relation to conflict-related damages, the law of reparations is broadly adequate but the application of PPP is riddled with difficulties. Further scrutiny leads to the conclusion that in practice, barring the one notable exception of the UNCC, affixing responsibility and awarding reparations under international law for war-related environmental damage are problematic as well. Not only are there political and diplomatic obstacles in holding parties responsible, there is also no obligation under international law to utilise any monetary reparation payment awarded for the benefit of the environment. In addition, although the UNCC was a success, part of its success was because the belligerent State held responsible was an oil-rich nation that could afford to fund such a compensation system.

- Chapter 5 highlights the fact that affixing liability and reparations, making the polluter pay or obtaining funding for post-conflict environmental recovery and management are difficult. It further concludes that in the absence of a permanent post-conflict environmental compensation system, the international community, in their commitment to achieving sustainable development, should enhance cooperative efforts to overcome the funding problems that hamper most attempts to provide effective post-conflict environmental remediation efforts. In addition, international cooperative efforts should include integration of the necessary environmental priorities together with other more traditional security, humanitarian and socio-economic development factors from the outset in order to prevent re-conflict in certain situations and contribute to a virtuous cycle of sustainable development post-conflict.

There is no doubt that there has been some measure of success with regard to protection of the environment relevant to security and armed conflict. This includes various MEAs that have not only reflected the components of sustainable development but, if effectively adhered to by States, could prevent, mitigate and manage the relevant environmental issues that could, if ignored, contribute to violent or armed conflict. In respect of the First Gulf War, the international community's action of holding Iraq responsible for conflict-related environmental damage and the subsequent establishment of the UNCC is considered a remarkable achievement and a success. Even when liability was not attached to conflict-related environmental damages, successes that contributed to the environment and sustainable development can be seen from scenarios illustrated within the case-studies. For example, where the international community collectively assisted and continues to assist financially and technically to clean-up, restore, manage and integrate capacity building for conflict-related environmental damages, including the management of environmental issues together with other socio-economic development factors within the war-torn countries.

Nonetheless, it is clear from this study that at each stage of the armed conflict life cycle, policy, law and enforcement on environmental protection relevant to security and armed conflict, falls short of the sustainable development model. At the pre-conflict and preventive stage, a distinct lack of urgency and a 'wait and see' attitude seems to be prevalent in the international community. This negates the preventive approach, for it exposes the district or region to a serious risk of irreparable damage, arising from a vicious cycle of environmental problems fuelling war, and war fuelling environmental problems. During actual armed conflict, the high, stringent and ambiguous thresholds of specific laws intended to protect the environment and the convenient justification of military necessity, allow belligerents to get away with a significant amount of environmental harm. It is also regrettable that thus far customary international law has not developed to a point where adequate protection is provided for the environment in times of armed conflict. Such environmental harm puts further obstacles in the path of sustainable development, having a negative impact on security, development, environmental and human well-being. Furthermore, the lack of prosecution or holding State parties liable for war-related environmental harm provides no deterrence or necessity for precaution with respect to the environment during times of armed conflict. As a direct result, not only are reparations for conflict-related environmental damages rare; at the post-conflict stage, obtaining funding for environmental clean-up, remediation and management is difficult and thus far, dependant on ad hoc voluntary donations. Furthermore, the integration of environmental priorities at the post-conflict stage to prevent recurrence of environmental-induced conflicts and the international community's efforts in doing so, are still in their infancy. These weaknesses hinder the international community's commitment to achieving sustainable development.

2. THE WAY FORWARD

Taking stock of the inherent weaknesses as discovered throughout this study, the international community needs to take note and step-up their collective efforts in protecting the environment in situations of conflict. The idea of this book is that the tools, objectives or guidelines provided by the principles under sustainable development and the overarching concept of sustainable development as the ultimate goal could assist the international community in improving policy and law to better achieve protection of the environment relevant to security and armed conflict. It is argued that sustainable development and its substantive principles could fill the gaps left by the weaknesses of policy and law in this field.

In their commitment to these principles, particularly the principles of precaution, public participation, good governance, common but differentiated responsibilities, intra- and inter-generational equity, integration and polluter pays, the international community should collectively improve their conflict prevention efforts, particularly from an environmental-conflict dimension. A better early warning and a corresponding early action system with an integrated international network is needed to facilitate tackling environmental pressures and challenges with consideration of other variable factors that may cause violent or armed conflict. As suggested in Chapter 3, a comprehensive environment-conflict EW system that could be administered and monitored by UNEP.

In respect of limiting unnecessary and unsustainable harm to the environment during the heat of armed conflict, short of clarifying or improving the existing laws that provide protection for the environment in times of conflict, better respect and adherence for the laws of armed conflict is required by belligerent forces. States should bear in mind that the increasing sophistication and advances in the means and methods of warfare could cause untold and long-term harm to the environment with associated uncertain and irreversible risks as a result. Such risks could not only cause further harm to the environment but also to the security, health and livelihoods of the human population. Thus, taking into consideration the spirit of the precautionary principle, inter- and intra-generational equity and sustainable development as a whole, States should ideally integrate and instil respect for the laws of armed conflict within the training of their armed forces and take into account these sustainable development issues when participating or entering armed conflict.

Chapter 5 brought home the difficulties in affixing liability for reparations under international law and making the polluter pay under international environmental law for conflict-related damages and in the event that liability cannot be attached, the difficulty in sourcing funds for post-conflict environmental recovery or environmental management programmes. UNEP's Post-Conflict and Disaster Management Branch (PCDMB) works effectively in coordinating and monitoring post-conflict environmental efforts but funding is a problem. In view of the life cycle of the armed conflict process and the holistic concept of sustainable development, a fund system for post-conflict environmental damage that would be dually applicable should be contemplated. Such a fund would first, compensate towards post-conflict environmental remediation and second, enable the integration of environmental priorities from the outset together with other more traditional security, humanitarian, political, socio-economic and development factors. Failure to do so may lead to these environmental issues becoming catalysts for re-conflict. Thus, aside from the possibility of obtaining funding from the new Peacebuilding Commission Fund, the international community, taking into account their commitment to sustainable development and its substantive principles, should increase their efforts collectively to establish a more comprehensive and effective post-conflict environmental funding system – a permanent post-conflict environmental fund with voluntary contributions from the donor community or a similar UNCC-like model where funding could be sourced on a case-by-case basis depending on the country's resources. For environmental-induced NIACs in particular, such a system could harness the environmental and natural resources available within the country concerned to be ploughed back into integrating environmental remediation and management programmes to prevent a relapse into conflict.

Index

Aarhus Convention (1998)
  public participation principle 36
Abe, K. *see* Donovan, D., Jong, W. D.
  and Abe, K.
Abuja Agreement (2000) 99
access to information and justice
      principle 35–7
  see also public participation principle
Africa
  Sub-Saharan region, population
      growth 74
  war of the well (2004) 79–80, 83, 88
  *see also individual countries and
      regional organisations*
African Union (AU) 93–4, 95
Agenda 21
  public participation principle 36
  WSSD affirmation of (2002) 14–15
Agricultural Revolution 11
Alexander, N. G. 177
Amnesty International 114
armed conflict *see* international armed
      conflicts (IACs)
ASEAN Convention (1985)
  sustainable development principles
      50
attribution, definition 153–4
Austin, J. E. *see* Bruch, C. E. and J. E.
      Austin

Barre, Siad 78, 88–9
Belgian Diamond High Council (DHC)
      100
Boyle, A. 187
Boyle, A. and D. Freestone 22
British Meteorological Office 144
Brodnig, G. 110
Bruch, C. E. and J. E. Austin 174
Brunée, J. 60, 61

Bruntland Commission
  establishment of 13
  Our Common Future report 9, 10,
      13–14, 20–21, 26, 35–6, 58–9,
      73

Caggiano, M. J. T. 145
Canada
  Cosmos-954 incident, *ex-gratia*
      payments 206–7
  transboundary air pollution 23
Cartagena Protocol (2000)
  precautionary principle 33
case studies *see* Darfur, Sudan, case
      study; First Gulf War (1990–
      1991), case study; Kosovo
      conflict, case study; Sierra Leone,
      case study; Somalia, case study
Chemain, R. 45–6
China
  Chinese Embassy incident, *ex-gratia*
      payments 206
  Chorzów Factory case 202
Chowdhury, N. and C. E. Skarstedt 40
Coalition forces
  transboundary environmental
      damage by, in First Gulf War
      145–6, 147
collective responsibility in preventing
      environmental-induced conflict
      principle
  overview 104–10
  common but differentiated
      responsibilities principle 104–5,
      110
  in Millenium Declaration 104
  post-conflict recovery 242
  public participation principle 110
  restitution 212–13

colonialism, European 11
command responsibility, definition
    159–60
common but differentiated
    responsibilities principle
    overview 28–31
    collective responsibility principle
        104–5, 110
    in compensation systems 217
    ENMOD provisions 132
    Gaines on environmental security 61
    Iraq/Kuwait bilateral talks 236
    polluter pays principle (PPP) 43
    restitution 212–13
    Voigt's sustainable development
        concept 21
common heritage of mankind principle
    28–9
compensation, for environmental
    damage *see* reparations, under
    international environmental law
Comprehensive Peace Agreement
    (CPA) (2005) 95–6, 220–21, 225
conflict, life cycle of 4
conflict prevention model (Cousens) 86
conflict resources
    as basis of First Gulf War *see* First
        Gulf War (1990–1991), case
        study
    definition 70
    in Sierra Leone 83–5, 99–101
    in Sudan 96
Conservation and Sustainable
    Development of all Types of
    Forests (Forest Principles) 14
Constitutional Court (South Africa)
    sustainable development principles in
        decisions 55
contingent valuation (CV) method 194,
    198–200
Convention on Civil Liability for
    Damage Resulting from Activities
    Dangerous to the Environment *see*
    Lugano Convention (1993)
Convention on the Prohibition of
    Military or Any Other Hostile Use
    of Environmental Modification

Techniques (ENMOD) (1976)
    130–32, 134–5
Convention on the Protection of the
    Ozone Layer (1985) 32
corporate social responsibility
    good governance principle and 39
Cosmos-954 incident 206–7
Cotonou Partnership Agreement
    good governance principle 39
Cousens, E. M. 86
Crawford, J. 191
criminal responsibility *see* individual
    criminal responsibility

damage cost avoided method 193–4
Danube River, release of toxic
    chemicals into 164–5, 167–70
Darfur, Sudan, case study
    Comprehensive Peace Agreement
        (CPA) (2005) 95–6, 220–21, 225
    conclusions and challenges 249–50
    death toll 82
    environment-conflict link 80–83
    international failure in 91–6
    migrations to Chad 82
    UNEP on environmental issues in
        80–81, 83
    see also Sudan
Darfur Integrated Water Resources
    Management (IWRM) 222, 240
De Beers 101
De Waal, A. 82
Declaration of the UN Conference on
    the Human Environment *see*
    Stockholm Declaration
Declaration on Environment and
    Development (Rio Declaration)
    common but differentiated
        responsibilities principle 29,
        30–31
    duty of States to ensure sustainable
        use of natural resources principle
        22–3
    equity principle and eradication of
        poverty 26
    good governance principle 38
    NGO participation in 49
    polluter pays principle (PPP) 44

precautionary principle 32–3
public participation principle 36
sustainable, definition 21
WSSD affirmation of (2002) 14
see also individual principles
Denmark
    funding of Kosovo post-conflict
        recovery 216–17
depleted uranium (DU) ammunition
    145–6, 217, 228, 239
Dernbach, J.C. 8, 19
diamond trade
    as conflict resource 70
    in Sierra Leone 83–5, 99–102
Dinstein, Y. 151
discrimination, as customary
        international law principle
    definition 140
    First Gulf War applicability 149–50
    Kosovo conflict applicability 170–71
    as source of environment protection
        138
distinction, as customary international
        law principle
    definition 138, 140
    Kosovo conflict applicability 170–
        72, 176
donor community, and permanent
        post-conflict environmental fund
    245, 254
Donovan, D., Jong, W. D. and Abe, K.
    104
duty of States to ensure sustainable use
        of natural resources principle
    overview 22–5
    restitution and 188–9

early warning (EW) systems 113–18
    conclusions and challenges 250
    definition 113
    early action efforts 117–18
    need for global unit managed by
        UNEP 115–17, 253
Earth Summit *see* UN Conference on
    Environment and Development
    (UNCED) (1992)
ecological marginalization, definition
    72

ECOMOG (Economic Community of
    West African States Monitoring
    Group) 98, 101
economic structure of States
    environment-conflict link 76
economic valuation methods, for
    environmental damages 192–5,
    206, 246
ecosystem services
    definitions of 2–3
    production function method of
        valuation 192–3
ECOWAS (Economic Community of
    West African States)
    early warning (EW) systems 114
    multilateral armed forces 98–9
enforcement
    challenges of 210, 217, 219, 235, 252
    Okowa on need for enforcement
        mechanisms 184–5
    *see also individual enforcement
        mechanims*
environment, definitions of 2
Environment and Security Initiative
    (ENVSEC) 238
environmental degradation
    environment-conflict link and 71–5
    in pre-conflict stage 4
    as security threat 60–61
environmental protection and
        sustainable development
    overview 1–7
    in-conflict stage *see* environmental
        security during armed conflict
        (in-conflict stage), IHL rules and
        principles
    post-conflict stage *see* sustainable
        development and environmental
        recovery (post-conflict stage)
    pre-conflict stage *see*
        environment-induced armed
        conflict, prevention of
        (pre-conflict stage)
environmental refugees 69, 93, 105,
    165, 205, 241, 242
    see also migration

environmental security during armed
conflict (in-conflict stage), IHL
rules and principles 120–82
overview 120–24
AP I provisions 126, 130, 132–5
compensation liability 137–8
conclusions and challenges 250–52
customary principles of 138–42
discrimination, principle of 138, 140,
149–50, 170–71
distinction, principle of 138, 140,
170–72, 176
ENMOD provisions 130–32, 134–5
evolution of concept 58–64
First Gulf War *see* First Gulf War
(1990–1991), case study
humanity, laws of 139
international humanitarian law
applicability 121–42
Kosovo conflict *see* Kosovo conflict,
case study
Lieber Code 141
military necessity, principle of 141–2,
174
precautionary principle 123–34
proportionality, principle of 140–41
sustainable development, cycle of
178–80
UNEP reports on armed conflict 1–2
environment-induced armed conflict,
prevention of (pre-conflict stage)
66–119
collective responsibility for 104–10
conclusions and challenges 249–50,
252
conflict prevention model (Cousens)
86
early warning (EW) systems 113–18,
250
environment-conflict link 67–85
international failure in 85–103; *see
also* Darfur, Sudan, case study;
Sierra Leone, case study;
Somalia, case study
lack of international law regime for
111–13
MEAs, function of 105, 107, 111–13,
250

equity principle and eradication of
poverty
overview 21, 25–8
AP I provisions and 133
during armed conflicts 123–4,
174
environmental security 61, 63–4
European Court of Justice (ECJ)
precautionary principle 33
European Union (EU)
early warning (EW) systems 114
Environmental Action Programmes
43, 107
good governance principle 39
polluter pays principle (PPP) 43
reconstruction efforts, post-Kosovo
conflict 219
as signatory of KPCS 107

failed state, definition 79
FAO Plant Treaty 27
Federal Republic of Yugoslavia (FRY)
(former)
filing of complaints with ICJ against
NATO states 166
nonsignatory to US drafted peace
accord for Kosovo 162
post-conflict clean-up responsibility
237–8
request of ICJ for cease-fire 175
see also Kosovo conflict, case study
Final Report to the Prosecutor by the
Committee Established to Review
the NATO Bombing Campaign
Against the Federal Republic of
Yugoslavia 163–70, 172, 173, 174,
176
financing recovery and management
213–26
First Gulf War applicability 213–16
future recommendations 245–6
Kosovo conflict applicability
216–19, 246
Sudan applicability 216–19, 220–26,
246
Finland
funding of Kosovo post-conflict
recovery 216–17

First Circuit Court (US)
environmental damages in oil spill cases 196–7
First Gulf War (1990–1991), case study 121, 143–61
applicable laws 147–52
conclusions and challenges 250–51
discrimination, principle of 149–50
individual criminal responsibility 156–61
military necessity, principle of 147–8, 149, 150–52
oil-well destruction 144, 147, 149–52, 158–9
proportionality, principle of 148–9, 150–52
regional lost GDP due to 147
release of oil into Persian Gulf waters 143–4, 147–9, 159
State responsibility 153–6, 158–9
transboundary environmental damage 143–7
UNCC financing recovery and management 213–16
UNCC-GC, category F4 assessment of State liability 201–6
UNCC-GC, category F4 compensation awards 215
Food and Agricultural Organization (FAO) 102
Forest Principles *see* Conservation and Sustainable Development of all Types of Forests (Forest Principles)
Founex Seminar on Environment and Development (1971) 12–13, 20, 48
France
AP I, nonbinding for during Kosovo conflict 170
FRY complaints to ICJ against 166–7
ICJ *Nuclear Tests* case 33
Freestone, D. *see* Boyle, A. and D. Freestone
French, D. 14, 16, 24, 31, 42, 57, 104–5, 245

Gaines, S. E. 61

G8 109
Geneva Convention of 1949 (GC IV)
as customary international law 135–8
First Gulf War applicability 158, 159
Kosovo conflict applicability 170
Geneva Conventions
as customary international law 135
First Gulf War applicability 147, 149
Martens Clause 139
see also Protocol Additional to the Geneva Conventions of 12 August 1949, and relating to the Protection of Victims of International Armed Conflicts (AP I)
Germany
FRY complaints to ICJ against 166–7
funding of Kosovo post-conflict recovery 216–17
Gleditsch, N. P. 76
good governance principle
overview 37–40
need for in Sudan recovery 95, 223, 224–5, 232
Government of Serbia and Montenegro
UNEP Clean-Up Programme 237–8
Gray, K. R. 15
Gulf States
regional lost GDP due to First Gulf War 147
UNCC financing recovery and management 214
see also individual countries

Haavisto, Pekaa 163
habitat equivalency analysis (HEA) method 194–5, 204–5
Hague Regulations
First Gulf War applicability 147, 149, 158–9
importance of 130
Kosovo conflict applicability 170
limitations on warfare 135–7, 170
Handl, G. 23
Hawke, L. D. *see* Magraw, D. B. and L. D. Hawke
hedonic pricing method 194

high-value resources *see* conflict
resources
Hirsch, J. L. 97
Homer-Dixon, T. F. 71–2
Hulme, K. 150, 158, 167, 168, 171
Human Rights Watch 114
humanity, laws of 139
Hungary
    ICJ Gabčikovo-Nagymaros case 33
Hussein, Saddam 147, 160–61

in-conflict stage, definition 4
    see also environmental security
        during armed conflict
        (in-conflict stage), IHL rules and
        principles
individual criminal responsibility
    First Gulf War applicability 156–61
    Kosovo conflict applicability 175–8
Industrial Revolution 11
Instructions for the Government of
        Armies of the United States in the
        Field *see* Lieber Code
integration and interrelationship
        principle
    overview 40–42
    in Arbitral Tribunal decision 42
    Iraq/Kuwait bilateral talks and 236
    UNEP, and Sudan recovery efforts
        241
inter-generational equity *see* equity
        principle and eradication of
        poverty
Intergovernmental Authority on
        Development (IGAD)
    Conflict Early Warning and Response
        Mechanism (CEWARN) 114,
        116–17
internally displaced persons (IDPs) 241,
        242
International Alerts 114
international armed conflicts (IACs)
    UNEP reports on 1–2, 127
    see also individual IAC case studies
International Atomic Energy Agency
        (IAEA) 228
International Committee of the Red
        Cross (ICRC)

Guidelines for Military Manuals and
        Instructions on the Protection of
        the Environment in Times of
        Armed Conflict (1994) 125
    impact of armed conflict on
        sustainable development 120
    natural environment, definition 133
    respect for IHL rules 122, 179
International Court of Justice (ICJ)
    environmental protection in armed
        conflict 125–7
    FRY complaints against NATO states
        166
    inter-generational equity as legal
        right 27
    jurisdiction issues 175
    precautionary principle 33
    State duty and environmental harm
        23
    sustainable development principles in
        decisions 52–4
International Criminal Court (ICC) 157
International Criminal Tribunals for
        Yugoslavia (ICTY) 156, 158, 172
    Office of the Prosecutor (OTP), war
        crimes investigation proposal
        175–7
International Crisis Group 114
international humanitarian law (IHL)
    see environmental security during
        armed conflict (in-conflict stage),
        IHL rules and principles;
        individual conventions and laws
International Law Association (ILA)
    Berlin Conference (2004) 20, 47
    Berlin Rules on Water Resources
        (2004) 127–30, 179
    Committee on Legal Aspects of
        Sustainable Development 16, 47
    New Delhi Declaration *see* New
        Delhi Declaration of Principles
        of International Law relating to
        Sustainable Development (2002)
        (ILA)
International Law Commission (ILC)
    case-by-case mix of remedies 187–8
    Draft Code of Crimes Against Peace
        and Security of Mankind 125

expansion of environmental protection in armed conflict laws 180
restitution 188–9
satisfaction 207–8
State responsibility for compensation for environmental damange 190–91
International Military Tribunals 156, 190
International North Sea Conference (1984) 32
International Treaty on Plant Genetic Resources for Food and Agriculture *see* FAO Plant Treaty
International Union for Conservation of Nature (IUCN)
Draft Convention on the Prohibition of Hostile Military Activities in Protected Areas 125
intra-generational equity *see* equity principle and eradication of poverty
Iran
compensation assessment for 205
territorial waters, damage due to Iraqi oil release 144
UNCC Follow-up Programme for Environmental Awards 235–6
Iraq
RERP, and bilateral talks with Kuwait 236
UNCC Follow-up Programme for Environmental Awards 235–6
see also First Gulf War (1990–1991), case study
Ireland
funding of Kosovo post-conflict recovery 216–17
Italian Development Cooperation 222
Italy
FRY complaints to ICJ against 166–7
Ivanov, A. and D. Nyheim 114

Janjaweed 82, 92
Japan International Cooperation Agency (JICA) 222
Jewell, T. *see* Steele, J. and T. Jewell

Johannesburg Declaration
Plan of Implementation (JPOI) 15, 38, 50
public participation principle 36
Joint UNEP/UNCHS-(Habitat) Balkan Taskforce (BTF) team
Final Report 163–70, 172, 173, 174, 176
UNEP/BTF Feasibility Studies 218
Jong, W. D. *see* Donovan, D., Jong, W. D. and Abe, K.
Jordan
compensation assessment for 204–5
UNCC Follow-up Programme for Environmental Awards 235–6

Khalfan, A. *see* Segger, M. C. Cordonier and A. Khalfan
Kiev Protocol (2003)
polluter pays principle (PPP) 44
Kimberly Process Certification Scheme (KPCS) 100–101, 107
Ki-Moon, Ban
on conflict prevention and sustainble development 118
on Darfur conflict and ecological crisis 83
on security as dependent on sustainable development 58
Kosovo conflict, case study 121, 162–78
affixing funds to environmental recovery 227–30
AP I applicability 166–70, 171
applicable laws 166–74
conclusions and challenges 250–51
distinction, principle of 170–72
financing recovery and management 216–19, 246
hot spots of pollution due to bombing 163–4, 174
individual criminal responsibility 175–8
military necessity, principle of 172
Pančevo, Serbia, NATO bombing of industrial complex 163–74
polluter pays principle (PPP) 217
proportionality, principle of 172–3

rebuilding of by international
community 219
recovery follow-up procedures
237–40
State responsibility 174–5
transboundary environmental
damage 165, 167
UNCC Follow-up Programme 237–9
UNDP recovery efforts 230
UNEP recovery efforts 216–19,
228–30
UNMIK, role of 219, 228, 239–40
Kosovo Protection Corps (KPC)
239–40
Kraska, J. 60
Kuwait
compensation assessment for 204–5
RERP, and bilateral talks with Iraq
236
territorial waters, damage due to Iraqi
oil release 144
UNCC Follow-up Programme for
Environmental Awards 235–6
war crime tribunals 160
see also First Gulf War (1990–1991),
case study

lex ferenda
precautionary principle as 31–4
liability, affixing of *see* State
responsibility; individual criminal
responsibility
Liberia 97
Lieber Code 141
Lomé Peace Accord (1999) 98–9
Lowe, V. 47–8
Lugano Convention (1993)
polluter pays principle (PPP) 44
Luxembourg
funding of Kosovo post-conflict
recovery 216–17

Maathai, Wangari 242
Magraw, D. B. and Hawke, L. D. 18
market price method 192
Marong, A. B. 61
Martens Clause (1899) 139
McCloskey, M. 20, 56

McGovern, F. E. 205
migration
due to ecological marginalization 72
due to warfare 66
environment-conflict link 73, 74–5
new ethnic tensions due to 83
see also environmental refugees
Mikovic, Srkjan 164
military necessity, principle of
overview 140–42
Berlin Rules and 129
CG IV 137–8, 158, 170
First Gulf War applicability 147–8,
149, 150–52
get out clause 174
Hague Regulations and 135–7, 170
Kosovo conflict applicability 172
Millennium Development Goals
(MDGs) 17–18, 231–2
Millennium Ecosystem Assessment
ecosystem, definition 2
minerals 68, 70
Momoh, Joseph 85
Multilateral Environmental
Aggreements (MEAs)
in European Union 107
during post-conflict stage 229, 252
during pre-conflict stage 105,
111–13, 250
Myers, N. 60

national security
definition 3
elements of 248
natural environment, definition 133
natural resources, definition 68
net factor income method 193
Netherlands
FRY complaints to ICJ against 166–7
funding of Kosovo post-conflict
recovery 216–17
New Delhi Declaration of Principles of
International Law relating to
Sustainable Development (2002)
(ILA) 16–46
duty of States principle 22, 24
equity principle and eradication of
poverty 25

good governance principle 37, 38
public participation principle 35
see also individual principles
New Zealand
ICJ *Nuclear Tests* case 33
nongovernmental organisations
(NGOs)
conflict diamonds trade and 99–100
policy-making, participation in 48–9
Somalia, relief efforts in 89
see also individual organisations
non-international armed conflicts
(NIACs)
lack of international law application
to 185
need for collective response in
post-conflict stage 212–13
need for permanent post-conflict
environmental fund 254
polluter pays principle 210
UNEP recommendations for 244
Non-Legally Binding Authoritative
Statement of Principles for a
Global Consensus on the
Management 14
non-use values, in damage assessment
191–2, 199–200, 203–4
North Atlantic Treaty Organization
(NATO)
environmental security forum 109
Final Report to the Prosecutor by the
Committee Established to
Review the NATO Bombing
Campaign Against the Federal
Republic of Yugoslavia 163–70,
172, 173, 174, 176
FRY complaints to ICJ against NATO
states 166
NATO Kosovo Force (KFOR) 228
see also Kosovo conflict, case study
Norway
funding of Kosovo post-conflict
recovery 216–17
Nuclear Weapons Advisory Opinion
(ICJ) 23, 53, 125–7, 139, 140, 141
Nuremberg Tribunals 156, 157, 190
Nyheim, D. *see* Ivanov, A. and Nyheim,
D.

oil resources
as basis of First Gulf War *see* First
Gulf War (1990–1991), case
study
as conflict resource in Sudan 96
Sudan, lack of transparency 220–21,
224–5
oil spills, and US courts 196–7
Oil-for-Food Programme 214–15
Okowa, P. 184–5
Organisation for Economic
Co-operation and Development
(OECD)
Guidelines for Multinational
Enterprises 39
polluter pays principle (PPP) 43
Organization for Security and
Cooperation in Europe (OSCE)
early warning (EW) systems 114
institution building, in post-conflict
Kosovo 219
workshops on environmental
security, co-sponsored with
NATO 109

Pakistan
transboundary environmental
damage in, due to First Gulf War
144
Pančevo, Serbia, NATO bombing of
industrial complex 163–74
participation principle *see* public
participation principle
Partnership Agreement between the
Members of the African,
Caribbean and Pacific Group of
States of the One Part, and the
European Community and its
Member States *see* Cotonou
Partnership Agreement
Peacebuilding Fund (PBC) 243, 246,
254
Permanent Court of Arbitration
integration and interrelationship
principle 42
sustainable development principles in
decisions 54–5

Persian Gulf, release of oil into by Iraq
        143–4, 147–9, 159
piracy 106
political instability
    environment-conflict link 75–6, 83–5
polluter pays principle (PPP)
    overview 21, 42–6, 208–9, 251
    as alternative to reparations 208–11
    EU endorsement of 43
    in funding of Kosovo environmental
        recovery 217
    in Kiev Protocol 44
    in Lugano Convention preamble 44
    noncodification of by US 45, 209
    OECD adoption of 43
    in Rio Declaration 44
population growth
    environment-conflict link 71–2
    future trends 69–70
    political instability 73–4
Portugal
    FRY complaints to ICJ against 166–7
post-conflict stage, definition 4
    see also sustainable development and
        environmental recovery
        (post-conflict stage)
poverty *see* equity principle and
        eradication of poverty
precautionary approach to human
        health, natural resources and
        ecosystems, principle of
    overview 31–4
    AP I provisions 133
    during armed conflicts 174, 178
    in compensation systems 200, 202,
        203, 217, 228
    in court decisions 33, 55
    in ENMOD efforts 132
    environment-conflict perspective 87
    international humanitarian law
        123–4, 128
    polluter pays principle (PPP) 43, 44
    restitution 188, 203
    UNEP, and Sudan recovery efforts
        239, 241
    in Voigt's sustainable development
        concept 21
pre-conflict stage, definition 4

    see also environment-induced armed
        conflict, prevention of
        (pre-conflict stage)
production function method 192–3
Programme for Further Implementation
        of Agenda 21 14
proportionality, as customary
        international law principle
    definition 138, 140–41
    First Gulf War applicability 148–9,
        150–52
    in ICJ decision 126
    Kosovo conflict applicability 172–3
Protocol Additional to the Geneva
        Conventions of 12 August 1949,
        and relating to the Protection of
        Victims of International Armed
        Conflicts (AP I) (1977)
    ICJ reference to 126
    Kosovo conflict applicability
        166–70, 171
    threshold criteria in Articles 35 and
        55 132–5, 179
Protocol on Civil Liability and
        Compensation for Damage
        Caused by the Transboundary
        Effects of Industrial Accidents on
        Transboundary Waters to the 1992
        Convention on the Protection and
        Use of Transboundary
        Watercourses and International
        Lakes and to the 1992 Convention
        on the Transboundary Effects of
        Industrial Accidents *see* Kiev
        Protocol
public participation principle
    overview 35–7
    Berlin Rules 128
    collective responsibility principle
        110
    conclusions and challenges 250, 253
    as process related 63
    UNEP, and Kosovo recovery efforts
        229
    UNEP, and Sudan recovery efforts
        238–9, 241

re-conflicts 184, 246

refugees *see* environmental refugees
Regional Environmental Centre (REC)
    168–70
Reid, D. 21
remedies and recovery *see* sustainable
    development and environmental
    recovery (post-conflict stage)
reparations, under international
    environmental law 186–208
  overview 186–8
  calculating costs for environmental
      damage 191–5
  compensation without admission of
      liability 206–7
  conclusions and challenges 251–3
  economic valuation methods 192–5,
      206
  future calculation model 205–8
  precautionary principle 188, 203
  restitution 188–9
  satisfaction 207–8
  State responsibility for compensation
      for environmental damange
      190–91
  UNCC compensation methods 191,
      200–206
  US compensation system 195–200
replacement cost method 193
resource capture, definition 71–2
resource scarcity
  environment-conflict link 73
  political instability 75–6
  in pre-conflict stage 4
  as security threat 60–61
Responsibility to Protect principle
    (R2P) 213
restitution 188–9
Revolutionary United Front (RUF) 84,
    85, 98–9
Rio Conference *see* UN Conference on
    Environment and Development
    (UNCED) (1992)
Rio+20 Summit (2012) 18, 48
Romania
  heavy metals in Danube waters 167
Rome Statute 156–8
Rwanda 156

Sahnoun, Mohammed 91
Sands, P. 20, 21
satisfaction, forms of reparations 207–8
Saudi Arabia
  compensation assessment for 204–5
  UNCC Follow-up Programme for
      Environmental Awards 235–6
Saundry, P. 123
Schmitt, M. N. 136, 161
Schrijver, N. 6, 18, 34, 40, 52
Schwabach, A. 163
scorched earth policy 158
Segger, M. C. Cordonier and A. Khalfan
    25–6, 28, 46, 48, 49, 52–3, 58
Shea, Jamie 166, 177–8
Sierra Leone, case study
  conclusions and challenges 249–50
  diamond resources in 83–5, 99–102
  ECOMOG intervention efforts 98
  environment-conflict link 83–5
  international failure in 96–103
  UNAMSIL peacekeeping forces in
      99
  UNDP economic development in 102
  UNEP environmental assessment in
      102
  UNSC Resolution 1132 98
Sierra Leone Government (GoSL)
    98–100
Skarstedt, C. E. *see* Chowdhury, N. and
    C. E. Skarstedt
social instability 76–7
Somalia, case study
  conclusions and challenges 249–50
  death toll 78, 80
  environment-conflict link 78–80
  as failed state 79, 89–90, 106
  international failure in 87–91
Soroos, M. S. 111
South Asia
  population growth 74
Southern Sudan 96, 221, 223–4, 225,
    232
  see also Darfur, Sudan, case study;
      Sudan
Spain
  FRY complaints to ICJ against 166–7
  ICJ, lack of jurisdiction against 175

Special Court for Sierra Leone (SCSL)
     101
Stake, R. E. 5
State responsibility
     overview 153–6
     compensation for environmental
          damage (ILC) 190–91
     ex-gratia compensation 206–7
     First Gulf War applicability 153–6,
          158–9
     Kosovo conflict applicability 174–5
     restitution (ILC) 188–9
     satisfaction (ILC) 207–8
     see also duty of States to ensure
          sustainable use of natural
          resources principle
State sovereignty
     natural resources 22–5
Statute of the International Criminal
     Tribunal for Rwanda (ICTR) 156
Steele, J. and T. Jewell 57
Stevens, Siaka 85
Stockholm Conference (1972)
     connectedness of environmental and
          development issues 12–13
     NGO participation in 48–9
     polluter pays principle 43
Stockholm Declaration
     connectedness of environmental and
          development issues 12–13
     duty of States principle 23
     equity principle and eradication of
          poverty 26
     integration and interrelationship
          principle 41
     Rio Conference affirmation of 14
Stub, S. 110
Sudan
     affixing funds to environmental
          recovery 230–32
     Comprehensive Peace Agreement
          (CPA) (2005) 95–6, 220–21, 225
     financing recovery and management
          220–26, 246
     lack of transparency in oil industry
          220–21, 224–5
     recovery follow-up procedures
          240–46

UNMIS/UNMISS peace support
     operations 225
     see also Darfur, Sudan, case study;
          Southern Sudan
Sudan People's Liberated Army (SPLA)
     82
Superfund compensation analogy
     195–200
Supreme Court (India)
     sustainable development principles in
          decisions 55
Supreme Court (Philippines)
     inter-generational equity as legal
          right 27
sustainable development and
     environmental recovery
     (post-conflict stage) 183–247
     overview 183–5
     affixing funds to environmental
          recovery 226–32, 251–3, 254
     conclusions and challenges 251–3
     financing recovery and management
          213–26, 245–6; *see also
          individual international
          organizations and case studies*
     polluter pays principle (PPP) 208–11,
          217, 251
     precautionary principle 217
     recovery follow-up procedures
          233–46
     reparations *see* reparations, under
          international environmental law
sustainable development, definition 3,
     8, 18–21
sustainable development, theoretical
     framework 8–65
     overview 8–10
     common but differentiated
          responsibilities principle 21,
          28–31
     conclusions and challenges 248–54
     definition 3, 8, 18–21
     duty of States principle 22–5
     as emerging norm, legal vs. political
          concept 47–58
     environmental security and armed
          conflict 58–64

equity principle and eradication of
poverty 21, 25–8
evolution of sustainable development
concept 10–18
good governance principle 37–40
integration and interrelationship
principle 21, 40–42
international court/tribunal decisions
52–6
international law and 21–2
participation principle 35–7
polluter pays principle (PPP) 21,
42–6
precautionary principle 31–4
scholarly publications 56–8
soft-law 48–50
treaties and conventions 50–52
see also individual principles
Sweden
funding of Kosovo post-conflict
recovery 216–17
Swedish International Development
Cooperation Agency (SIDA) 223
Switzerland
funding of Kosovo post-conflict
recovery 216–17, 218

Taylor, Charles 84
Toepfer, Klaus 180
Trail Smelter Arbitration 23, 126,
191–2, 202
travel cost method 194, 204
Tresac, Ing Slobodan 171
Turkey
AP I, nonbinding for during Kosovo
conflict 170

Ullman, R. H. 60
UN Commission on Sustainable
Development (CSD)
establishment of 14
UN Conference on Environment and
Development (UNCED) (1992)
14–15, 21
UN Convention against Corruption
good governance principle 39–40
UN Convention on Biological Diversity
(UNCBD) 24

equity principle and eradication of
poverty 26
integration and interrelationship
principle 41
public participation principle 36
UN Convention on the Law of the Sea
(UNCLOS)
duty of States 23–4
precautionary principle 32
UN Convention to Combat
Desertification (UNCCD)
common but differentiated
responsibilities principle 30
integration and interrelationship
principle 41
public participation principle 36
sustainable development principles
50, 112
UN Development Programme (UNDP)
economic development in Sierra
Leone 102
good governance principle 38
Kosovo post-conflict recovery 230
UN Environmental Mediation
Programme (UNEMP) proposal
108
UN Framework Convention on Climate
Change (UNFCCC)
common but differentiated
responsibilities principle 30
eradication of poverty 26
integration and interrelationship
principle 41
precautionary principle 32–3
protection of global climate 24,
29–30
public participation principle 36
State of the Future Report (2009) 112
sustainable development principles
50, 112
UN General Assembly (UNGA)
climate change discussions 109
Resolution 38/161 13–14
Resolution 60/1, adoption of 2005
World Summit Outcome 17–18
UN High Commissioner for Refugees
219

UN Interim Administration in Kosovo
(UNMIK) 219, 228, 239–40
UN International Children's Emergency
Fund (UNICEF) 241
UN International Panel for Sustainable
Resource Management (IPSRM)
108
UN Mission in Sierra Leone
(UNAMSIL) 99
UN Mission in Sudan (UNMIS) 225
UN Mission in the Republic of South
Sudan (UNMISS) 225
UN Observer Mission in Sierra Leone
(UNOMSIL) 98
UN Office for Project Services
(UNOPS) 223, 229–30, 240
UN Peacebuilding Commission (PBC)
213, 243–4, 246, 254
UN Refugee Agency (UNHCR) 93
UN Security Council (UNSC)
collective responsibility principle
108
complaint procedure 132
mandated government certification of
diamonds 100, 101–2
Resolution 674 154
Resolution 687 154–6
Resolution 1132 98–9
Resolution 1244 219
Somalia intervention, critique of
90–91
UN-EU Partnership on Natural
Resources and Conflict Prevention
109
Union of Soviet Socialist Republics
(former)
Cosmos-954 incident, *ex-gratia*
payments 206–7
transboundary environmental
damage in, due to First Gulf War
144
United Kingdom (UK)
Department for International
Development (DFID) 222–3,
240
FRY complaints to ICJ against 166–7
funding of diamond certification
system 100

nonfunding of Kosovo environmental
recovery 216–17
United Nations
A More Secure World Report (2004)
68
agency collaboration in Sudan's
recovery 241–2
Charter 25–6, 154–5
collective responsibility principle
107–10
creation of body to monitor
conflict-related environmental
damage 180
Darfur intervention, critique of 92–5
early warning (EW) systems 114, 116
Global Compact 39
High-Level Panel on Threats,
Challenges and Change 68
Millennium Development Goals
Report 17
Somalia intervention, critique of
90–91
Special Court for Sierra Leone
(SCSL) 101
United Nations Compensation
Commission (UNCC)
advantages of calculation model of
205–6
affixing funds to environmental
recovery 226–7
calculating compensation 191,
200–205
Clean-Up Programme, post-Kosovo
conflict 237–9
establishment of 252
financing recovery and management
213–16
Follow-up Programme for
Environmental Awards, Gulf
region 234–7, 243
recovery follow-up procedures 233–7
Regional Remediation Programme
(RERP) 235–6
UNCC-GC, category F4 assessment
of Iraq's liability 201–5
United Nations Environment
Programme (UNEP)

Clean-Up Programme, post-Kosovo
conflict 228–30
From Conflict to Peacebuilding
Report (2009) 116, 184
Division of Early Warning and
Assessment (DEWA) 115
environmental assessment in Sierra
Leone 102
environmental security, definition 59
environment-conflict link in Darfur
80–81, 83, 95, 96
environment-conflict link, overview
1–2, 68
financing recovery in Kosovo 216–19
financing recovery in Sudan 220–26
global environment-conflict EW
system proposal 115–17, 253
International Law Report 127,
179–80, 244–5
Post-Conflict and Disaster
Management Branch (PCDMB)
96, 115–16, 212, 233, 254
post-conflict depleted uranium (DU)
assessments 217, 228, 239
post-conflict environmental
assessment (PCEA) in Sudan
220–21, 230–31, 243
Sudan Programme, post-conflict
239–46
on Taylor's support for RUF 84
UN Joint Vision of Sierra Leone 102
United States of America (US)
AP I, nonbinding for during Kosovo
conflict 170
Chinese Embassy incident, *ex-gratia*
payments 206
compensation system 195–200, 209
Department of Interior (DOI)
compensation regulations 197–9
FRY complaints to ICJ against 166–7
funding of diamond certification
system 100
ICJ, lack of jurisdiction against 175
noncodification of PPP 45, 209
nonfunding of Kosovo post-conflict
environmental recovery 216–17
Operation Allied Force 162
polluter pays principle (PPP) 45

Somalia intervention, critique of 90
transboundary environmental
damage by, in First Gulf War
145–6
Urdal, H. 75
US Agency for International
Development (USAID)
continuing humanitarian aid to Sudan
232
Darfur Timber and Energy project
222, 240
Sudan Transitional Environment
Programme (STEP) 223–4, 232
US Army, Office of the Judge Advocate
General (JAG) 159–60
US Comprehensive Environmental
Response, Comprehensive, and
Liability Act (CERCLA) 197–8,
209
US Court of Appeals (DC)
on DOI compensation regulations
198

Vietnam War 131, 132, 162–3
Voigt, C. 21

war crimes *see* individual criminal
responsibility
war of the well (2004) 79–80, 83, 88
warfare *see* environmental security
during armed conflict (in-conflict
stage), IHL rules and principles
weapons of mass destruction see
Hussein, Saddam; *Nuclear
Weapons* Advisory Opinion (ICJ)
Weeramantry, C. G.
on balancing competing interests 21
on customary law status 53
on history of sustainable
development 10
on integration principle 41–2
on inter-generational equity principle
27
Weiss, E. B. 28, 35, 107
Westing, A. H. 60
World Bank
World Development Report (1989) 38
World Charter of Nature 184

World Commission on Environment
and Development (WCED) *see*
Bruntland Commission
World Health Organization (WHO)
102
World Summit on Sustainable
Development (WSSD)
NGO participation in 49
purpose of 14–15

World Trade Organization (WTO)
common but differentiated
responsibilities principle 30–31
sustainable development principles in
decisions 54

Yugoslavia (former) 156

Zartman, I. W. 115